Premerger Notification Practice Manual

Third Edition

Neil W. Imus, Editor

Section of Antitrust Law

This volume should be officially cited as:

ABA SECTION OF ANTITRUST LAW,
PREMERGER NOTIFICATION PRACTICE MANUAL
(3D ED. 2003)

Cover design by ABA Publishing.

The materials contained herein represent the opinions of the authors and editors and should not be construed to be the action of either the American Bar Association or the Section of Antitrust Law unless adopted pursuant to the bylaws of the Association.

Nothing contained in this book is to be considered as the rendering of legal advice for specific cases, and readers are responsible for obtaining such advice from their own legal counsel. This book and any forms and agreements herein are intended for educational and informational purposes only.

© 2003 American Bar Association. All rights reserved.
Printed in the United States of America.

Library of Congress Control Number: 2003108096
ISBN 1-59031-255-4

Discounts are available for books ordered in bulk. Special consideration is given to state bars, CLE programs, and other bar-related organizations. Inquire at ABA Publishing, American Bar Association, 750 North Lake Shore Drive, Chicago, Illinois 60611.

06 05 04 03 02   5 4 3 2 1

Dedicated to the memory of Thomas F. Hancock, a long time member of the Premerger Notification Office of the Federal Trade Commission and a devoted antitrust scholar and practitioner.

CONTENTS

Foreword xiii

Preface xv

Introduction xvii

Commonly Used Terms and Abbreviations xxv

INTERPRETATIONS RELATING TO SECTION 7A

7A(a)(2) 3

Transfers of goods or realty in the ordinary course
of business – § 7A(c)(l) 5

Acquisition of bonds, mortgages, etc. – § 7A(c)(2) 12

Transfers to or from a federal or state agency – § 7A(c)(4) 14

Transactions specifically exempted by agency
approval – § 7A(c)(6) 17

Transactions requiring banking agency
approval – §§ 7A(c)(7) and 7A(c)(8) 18

Acquisitions of voting securities solely for
purpose of investment – § 7A(c)(9) 21

Acquisitions that do not increase the person's
per centum share – § 7A(c)(10) 24

Civil penalty actions – § 7A(g)(1) 27

Confidentiality – § 7A(h) 29

INTERPRETATIONS RELATING TO PART 801

THE COVERAGE RULES

801 generally 33

Definitions – Entity – § 801.1(a)(2) 44
       – Ultimate Parent Entity – § 801.1(a)(3) 47
       – Control – § 801.1(b) 49
       – Hold – § 801.1(c) 62
       – Foreign Issuer – § 801.1(e) 83
       – Voting Securities – § 801.1(f) 84
       – Tender Offer – § 801.1(g) 96

Acquiring and acquired persons – § 801.2 99

Secondary acquisitions – § 801.4 110

Value of voting securities and assets to be acquired – § 801.10 111

Annual net sales and total assets – § 801.11 154

Voting securities or assets to be held as a
result of acquisition – § 801.13 185

Aggregate total amount of voting securities
or assets – § 801.14 194

Acquisitions subsequent to exceeding threshold – § 801.20 197

Securities and cash not considered assets
when acquired – § 801.21 198

Tender offers and acquisitions of voting securities from
third parties – § 801.30 202

Acceptance of tendered shares for payment – § 801.33 206

Formation of a joint venture or other corporations – § 801.40 207

Transactions or devices for avoidance – § 801.90 227

INTERPRETATIONS RELATING TO PART 802

THE EXEMPTION RULES

Acquisitions of goods or realty in the ordinary course of business – § 802.1 243

Certain acquisitions of real property assets – § 802.2 247

Acquisitions of carbon-based mineral reserves – § 802.3 259

Acquisitions of voting securities of issuers holding certain assets the direct acquisition of which is exempt – § 802.4 260

Acquisitions of investment rental property assets – § 802.5 264

Acquisitions of voting securities not meeting or exceeding greater notification threshold – § 802.21 269

Amended or renewed tender offers – § 802.23 275

Intraperson transactions – § 802.30 278

Acquisitions of foreign assets – § 802.50 287

Acquisitions of voting securities of a foreign issuer – § 802.51 293

Acquisitions by creditors and insurers – § 802.63 300

INTERPRETATIONS RELATING TO PART 803

THE TRANSMITTAL RULES

803 generally 305

Instructions applicable to Notification and Report Form – § 803.2 313

Statement of reasons for noncompliance – § 803.3 314

Contents

Affidavits required – § 803.5 316

Expiration of notification – § 803.7 323

Running of time – § 803.10 327

Termination of waiting period – § 803.11 329

Formal and informal interpretations of requirements under the Act
and the rules – § 803.30 331

INTERPRETATIONS RELATING TO THE NOTIFICATION AND REPORT FORM

Form generally 335

Names of all ultimate parent entities – Item 2(a) 336

Description of acquisition – Item 3 337

Documents to be supplied: annual reports, audit reports, and balance sheet – Item 4(b) 339

Documents to be supplied: documents analyzing the
transaction – Item 4(c) 342

Revenue data by NAICS code – Items 5(a) – (c) 347

Description of formation of joint venture or
other corporation – Item 5(d) 355

Shareholders and shareholdings – Item 6 356

Dollar revenues and geographic market information – Item 7 358

ENFORCEMENT ACTIONS DEALING WITH THE HART-SCOTT-RODINO ACT

A. United States v. Smithfield Foods, Inc. 363

B. United States v. Gemstar-TV Guide International, Inc. and
   TV Guide, Inc. 364

C. United States v. Computer Associates International, Inc. 366

D. United States v. The Hearst Trust:
   FTC v. The Hearst Trust 368

E. United States v. Input/Output, Inc. 370

F. United States v. Blackstone Capital Partners II
   Merchant Banking Fund L.P. 371

G. United States v. Loewen Group, Inc. 373

H. United States v. Mahle GmbH 375

I. United States v. Figgie International Inc. 376

J. United States v. Foodmaker, Inc. 377

K. United States v. Titan Wheel International, Inc. 379

L. United States v. Automatic Data Processing, Inc. 380

M. United States v. Sara Lee Corp. 382

N. United States v. Farley 383

O. United States v. Pennzoil Co. 384

P. United States v. Anova Holding AG 385

Q. United States v. Honickman 386

R. United States v. Beazer plc 387

x *Contents*

S. United States v. Atlantic Richfield Co. 389

T. United States v. General Cinema Corp. 391

U. United States v. Cox Enterprises, Inc. 392

V. United States v. Aero Limited Partnership 393

W. United States v. Atlantic Richfield Co. 394

X. United States v. Equity Group Holdings 395

Y. United States v. Service Corp. International 396

Z. United States v. Reliance Group Holdings, Inc. 397

AA. United States v. Baker Hughes Inc. 398

BB. United States v. Tengelmann Warenhandelsgesellschaft 400

CC. FTC v. Illinois Cereal Mills, Inc. 401

DD. United States v. Lonrho PLC 403

EE. United States v. Roscoe Moss Co. 404

FF. United States v. Wickes Cos. 405

GG. United States v. Trump 406

HH. United States v. First City Financial Corp. 407

II. United States v. Bell Resources Ltd. 408

JJ. United States v. Coastal Corp. 409

APPENDIX: FORMAL INTERPRETATIONS

Formal Interpretation 1 413

Formal Interpretation 2 416

Formal Interpretation 3 424

Formal Interpretation 4 428

Formal Interpretation 5 435

Formal Interpretation 6 437

Formal Interpretation 7 439

Formal Interpretation 8 445

Formal Interpretation 9 450

Formal Interpretation 10 452

Formal Interpretation 11 454

Formal Interpretation 12 456

Formal Interpretation 13 467

Formal Interpretation 14 469

Formal Interpretation 15 473

Formal Interpretation 16 487

Formal Interpretation 17 491

FOREWORD

The Section of Antitrust Law of the American Bar Association is pleased to publish this third edition of the *Premerger Notification Practice Manual*. The *Manual* collects and discusses summaries of informal interpretations by the staff of the Federal Trade Commission and enforcement actions regarding the premerger notification requirements contained in Title II of the Hart-Scott-Rodino Antitrust Improvements Act of 1976 and the Commission's implementing regulations.

Like the first two editions, published in 1985 and 1991, this third edition of the *Manual* continues to be the most comprehensive published source for such materials. The extensive involvement of the Federal Trade Commission's Premerger Notification Office staff in the review of the drafts of this edition, for which the Section is most grateful, assures that its contents are as accurate and as current as possible.

This edition of the *Manual* was prepared by a working group, headed by Neil W. Imus, within the Section's Mergers & Acquisitions Committee. The Section appreciates the experience, expertise, and effort resulting in this new edition, which we believe will be invaluable to premerger notification practice.

                                              Robert T. Joseph
                                              Chair, 2002-2003
                                              Section of Antitrust Law

PREFACE

In 1985 the Section of Antitrust Law published the first edition of the *Premerger Notification Practice Manual*, which contained a collection and discussion of Federal Trade Commission informal staff interpretations relating to the Hart-Scott-Rodino Antitrust Improvements Act of 1976 and the FTC's implementing rules. This *Manual* quickly became a valuable reference tool for HSR practitioners that continued with the publication of the second edition of the *Manual* in 1991.

Since 1991 the HSR Act has been amended, many of the HSR rules have changed, and the body of informal HSR Act "lore" has evolved significantly and expanded enormously. A working group coordinated by Neil W. Imus began collecting materials for a new edition of the *Manual* in 1997. Assimilating the additional lore, drafting the new *Manual*, and reviewing the draft with the staff of the FTC's Premerger Notification Office ("PNO") required several more years. This third edition replaces the 1991 version of the *Manual*. Interpretations have been revised and expanded as necessary and, in a few cases, deleted as obsolete. A great many new interpretations have been added.

Like the earlier editions, the third edition of the *Manual* is organized by specific sections of the HSR Act and rules. This edition also adds summaries of certain agency enforcement actions relating to HSR issues. Each numbered interpretation describes the issue and analysis, identifies some of the documents that deal with the issue, and may comment on the issue and the interpretation. Like the second edition, this edition was reviewed and discussed in detail with the staff of the PNO. It attempts to present as accurately as possible the current position of that office on all of the issues that it discusses.

Special thanks are due to Neil W. Imus, who coordinated preparation of the new edition; to John Sipple and Marian Bruno, PNO Assistant Directors at different times during the work on this *Manual*; and Richard Smith and Michael Verne in the PNO office, for countless hours and assistance. Thanks also go to many people in Vinson & Elkins's administrative staff, especially Jill Maguire and Linda Sheffield. There were literally scores of other individuals in the private bar and in the government who assisted in this project, including:

Roberta Baruch	Daniel Ducore
William Blumenthal	Janet Durholz Ridge
Dale Collins	Theodore Edelman
Ken Davidson	David Fierst

Ilene Knable Gotts
Michele Harrington
Howard Iwrey
Jonathan Jacobson
Michael Jahnke
Robert Jones
William Kolasky
Jonathan Konoff
Bruce McCulloch
John McLean
Joseph Nisa
Alexander Okuliar
Nancy Ovuka
Debra Pearlstein
Malcolm Pfunder

Bruce Prager
Hy Rubenstein
Robin Sampson
Robert Schlossberg
Keith Shugarman
Jack Sidorov
Jim Sonda
Kenneth Starling
Charles Stormont
Nancy Strick Hawkins
Anthony Swisher
David Wales
Valarie Williams
Edward Zimmerman

As a result of their labors, the new third edition of the *Manual* is the most comprehensive collection and explanation of Hart-Scott-Rodino lore available to company counsel and antitrust practitioners. We believe it will provide a valuable service to members of the antitrust bar for years to come.

Joseph G. Krauss
Chair, 2002-2003
Mergers & Acquisitions
  Committee
Section of Antitrust Law

INTRODUCTION

This *Premerger Notification Practice Manual* (*"Manual"*) contains interpretations as well as summaries of cases relating to the premerger notification requirements under Section 7A of the Clayton Act, 15 U.S.C. § 18a (2000), enacted as Title II of the Hart-Scott-Rodino Antitrust Improvements Act of 1976 ("HSR Act" or the "Act") and the Federal Trade Commission's ("FTC") implementing rules. The interpretations are based on guidance from the FTC staff, which is charged with administering the Act. The case summaries are of enforcement actions, most of which are filed by the United States Department of Justice ("DOJ") based on a referral by the FTC.

The HSR Act and Rules

Section 7A of the Clayton Act specifies that certain proposed acquisitions must be reported to the DOJ and FTC in advance of their consummation. Reportability is governed in some cases by the sizes of the parties to the proposed transaction and always by the size of the contemplated transaction.

Where premerger notification is filed, the parties must thereafter wait a period of time (normally about thirty days) before completing the proposed acquisition. That waiting period may be extended if either of the federal antitrust enforcement agencies, the DOJ or the FTC, issues a request for additional information or documentary material (a "Second Request") to either or both of the parties. The purpose of the statute is to facilitate evaluation of the antitrust implications of the proposed transaction and, where after investigation the anticompetitive consequences appear substantial, to permit either agency to challenge the legality of the transaction in federal district court and seek a preliminary injunction to block its consummation. A detailed explanation of the entire merger review process can be found in ABA SECTION OF ANTITRUST LAW, THE MERGER REVIEW PROCESS: A STEP-BY-STEP GUIDE TO FEDERAL MERGER REVIEW (2d ed. 2001). A discussion of many of the substantive antitrust issues that arise in merger investigations can be found in ABA SECTION OF ANTITRUST LAW, MERGERS AND ACQUISITIONS: UNDERSTANDING THE ANTITRUST ISSUES (2000).

The initial rules implementing the Act were promulgated by the FTC in 1978 and are codified at 16 C.F.R. Parts 801 through 803 (the "Rules"). The FTC's Statement of Basis and Purpose, 43 Fed. Reg. 33,450 (July 31, 1978), here often referred to as the "SBP," provides a lengthy, detailed explanation of those initial Rules and is frequently discussed in these interpretations. The Rules have been modified numerous times over the years, and each time, an SBP explaining the rule changes is published in the Federal Register. Part 801 of the Rules deals generally with the reporting requirements; Part 802 contains a number of exemptions from those requirements; and Part 803 contains procedural rules for completing and filing the notification itself. The Notification and Report Form, which is used to provide information to the agencies concerning a specific transaction, is an appendix to Part 803.

Informal Interpretations of the HSR Act and Rules

By agreement between the two enforcement agencies, the FTC has the primary responsibility for explaining and interpreting the Rules and for responding to inquiries from the public concerning their application. Since the premerger notification program became effective in 1978, the FTC's Premerger Notification Office ("PNO") has received tens of thousands of letters and telephone inquiries. Because of the volume of these inquiries and the limited number of staff, most of these inquiries have received oral responses, and the FTC staff has generally declined to provide written interpretations, even when requested to do so. While the FTC has, with the concurrence of the DOJ, issued a small number of formal written interpretations, the vast majority of the informal, oral interpretations have not been publicized. Thus a substantial body of unwritten HSR lore has grown up and been passed along by word of mouth among antitrust practitioners.

Sources of Information for the Manual

This *Manual* attempts to capture and document HSR "lore" and provides a unique source of information about interpretations of the HSR Act and the Rules.

The HSR practitioner has a number of published resources to use in interpreting the HSR requirements. The Rules themselves along with the SBP often provide sufficient guidance. Over the last few years the PNO has placed a significant amount of additional HSR information on the FTC Web site. The Web site contains Introductory Guides, the HSR form and instructions, the HSR Act, the Rules, the Formal Interpretations, FTC annual reports, frequently asked questions and other helpful tips, speeches by FTC staff regarding HSR issues, a database of informal interpretation letters, and PNO staff contact information. The address for the FTC web page containing the HSR material is www.ftc.gov/bc/hsr/hsr.htm. There also are a few treatises that deal with HSR matters. Despite the existence of this information there are still a large number of transactions that raise HSR filing questions not specifically addressed by these materials. This *Manual* compiles almost 300 examples providing further guidance on the PNO's current views on the application of the HSR Act to a variety of situations.

The sources of information used to prepare the interpretations contained in the *Manual* have changed with each edition. The first edition of the *Manual*, published in 1985, reflected primarily the information contained in documents obtained from the FTC through a Freedom of Information Act ("FOIA") request. Most of those documents were letters received by the PNO purporting to confirm telephonic advice provided by attorneys and other members of the staff of that office. Certain internal PNO memoranda also were supplied. In addition, the original *Manual* contained interpretations furnished by law firms and individual lawyers, some reflecting advice received from the PNO staff, others embodying advice which attorneys had given to their clients. The original *Manual* relied on materials covering the period from the inception of the HSR Act program until mid-1983.

The second edition of the *Manual*, published in 1991, also reflected materials obtained from the FTC in response to FOIA requests, along with other interpretations gathered from law firms and various other sources. But PNO positions had evolved over the years, in some cases significantly, and the materials that were collected included inconsistent or incorrect staff advice. Furthermore, the materials failed to address some important issues entirely, while containing tremendous duplication on other issues. For these reasons, it was decided that the systematic effort to collect and report more than ten years of HSR lore would be better served by altering the approach used in the first edition. The editors identified as many interpretative issues as possible and then summarized what they understood to be the PNO positions on them. The interpretations made selective reference to confirming letters and other documents obtained from the PNO and elsewhere, but did not identify all of the relevant documents that were examined. Nor did they systematically review all materials potentially available from the FTC through FOIA requests. The various drafts of the revised *Manual* were reviewed in detail with the PNO, whose views were sought as to all issues discussed.

The group formed to write the third edition of the *Manual* also recognized the limitations of relying solely on existing written material—letters written to the PNO and internal memoranda and letters from law firms—to update the interpretations. As the second edition editors had noted, the existing written materials were sometimes inconsistent and often duplicative. But importantly, there were huge gaps in coverage. Only a fraction of the interpretations made by the PNO each year are documented in letters sent to the PNO or internal memoranda that firms are willing to share. Furthermore, the HSR Act itself had been amended and many sections of the Rules had been changed since the second edition was published. In many cases there were no written materials dealing with important interpretative issues relating to the changes in the Act or the Rules.

The third edition authors started their work by examining collected written materials, the second edition interpretations, and the new rules and revised statute to identify issues that were either missing from the second edition or needed to be revised. They then began a series of meetings with the PNO to discuss each proposed interpretation. The authors prepared several drafts, which were discussed with the PNO at each stage. In the course of these discussions, the PNO identified additional and related issues that were added to the *Manual*. This third edition not only reflects information contained in various written materials but also includes substantial input from experienced HSR practitioners in the private bar and from the PNO.

One of the primary goals of the *Manual* is to provide the HSR practitioner with information about PNO positions on HSR issues as faithfully as possible. Of course, as with the earlier edition of the *Manual*, views expressed herein are not necessarily those of the Commission itself, of any individual Commissioner, or of the Bureau of Competition.

Caveats

This *Manual* attempts to provide the current views of the PNO on the HSR analysis of the facts presented in the various interpretations. It is important, however, that the HSR practitioner using the *Manual* understand the limits of the information contained in the book.

First, even though the PNO has had substantial input in this publication, the interpretations in the Manual do not bind the FTC or the PNO. As noted earlier, the PNO cannot bind the Commission, and the PNO's position may be superseded at any time, either by a formal change to the HSR Act or the Rules, or as a result of its own internal decision-making. Changes in the PNO views on the interpretations in the *Manual* do not happen frequently, but they do happen.

Introduction xxi

The 1985 *Manual* quoted at length from an FTC letter that cautioned that letters purporting to confirm advice received from the staff may not accurately reflect the advice given, that internal staff memoranda may not state the interpretation ultimately adopted, and that, in any case, staff positions may have changed over time. Those cautions obviously remain equally relevant today.

Similarly, a 1990 letter from a former director of the FTC's Bureau of Competition emphasized that the *Manual* is not a compilation of policy formulations or interpretations issued or adopted by the FTC or its Bureau of Competition. Instead, the *Manual* presents broad and accessible summaries of advice given by the PNO. Thus, the letter warned, there are limitations on the usefulness of these summaries. The letter stated:

> The advice reflected in the ABA *Manual* is, most commonly, the product of responses to questions from persons that were in the process of negotiating transactions. Because of their need for a fast turnaround, the responses of the Premerger Notification Office must be limited to the specific facts presented, are not necessarily applicable to transactions with other facts and do not comprehensively reflect the views of the Premerger Notification Office. Moreover, unlike telephone advice from the Premerger Notification Office, advice summarized in the *Manual* may have been superseded by the time it is read. Conflicts, or apparent conflicts, between these summaries may or may not have been fully rationalized. Also, the summaries may be misleading where the underlying written documents do not identify all relevant facts. Furthermore, in summarizing advice the ABA may have introduced some distortions, either by characterizing the facts and advice too broadly or by inadvertent errors.
>
> In view of these limitations, persons examining prior advice from the Premerger Notification Office or the ABA *Manual* must be wary of relying heavily on one or two interpretations; they need to look at the totality of relevant materials in the ABA *Manual* and, more particularly, at § 7A of the Clayton Act, the premerger notification rules, their examples and the statements of basis and purpose for the rules. If, after examining these materials, a person has questions about its obligations under § 7A of the Clayton Act, the person would do well to seek specific advice from the Premerger Notification Office.

Thus, the reader must remember that what is published in this *Manual* today may no longer be the PNO's position on the issue at a later time. Practitioners can usually keep abreast of changes and proposed changes in the HSR Act and the Rules by reviewing the FTC's Web site.

xxii *Introduction*

Attorneys also are always encouraged to contact the PNO directly by telephone or letter for specific advice on particular facts. This contact can ensure that an interpretation is still followed by the PNO. The PNO staff is readily accessible and normally very responsive to questions from the bar.

Just as the interpretations in the *Manual* are not formal positions of the FTC, neither are they formal positions of the ABA, the Section of Antitrust Law, or the private bar. As noted above, the primary goal of this *Manual* is to provide what is believed to be the current position of the PNO on the application of the HSR regulations to various situations. In a few instances the authors and editors of this third edition have provided their comments about an interpretation. But no comment, or lack of comment, should be interpreted as general acceptance or rejection by the authors or editors (much less the Section of Antitrust Law) of the analysis contained in an interpretation. There was no attempt to reach a consensus among the bar as a whole (or even among the authors) on each interpretation.

Finally, it is not inconceivable that a party could take a defensible HSR position that differs from a PNO position. Reasonable, experienced HSR practitioners can (and do) disagree among themselves and with the PNO about the "correct" application of HSR regulations to a given transaction. This is because the Act and the Rules have some inherent inconsistencies. Some of these are due to the varied treatment afforded different forms of entities (e.g., corporate versus partnership). Some arise because of longstanding PNO interpretations that create consistent treatment among certain transactions but inconsistent treatment among other transactions with similar substantive results (e.g., difference in valuation in asset versus stock transactions). It is not possible to resolve every inconsistency in the Rules. But the PNO's interpretations of the HSR Act and the Rules are not always without controversy. Of course, taking a position contrary to the PNO's views runs the risk that the agency will institute an investigation and initiate an enforcement action for failure to file the HSR form and observe the HSR waiting period.

Format of Summaries and Citation Procedures

The *Manual* contains summaries, which are arranged into six groups: statutory interpretations of Section 7A; interpretations relating to Parts 801, 802, and 803 of 16 C.F.R.; discussions of individual items on the Notification and Report Form; and enforcement actions. Each of these summaries begins with a citation to the specific section or subsection of the Act, the Rules, or the Form. Where multiple sections or subsections are cited, they appear in order of relevance to the summary, from most relevant to least. A brief statement of the issue and a description of the facts are followed by an analysis and discussion. In some instances an "Editor's Note" has been included to provide additional perspective.

Users of previous editions of the *Manual* told the authors of the third edition that they used prior editions to record notes about conversations with PNO staff on various interpretations and issues. Therefore, it was decided to start each interpretation in this edition on a new page to provide plenty of space for notes.

Correlation of Interpretations in Prior and Present Manuals

This edition of the *Manual* is intended to replace the earlier versions. Thus, interpretations contained in the 1985 and 1991 *Manuals* have been incorporated into the present publication to the extent that they remain the present views of the PNO staff. Some of these earlier interpretations have been reprinted without change, though most have been revised. A few prior interpretations have been superseded and therefore do not appear in this edition at all.

COMMONLY USED TERMS AND ABBREVIATIONS

Bureau	FTC Bureau of Competition
DOJ	United States Department of Justice
Exchange Act	The Securities Exchange Act of 1934
FDIC	Federal Deposit Insurance Corporation
FOIA	Freedom of Information Act
FTC	Federal Trade Commission
GAAP	Generally-accepted accounting principles
HSR Act or Act	Hart-Scott-Rodino Antitrust Improvements Act of 1976
IPO	Initial public offering
LLC	Limited liability company
MLP	Master limited partnership
PNO	The Premerger Notification Office of the FTC
REIT	Real Estate Investment Trust
Rules	16 C.F.R. Parts 801 through 803
SBP	Statement of Basis and Purpose
SEC	U.S. Securities and Exchange Commission
Second Request	A request for additional information or documentary material issued by the DOJ or FTC pursuant to § 7A(e)(1)(A)
UPE	Ultimate Parent Entity

INTERPRETATIONS RELATING TO SECTION 7A

1 Applicable provisions. 7A(a)(2), 801.1(j).

Issue. When is a person "engaged in manufacturing" for determining the size-of-person requirement in Section 7A(a)(2) of the Act?

Analysis. The PNO's position is that, within the meaning of Section 7A(a)(2) and Section 801.1(j), a company is engaged in manufacturing if there is any manufacturing by *any* entity within the person *anywhere* in the world, regardless of whether the product is sold in or into the United States or how the revenue would be reported in Item 5, if at all. *See* Int. 281.

| 2 | **Applicable provisions.** 7A(a)(2), 801.1(j).

Issue. Is a company "engaged in manufacturing" if it supplies raw ingredients (as distinguished from manufactured components) to an unrelated company that manufactures a finished product under a contractual arrangement, such as a tolling arrangement, which the first company then resells?

Analysis. Such an entity is not engaged in manufacturing. It is simply a reseller and does not control the manufacturer. The fact that the product it sells is manufactured specifically for it under contract and with raw materials provided by it is irrelevant.

3 **Applicable provisions.** 7A(c)(l), 802.2(h), 802.3, 802.1, 802.4, 802.5.

Issue. Is the transfer of shopping center sites to a limited partnership created solely to acquire and develop such sites exempt under Section 7A(c)(1) as a transfer of realty in the ordinary course of business?

Analysis. Rather than having to rely on the "ordinary course" language of 7A(c)(1), in this case one can look at Section 802.2 of the Rules. (This is one of the rules promulgated to provide specific examples of transactions qualifying for the ordinary course exemption. *See* Editor's Note below.) The PNO position is that the shopping center sites, as "retail rental spaces," would be considered realty under Section 802.2(h) and would be exempt. However, if the acquisition included a business, then the portion of the shopping center sites used by the business would be separately subject to the notification requirements as part of the business being acquired. For example, the Section 802.2(h) exemption would not apply when a person acquires a store with its inventory and intends to operate the store under a new name. However, the exemption would apply if the person buys the store space and acts as a landlord for the operators of the store.

In addition, the Section 802.2 and 802.3 exemptions apply to the purchase of leasehold interests as well as asset purchases. Even though not explicit in the Rules, the PNO's position is that, if the asset would qualify for the exemption if purchased outright, the purchase of a lease is similarly exempt.

Editor's Note. *In 1996, the FTC replaced and expanded former Section 802.1, which described the application of the ordinary course exemption granted by Section 7A(c)(1) of the Act, with five new rules (Sections 802.1 through 802.5) that were intended, among other things, to provide examples of specific transactions that would qualify for the ordinary course exemption. See SBP, 61 Fed. Reg. 13,666 (Mar. 28, 1996). While these rules clarified the application of the 7A(c)(1) exemption, see, e.g., Ints. 197 through 218, the FTC acknowledged that the five new sections do not cover the entire statutory exemption created by Section 7A(c)(1). See 61 Fed. Reg. at 13,669. Thus, there are transactions that will qualify for the statutory exemption of Section 7A(c)(1) that are not covered by the Part 802 rules. The SBP itself provides one example. It states, "certain acquisitions of credit card receivables may qualify for exemption as transfers in the ordinary course of business."* Id.

4 Applicable provision. 7A(c)(1).

Issue. Does entering into a long-term lease constitute an exempt acquisition of realty within the meaning of Section 7A(c)(1)?

Facts. The buyer of corporation X, which operates on premises leased from a partnership whose members also control X, enters into a new long-term (twenty-year) lease of those premises. It is in the ordinary course of business for the partnership to lease this property to the owner of the corporation, and it is the buyer's practice to lease all premises on which its businesses are operated.

Analysis. The PNO position is that entering into a lease generally does not constitute an acquisition of the underlying assets. Exceptions to this position are where the lease amounts to an installment sale of the property or where a lease exhausts the useful life of the property. *See* Int. 28. If the facts suggest that entering into the lease would constitute an acquisition of the underlying assets, a Section 7A(c)(1) analysis would be applied to determine whether the acquisition was in the ordinary course of business for the parties.

The PNO has never viewed entering into an executory contract negotiated at arm's length as the acquisition of an asset. Thus, the PNO generally appears to distinguish between entry into a new lease (which typically is not covered by the Act) and transfer of an existing lease, which will be reportable if the lease has a "value" of more than $50 million and the underlying property is not otherwise exempt. The value of the lease will not include the ordinary payments over the life of the lease; rather, the value of the lease will be the additional payment for the transfer, the premium (if any) that the purchaser will pay for the assignment of the lease interests. *Compare* Ints. 103, 104. Even if the person is making a premium payment for assignment of the lease, the value of which exceeds $50 million, the transfer of the lease is exempt if transfer of the underlying property would be exempt. *See* Int. 3.

5 | Applicable provisions. 7A(c)(l), 801.21(a), 802.1(a), 801.15.

Issue. Is the acquisition of inventory assets aggregated with the acquisition of related productive assets in determining whether the size-of-transaction test is met?

Facts. In this asset acquisition of several supermarkets, there are three components of the purchase price: a component for cash and cash equivalents on hand at the time of closing, a component for the asset value of the supermarkets themselves, and a component for the inventory on hand at the supermarkets.

Analysis. The PNO's position is that the value of the supermarkets and the value of the inventory must be aggregated in this case. The acquisition of cash and cash equivalents is not subject to the Act because they are not considered assets when acquired. *See* Section 801.21(a). If the purchase price attributable to the inventory on hand at the supermarkets, coupled with the price for the supermarkets, takes the purchase price over $50 million, the transaction would be reportable.

The PNO position is that an acquisition of inventory cannot be treated separately as an acquisition in the ordinary course of business when all of the assets of an operating unit, including the inventory, are being purchased. *See* Section 802.1(a). The FTC defines "operating unit" to mean "assets that are operated by the acquired person as a business undertaking in a particular location or for particular products or services, even though those assets may not be organized as a separate legal entity."

On the question of whether the purchase of the supermarket is considered an acquisition of an operating unit within the meaning of the Rules, the PNO has indicated that normally the purchase of a supermarket will be considered the acquisition of an operating unit when the acquisition includes the supermarket's inventory. *See* Section 802.1, Example 1.

| 6 | **Applicable provisions.** 7A(c)(1), 802.3, 802.1, 802.2, 802.4, 802.5.

Issue. Is the purchase of several movable oil and gas drilling rigs exempt where both buyer and seller have previously bought and sold such rigs in the course of their contract oil and gas drilling businesses?

Analysis. The acquisition is not exempt. The PNO takes the position that the 7A(c)(1) ordinary course exemption does not apply because the assets do not fall within the parameters of the rule that deals with oil and gas assets. Movable oil and gas drilling rigs are not considered "associated exploration or production assets" otherwise exempt under Section 802.3(a). The PNO considers permanent derricks exempt but not movable rigs, unless they are "integral and exclusive" to a particular oil or gas field. Section 802.3(c).

Editor's Note. This interpretation highlights one aspect of the PNO's approach in applying the "ordinary course" exemption as stated in Section 7A(c)(1) and the Rules. Since drilling rigs are involved in exploration and production activities and are thus dealt with by Section 802.3, if the transaction does not qualify for the exemption under that Section, it cannot otherwise qualify under Section 7A(c)(1). In other words, where one of the rules that were adopted to elaborate on the Section 7A(c)(1) ordinary course exemption (see Editor's Note to Int. 3) arguably applies to a particular asset, the PNO will look to the specific application of those rules to determine whether an exemption ought to apply. The PNO will not expand the "ordinary course" exemption beyond the scope of Sections 802.1 through 802.5 if those rules apply to the particular assets involved in the transaction. It is only where Sections 802.1 through 802.5 do not cover the assets involved that the PNO will consider whether Section 7A(c)(1) will apply independently.

| 7 | **Applicable provisions.** 7A(c)(1), Formal Interpretation 9, 802.21, 802.1(a).

Issue. Is the transfer of more than $50 million worth of retail installment receivables exempt as a transfer of goods in the ordinary course of business?

Facts. The seller had acquired receivables from the retail sales business conducted in its own stores and those of its dealers. The acquiring entity was regularly engaged in making consumer loans and regularly acquired retail installment receivables as part of that business.

Analysis. The acquisition is exempt under Section 7A(c)(1). The original PNO position had been that accounts receivable were for practical purposes the equivalent of cash and therefore could, by reason of Section 801.21, be acquired without notification. After the DOJ successfully challenged an acquisition of finance companies in *United States v. Household Finance Corp.*, 1981-2 Trade Cas. (CCH) ¶ 64,301 (N.D. Ill. 1980), the FTC in March 1980 issued Formal Interpretation 9 (*see* Appendix), which stated that accounts receivable would no longer be treated as a cash-equivalent under Section 801.21. The formal interpretation thus assumed the possibility of competitive significance in any transfer of accounts receivable, a position far more extreme than the *Household Finance* case seemed to justify.

The PNO position that has evolved since that time is that accounts receivable may be transferred in the ordinary course of business under Section 7A(c)(1). But transfer of such receivables in the context of an acquisition of a retail lending company (the *Household Finance* situation) or of substantially all the assets of any other entity, would not be in the ordinary course of business (and therefore not exempt), by reason of Section 802.1(a).

8 **Applicable provisions.** 7A(c)(1), 802.1(a), Formal Interpretation 9.

Issue. Is the acquisition of consumer loans exempt?

Facts. Bank A plans to acquire a portfolio of consumer loans of Bank B. The loans comprise all of Bank B's business in a particular state but not all of its assets and not even all of its consumer loans.

Analysis. The acquisition is exempt. Unlike other ordinary course of business acquisitions, (and unlike its treatment of accounts receivable, *see* Int. 9) the PNO allows the exemption for these types of financial portfolios, even if the portfolio represents all of the assets of an operating unit. For example, if a bank were to sell its home improvement loan portfolio, but retain its boat loan and car loan portfolios, the sale of the home improvement loan portfolio would be exempt as a sale in the ordinary course of business, even if the portfolio to be acquired represented all of the assets of a corporate subsidiary of the bank. Likewise, if the bank were selling all of the assets of a subsidiary that represented all of its consumer loans, but retained another subsidiary that handled its commercial loan business, the transaction would be exempt in the ordinary course. If the bank had no other loan business, however, the sale of the home improvement loans would not be in the ordinary course, since the bank would be exiting the loan business as a result of the sale.

Note that the PNO considers credit card receivables to be in a different category from other loan products. If the bank were selling all of its credit card business, the transaction would not be in the ordinary course of business, even if the bank continues to provide other types of loans. *See also* Int. 9.

9 **Applicable provisions.** 7A(c)(2), 802.4, 801.21, 802.2, Formal Interpretation 9.

Issue. Is the acquisition of mortgage loans exempt under Section 7A(c)(2)?

Facts. In light of Formal Interpretation 9 (*see* Appendix), which stated that accounts receivable would not be treated as exempt assets when acquired, the acquiror questioned if the value of a portfolio of mortgage loans, obtained as part of an acquisition of a mortgage banking business, could be excluded from the size-of-transaction computation for that acquisition.

Analysis. Shortly after issuance of Formal Interpretation 9 stating that accounts receivable were not "exempt assets" under Section 801.21, the PNO took the position that an acquisition of mortgage loans was nevertheless exempt under Section 7A(c)(2).

Under Section 802.4, the acquisition of the voting securities of an issuer whose assets consist of mortgage loans would be exempt unless the business entity and all of the entities it controls hold other nonexempt assets with a fair market value of more than $50 million.

10 | Applicable provisions. 7A(c)(2), 801.1(f), 802.31, 801.32.

Issue. Is the acquisition of "junior subordinated notes" that are convertible into common stock, exempt?

Analysis. Section 7A(c)(2) of the Act exempts "acquisitions of bonds, mortgages, deeds of trust, or other obligations that are not voting securities." Thus the first question is whether notes that are convertible into common stock are "voting securities."

Section 801.1(f)(1) (as amended in 1983) defines "voting securities" to include securities which "upon conversion entitle the owner or holder thereof to vote for the election of directors . . . ." The term "conversion" is defined by Section 801.1(f)(3) to mean:

> the exercise of a right inherent in the ownership or holding of particular voting securities to exchange such securities for securities which presently entitle the owner or holder to vote for directors . . . .

Thus, because at present or at some future time these notes are exchangeable for voting securities, they are themselves voting securities, and their acquisition is not exempt under Section 7A(c)(2).

Section 802.31, however, exempts the acquisition of convertible voting securities from the requirements of the Act. Section 801.1(f)(2) defines a *convertible* voting security as a *voting* security that carries no present right to vote for the board of directors. Therefore, so long as the "junior subordinated notes" carry no present voting rights, they are "convertible voting securities," and their acquisition is exempt.

Subsequent conversion of the notes into common stock would itself be a potentially reportable event. *See* Section 801.32.

11 Applicable provisions. 7A(c)(4), 801.1(a)(2).

Issue. What federal, state, and foreign governmental units are not considered entities under 7A(c)(4) and Section 801.1(a)(2) and, thus, cannot be considered acquired or acquiring persons under the Act?

Analysis. Section 7A(c)(4) exempts "transfers to or from a Federal agency or a State or political subdivision thereof." Section 801.1(a)(2) defines the term "entity" under the Act and provides that "the term 'entity' shall not include any foreign state, foreign government, or agency thereof (other than a corporation engaged in commerce), nor the United States, any of the States thereof, or any political subdivision or agency of either (other than a corporation engaged in commerce)." If the government organization is not an "entity" under the Act, it cannot be an acquired or acquiring person subject to the Act.

The fact that a government agency, such as the FDIC, is a corporation "engaged in commerce," does not change its status as a nonentity for purposes of the Act. The PNO's position is that the FDIC is a federal agency, and therefore, cannot be an entity under Section 801.1(a)(2). Similarly, many state organizations, such as universities and municipal hospitals, are state agencies and are not considered entities under the Act. The federal or state enabling legislation will determine whether the organization was created as an agency of the government or as a quasi-independent corporation controlled by the government. If the enabling legislation is ambiguous, the PNO will consider judicial decisions from the highest state court declaring that an organization is or is not a state agency and examine whether the organization holds itself out as a government agency or an independent body.

For example, an organization that manages a state pension fund may or may not be an entity for purposes of compliance with the Act. The organization may be controlled by the state, but if it was not created as a state agency, it will be considered an entity under Section 801.1(a)(2). The SBP makes clear that "corporations controlled by [federal, state, and foreign governments] and engaged in commerce are entities, and may be subject to the requirements of the act." 43 Fed. Reg. 33,450, 33,456 (July 31, 1978). The state pension fund's charter or the enabling legislation that created the pension fund will determine its status as an entity within the definition of Section 801.1(a)(2). *See* Ints. 12, 34, 35, and 36.

| 12 | **Applicable provisions.** 7A(c)(4), 801.1(a)(2).

Issue. If an organization is a state or federal agency and not an entity under the Act, under what circumstances are acquisitions of assets or voting securities from the agency exempt from premerger notification requirements?

Analysis. Section 7A(c)(4) exempts "transfers to or from a Federal agency or a State or political subdivision thereof." Under the plain language of the Section 7A(c)(4) exemption, all transfers to or from federal agencies and state or political subdivisions would be exempt from the requirements of the Act. The PNO's position, however, is that Section 7A(c)(4) must be read in conjunction with Section 801.1(a)(2) of the Rules and the SBP for Section 801.1(a)(2). Section 801.1(a)(2) and the applicable SBP define what organizations are considered government agencies, and only those organizations are eligible for the Section 7A(c)(4) exemption.

If the government organization is not an entity under Section 801.1(a)(2), the Section 7A(c)(4) exemption applies to all asset transfers to or from the government organization. Any asset transfer, no matter the size of the assets involved, to or from a federal or state agency, as defined by Section 801.1(a)(2), is exempt from the reporting requirements of the Act. Moreover, any voting securities acquisition by the federal or state agency is subject to the same exemption. This is supported by the SBP for Section 801.1(a)(2) that provides: "acquisitions by [nonentities] are not subject to the Act, because the Act applies only to acquisitions involving persons." *See* 43 Fed. Reg. 33,450, 33,456 (July 31, 1978).

The conflict between Section 7A(c)(4) and Section 801.1(a)(2) arises when the federal or state agency *sells* the voting securities of a corporation that is considered an entity under the Act. This could arise if the Internal Revenue Service decided to sell the previously seized voting securities of corporation X. The SBP to Section 801.1(a)(2) observes that "[s]tock acquisitions . . . are not excluded under this rule, since the issuer of the stock, not the State or government, would be the acquired person." *See* 43 Fed. Reg. at 33,456. (This is true whether the state or federal entity holds a minority or majority of the voting securities of the stock.) Thus, if a state or federal agency sells voting securities, the transfer is not automatically exempt under Section 7A(c)(4). The transaction will be subject to the Act if the acquired person, the issuer of the voting securities, is an entity under Section 801.1(a)(2) and otherwise subject to the Act. If, however, the federal or state agency is itself the issuer of the voting securities being acquired, the transfer will always be exempt because the acquired person would be the agency, a nonentity under the Act. *Compare* Int. 11.

13 | Applicable provisions. 7A(c)(6), 7A(c)(8), 802.6, 802.8.

Issue. Where the parties to an acquisition requiring regulatory agency approval have supplied the FTC and the DOJ with copies of their initial filings, pursuant to Section 7A(c)(6) and Section 802.6, is there any obligation to provide the FTC and the DOJ with copies of any additional documents or other information that may thereafter be required by or filed with that agency?

Analysis. It is the position of the PNO that no additional filings are required once the initial submissions are made in accordance with the Act and the Rules. The position applies equally to Section 7A(c)(6), Section 7A(c)(8), Section 802.6, and Section 802.8. The parties need not continue sending the FTC and the DOJ additional materials submitted as part of the regulatory proceeding.

14 Applicable provisions. 7A(c)(7), 7A(c)(8), 7A(c)(6), 802.6(b).

Issue. Is a filing required when the transaction is exempt under both Section 7A(c)(7), which does not require a filing, and Section 7A(c)(8), which requires that all information and documentary materials filed with the appropriate regulatory agency be filed contemporaneously with the FTC and DOJ at least thirty days prior to consummation of the proposed transaction?

Analysis. When a transaction is subject to both Sections 7A(c)(7) and 7A(c)(8), and is not a "mixed transaction" – part of which is not exempt under Sections 7A(c)(6)-(8), *see* Section 802.6(b) – no filing is required. Assuming that all portions of the transaction are exempt under Section 7A(c)(7), no filing is required even with respect to the portion of the transaction subject to Section 7A(c)(8).

| 15 | **Applicable provisions.** 7A(c)(8), 802.6, Formal Interpretation 17.

Issue. Is an acquisition requiring Federal Reserve Board ("Fed") approval under Section 4(c)(8), and possibly under Section 4(c)(9), of the Bank Holding Company Act of 1956, 12 U.S.C. § 1843 ("BHCA"), always exempt from premerger notification by reason of Section 7A(c)(8)?

Analysis. Banking and financial services industry transactions requiring Fed or Treasury Department approval are no longer automatically exempt from notification under the Act. The Gramm-Leach-Bliley Act of 1999 ("GLBA"), Pub. L. No. 106-102, 113 Stat. 1338 (1999), altered the legal and regulatory structure of the financial services industry by repealing key provisions of the Glass-Steagall Act, which prohibited affiliations between a member bank and a company principally engaged in securities activities. Under the new law, authorized bank holding companies and banks can expand their activities to include insurance and securities underwriting and agency activities, merchant banking, and insurance company portfolio investment activities. Companies that take advantage of the GLBA to expand their services will be classified as "financial holding companies" under Section 4(k) of the BHCA.

As part of the regulatory changes, certain banking industry transactions will become subject to the notification and waiting period requirements of the Act. Prior to the enactment of the GLBA, banking industry mergers were exempt from notification under Sections 7A(c)(7) and 7A(c)(8) of the Act, which exempted certain transactions that require agency approval under the BHCA, the Federal Deposit Insurance Act, and the Home Owners' Loan Act. Review under the HSR Act was deemed unnecessary considering the complete regulatory and competitive review of banking mergers undertaken by the Treasury Department and the Fed.

Section 133(c) of the GLBA amends the Section 7A(c)(7) and 7A(c)(8) exemptions for transactions involving banks that will offer the expanded services authorized by the GLBA. The change to the GLBA limits the Act exemptions to those portions of transactions that are actually reviewed by the relevant agencies. On April 3, 2000, the PNO, with the concurrence of the DOJ, adopted Formal Interpretation 17 (*see* Appendix) to address the reportability under the Act of "mixed" transactions involving banking and nonbanking financial institutions.

Formal Interpretation 17 confirms the PNO's longstanding position that nonbanking portions of mixed transactions are subject to review under the Act. The nonbank portion of a mixed transaction is subject to the reporting requirements of the Act, regardless of whether the nonbank business is housed in an affiliate of a financial holding company or a financial subsidiary of a bank.

For example, a merger of two newly authorized financial holding companies that involves banks and nonbanking financial institutions potentially will be subject to review under the bank merger statutes and the Act. The banking portion of the transaction will continue to be reviewed by the Fed while the nonbanking portion will be subject to HSR review by the FTC and the DOJ. See Section 802.6 for the treatment of "mixed" transactions.

16 | Applicable provisions. 7A(c)(9), 802.9, 801.1(i)(1), 802.64(b)(3), 7A(g)(1).

Issue. Will certain expressions of an acquiring person's intentions in its Schedule 13Ds that are inconsistent with the acquiror's assertion that its purchase of the stock of another company was "solely for the purpose of investment," result in a filing obligation?

Facts. Acquirer made certain purchases of Company's stock that resulted in its holding less than 10 percent of the voting securities of Company valued in excess of $50 million. Acquirer did not file notification or comply with a waiting period but filed Schedule 13Ds with the SEC in connection with its purchases. These filings stated that (1) Acquirer might seek control of Company; (2) although Acquirer had no present plans to merge with, liquidate, or reorganize Company, it might formulate such plans or proposals in the future; (3) Acquirer had demanded Company's shareholder list for the purpose of communicating with Company shareholders about a proposed transaction between Company and another entity; and (4) Acquirer had retained the services of a proxy solicitation concern.

Analysis. The PNO position is that the activities disclosed in the Schedule 13Ds are inconsistent with an intent to purchase voting securities "solely for the purpose of investment" as that term is used in the Act and the Rules. In this case, the purchase of the voting securities would constitute a violation of the Act, subjecting the Acquirer to a potential enforcement action under Section 7A(g)(1) of the Act.

For purposes of the Section 802.9 exemption, the PNO construes the term "solely for the purpose of investment," as used in the Act and the Rules, to apply only to purchasers who intend to hold the voting securities as passive investors. If an acquiring person purchases voting securities with the intention of influencing the basic business decisions of the issuer, or with the intention of participating in the management of the issuer, the exemption is not available. Merely voting the stock will not be considered evidence of an intent inconsistent with investment purpose, but the SBP for Section 801.1(i)(1) (43 Fed. Reg. 33,450, 33,465 (July 31, 1978)) lists certain types of conduct that could be so viewed. These include but are not limited to:

(1) nominating a candidate for the board of directors of the issuer; (2) proposing corporate action requiring shareholder approval; (3) soliciting proxies; (4) having a controlling shareholder, director, officer, or employee simultaneously serving as an officer or director of the issuer; (5) being a competitor of the issuer; or (6) doing any of the foregoing with respect to any entity directly or indirectly controlling the issuer.

The PNO's position is that the presence of any of this conduct creates a rebuttable presumption that the securities are not being held solely for the purpose of investment. The PNO has stated that seeking a presence on the board of directors of the issuer, a subsidiary of the issuer, or any other affiliated entity creates an irrebuttable presumption of intent inconsistent with passive investment. See Int. 21 for a discussion of the circumstances under which the FTC might not pursue an enforcement action.

The FTC has obtained civil penalties in a number of cases relating to the investment exemption. *See United States v. Smithfield Foods, Inc.*, Case No. 1:03CV00434 (D.D.C. filed Feb. 28, 2003) (Enf. Action A); *United States v. Farley*, 1995-1 Trade Cas. (CCH) ¶ 70,833 (N.D. Ill. 1995) (Enf. Action N); *United States v. Pennzoil Co.*, 1994-2 Trade Cas. (CCH) ¶ 70,760 (D.D.C. 1994) (Enf. Action O); *United States v. General Cinema Corp.*, 1991-2 Trade Cas. (CCH) ¶ 69,681 (D.D.C. 1992) (Enf. Action T); *United States v. Aero Ltd. P'ship*, 1991-1 Trade Cas. (CCH) ¶ 69,451 (D.D.C. 1991) (Enf. Action V); *United States v. Cox Enter., Inc.*, 1991-2 Trade Cas. (CCH) ¶ 69,540 (N.D. Ga. 1991) (Enf. Action U); *United States v. Reliance Group Holdings, Inc.*, 1990-2 Trade Cas. (CCH) ¶ 69,248 (D.D.C. 1990) (Enf. Action Z); *United States v. Bell Resources Ltd.*, 1986-2 Trade Cas. (CCH) ¶ 67,321 (D.D.C. 1986) (Enf. Action II); *United States v. Coastal Corp.,*1985-1 Trade Cas. (CCH) ¶ 66,425 (D.D.C. 1984) (Enf. Action JJ).

17 | Applicable provisions. 7A(c)(9), 802.9, 801.1(i)(1), Formal Interpretation 4.

Issue. May an acquiring person that has made an HSR filing to acquire in excess of 10 percent of the voting securities of an issuer acquire up to 10 percent of such voting securities (worth more than $50 million) prior to termination of the HSR waiting period relying on the "solely for purpose of investment" exemption of 7A(c)(9) and 802.9?

Analysis. Relying on the "solely for investment" exemption and acquiring up to 10 percent of the voting securities prior to termination of the waiting period is not necessarily precluded in this situation.

The key is the investment intention of the acquiring person. *See* Formal Int. 4, at Appendix. The "solely for investment" exemption would not be withheld merely because the acquiring person has filed an HSR Notification and Report Form stating an intention to acquire sufficient voting securities to exceed the 10 percent investment threshold. As the Formal Interpretation explains, to qualify for the exemption the acquiring person must hold 10 percent or less of the voting securities of the issuer and the acquisition must be solely for the purpose of investment, as defined by Section 801.1(i)(1). One of the keys is the intention of the acquiring person vis-à-vis the basic business decisions of the acquired person. "The fact that the reporting person has indicated through a filing that it intends to exceed the 10 percent investment threshold after expiration of the statutory waiting period does not, of itself, constitute an intention inconsistent with that of investment." Formal Int. 4, at Appendix. The Formal Interpretation does conclude, however, that "an intention (indicated in an HSR filing or otherwise) to acquire shares resulting in holdings of 50 percent or more of the shares of the issuer would necessarily eliminate the applicability of the exemption." An intention to acquire less than 50 percent might still preclude the applicability of the exemption depending on the circumstances (e.g., holding less than 50 percent but enough stock to obtain "working control of the issuer").

| 18 | **Applicable provision.** 7A(c)(10).

Issue. When does an acquiring person have to make an HSR filing for an acquisition of voting securities in an IPO where the acquiring person holds stock of the issuer prior to the IPO?

Facts. A holds securities in issuer B. B is its own UPE. B is planning an IPO of its stock. A is planning to acquire additional shares of B's voting securities during the IPO. If the actual IPO price is at the midpoint of the price range that has been set, A's percentage of B's total outstanding voting securities will actually decrease on the day of B's IPO when A acquires additional shares of B stock.

Analysis. When an acquiring person holds voting securities of an issuer before an IPO, and acquires additional voting securities of that issuer during the IPO, the acquiring person need not make an HSR filing so long as the acquiring person's percentage of that issuer's outstanding voting securities does not increase at the closing of the IPO. The PNO has applied the Section 7A(c)(10) exemption to such acquisitions.

19 | Applicable provisions. 7A(c)(10), 802.10, 802.30.

Issue. Does Section 802.30 of the Rules or Section 7A(c)(10) of the Act provide an exemption for a transaction in which an independent corporation organized to become a one-bank holding company issues its shares in precisely the same proportions to existing shareholders of the organizing corporation and then merges with the organizing corporation?

Analysis. The transaction is not exempt under Section 802.30, unless only one shareholder will control both corporations before the merger, in which case the acquiring and acquired persons would be the same. However, as the merger between the preexisting and newly formed entities will result in a single issuer, the exemption in Section 7A(c)(10) would apply. Section 7A(c)(10) provides an exemption for the "acquisitions of voting securities, if, as a result of such acquisition, the voting securities acquired do not increase, directly or indirectly, the acquiring person's per centum share of outstanding voting securities of the issuer." Section 7A(c)(10) is not necessarily limited by Section 802.10, which only exempts pro rata stock dividends or stock splits by a single issuer. Although the PNO reads Section 7A(c)(10) narrowly, it does interpret that exemption to permit acquisitions of the stock of a new shell parent by the shareholders of the existing entity, in the same percentage held prior to the transaction, even though the shareholders receive shares of a different issuer. Similarly, if a corporation reincorporates in a different state and shares of the new successor company are distributed to shareholders in the same percentage held prior to the reincorporation, the acquisition will be exempt under Section 7A(c)(10), even though the shareholders receive shares of a different issuer.

The PNO has extended Section 7A(c)(10) to exempt the spin-off of a wholly owned corporate subsidiary to the shareholders of the parent corporation as long as the percentage of shares of the subsidiary received by each shareholder is pro rata to its holdings in the parent. Additionally, the spin-off of a less than 100 percent controlled corporate subsidiary to the shareholders of the parent on a pro rata basis would also be exempt under Section 7A(c)(10), except for any shareholders of the parent who also held voting securities directly in the subsidiary. Those shareholders would be increasing their percentage held in the subsidiary as a result of the spin-off, and their acquisitions would not be exempt under Section 7A(c)(10).

20 Applicable provisions. 7A(c)(10), 802.30.

Issue. Is the transfer of shares between subsidiaries of a corporation exempt under Section 802.30 or 7A(c)(10)?

Facts. Company B, a wholly owned subsidiary of company A, holds less than 50 percent of the voting securities of X. A creates C, another wholly owned subsidiary, and B transfers the X voting securities to C.

Analysis. The PNO has confirmed that the intraperson exemption (802.30) is not applicable in this scenario because the acquired person is not A, so the acquiring and acquired persons are not the same person. However, the transfer of X's voting securities is exempted by Section 7A(c)(10), because A will hold the same percentage of X's voting securities both before and after the transfer. *See* Int. 19.

21 Applicable provisions. 7A(g)(1), 802.9, 802.64.

Issue. What are the factors that may lead the FTC, in the exercise of its prosecutorial discretion, to recommend against commencing a civil penalty action under Section 7A(g)(l)?

Analysis. An institutional investor purchased voting securities of an issuer after taking certain actions that the Bureau interpreted as inconsistent with the "solely for the purpose of investment" exemption in Section 802.9. See Int. 16 for a description of the background facts. The Bureau found a violation of the Act, but in the exercise of its prosecutorial discretion, declined to recommend commencement of a civil penalty action under Section 7A(g)(l).

In explaining its decision not to recommend a civil penalty action, the Bureau cited the following factors:

1. The purchaser's actions were undertaken to protect its investment with the good faith belief that its conduct was not inconsistent with the "investment purpose" exemption for institutional investors in Section 802.64;

2. The Section 802.64 exemption had not previously been the subject of any public formal interpretation or legal opinion by the Bureau, the FTC, or the courts;

3. When apprised of the violation, the purchaser agreed to file notification within three working days; and

4. The purchaser agreed to refrain from voting the newly purchased securities and to refrain from making additional purchases until expiration of any applicable waiting period.

22 | Applicable provision. 7A(g)(1).

Issue. Does a person that in good faith inadvertently fails to file notification have a defense to an action for civil penalties under Section 7A(g)(1)?

Analysis. The PNO's position is that the inadvertent failure to comply with the Act is not a defense to an agency action for civil penalties. One PNO staff memorandum discussing this issue stated that "inadvertence is not a defense in an action for civil penalties brought by a government agency. Good faith or inadvertence can only be used by a defendant to attempt to persuade the court to lessen the amount of penalty it assesses."

In *United States v. Lonrho PLC,* 1988-2 Trade Cas. (CCH) ¶ 68,232 (D.D.C. 1988) (Enf. Action DD), the government obtained a civil penalty where failure to file was not intentional. In this case, however, the inadvertence was careless to a point warranting sanction, according to the government.

The FTC has published procedures for correcting an inadvertent failure to file. *See* "Procedures for Submitting Post-Consummation Filings," *available at* www.ftc.gov/bc/*hsr*/postconsumfilings.htm. In notifying the FTC of a failure to file, the person must explain how the violation occurred and what steps will be taken to ensure that the failure to file does not reoccur. If the FTC is convinced that the violation was inadvertent (that is, the result of understandable, simple negligence and not gross negligence or reckless disregard for the filing requirement), the FTC will send a letter stating that the person must bear responsibility for the violation, that no enforcement action will be initiated, but that the person's compliance in the future will be monitored and any other violation may incur an enforcement action for all violations, including the earlier one.

23 | Applicable provision. 7A(h).

Issue. Is the fact that a premerger notification filing has been made with the agencies itself confidential information?

Analysis. The PNO has consistently taken the position that the fact of filing is itself "information . . . filed with the Assistant Attorney General or the Federal Trade Commission pursuant to this section" and therefore exempt from disclosure under FOIA. *See* Section 7A(h).

Note, however, that the fact that a filing has been made becomes public information if early termination is granted. The day after the grant of early termination, the PNO makes available the names of the acquiring and acquired persons, and the acquired entities (if any), on its Web site and in a recorded phone message. There is also a statutory requirement of publication of the same facts in the Federal Register. *See* Int. 269.

Two federal circuit courts of appeals have held that state attorneys general, as members of the "public," may not obtain preacquisition notification materials. *See Lieberman v. FTC,* 771 F.2d 32 (2d Cir. 1985); *Mattox v. FTC,* 752 F.2d 116 (5th Cir. 1985). As a result of these decisions, and congressional unwillingness to change the strict confidentiality protections under the Act, the National Association of Attorneys General ("NAAG") has developed a voluntary compact whereby any premerger filing voluntarily shared with a state would be shared with other signatory states, but would be destroyed or returned after completion of the investigation. *See* www.ftc.gov/os/1998/03/mergerco.op.htm. The signatory states would agree to serve no investigative subpoenas, civil investigative demands, or other compulsory precomplaint demands for disclosure during the pendency of the HSR waiting period, if the initial HSR notification is voluntarily supplied.

24 Applicable provision. 7A(h).

Issue. May information or documentary materials filed with the enforcement agencies be disclosed in the context of litigation to which neither agency is a party but receives a subpoena as a nonparty?

Analysis. The SBP provides the following discussion of Section 7A(h), which clearly contemplates that such disclosure should only occur where the FTC or DOJ is a party to the litigation:

> The Commission interprets the provision of section 7A(h) that the information submitted may be made public "as may be relevant to any administrative or judicial action or proceeding" to authorize making it public, in the agency's discretion, in any proceeding brought by or against the Commission or the Assistant Attorney General, whether the submitting person is a party or not.

43 Fed. Reg. 33,450, 33,519 (July 31, 1978).

INTERPRETATIONS RELATING TO PART 801 OF THE RULES

| 25 | **Applicable provisions.** 801 generally, 7A generally, 801.33.

Issue. In an open market stock purchase, when does the "acquisition" take place: on the date that a purchase order is executed (the "trade date"), or when the stock is delivered and paid for (the "settlement date")?

Analysis. Neither the FTC nor the PNO staff has ever formally defined the crucial Section 7A term "acquisition." Because a person "holds" voting securities if he or she has beneficial ownership thereof, it is appropriate to interpret an "acquisition" of voting securities to take place at the time that beneficial ownership is obtained by the acquiring person. *See* 43 Fed. Reg. 33,450, 33,458-59 (July 31, 1978). The PNO has indicated that in market transactions beneficial ownership is deemed to transfer as of the trade date, rather than the settlement date. In part, this view is based upon Section 801.33, which provides that, in the case of a tender offer, acceptance for payment constitutes the acquisition.

| 26 | **Applicable provisions.** 801 generally, 801.1(b).

Issue. Two or more persons wish to form a partnership for purposes of acquiring the voting securities of an issuer. What procedures or formalities must be completed prior to the acquisition in order to assure existence of an "entity" distinct from the two persons?

Analysis. The question is a matter of local law. Generally, formation of a partnership may be accomplished by an agreement of the participants to share the benefits and risks of a joint undertaking. The agreement need not be in writing.

Proving the existence of such an entity may be difficult, however, if some additional formalities are not employed. If, for example, three or more persons are forming a partnership such that the resulting entity will be deemed to be a separate "person" for HSR purposes (because no one individual will control it under the Rules, see Section 801.1(b)), a written agreement would be advisable. The existence of additional formalities (e.g., office, letterhead, telephone listing, registration to do business, and the like) could be helpful.

If the existence of the partnership cannot be proven, transfers by the partnership may be analyzed as transfers by the individual partners.

27 | Applicable provisions. 801 generally, 801.1(b)(1), 801.90.

Issue. Is it a reportable event if company A contributes half of its interest in a plant, equipment, and technology to a newly formed partnership and transfers the other half interest to its future partner B on the condition that the future partner immediately contribute it to the partnership?

Analysis. B's acquisition of the half interest from A was subject to the Act regardless of its obligation to contribute it to the partnership and regardless of how B treated the transaction for accounting purposes. The PNO recognized that the transaction would not have been reportable had A contributed its entire interest directly to the partnership.

The initial contributions of capital by partners to a newly formed partnership are generally not reportable. *See* Int. 73. However, if one partner contributes assets and receives cash directly or indirectly from another partner in connection with the formation, the partner receiving the cash will generally be deemed by the PNO to have sold assets to the partner providing the cash, unless the cash represented a bona fide equalization payment (see examples below). Therefore, that sale of assets may be reportable if the Act's jurisdictional tests are met. This will not be the result if several participants first establish a partnership to which they contribute assets and then in a second step sell a partnership interest for cash to another party. The avoidance provision of Section 801.90 may be considered in determining the reportability of such transactions, however, unless the parties have a valid business reason (i.e., a reason other than avoiding HSR filing) for structuring the transaction in this way.

A similar issue is raised where a partnership is formed and the partnership borrows money and distributes it to the partners. As long as the distribution is in proportion to the relative partnership interests, the PNO has said that no asset sale will be imputed. This transaction is the functional equivalent of a contribution by each partner of assets subject to liabilities. By contrast, if the distribution is not in proportion and results in a shifting of partnership interests, it may be viewed as a purchase of assets by a partner at the time of formation, depending upon all of the facts and circumstances.

Two examples may illustrate the issue. In the first example, the parties plan to form a 50-50 partnership. One party contributes a $102 million plant, the other $51 million in cash. The partnership then gives $51 million cash to the party who contributed the plant. This distribution is not reportable as it is deemed to be an equalization payment related to the initial formation of the partnership. In the second example, Party A creates a wholly owned partnership into which it contributes a plant valued at $60 million. (Note: the PNO does not consider the partnership to be formed at this point since only one person holds interests in it.) Party B contributes $60 million in cash to the partnership in exchange for a 99.9 percent interest, and the $60 million is immediately distributed to Party A, which retains a 0.1 percent interest in the partnership. In the view of the PNO, this would be reportable as the sale of an asset by Party A to Party B, not a partnership formation involving a bona fide equalization payment.

Editor's Note. *Subject to Section 801.90 considerations, it appears that a legitimate "equalization payment" can normally be made anywhere along the spectrum of percentage ownership interests, except perhaps at the extremes, where the arrangement may be viewed as an outright sale of assets. See, however, Int. 191 where a partnership formation with a purported "equalization payment" combined with an option to buy out the minority partner after one year was viewed as an avoidance scheme by the PNO.*

28 | Applicable provision. 801 generally.

Issue. Does entering into a lease constitute a potentially reportable acquisition?

Analysis. Generally the PNO does not treat the signing of a lease as an acquisition of an asset, unless the lease will result in the present transfer or installment purchase of the underlying asset. Where, for example, an unduly high rental charge is coupled with an option under which the lessee may subsequently purchase the property at a nominal price, the lease would be regarded as a present acquisition of the underlying asset.

Where a lease agreement provides for rental payments considered normal for that kind of property and/or a subsequent purchase option at fair market value, the PNO has stated that the transaction is not an "acquisition" subject to the filing requirements of the Act. However, the PNO has taken the position that the sale or assignment of an existing lease may constitute an "acquisition" of an asset, namely the acquisition of an existing leasehold interest. (Note: the transfer or assignment of a lease that was not considered to be a transfer or installment purchase of the underlying asset at the time it was initially signed is not considered an acquisition of the underlying asset).

For purposes of distinguishing a "purchase styled as a lease" from a "routine leasing transaction," the PNO looks to see whether the lease amounts to a present transfer of beneficial ownership. The duration of the lease might be relevant to a determination of whether an acquisition (i.e., a transfer of beneficial ownership) is in fact intended. Leases for extraordinarily long periods of time that might encompass the useful life of the asset may be deemed reportable acquisitions. In addition, how the parties to the lease allocate the risk of loss or damage to the underlying property during the lease term may indicate whether an acquisition is involved. Other potentially relevant indicia of a lease or sale are whether the lessee has a right to transfer its interest without the consent of the lessor, whether the lease is or will be shown as an asset on the financial books of either party, and how the lease is treated for tax purposes.

Note that even if entering into a lease is deemed the acquisition of an asset, the transaction may still qualify for exemption under the Act or the Rules. *See, e.g.*, Int. 4.

29 Applicable provision. 801 generally.

Issue. Is the grant of a patent or trademark license a reportable acquisition of assets?

Analysis. The PNO position is that the grant of an exclusive license is the transfer of an asset to the licensee, which may be reportable if the size-of-person and size-of-transaction criteria of Section 7A(a) are met. *See* Int. 91 (regarding valuation of exclusive licenses). To be treated as an acquisition, the license must be exclusive even against the grantor. On the other hand, the grant of a nonexclusive patent or trademark license does not involve acquisition of an asset, since the grantor retains the right to use the patent or trademark and/or to grant additional nonexclusive licenses. Termination rights alone do not make the grant nonexclusive. Similarly, march-in rights, where the licensor reserves the right to assume the license under certain regulatory conditions, do not render the license nonexclusive.

The PNO has extended this position to partial or limited exclusivity, sometimes called "field-of-use" exclusivity. For example, if a license grants exclusive geographic territories or exclusivity for specific uses, it may be considered an acquisition of an asset. If the license has no exclusive aspects, it is not viewed as an acquisition of an asset. In addition, the grant of marketing and distribution rights, even if granted on an exclusive basis, does not constitute the acquisition of an asset.

| **30** | **Applicable provisions.** 801 generally, 801.13, 801.90, 7A generally.

Issue. Does a temporary consignment of goods constitute a potentially reportable acquisition of assets?

Facts. A company that is going out of business transfers its widget-making technology to a purchaser for a stated sum. The purchaser also agrees to accept a consignment of the transferor's inventory of widgets for a four-month period and to supply them to the transferor's customers during that time. The consignor retains title to its inventory and pays the consignee a fee for the delivery and servicing by the consignee of widgets sold to customers. At the end of the four months, the consignee would purchase any of the inventory that remained unsold.

Analysis. The PNO takes the position that a consignment of goods is not an acquisition of assets within the meaning of Section 7A so long as the consignee does not acquire beneficial ownership of the goods during the consignment period. If the consignment is considered to be a transfer of beneficial ownership of the goods to the buyer, the value of the goods would be included in the size-of-transaction calculation. Assuming that the consignment did not transfer beneficial ownership of the goods to the consignee, the PNO noted that the subsequent purchase of the remaining inventory might trigger a reporting obligation under the aggregation provisions of Section 801.13(b)(2), if the size-of-transaction test were met at that time.

Whether beneficial ownership of the goods is considered to transfer to the consignee will depend on the facts. The Rules do not provide a definition of "beneficial ownership." In determining who has beneficial ownership, the SBP lists as one factor the right to gains and the risk of loss. 43 Fed. Reg. 33,450, 33,458 (July 31, 1978). The PNO has also looked at such factors as who maintains insurance for the goods and what happens to the goods if they are not sold. If the consignor is obligated to take them back there is a stronger argument to be made that beneficial ownership has not transferred. But even if the consignor buys unsold goods at some point, as long as the consignor has retained a title, has had the risk of loss during the consignment period and has paid a fee for the services, the PNO will likely consider the arrangement to be a legitimate consignment and not a transfer of beneficial ownership.

As noted above, if the consignee is obligated to purchase unsold goods after a certain period, and in fact does so, the aggregation provisions of Section 801.13 could require reporting at that time. The PNO takes the position that an issue under Section 801.90 could arise if the consignment has been entered into for avoidance purposes (i.e., the consignment period was set to go beyond 180 days to avoid the aggregation rules). In the fact situation described in this interpretation, the fact that the consignment is of four-month duration would seem to negate any possible suggestion of avoidance, since any consignee purchases would be subject to aggregation under Section 801.13(b)(2).

| 31 | **Applicable provisions.** 801 generally, 7A(b)(3)(A), 801.1(f)(1) and (3), 802.31, Formal Interpretation 12.

Issue. Is granting an option to purchase voting securities a reportable transaction? Further, is the acquisition of an option to purchase voting securities reportable where the option also conveys a present right to vote the underlying securities?

Analysis. The granting of an option to purchase voting securities at some future time is, by itself, generally not reportable, although the exercise of that option may give rise to reporting and waiting period obligations. The PNO position, however, is that the grant of an option to purchase voting securities, coupled with the grant of a present irrevocable proxy to vote those securities, constitutes transfer of a voting security, and thus is an acquisition of "voting securities" within the meaning of Section 7A(b)(3)(A) and Section 801.1(f)(1). The PNO cited the formal interpretation issued on June 2, 1981, concerning certain subordinated exchangeable debentures issued by Sun Company, Inc. *See* Formal Int. 12, at Appendix.

Note that the conferral of limited voting rights, such as in change-of-control situations, does not make securities or options "voting securities." The only relevant voting right in this determination is the right presently to cast votes for members of the board of directors of a corporation or persons exercising similar functions. *See* Section 801.1(f)(1); Int. 70.

Example 2 to Section 801.1(f)(3) makes it clear that the acquisition of an option to purchase voting securities is an acquisition of voting securities but is exempt under Section 802.31. Acquisition of an option to acquire assets would not be treated by the PNO as an acquisition of assets, even if the option were valued at more than $50 million and the Act's other tests were satisfied.

| 32 | **Applicable provisions.** 801 generally, 801.10(b).

Issue. How does the granting of a covenant not to compete affect the reportability and valuation of a transaction?

Analysis. It is clear that entering into an agreement for performance of future services does not by itself constitute the acquisition of an asset. Thus, the value of such an agreement is relevant only where it reflects part of the value of assets or voting securities being acquired contemporaneously.

The PNO's position is that when a covenant not to compete is entered into in connection with the transfer of a business (either through the transfer of voting securities or assets) and a resulting payment is made to an employee who is not a selling shareholder, the payment will not be considered part of the purchase price for the acquisition.

If, however, the recipient is a controlling shareholder (or all selling shareholders are receiving payments), there generally will be a presumption that the payment is partial consideration for the sale of securities or assets. This presumption can in some cases be overcome by clear proof that the covenant was negotiated at arm's length or that the obtaining of noncompete agreements is standard practice for the acquiring company in its acquisitions. *See* Int. 33.

33 | Applicable provisions. 801 generally, 801.10(b).

Issue. Is the value of consulting agreements and retirement plans negotiated in connection with acquisition of a business (through the transfer of voting securities or assets) included in the purchase price for purposes of the size-of-transaction test?

Analysis. If consulting agreements and retirement plans reflecting the value of services actually to be performed *in the future* are negotiated at arm's length in connection with the sale of a business or assets, their value is not to be included. Conversely, to the extent that such arrangements reflect present or future remuneration paid to the seller as consideration for its transfer of the business or assets, they must be included in the acquisition price. *See* Ints. 32, 53.

34 | Applicable provision. 801.1(a)(2).

Issue. Is an acquisition of voting securities by an unincorporated agency of a foreign government engaged primarily in nongovernmental, commercial functions potentially subject to the Act?

Analysis. Under Section 801.1(a)(2), an agency of a foreign state or government is not an "entity" and therefore is not a "person" capable of making a reportable acquisition. An agency's acquisitions are never reportable, but corporations controlled by agencies that are engaged in commerce are entities under the Rules and may be subject to the Act unless the corporation is itself an agency. If the corporation is required to file, it would be its own UPE. *See* Ints. 11, 35, and 36.

35 | Applicable provision. 801.1(a)(2).

Issue. Is an acquisition of assets by a federally recognized tribe of Native Americans potentially subject to the Act?

Analysis. The acquisition is not reportable. Under Section 801.1(a)(2), the term "entity" does not include any foreign state, foreign government, or agency thereof. Because a federally recognized tribe of Native Americans is a sovereign entity under federal law, it should be treated the same as a foreign state or foreign government. Thus, acquisitions by the tribe itself are not covered, but acquisitions by tribe-controlled corporations engaged in commerce that do not qualify as agencies of the tribe may be reportable. *See* Ints. 11, 36.

Editor's Note. Not only acquisitions by the tribe, but acquisitions from the tribe, would be exempt. Likewise, acquisitions of the stock of a corporation controlled by a tribe would be exempt, unless the corporation is engaged in commerce (in which case the corporation would be its own UPE).

36 Applicable provision. 801.1(a)(2).

Issue. Is a foreign governmental corporation (i.e., a corporation controlled by a foreign government) that is a holding corporation for various operating companies "engaged in commerce" so as to make its acquisitions potentially reportable?

Analysis. Regardless of whether the activities of the holding corporation are sufficient for it to be deemed directly engaged in commerce, the holding corporation is considered engaged in commerce through its subsidiaries. *See* Ints. 11, 35.

| 37 | **Applicable provisions.** 801.1(a)(3), 801.1(b), 801.1(c)(2).

Issue. Does the familial relationship of a corporation's shareholders affect the determination of the UPE of that corporation?

Facts. Three individuals related by blood or marriage each own a one-third interest in a corporation.

Analysis. The Rules provide that a corporation is its own UPE if no one individual or entity holds 50 percent or more of its outstanding voting securities or has the contractual power presently to designate 50 percent or more of the board of directors. Although family members may act in concert, if the parties involved are adults and not spouses of each other, each individual will be deemed a separate entity and their holdings will not be aggregated based solely on their familial relationship. Unless the holdings of two of the three individuals are aggregated, the family-owned corporation is its own ultimate parent.

Section 801.1(c)(2) states that the holdings of spouses and their minor children are deemed the holdings of each of them. Thus, if one of the three individuals is the spouse or minor child of one of the others, their holdings would be aggregated. If the holdings of two of the shareholders are aggregated pursuant to Section 801.1(c)(2), each would be deemed to hold the aggregated shares. Therefore, each would hold two thirds of the corporation's shares and would control the corporation.

Other than Section 801.1(c)(2), the Rules do not aggregate the holdings of individuals. For example, the familial relationship between a parent and any adult child (the age of adulthood is determined under the law of the state or foreign country where the child resides) is irrelevant to any determinations under the Act. A parent does not control his or her adult child, nor are any holdings of adult children considered holdings of their parents. Similarly, the holdings of adult siblings are not aggregated.

| 38 | **Applicable provisions.** 801.1(a)(3), 801.1(b), 801.1(c)(2).

Issue. Is a natural person invariably its own UPE?

Analysis. Yes. A natural person is incapable of being "controlled" by any other entity within the meaning of Section 801.1(b). Pursuant to Section 801.1(c)(2), in determining their holdings natural persons must aggregate the holdings, if any, of their spouses and minor children. *See* Int. 37.

39 | Applicable provisions. 801.1(b), 801.1(c).

Issue. Are the holdings of a voting trust aggregated with the holdings of the individual who is both settlor and trustee of that trust?

Facts. An individual X and his spouse own 15 percent of the voting securities of a corporation and that 15 percent plus an additional 45 percent of the voting securities are held in a voting trust of which X is settlor and trustee.

Analysis. The analysis is dependent upon the special control rules for trusts. While it is correct to aggregate the holdings of X and his spouse, *see* Section 801.1(c)(2), X may or may not be deemed to hold the 45 percent voting stake held in the voting trust. If X is deemed to hold the voting securities subject to the voting trust, X would aggregate the direct holdings with the shares held by the voting trust.

The general rule is that a trust is deemed to hold all assets and voting securities constituting the corpus of the trust, and the trust itself becomes a potential reporting party under the Act. However, there are a few situations in which someone other than the trust may be deemed to hold the trust assets.

First, a settlor is deemed to hold the corpus of the trust if the trust is a revocable trust or if it is an irrevocable trust in which the settlor retains a reversionary interest in the corpus. *See* Section 801.1(c)(3); 43 Fed. Reg. 33,450, 33,458 (July 31, 1978); Int. 61. Second, a person "controls" a trust, and thus holds the corpus of the trust, if it has the contractual power to appoint 50 percent or more of the trustees. *See* 43 Fed. Reg. at 33,459; Int. 61 (X will not be deemed to control the voting trust solely because of his position as trustee).

Therefore, if X is deemed to "hold" the corpus of the trust in any of these circumstances, X would have to aggregate the shares in the corpus of the trust with the shares X held directly. Thus, X would be deemed to hold 60 percent of the voting securities and would control the corporation.

Note that the prior analysis assumes that the trust itself holds the shares of the corporation. In some cases "voting trusts" do not actually hold the shares of the corporation, (beneficial ownership of the voting securities have not been transferred to the trust). Instead, the voting trust merely functions as an irrevocable proxy giving the "trustee" the power to vote all of the shares of the voting trust. In that case, the trustee's ability to vote the shares may give the trustee "control" of the corporation merely because the trustee could elect 50 percent or more of the directors. *See* Ints. 40, 43, and 58. The control definition in Section 801.1(b)(2) does not refer to the power to vote shares, rather, it refers to the power "presently to designate" 50 percent or more of the board. Therefore, the contractual power to vote shares will constitute control only under certain circumstances. First, the proxy or other voting right must be irrevocable, or if it is revocable only after the satisfaction of some condition precedent (*see* Int. 43) that condition must not have occurred. Second, taking into account provisions of corporate law and governance such as cumulative voting or a staggered board, the voting rights must actually give the ability to elect 50 percent or more of the board, without the voluntary concurrence of any other shareholder. (In practice, the PNO sets up a rebuttable presumption at the 50 percent voting level and requires that the parties carefully examine the circumstances to determine whether control exists.) *See* Ints. 51, 58.

| **40** | **Applicable provisions.** 801.1(b), 801.12(b).

Issue. Can a person control a corporation through a combination of holding less than 50 percent of the voting securities and having the contractual power presently to designate fewer than half the directors of the corporation?

Analysis. Yes, but only when the corporation has cumulative voting. (Cumulative voting is the type of voting in which a stockholder may cast as many votes for directors as he has shares of stock multiplied by the number of directors to be elected. The stockholder may cast all his votes for one or more but fewer than all the directors on the slate). Absent this, less than 50 percent of the voting securities can elect no directors without the concurrence of other shareholders. In 1987, the FTC adopted the PNO's interpretation as part of the SBP to amended Section 801.1(b), stating:

> The Premerger Notification Office deems a corporation controlled if a person can designate a *majority* of the board as a result of both holding voting securities and having contractual power to designate directors. In other words, in determining whether an entity is controlled pursuant to § 801.1(b)(2), the staff adds directors elected to the board as a result of holding voting securities to directors designated as a result of a contractual power. Under the amendment, the staff will deem the entity controlled by a person who, as a result of such combined rights, has the power to designate 50 percent or more of the directors.

52 Fed. Reg. 20,058, 20,062 (July 3, 1987) (emphasis added).

The PNO has indicated that application of this interpretation requires a calculation analogous to that called for in Section 801.12(b) if the corporation has cumulative voting. Assuming only a single class of voting securities, the person would multiply the percentage of voting securities held by the number of directors eligible to be elected by the shareholders. If the sum of that product and the number of directors that the person has the contractual power to designate, appoint, or elect meets or exceeds 50 percent of all directors, the person is presumed to control the corporation.

41 **Applicable provision.** 801.1(b).

Issue. Does a voting agreement under which three shareholders, each holding one-third of a corporation's voting securities, agree to vote for a board of directors composed of the three shareholders, mean that the corporation is "controlled" by any entity or entities?

Analysis. The corporation remains its own UPE and is not controlled by any other entity. No shareholder holds 50 percent or more of the voting securities of the corporation (assuming that no other rule requires aggregation) and the voting agreement does not give any person the contractual power to designate 50 percent or more of the board of directors. (If the voting agreement gave the irrevocable right to appoint the board to just one of the shareholders, that person would control the corporation. *See* Int. 46.)

| 42 | **Applicable provisions.** 801.1(b), 801.1(c)(8), 801.1(f)(1), 802.30.

Issue. If a nonprofit corporation (with members as opposed to shareholders) has several members but is deemed to be "controlled" by only one of those members (because the member has the right to appoint a majority of the board of directors), would a transaction between that controlling member and the corporation be exempt from notification obligations by reason of Section 802.30?

Analysis. Control over a member-only nonprofit corporation is established by having the right to appoint 50 percent or more of the board of trustees or board of directors of the nonprofit corporation. Thus, if one member has the right to appoint a majority of the board of the nonprofit, that member would control the corporation for purposes of the Act.

A transaction between a member controlling a nonprofit and the nonprofit is not covered explicitly by the intraperson transaction exemption of Section 802.30 because that exemption is available only where control is the result of holdings of voting securities. Here control is maintained by the right to appoint a majority of the board. However, if a nonprofit is deemed to be controlled by one member, the PNO has stated that Section 801.1(c)(8) is applied literally, and no filing is required. Section 801.1(c)(8) states that "A person holds all assets and voting securities held by the entities included within it . . . and all assets and voting securities held by the entities which it controls directly or indirectly." This analysis also applies to the merger of two nonprofits with the same controlling member (i.e., no filing would be required).

Editor's Note. *This interpretation appears to be a concession to nonprofit corporations. The PNO does not apply this principle to transfers of assets between controlled partnerships and LLCs unless they are wholly owned by the parent. The PNO treats any partnership or LLC that is wholly owned as indistinguishable from its parent. However, if any other person holds even a very small interest in the partnership or LLC then the partnership or LLC is distinguishable from the controlling entity and asset transfers between them would be subject to the HSR Act.*

| 43 | **Applicable provisions.** 801.1(b), 801.90.

Issue. In what circumstances will proxies be aggregated with voting securities held to determine whether the holder of the voting securities and proxies has control of an issuer?

Analysis. The PNO position distinguishes between revocable proxies, which generally are not included in the control calculation, and irrevocable proxies, which are viewed as counting toward control. A combination of the holding of voting securities and the irrevocable contractual right to vote other securities (even though not constituting beneficial ownership of those securities) can constitute control. For example, a person holding 40 percent of the voting securities of an issuer and an irrevocable proxy to vote an additional 10 percent of the issuer's voting securities would be deemed to control that issuer.

The PNO also has indicated that a proxy revocable only under certain specified circumstances (e.g., a proxy irrevocable until a certain date or until the happening of a certain event) may be treated as an irrevocable proxy. If treated as an irrevocable proxy, such a proxy will be counted toward control unless and until the conditions permitting revocation have been met. *See* Ints. 40, 46, and 58.

Editor's Note. Control in this case is not conferred by "holding" 50 percent or more of the voting securities since an irrevocable proxy normally does not transfer beneficial ownership of the voting securities. See Int. 58. Rather, the PNO takes the position that the 40 percent of the voting securities held combined with the voting rights to an additional 10 percent conferred by the irrevocable proxy provide the contractual power presently to designate 50 percent or more of the directors.

44 Applicable provisions. 801.1(b), 801.1(c).

Issue. Is it a violation of the Act to (a) enter into a contract to acquire a company that requires the buyer to make a nonrefundable payment of the entire purchase price to the seller upon signing the merger agreement and (b) make the required payment in a case where the acquisition agreement provides that the seller will continue to operate the business in accordance with its existing business plan?

Facts. A complaint was filed on similar facts charging that beneficial ownership passed at the time the acquisition agreement was signed and the purchase price paid. *See United States v. Atlantic Richfield Co.*, 1991-1 Trade Cas. (CCH) ¶ 69,318 (D.D.C. 1991) (Enf. Action W). The complaint alleged that: (1) the payment was made upon execution of the merger agreement; (2) the payment was nonrefundable, even if the buyer was later blocked from taking title to the assets as a result of the antitrust review; (3) the seller was required to operate the business in the ordinary course and in accordance with its existing business plan; (4) the buyer would cover liabilities from the continued operation after the date of signing; (5) if the buyer were prevented from taking title, a trustee would be required to sell the assets with the proceeds paid to the original buyer; (6) the purchase price would be adjusted at closing to account for net cash flow between signing and closing; and (7) the acquisition agreement had the effect, upon execution, of transferring beneficial ownership of the assets to buyer so that buyer acquired those assets on the date of signing and payment. The FTC press release says that under this agreement, ARCO stood to reap the benefit of gain or loss during the waiting period. In addition to the divestitures and other remedial provisions required to resolve the Section 7 concerns, the acquiring person and the acquired person each paid a $1 million civil penalty to settle the charges that the merger agreement violated the HSR Act.

Analysis. Although every purchase contract in some way allocates risk between buyer and seller, the parties must be careful that the risk allocation measures do not transfer beneficial ownership to the buyer prior to observing the Act's waiting period(s). Even though the right to vote the stock and dispose of assets were not transferred (two of the four indicia of beneficial ownership listed in the SBP (43 Fed. Reg. 33,450, 33,458 (July 31, 1978)) and even though the seller was obligated to continue operating the business in the ordinary course, the transfer of the risk and potential benefits of a change in value of the company prior to expiration of the waiting period was apparently deemed by the *Atlantic Richfield* court to be sufficient to transfer beneficial ownership of the company from the seller to the buyer. There is some question about how much risk of gain or loss may be transferred prior to expiration of the waiting period. The merger agreement in *Atlantic Richfield* contained two routine merger provisions: (i) the seller had to operate the business in the ordinary course, and (ii) the purchase price was to be adjusted by the net cash flow during the waiting period. These two provisions indicate that the seller retained at least some degree of risk of gain or loss in the value of the business during the waiting period. Neither the FTC nor the PNO has addressed exactly where the line will be drawn. *See, e.g.*, M. Howard Morse, *Mergers and Acquisitions: Antitrust Limitations on Conduct before Closing*, 57 BUS. LAW. 1463 (2002); William Blumenthal, *The Scope of Permissible Coordination Between Merging Entities Prior to Consummation*, 63 ANTITRUST L.J. 1 (1994).

45 | Applicable provisions. 801.1(b)(2), 801.1(c).

Issue. Where a common trustee of several trusts has the power under the respective trust agreements to vote all of the shares representing a majority interest in an issuer held by the trusts, does the common trustee "control" the issuer?

Analysis. Unless a trust is revocable or the settlor retains a reversionary interest or is a beneficiary of the trust, Section 801.1(c)(3) specifies that the trust holds the assets or stock constituting the corpus of the trust. Only if another person has the contractual power presently to designate 50 percent or more of the trustees can a trust be controlled under Section 801.1(b)(2), in which case the controlling person holds the corpus of the trust. But a trustee who holds voting power with respect to stock held by the trust does not control either the trust or the issuer, even if the trustee's voting power covers 50 percent or more of the issuer's outstanding voting securities.

In amending the definition of control in Section 801.1(b), the FTC made clear in the SBP that it did not intend to amend the original provisions of Section 801.1(c) relating to trust assets.

> Comment 3 asks how to resolve the apparent conflict between the amended definition of control and the definition in § 801.1(c)(5), which states that the beneficiary of a trust (regardless of the percentage of its profits to which he is entitled) does not hold the assets of the trust. *It is the Commission's intention that the control amendments, although adopted more recently, do not supersede the more specific treatment of trust assets mandated by § 801.1(c).*

52 Fed. Reg. 20,058, 20,063 (July 3, 1987) (emphasis added).

| 46 | **Applicable provisions.** 801.1(b)(2), 7A(a)(2).

Issue. Can a shareholders' agreement confer control of a corporation to an individual designated to appoint a majority of the corporation's board of directors?

Facts. A group of individual investors has previously purchased nonvoting preferred shares of the issuer, which has neither annual sales nor assets of $10 million. The investor group is not itself an entity; each investor holds a noncontrolling interest in the issuer. At the time of their purchase, the investor group obtained the contractual right to designate a majority of the board of directors of the issuer, and the group, through a shareholders' agreement, designated one individual investor to exercise this right on behalf of, and for the benefit of, the group. This individual has assets of more than $10 million. The assets of the issuer are now to be sold (for more than $50 million but less than $200 million) to a $100 million buyer.

Analysis. If the individual investor designated by the investment group has an irrevocable contractual right to appoint a majority of the issuer's board of directors, the designated individual would be deemed to control the issuer, and the individual's size-of-person would determine whether the acquired person met the size-of-person test. *See* Int. 41. With an irrevocable contractual right to appoint a majority of the board, the size-of-person test would be satisfied because the designated individual is a $10 million person. (There may be an argument that from a practical perspective the issuer is "controlled" by the group of investors as a result of the group's contractual power to designate a majority of the directors of the issuer, but the Rules do not recognize a "group" as an "entity.")

If, however, under the terms of the shareholders' agreement, the other investors could revoke the designation of the individual at will (i.e., without any adverse consequences), neither the investors as a group nor the designated investor would be deemed to control the issuer, and if no other person controlled the issuer, it would be its own UPE for HSR purposes. As a result, the issuer's size-of-person would be determined by examining its annual net sales and total assets (including the annual net sales and total assets of all entities controlled by the issuer) pursuant to the requirements of Section 801.11. Under these facts, the size-of-person test would not be satisfied for this transaction.

Note, however, that the PNO will consider a proxy or a contractual right revocable only if it can be revoked without adverse consequences. (For example, the PNO takes the position that the fact that an irrevocable contractual right might be breached, subjecting the breaching party to a potential lawsuit or liquidated damages, does not turn an irrevocable agreement into a revocable agreement.)

| 47 | **Applicable provisions.** 801.1(b)(2), 801.1(c)(3)-(5), 802.71, 801.11(e)(1), 7A(a).

Issue. How do the Rules treat acquisitions relating to trusts?

Analysis. Application of the Rules to trusts depends upon the type of trust involved. Two types of trusts are viewed as ineffective in creating any interest separate from that of the settlor: (1) revocable trusts and (2) trusts in which the settlor retains a reversionary interest. Furthermore a trust in which the settlor (or any other person, as described in the next paragraph) retains the contractual power to replace the trustee (or 50 percent or more of the trustees if there are multiple trustees) would be "controlled" by the settlor (or other person). In each of these situations, assets in the corpus of the trust are held by the settlor for HSR purposes under Sections 801.1(c)(4) and 801.1(b)(2). Note, however, that a trust instrument that designates the settlor as trustee does not, by itself, confer power to control the trust on the settler/trustee.

Where any person other than the settlor has the contractual power to replace the trustee (or 50 percent or more when there are multiple trustees), that person controls the trust and holds the assets in the corpus of the trust. *See* Section 801.1(b)(2). The kind of contractual power necessary to confer control of a trust is the power under the trust indenture to remove and replace the trustee (or 50 percent or more of the trustees if there are multiple trustees) at any time. The power merely to designate a successor in the event the trustee resigns or is unable to continue to serve does not constitute control of the trust.

Trusts that (a) are irrevocable and in which (b) the settlor does not retain a reversionary interest and (c) no person controls the trust by reason of a contractual power to replace the trustee(s) are their own ultimate parent entities, and are thus persons under the Rules. Assets comprising the corpus of such a trust are held by the trust and are not aggregated with assets held by any other person. Thus, assets held in such a trust are not aggregated with those of the settlor or of his or her spouse or minor children, even if the spouse or minor children are trustees or beneficiaries of the trust. Acquisitions of assets or voting securities by or from a trust are subject to normal HSR treatment.

Formation of a trust is usually nonreportable because Section 802.71 exempts transfers by a settlor to an irrevocable trust, and because transfers by a settlor to a revocable trust or a trust in which the settlor retains a reversionary interest are viewed as ineffective to divest the settlor of beneficial ownership. In addition, an irrevocable trust, at the time of its formation, will not satisfy the statutory size-of-person test, and so the transfer of assets or voting securities to the trust will not be reportable unless their value exceeds $200 million. *See* Sections 7A(a), 801.11(e)(1).

Special rules govern common trust funds and collective investment funds within the meaning of 12 C.F.R. § 9.18(a). *See* Section 801.1 (c) (3); Ints. 61, 63.

| 48 | **Applicable provisions.** 801.1(c), 801.1(b).

Issue. Where two parties to a voting securities transaction have already made a premerger notification filing, but then restructure the transaction after the expiration of the waiting period to become an asset acquisition whereby the assets will flow through an intermediary, must the parties file a new premerger notification reflecting the inclusion of the intermediary or the change from a voting securities transaction to an asset transaction?

Facts. Corporation A has agreed to sell all of its stock to Corporation C. Premerger notification filings are made, and the waiting period expires. The parties then decide to restructure the proposed transaction as a sale of all of Corporation A's assets to Corporation C. But such a transfer would violate the terms of a contractual arrangement securing a liability of Corporation A to a third party, which may not convey all of its assets without assuring assumption of its liability by someone acceptable to that third party.

Corporation A proposes to transfer all of its assets to Corporation B, which would also assume this liability. At the closing, Corporation B would simultaneously transfer all of Corporation A's assets to Corporation C, retaining the obligation to the third party.

Analysis. The PNO stated that the critical issue is whether the transfer from B to C could be assured. Where an intermediary is involved, a new filing reflecting the transaction involving the intermediary will be required except where the intermediary's ownership will be only transitory and where the subsequent transfer is an integral part of the transaction such that the second step is a virtual certainty. Even then, if for some unanticipated reason the transaction stalls temporarily, leaving the intermediary holding the stock or assets, that may be a violation of the Act if the intermediary has not filed.

In previous informal interpretations, the PNO has indicated that an intermediary like B would normally be the beneficial owner of A's assets (albeit only for an instant), and thus the transfer from A to B would be reportable if A and B satisfied the statutory tests. In those cases, the PNO's concern had been that, if for some reason only the transfer from A to B were to occur, a violation would arise. In these situations, the PNO requests that the parties demonstrate convincingly that the second step transfer actually will occur if they choose to file only for the transfer from A to C. Contracts requiring that transfer, coupled with an explanation of the need for an intermediary, are generally satisfactory. Since in this case a filing had already been made for the transfer from A to C (and the change from a voting securities transaction to an asset transaction would not normally require a refiling – see below) the parties would merely be required to send a letter explaining the intermediary step.

As just noted, the restructuring of the above transaction from an acquisition of C's voting securities to an acquisition of substantially all the assets of C would not, without more, require the filing of a new premerger notification. *See* Int. 249; *cf.* Int. 57.

Editor's Note. *The PNO usually adopts a step-by-step approach to analyzing the reporting requirements in a given transaction, i.e., it will treat simultaneous events as occurring in a sequence and require a filing for each notifiable step, rather than looking at just the before-and-after picture. The parties can choose any sequence of events they please (for instance, organizing the sequence so as to minimize the number of filings required), so long as the PNO receives at least one filing for the transaction. See Int. 80.*

49 | Applicable provisions. 801.1(c), 802.9, 802.64.

Issue. Under what circumstances are stock purchases under a put-call option agreement with an investment bank reportable by the option holder and/or the investment bank?

Analysis. Three enforcement actions brought by the DOJ at the request of the FTC indicate that under certain circumstances acquisitions pursuant to put-call option agreements result in the transfer of beneficial ownership, which is potentially reportable under the Act. *See United States v. Wickes Cos.,* 1988-1 Trade Cas. (CCH) ¶ 67,966 (D.D.C. 1988) (Enf. Action FF); *United States v. Trump,* 1998-1 Trade Cas. (CCH) ¶ 67,698 (D.D.C. 1988) (Enf. Action GG); *United States v. First City Financial Corp.,* 1988-1 Trade Cas. (CCH) ¶ 67,967 (D.D.C. 1988) (Enf. Action HH). Because each case was settled when brought, the details of the FTC's interpretation of these agreements are unclear. Bureau of Competition Associate Director James Mullenix, in a speech before the ABA Antitrust Section 1988 Spring Meeting, characterized such agreements as devices for avoiding filings, seemingly implicating Section 801.90. *See* James Mullenix, *The Premerger Notification Program at the Federal Trade Commission,* 57 ANTITRUST L.J. 125 (1988).

Typically these agreements work as follows: A person, usually an investment bank, purchases voting securities of an issuer valued in excess of the size-of-transaction threshold. The investment bank does not file HSR notification, presumably in reliance on the investment exemption, Section 802.9, or the institutional investor exemption, Section 802.64. Prior to making the purchases, the investment bank enters into an agreement or a tacit understanding with the buyer whereby the investment bank grants the buyer a call option, i.e., the right to buy the voting securities at the investment bank's cost, for a fixed period. The buyer grants the investment bank a put option, i.e., the right to sell the securities to the buyer at the same price for the same period. Exercise of either the put or the call is explicitly conditioned on compliance with the Act by the buyer and issuer. The investment bank retains the right to vote the securities and the right to receive dividends, although the put-call exercise price is reduced by the dividends received. If the buyer is unable to acquire the shares, the buyer agrees to pay the investment bank the difference, if any, between the agreed-upon purchase price and the price at which the investment bank disposes of the shares. If the disposition price exceeds the agreed-upon purchase price, the investment bank will pay the buyer the difference. The buyer also agrees to pay the investment bank a set interest rate and to place funds in an account with the investment bank sufficient to purchase the securities on margin.

The PNO has subsequently indicated that it looked at a combination of agency theory (*see* Section 801.1(c)(1)) and beneficial ownership under the Rules to conclude that the client and not the investment bank held the shares purchased by the bank. The PNO theory was based on evidence that there was at least an informal understanding between the investment bank and its client before the securities were purchased that the client would later purchase the securities and hold the bank harmless for any loss. Thus, the client could be deemed to be the beneficial owner of the securities purchased by the bank. It is not clear whether, absent such an understanding prior to the purchases, the execution of the option agreement itself would be held to transfer beneficial ownership.

| **50** | **Applicable provisions.** 801.1(c), 801.1(b), 801.1(a)(3).

Issue. Under what circumstances are the holdings of a person aggregated with the holdings of the pension trust of a company controlled by that person?

Analysis. If the pension trust is deemed to hold the securities constituting the corpus of the trust, and if the pension trust is controlled by the company or by the person who controls that company, then the holdings of the company, its controlling person, and the pension plan holdings must all be aggregated. Under Section 801.1(c)(3), a pension trust holds the voting securities that constitute the corpus of that trust. Furthermore, the holdings of a trust are not aggregated with the holdings of another entity unless the entity controls the trust. This conclusion follows from the definition of ultimate parent entity – if no person or entity can be deemed the ultimate parent entity of the trust, then the trust is its own ultimate parent entity and its holdings will not be aggregated. *See* Section 801.1(a)(3). The control of the pension trust will be determined by whether the company or any other person or entity has contractual power to remove and replace 50 percent or more of the trustees of the trust. *See* 43 Fed. Reg. 33,450, 33,459 (July 31, 1978). Under Section 801.1(c)(8), if the pension plan is controlled by the company, the pension plan's holdings are the holdings of the company, and the holdings of the individual (if any) who controls the company.

| 51 | **Applicable provisions.** 801.1(c), 801.1(b)(2), 802.30.

Issue. Does a person who controls an issuer by reason of a contractual power presently to designate 50 percent or more of its directors hold the issuer's voting securities and has the person crossed a notification threshold?

Analysis. A person does not hold voting securities under Section 801.1(c)(1) unless that person has beneficial ownership of the securities. A contractual power presently to designate 50 percent or more of the directors of the issuer gives the person control of the issuer but does not, by itself, confer beneficial ownership of the issuer's voting securities. Thus, a person having a contractual power to appoint 50 percent or more of the issuer's directors does not necessarily hold its stock and no notification threshold has been crossed purely as a result of the contractual right.

Whether a person has met or exceeded a notification threshold is determined by the amount of voting securities held, not by whether a person has been given the right to vote the stock or entered into an agreement with the others as to how the stock will be voted. If a person who has obtained voting control of a corporation through such an agreement wishes to purchase shares of the corporation, reporting requirements are determined by the amount of voting stock that will be held by that person as a result of the acquisition. Therefore, individual shareholders (other than husband and wife and minor children) look only to their own holdings when determining reportability of acquisitions of additional shares, even if those shareholders have previously agreed to pool their voting power through an agreement with other shareholders. Thus, an HSR filing by such a person may be required even if that individual already controls the issuer by virtue of the person having the contractual power to designate 50 percent or more of the directors; in this situation, the party making the filing will report as both the acquiring and the acquired person.

Note that the Section 802.30 exemption does not apply here because the acquiring and acquired persons are not the same "by reason of holdings of voting securities," but rather by reason of a contractual arrangement.

52 | Applicable provision. 801.1(c).

Issue. Who are the holders of voting securities held in an employee savings and profit-sharing trust, where each employee has the right to vote all shares credited to his or her individual account?

Analysis. The PNO position is that the trust (and not the employees) is the beneficial owner of the voting securities held in the trust. The trust must be analyzed under Section 801.1(c). Section 801.1(c)(3) provides that "a trust, including a pension trust, shall hold all assets and voting securities constituting the corpus of the trust." Moreover, Section 801.1(c)(5) states that normally "beneficiaries of a trust including a pension trust . . . shall not hold any assets or voting securities constituting the corpus of such trust."

53 | Applicable provisions. 801.1(c), 801.2.

Issue. Is entering into a management agreement a reportable transaction?

Facts. Company A seeks to enter into a management agreement with a hospital for the management of an acute care hospital facility.

Analysis. The agreement is not reportable because entry into a management agreement is not an "acquisition" and no change in beneficial ownership results from entry into the agreement.

Note, however, that the PNO position is that a management agreement may violate the Act if it is executed in conjunction with a purchase of the underlying business. A management agreement entered into along with an agreement to purchase the managed company may, in the PNO's view, amount to the transfer of beneficial ownership at the time the management agreement takes effect, and hence a violation of the Act if this occurs prior to HSR clearance. Similarly, if the management agreement becomes effective during the HSR waiting period for the acquisition of the underlying business, or even during negotiations to purchase the business, the PNO may consider the parties to be "jumping the gun" prior to receiving HSR approval for the acquisition.

The PNO has acceded to the DOJ's stated position that local marketing agreements ("LMAs"), in which radio station owners transfer the right to set programming and to sell advertising on a station, entered into in connection with an acquisition, "may prematurely transfer beneficial ownership and require an HSR filing." *See* Lawrence R. Fullerton, Current Issues in Radio Station Merger Analysis, Address Before the Business Development Associates Antitrust 1997 Conference (Oct. 21, 1996), *available at* www.usdoj.gov/atr/public/speeches/8210.pdf.

54 | Applicable provision. 801.1(c).

Issue. Are the voting securities in the portfolio of an investment fund "held" by the fund's investment advisor, who has the voting rights to the securities (by reason of the proxies) and investment discretion with respect to the portfolio's securities?

Analysis. Under ordinary circumstances, the investment advisor will not be deemed to hold the voting securities in the investment fund's portfolio. The issue is one of "beneficial ownership." Since the fund's investors have the ultimate risk of gain or loss, and have the power to replace the investment advisor, they will "hold" the voting securities in the fund's portfolio. The indicia of beneficial ownership include the right to any increase "in value or dividends, the risk of loss of value, the right to vote the stock or to determine who may vote the stock, and investment discretion (including the power to dispose of the stock)." SBP, 43 Fed. Reg. 33,450, 33,458 (July 31, 1978). Although managers often have broad investment discretion, that alone does not establish beneficial ownership. While the investment advisor has proxies allowing it to vote the securities in the fund, those proxies are ultimately controlled by the fund's board of directors and are therefore revocable. *See* Int. 43. Also, the other indicia of beneficial ownership are unlikely to reside with the manager in these cases.

If the investment fund had been organized as a trust, the voting securities in the fund portfolio would ordinarily be held by the trust by reason of Section 801.1(c)(3), unless the fund is a "common trust fund or collective investment fund within the meaning of 12 C.F.R. § 9.18(a)." Under Section 801.1(c)(6), a bank or trust company that administers one or more such funds holds all of the assets and voting securities constituting the corpus of each such fund and must aggregate all such holdings with its own holdings for purposes of the Act. This is a special rule applicable only to investment funds (that must be organized as trusts) administered by a bank or trust company, as specified by 12 C.F.R. § 9.18(a). Such aggregation is not required of investment funds that are not "common trust funds" or "collective investment funds" within the meaning of 12 C.F.R. § 9.18(a).

Another special rule applies to insurance companies' general accounts or separate accounts that they administer. Under Section 801.1(c)(7), the insurance company is deemed to hold the assets and voting securities in such accounts.

55 Applicable provision. 801.1(c)(1).

Issue. Has an individual who obtains a one-third share in any gain or loss in voting securities held by another person made a potentially reportable acquisition?

Analysis. Because the individual does not have title to, or the power to vote or dispose of, the acquired securities, the individual has no reporting obligation. The PNO's position is that a derivative agreement like this where an individual realizes a gain or loss derived from the gain or loss of the underlying assets (in this case voting securities) that is held by an unrelated person, standing alone, does not confer beneficial ownership on that individual within the meaning of Section 801.1(c)(1). The holder of the derivative in this case has only one indicium of beneficial ownership and will not receive any other indicia of ownership in the voting securities such as the right to vote or dispose of the acquired securities.

56 | Applicable provision. 801.1(c)(1).

Issue. Does the buyer of shares under a contingent purchase arrangement have an HSR reporting requirement?

Facts. A person who is a residual beneficiary of a trust under the will of a deceased shareholder agrees to sell any of the shares that he may inherit to the buyer. The trustee has the power both to vote and to sell the shares held in trust.

Analysis. Since the seller may never come into possession of the shares, the buyer has no present reporting obligation under these facts. The buyer's contingent purchase right does not confer sufficient indicia of beneficial ownership to result in his "holding" the shares. At such time as the seller actually inherits the shares and a transfer to the buyer then occurs, notification may be required by the buyer and the appropriate acquired person.

Note however that the buyer could file notification if it wished to do so. Otherwise the purchase would not be notifiable until the contingency actually occurred, and the buyer would not be able to take possession at that time without creating an HSR reporting violation. The PNO has indicated that a filing made while the purchase was still contingent would be acceptable, although Section 803.7 would result in expiration of that notification if the transaction were not consummated within one year.

| 57 | **Applicable provision.** 801.1(c)(1).

Issue. In a multi-step transaction, does an intermediary acquiring person, which will sell stock or assets simultaneously with its acquisition, have a reporting requirement?

Facts. In connection with the sale of all of its assets, Z Corporation will receive voting securities of the purchaser. Simultaneously, Z will liquidate and transfer those voting securities to its own shareholders. The question arises whether Z's receipt of voting securities is subject to reporting and waiting-period requirements.

Analysis. The PNO's position is that where the sale or liquidation by which the intermediary acquiring person (which will merely be a shell after the liquidation) will dispose of stock or assets occurs simultaneously with the acquisition and is an integral, unconditional part of the transaction, no filing by the intermediary will be required. Thus, the party from whom the intermediary is acquiring, and the party to whom the intermediary is transferring, may be required to file. The PNO stresses, however, that if for any unanticipated reason the intermediary Z should hold the stock or assets for more than the transitory period, its failure to file and observe the waiting period will be a violation of the Act. *See* Int. 48.

58 Applicable provisions. 801.1(c)(1), 801.1(b)(2).

Issue. Does a person who has an irrevocable power of attorney giving a right to vote 25 percent of the voting securities of an issuer "hold" those securities?

Analysis. The PNO has indicated that an irrevocable contractual right to vote securities is not, by itself, an interest sufficient to constitute beneficial ownership of those securities; voting rights are only one indicium of ownership. The irrevocable contractual right will, however, be relevant to determine whether the person controls the issuer. If the person holds 25 percent or more of the voting securities of the issuer coupled with the irrevocable contractual right to vote an additional 25 percent, the person would be deemed to control the issuer. *See* Int. 43.

It should be noted that, because entering into a contract to vote or receipt of a proxy alone does not transfer beneficial ownership, transfer of control in such a manner does not necessitate a filing. Only acquisitions of voting securities trigger such filing requirements. *See* Int. 43.

59 Applicable provision. 801.1(c)(1).

Issue. Does a bank, investment banker, or broker who invests and manages its client's money "hold" the voting securities that it purchases for the client's account?

Analysis. Although the banker, investment banker, or broker is delegated the authority to purchase, sell, and vote the securities, the client can revoke this power at any time; can direct the bank to purchase, sell, and vote the securities; and retains the benefit of any gain in value and risk in loss of value of the stock. Therefore, the client, and not the investment banker, bank, or broker, has beneficial ownership of any voting securities purchased for the client's account. The obvious corollary to this position is that any acquisition by the banker or broker for the account of the client is an acquisition by the client. *See* Int. 54.

| 60 | **Applicable provision.** 801.1(c)(1).

Issue. Is the transfer of an undivided interest in an asset potentially reportable?

Analysis. If the other requirements of the Act are met, a filing will be required for the transfer of an undivided interest in an asset. Because undivided interests are treated as separate assets, however, there is no aggregation of a single buyer's purchases of undivided interests in a single asset from different ultimate parent entities. The size-of-transaction test is applied separately to the interests of each owner. Thus, if three unrelated entities were each selling their interests constituting 100 percent of the asset for $50 million or less, each transaction would be nonreportable.

In contrast, if the asset were held by a corporation, partnership or LLC, the sale of the entity or the asset to a single acquiring person for more than $50 million would meet the size-of-transaction test, and might be reportable if the other jurisdictional requirements are met. The sale of less than 100 percent of the interests in a partnership or LLC for cash is always exempt from the Act's reporting requirements (so long as the buyer will not as a result hold 100 percent of the partnership or LLC interests). Any sale of partnership or LLC interests where a single buyer will end up holding 100 percent of the interests in a partnership or LLC is treated as the acquisition of all of the assets of the partnership or LLC by the acquiring person. *See* Int. 73.

However, the acquisition by one buyer of three one-third undivided interests in an asset from three different sellers for less than $50 million each will be exempt even if the aggregate acquisition price is more than $50 million.

61 Applicable provisions. 801.1(c)(3), 801.1(c)(4), 801.1(b)(2).

Issue. When does an individual who creates a trust for his or her children "hold" the voting securities constituting the corpus of the trust, and when does he or she "control" the trust?

Facts. An individual creates an irrevocable trust for his children, retains no reversionary interest, serves as trustee of that trust, has the contractual power to designate the successor trustees of the trust, and may by operation of state descent and distribution law have a remote possibility of receiving an inheritance from the trust.

Analysis. Under the facts as stated, the individual neither "holds" the corpus of the trust, nor "controls" the trust; rather, the trust itself is deemed to hold the trust's assets.

The PNO's position is that there are two ways that a person can be deemed to hold the assets of an irrevocable trust: (1) the settlor retains a reversionary interest in the corpus of the trust so that the settlor is also a beneficiary of the trust (*see* SBP, 43 Fed. Reg. 33,450, 33,458 (July 31, 1978)), or (2) the settlor (or any other person for that matter) has the right to remove and replace 50 percent or more of the trustees and therefore controls the trust.

In this scenario, although it is possible that the settlor-trustee could inherit the securities that constitute the corpus of the trust if his children predecease him without issue, the possibility of inheritance is not a reversionary interest within the meaning of Section 801.1(c)(3).

The PNO's position is that where the terms of the trust empower a person or entity to remove and replace 50 percent or more of the trustees, that person or entity controls the trust. Without more, the settlor's power to designate the trustee upon the trust's creation does not confer control, as this power adds very little to the actual control the settlor already exercises over the trust assets. Similarly, no control over the trust exists simply by having the right to appoint a successor trustee in the event the trustee resigns or is unable to continue to serve. Again, there must be some mechanism by which the original trustee can be removed and replaced in order for another person to have control over the trust. Note the PNO's position that, if the power to designate a replacement trustee is shared or subject to the consent of a third-party, no one person has a power to appoint 50 percent or more of the trustees and no one would be deemed to control the trust. *See* Int. 47.

Editor's Note. *The PNO's current position on what it takes to control a trust is different (and in some ways more limited) than what is described in the SBP. The SBP states that a trust can be controlled if another entity "has a contractual power, under the trust indenture, to designate the trustee or, if there is more than one, a majority of the trustees." 43 Fed. Reg. 33,450, 33,459 (July 31, 1978). The PNO's current position differs from the SBP position in two ways. First, the PNO now asserts that "control" requires more than just the right to designate when the trust is created or if and when a vacancy arises. A controlling entity must have the right to "remove and replace" the trustees. Second, the PNO's current position is that an entity has control of the trust if it can remove and replace **50 percent** or more of the trustees, in accordance with the language of Section 801.1(b)(2), rather than a **majority** of the trustees (i.e., **more than** 50 percent) as stated in the SBP.*

| 62 | **Applicable provisions.** 801.1(c)(3), 801.1(c)(6).

Issue. Is the treatment of collective investment funds in Sections 801.1(c)(3) and (6) limited to those funds that are administered by a *national* bank, since 12 C.F.R. § 9.18(a) is a rule promulgated by the Comptroller of the Currency for regulation of national banks?

Analysis. The treatment of collective investment funds in Sections 801.1(c)(3) and (6) is not so limited. The PNO's position is that all common trust funds or collective investment funds operated in accordance with the guidelines provided for national banks in 12 C.F.R. § 9.18(a) are covered by the Rules. Referring to Sections 581 and 584 of the Internal Revenue Code, the PNO's position is that national banks, trust companies, state banks, territorial banks, and banks organized under the laws of the District of Columbia may administer such funds, and the Rules apply to all such funds. *See* Int. 64.

63 Applicable provisions. 801.1(c)(3), 801.1(b)(2).

Issue. What is the effect of owning stock outright and also having the voting power of additional shares by virtue of being a trustee of a trust?

Facts. An individual with the authority to vote 21 percent of the voting securities of a corporation in his capacity as trustee of a trust will acquire 33 percent of the voting securities of the same corporation.

Analysis. The HSR analysis of such a transaction would depend on the nature of the trust and the individual's interest in the trust.

First, if the trust is an irrevocable "voting trust" the trustee may be deemed to "control" the corporation in this case. A "voting trust" is normally one created by an agreement between a group of stockholders and the trustee in which certain of the rights of the shareholders is lodged in the trustee. If the shareholders have not transferred beneficial ownership of the stock to the trust but have merely given the trustee the irrevocable right to vote the shares, the PNO has taken the position that it will treat the arrangement for HSR analysis purposes as an irrevocable proxy. In that case the trustee would not "hold" the shares but might be able to "control" the corporation by means of its ability to elect 50 percent or more of the directors. *See* Int. 51.

On the other hand, if the trust holds beneficial ownership of the shares, the PNO will look to the usual HSR rules dealing with trusts to analyze the effect of the trustee's rights. The general rule is that a trust, not the trustee, holds the corpus of a trust. Unless the trustee was deemed to control the trust and "hold" the underlying voting securities, the individual/trustee in this case would hold only 33 percent of the corporation's voting securities after consummating the transaction.

If, however, the individual was deemed to control the trust (e.g., the individual has the right to remove and replace the trustee of the trust), the individual would hold in excess of 50 percent of the corporation's voting securities, and thus control the corporation.

64 Applicable provision. 801.1(c)(6).

Issue. When an acquisition of assets includes collective investment trusts within the meaning of 12 C.F.R. § 9.18(a), must the assets in the trusts be aggregated with the other assets being acquired for purposes of the size-of-transaction test?

Facts. An entity proposes to acquire all of the assets of the acquired person's trust department. Some of those assets include collective investment trusts.

Analysis. The PNO's position is that the assets held in the collective investment trusts are not to be aggregated with the acquired person's other assets. The rationale is apparently that Section 801.1(c)(6) was intended to require aggregation of a trust company's fiduciary holdings of assets or voting securities of an acquired company only when either the trust company or its fund makes an additional investment in the acquired person. In contrast, when the trust company is itself the acquired person, the collective investment fund assets held in a fiduciary capacity are not also included in the trust company's assets.

65 Applicable provision. 801.1(c)(7).

Issue. Does an insurance company "hold" the assets and voting securities held for the benefit of separate accounts administered by that company when the owners of the variable contracts funded by the separate accounts have the right to vote the separate accounts' holdings of the shares of the underlying mutual funds?

Analysis. Yes. The contract owner's right to provide voting instructions is typical of insurance company separate accounts, and as such does not exempt it from the coverage of Section 801.1(c)(7).

66 Applicable provision. 801.1(e).

Issue. What constitutes "principal offices" for purposes of determining whether an issuer is a foreign or U.S. issuer?

Facts. Two separate scenarios were presented. In scenario one, the issuer was organized under the laws of Jamaica. Its legal address was in Kingston, Jamaica; however, its only presence in that country was a mailbox. Its officers all maintained offices in New York.

In scenario two, the issuer was organized under the laws of Mexico and its headquarters, including the offices of all of its officers, was located in Mexico City. All of its operations, including six manufacturing plants and a distribution center, were located in the United States.

Analysis. A foreign issuer is defined in Section 801.1(e)(2)(ii) as an "issuer which is not incorporated in the United States, is not organized under the laws of the United States and does not have its principal offices in the United States." Because the issuer in scenario one is not incorporated in the United States or organized under the laws of the United States, the only remaining issue is whether the legal address is the principal office of the issuer. In this instance, the PNO's position is that the physical location of the offices of the officers of the corporation constitutes the principal offices of the issuer, notwithstanding the foreign legal address. The mailbox presence in Jamaica does not constitute a sufficient nexus with the foreign jurisdiction of that country to qualify as the issuer's principal offices.

In scenario two, the PNO found that the issuer is a foreign issuer despite the fact that all of the operations of the issuer were located in the United States, because the principal offices of the issuer were located outside of the United States. The SBP defines principal office as "that single location which the person regards as the headquarters office of the ultimate parent entity." 43 Fed. Reg. 33,450, 33,461 (July 31, 1978). This location may or may not coincide with the location of incorporation or the location of principal operations.

67 | Applicable provisions. 801.1(f), 802.31.

Issue. Is the acquisition of convertible securities that have no present voting rights but that carry certain veto rights a reportable transaction?

Facts. Various veto rights may attach to convertible securities, including for instance the right to veto the acquired person's entry into certain businesses, the right to veto the sale or liquidation of the business, and the right to veto the issuance of debt above a given level.

Analysis. None of these veto rights makes the acquisition of the underlying convertible voting securities reportable. Although convertible voting securities are within the definition of voting securities in Section 801.1(f)(1), the acquisition of such securities is exempt under Section 802.31. The fact that nonvoting convertible securities have certain veto rights does not eliminate the availability of the exemption. Consequently, only the acquisition of securities with a presently exercisable right to vote for the election of a director of the issuer (or of a subsidiary, or in the case of an unincorporated entity, individuals exercising similar functions) is reportable. *See* Section 801.1(f)(1); *cf.* Int. 70.

If the acquiring person takes affirmative steps to convert the securities into securities having a present right to vote for directors, that event may be reportable.

| **68** | **Applicable provisions.** 801.1(f), 802.31.

Issue. If a lender financing the sale of one corporation to another corporation will acquire newly issued, nonvoting, nonconvertible, cumulative preferred stock and warrants with the power to purchase 70 percent of the common stock (upon payment of additional consideration) of the acquired corporation, is the transaction reportable?

Analysis. Neither the acquisition of the warrants nor the acquisition of the nonvoting, nonconvertible preferred stock is presently reportable. Warrants are convertible voting securities within the meaning of Section 801.1(f), which defines "voting securities," but, because they confer no present voting rights, their acquisition is exempt under Section 802.31. Of course, the subsequent conversion of those warrants into voting securities could be reportable. By contrast, no exemption is needed for shares of nonvoting, nonconvertible preferred stock because they are not voting securities within the definition in Section 801.1(f).

69 | Applicable provision. 801.1(f).

Issue. Do shares of nonvoting preferred stock, which gives holders voting rights only upon the occurrence of certain events (e.g., failure to pay dividends for a certain number of quarters) constitute "voting securities"?

Analysis. The PNO's position is that the nonvoting preferred shares are not "voting securities" unless or until the stated events give the holders a present right to vote for directors of the issuer.

Note that no "acquisition" takes place when the events occur that confer present voting rights, and no reporting obligations arise. (Existence of those voting rights may result in a change of control of the issuer, however, which could affect reporting obligations with respect to subsequent acquisitions.) Underlying this conclusion is the view that the occurrence of the events that gives the right to vote for directors is not a "conversion" within the meaning of Section 801.1(f)(3) because the events are not the "exercise of a right inherent in the ownership or holding of particular voting securities to exchange such securities for securities which presently entitle the owner or holder to vote for directors . . . ." Examples of conversions that do fall within the 801.1(f)(3) definition and could trigger reporting obligations are when options, warrants, or convertible securities are exchanged for securities that presently entitle the holder to vote for directors. The PNO takes the position that situations where the event that gives the right to vote for directors is certain, or virtually certain, to occur at the time the security is acquired (e.g., voting rights granted after one year of holding the stock) are considered to be 801.1(f)(3) conversions that could trigger reporting obligations.

A variation of this question has arisen with respect to "white squire" preferred shares, which give the shareholder the right to vote on all issues other than the election of directors. Because Section 801.1(f)(1) defines voting securities in terms of the right presently to vote for the election of directors, the acquisition of shares that presently have the right to vote only on other issues, such as mergers, charter amendments, etc., is not reportable. It also is not a reportable event to acquire shares that will only have the right to vote for directors after expiration of an HSR waiting period. In those circumstances, the acquiring person can file under the Act after it acquires the shares; the PNO treats the expiration of the HSR waiting period as a "conversion" under the Rules.

70 | Applicable provisions. 801.1(f), 802.31.

Issue. Is an acquisition of convertible nonvoting securities coupled with irrevocable proxies to vote the underlying shares or a contractual right to designate directors reportable under the Act?

Facts. Two scenarios: in one, Shareholder A acquires convertible nonvoting stock and also receives irrevocable proxies to vote the same number of shares it would hold upon conversion. In the second, Shareholder A acquires nonvoting convertible stock that upon conversion will represent 20 percent of the voting securities of the corporation. A also receives a contractual right to designate one of five directors of the corporation.

Analysis. Standing alone, the acquisition of any nonvoting, convertible securities is exempt from reporting prior to the time of conversion under Section 802.31. Similarly, receiving irrevocable proxies or the contractual right to designate directors is not, by itself, an acquisition of voting securities or assets under the Act and is not reportable. However, the PNO's position is that the combination may be reportable.

The PNO considers that the acquisition of a combination of present irrevocable voting rights and convertible voting securities may be deemed to be the acquisition of voting securities. In scenario one, the convertible securities are deemed to be voting securities prior to their conversion, since Shareholder A has irrevocable proxies to vote the same number of shares that it would be able to vote upon conversion, and thus their acquisition may trigger an HSR filing obligation if the various size tests are met.

The PNO will treat the acquisition of the nonvoting convertible stock coupled with an irrevocable proxy as an acquisition of voting securities even if the number of shares to be voted under the terms of the irrevocable proxy does not equal the number of shares of voting securities the acquiring person would hold upon conversion of its nonvoting convertible stock. For example, if Shareholder A planned to acquire convertible nonvoting stock that would convert into 10 percent of the voting securities of the company and would also receive an irrevocable proxy that entitled it to vote 20 percent of the company's shares, the PNO would treat Shareholder A's acquisition of the nonvoting convertible securities as an acquisition of ten percent of the company's voting securities. On the other hand, if Shareholder A planned to acquire convertible nonvoting stock that would convert into 25 percent of the voting securities of the company and would also receive an irrevocable proxy that entitled it to vote 20 percent of the company's shares, the PNO would treat Shareholder A's acquisition of the nonvoting convertible securities in two parts on a proportional basis. The amount of nonvoting convertible stock that would convert into 20 percent of the company's voting securities would be treated as the acquisition of voting securities. The remainder would be treated as merely the acquisition of nonvoting convertible stock.

In scenario two, the convertible securities would not be deemed to be voting securities if there was no cumulative voting since, in that case, 20 percent of the voting securities of the corporation would elect no directors on its own (cumulative voting permits the stockholder to cast all of his or her votes for one or more, but fewer than all, of the directors on the slate). On the other hand, with cumulative voting, A could elect one director when the shares were converted and there would be a direct correlation between the number of directors that A currently can appoint, and the number of directors it could elect unilaterally upon conversion. In this case, the convertible securities would be deemed to be voting securities at the time of their acquisition.

As in the case of the irrevocable proxy described above, the nonvoting convertible shares may be treated as voting securities even if the number of directors to be appointed does not exactly equal the number of directors that could be elected by the voting securities that would be held at the time of conversion. For example, if the number of directors that currently can be designated under the terms of the contractual agreement is greater than or equal to the number of directors that could be elected by voting the shares postconversion (assuming the shares can unilaterally elect at least one director), then the convertible securities will be deemed to be voting securities at the time of their acquisition. If the number of directors that currently can be designated under the contractual right is less than the number of directors that could be elected by voting the shares postconversion (assuming the shares can unilaterally elect at least one director), then that portion of the convertible securities that would convert into enough shares to appoint that smaller number of directors will be treated as an acquisition of voting securities. The remainder would be treated as the acquisition of nonvoting convertible stock.

In any scenario, if at a later date any of the convertible shares that were treated as voting securities initially are converted, no filing would be required unless their voting power increased as a result of the conversion.

71 | Applicable provision. 801.1(f)(1).

Issue. Is the acquisition of an interest in a publicly traded MLP potentially reportable?

Analysis. No, unless as a result of the acquisition the acquiring person would hold 100 percent of the interests in the MLP. *See* Int. 73. MLP interests are treated like any other partnership interest. The fact that MLP units are traded on exchanges like conventional voting securities does not make them voting securities.

The term "voting securities" is defined in Section 801.1(f)(1). "'[V]oting securities' means any securities which at present or upon conversion entitle the owner or holder thereof to vote for the election of directors of the issuer . . . or with respect to unincorporated entities, individuals exercising similar functions." *Id.* The key is not whether a security is publicly traded, but whether it entitles the holder to vote for directors or "with respect to unincorporated entities, individuals exercising similar functions." When the FTC revised the control rules in 1987, the SBP took the position that "partnerships do not possess 'individuals exercising similar functions' to directors." 52 Fed. Reg. 20,058, 20,062 (May 29, 1987). As a result, partnership interests are never considered to be voting securities, irrespective of the form of management used by the partnership. Thus, the acquisition of MLP units will not be reportable (absent a transaction that results in one person holding 100 percent of the MLP interests) because they are not considered voting securities.

Editor's Note. The PNO takes the position that interests in "business trusts" may be "voting securities" if they are organized in such a way as to have "directors" or "individuals exercising similar functions to directors" and the holders of the interests in the business trust are entitled to vote for these individuals. The PNO uses this same analysis for determining whether interests in non-U.S. entities (including LLCs organized under laws outside the United States) will be considered to be "voting securities." Transactions involving U.S. LLCs are always analyzed under Formal Interpretation 15 (see Appendix), even if they arguably have "individuals exercising similar functions to directors." See also, e.g., Ints. 81, 82, and 177. Formal Interpretation 15 does not apply to foreign LLCs, so a foreign LLC will either be treated for HSR purposes as a corporation or a partnership (depending on the "voting securities" analysis), but never as a limited LLC. See Int. 177.

72 Applicable provisions. 801.1(f)(1), 802.31.

Issue and Facts. Securities issued by a corporation are nonvoting while held by the original purchaser, but may be converted to voting securities when transferred to a subsequent holder. Are these securities considered "voting securities"? Does the HSR treatment change if the securities held by the original purchaser automatically become voting securities upon transfer?

Analysis. The securities are not "voting securities" while they are held by the original purchaser, because they carry no present voting rights and cannot be converted into voting securities. An acquisition of such securities by an unaffiliated purchaser would be treated as an acquisition of *convertible* voting securities and would be exempt (until conversion) under Section 802.31.

If the securities *automatically* convert to voting securities upon transfer by the original purchaser, the transfer is treated as an acquisition of voting securities (with present voting rights) and may be immediately reportable if the requirements of the Act are satisfied. Thus the parties would have to file for and obtain HSR clearance before the transaction takes place, unless the PNO permitted them to close the transaction in escrow before filing. *See* Int. 88 regarding escrows.

Interpretations Relating to Part 801 93

| 73 | **Applicable provisions.** 801.1(f)(1), 801.90, 7A(c)(3), 802.30.

Issues. Are partnership interests considered assets or voting securities under the Act? When is the acquisition of a partnership interest potentially reportable?

Analysis. In an interpretation that is almost as old as the Rules themselves, the PNO set forth the view that an acquisition or any other transfer of partnership interests where the acquiring person will hold less than all of the interests in the partnership is not reportable. The reason is that the transfer of any partnership interest or interests that results in the acquiring person holding less than 100 percent of the interests in such partnership is not regarded as an acquisition of an asset or voting security within the meaning of the Rules. If, however, as a result of an acquisition one person holds 100 percent of the partnership interests, the transaction is deemed an acquisition of 100 percent of the partnership's assets and is reportable if the size-of-person and size-of-transaction tests of Section 7A(a) are met (and if no exemption applies to the assets). Note that the size-of-transaction test is determined by the value of 100 percent of the partnership's assets, not by the purchase price for the partnership interests being acquired. *See* Int. 110. However, the value of assets that are otherwise exempt under the Rules may be excluded from the size-of-transaction calculation. For example, the acquisition of cash is exempt (Section 801.21) and would not be part of the size-of-transaction calculation. *See also, e.g.*, Section 802.2(d) (offices); Section 802.2(e) (hotels); and Section 802.3 (carbon-based mineral reserves). Likewise, if the assets of the partnership being acquired include partnership interests of other partnerships, the value of those partnership interests are excluded from the size-of-transaction calculation unless, of course, the acquiring person will also hold 100 percent of the partnership interests of this second partnership as a result of the transaction. Where one person will hold 100 percent of the partnership interests, the person is deemed to be acquiring all of the assets of the partnership, even if the partnership continues to exist as a separate legal entity and even if the acquiring person previously held a minority (or majority) interest in the partnership.

Several conclusions follow from these interpretations. First, because partnership interests are not voting securities, a partnership is never an "issuer" within the meaning of the Rules. Second, although limited partnership interests may be treated as securities in other contexts (e.g., cash tender offers for publicly traded partnership interests), such interests are not "voting securities" under Section 801.1(f)(1). Third, formation of a partnership is never reportable, unless it is a disguised asset sale, deemed reportable under Section 801.90. *See* Int. 27.

Editor's Note. *This interpretation causes significant discrepancies between the treatment of partnerships and the treatment of corporations for HSR reporting purposes. The acquisition of minority interests in a partnership is always exempt (so long as less than 100 percent of the interests are held by the acquiror), whereas acquisitions of minority interests in corporate stock are potentially reportable if the statutory thresholds are met. The acquisition of 100 percent of the interests in a partnership by a majority member, for instance a 70 percent interest holder, would be reportable as an acquisition of all of the partnership's assets, whereas the acquisition of 100 percent of the interests in a corporation by a 70 percent shareholder would be exempt under Sections 7A(c)(3) and 802.30.*

74 Applicable provisions. 801.1(f)(1), 801.2(d).

Issue. Is the acquisition of a nonstock membership corporation (profit or nonprofit), or the acquisition of control of such an entity, subject to the Act? If so, should it be viewed as an acquisition of assets or as an acquisition of voting securities?

Facts. This transaction involved the transfer of control of a hospital operated by one religious order to another religious order. Apparently, no consideration was given for the transfer.

Analysis. The PNO treats this form of transaction as a merger or consolidation under Section 801.2(d), but views it as an acquisition of assets for valuation purposes. *See* Ints. 79, 102.

| 75 | **Applicable provisions.** 801.1(g), 803.10(b).

Issue. Is a cash tender offer for control of a foreign issuer (which is not subject to Section 14 of the Exchange Act) entitled to a fifteen-day waiting period?

Analysis. The PNO applies the fifteen-day waiting period to these situations. In the SBP to Section 801.1(g), the FTC "specifically adopts th[e] broader meaning of the term 'tender offer,'" which includes transactions that may be subject to the requirements of Section 14(e) of the Exchange Act but that may not be conventional tender offers within the meaning of Section 14(d) of the Exchange Act. *See* 43 Fed. Reg. 33,450, 33,464 (July 31, 1978). But it is the view of the PNO that if the consideration offered is anything other than a present cash payment (e.g., a promissory or loan note option), the offer does not qualify as a cash tender offer.

76 Applicable provisions. 801.1(g)(1), 801.30.

Issue. Does a proposed acquisition qualify as a cash tender offer subject to Section 801.30 where the holder of 51 percent of the securities of the acquired person intends to tender its shares in response to the tender offer, but is contractually obligated to sell its shares to the acquiring person in any case?

Analysis. Existence of a purchase agreement between the acquiring person and the majority shareholder is not inconsistent with cash tender offer treatment. Whether the transaction is a cash tender offer is determined by reference to applicable federal securities law or the laws of the jurisdiction in which the cash tender offer will be conducted. This transaction is likely to be governed by Section 801.30.

| 77 | **Applicable provisions.** 801.1(g)(1), 803.5(a)(2).

Issue. Is a tender offer for the shares of a privately held company a tender offer for HSR purposes? What kind of public announcement is required under these circumstances?

Analysis. Provided the offer otherwise satisfies the definition of a tender offer under federal securities laws, the fact that the issuer's shares are not publicly traded will not prevent the transaction from being treated as a tender offer under the Act. Thus, if the offer is for cash, the waiting period is fifteen days, rather than thirty.

Under Section 803.5(a)(2) of the Rules and the Exchange Act, all tender offers must be publicly announced. Tender offers to publicly held companies must be publicly announced in newspapers or other media, but the announcement requirement is different for tender offers to privately held companies. Section 14E of the Exchange Act states that the public announcement requirement for privately held companies may be satisfied by additional means (other than publication in the media), such as a letter to all shareholders. For privately held companies, the PNO accepts the procedures that satisfy federal securities law requirements. Thus, the Section 803.5(a)(2) requirement can be satisfied, for privately held companies, with a letter to all the shareholders of the issuer.

| 78 | **Applicable provisions.** 801.2(a), 801.1(c).

Issue. How does the Act apply to acquisitions by an agent acting on behalf of a principal?

Analysis. Acquisitions of assets or voting securities are reportable by the person who obtains beneficial ownership of those assets or voting securities. If the acquisition is made by a person acting as agent, the transaction is reportable by the principal on whom beneficial ownership is conferred, and is not reportable by the agent. The language of Section 801.2(a) and the SBP clearly indicate that agents, brokers, or other entities acquiring voting securities on behalf of another person do not "hold" those securities within the meaning of Section 801.1(c)(1) and that the person on whose behalf such securities are acquired is the acquiring person. *See* 43 Fed. Reg. 33,450, 33,467 (July 31, 1978); Int. 59.

| 79 | **Applicable provisions.** 801.2(d), 802.30, 7A(c)(3).

Issue. Are consolidations of not-for-profit membership corporations potentially reportable?

Analysis. Consolidations of not-for-profit membership corporations are subject to Section 801.2(d), which states that "[m]ergers and consolidations are transactions subject to the act and shall be treated as acquisitions of voting securities." Section 801.2(d)(1)(i).

Although it can be argued that a merger or consolidation of nonprofit corporations is not an acquisition of voting securities because such entities do not issue voting securities, the PNO's position is that any merger, consolidation, or other combination of the business or operations of any two persons may be reportable under Section 801.2(d) if the other jurisdictional criteria of the Act are met. In the case of nonprofits, the combinations have been effected in a number of different ways: trustees resign and are replaced by the trustees of the acquiring organizations, one organization becomes the sole voting member of the other, or members of one organization vote to become members of the acquiring organization. *See* Int. 102.

Note, however, that if two nonprofit companies with the same controlling member merge or transfer assets between themselves, it is the PNO's position that no HSR notification is required for the transaction, even though the transaction is not specifically exempted by Section 802.30 or Section 7A(c)(3) of the Act. *See* Ints. 42, 102.

80 | Applicable provisions. 801.2(d), 801.40(b).

Issue. How is the simultaneous consolidation of more than two corporations into a new parent entity analyzed for HSR reportability purposes?

Facts. In a simultaneous transaction, four independent manufacturing companies (A, B, C, and D) are going to consolidate into a new parent company. All four will consolidate at one time. Each of the companies has the following assets and sales:

Company	Revenue	Assets
A	$12mm	$10mm
B	$14mm	$10mm
C	$21mm	$24mm
D	$84mm	$46mm

Analysis. The PNO analyzes consolidations of more than two corporations sequentially, as if the transaction were a series of mergers, and does not recognize simultaneous consolidations. If the parties do not spell out the sequence of the consolidation in the consolidation agreement, the PNO advises the parties to analyze the transactions in all possible sequences. If any sequence would result in a filing obligation, the parties should then file for the minimum number of reportable transactions. For example, if A acquires B, AB acquires C, and ABC acquires D, there is no reportable transaction (even assuming the size-of-transaction test is met) because there is no $100 million person in any of the transactions. But if A acquires B, AB acquires D, and ABD, a $100 million person, acquires C, then there is a minimum reporting obligation (one notification) in this sequence, and the PNO has advised parties to file. In its filing, ABD must include all of the HSR information required for A, B, and D including certification by respective company officials if the deals have not closed. On the other hand, if the parties spell out the sequence in the agreement in such a way as to not be reportable and there are valid business reasons (tax, etc.) for the sequence, then no filing is required.

| 81 | **Applicable provisions.** 801.2(d); Formal Interpretation 15.

Issue. Is the formation of an LLC a "merger or consolidation" and thus reportable?

Analysis. As a result of Formal Interpretation 15 (*see* Appendix) the formation of an LLC is reportable if the jurisdictional tests are met, and if (1) two or more preexisting, separately controlled businesses will be contributed to the LLC, and (2) at least one of the members will control the LLC. Control is defined as having the right to 50 percent of the profits of the LLC or 50 percent of the assets of the LLC upon dissolution. The staff of the PNO uses the definition of "operating unit" under Section 802.1(a) of the Rules to define a business for purposes of Formal Interpretation 15. Thus, if all the parties to the formation are contributing only cash, no HSR filing is required. Furthermore, if one of two parties in an LLC formation is contributing a business and the other only cash, no HSR filing is required because two businesses are not being combined. Furthermore, if three parties are forming an LLC, and no one will control the new LLC, no filing will be required no matter what the parties are contributing.

On the other hand, if there are three parties, with two of them contributing businesses and one contributing cash, the formation is potentially reportable if one of the parties will control the LLC. The contribution of an interest in intellectual property, such as a patent, a patent license, or know-how, that is exclusive against all parties including the grantor, is the contribution of a business, whether or not the intellectual property has generated any revenues. The contribution of something less than an "operating unit," such as a manufacturing line without sales, distribution, or payroll, is not the contribution of a business.

The SBP accompanying Formal Interpretation 15 states that the "formation of an LLC into which two or more businesses are contributed, like other unions of businesses under common control, is a kind of merger or consolidation." 64 Fed. Reg. 5,808, 5,809 (Feb. 5, 1999). Although combining businesses in an LLC may not be a "merger" or "consolidation" in the strictest sense because they do not involve corporations (and voting securities), the FTC stated that its rationale for basing the formation of LLCs upon Section 801.2(d) was similar to the PNO's requiring filings for acquisitions of nonprofit corporations, which, like LLCs, typically do not issue voting securities. *See* Ints. 79, 102.

| 82 | **Applicable provision.** Formal Interpretation 15.

Issue. If two parties contribute jointly controlled assets (each owns 50 percent) to a newly created LLC, and a third party buys 51 percent of that LLC for cash, is there either a reportable formation or acquisition (assuming size thresholds are satisfied)?

Facts. Two adult brothers placed the assets of four separate corporations, jointly controlled (50 percent by each brother), into four newly created LLCs. The membership interests in the four LLCs were then contributed to a newly created holding company LLC, also controlled 50-50. Thereafter, a third party purchased 51 percent of the holding company LLC for cash, with the brothers retaining 49 percent.

Analysis. There is no reportable formation because, under Formal Interpretation 15 (*see* Appendix), a filing is required for an LLC formation only if two or more preexisting, separately controlled businesses are combined under common control in a new LLC. Here, the businesses contributed to the LLC were controlled by each of the two brothers both before and after the formation.

As this scenario illustrates, just because a business is not "solely" controlled does not mean it is "separately" controlled for purposes of Formal Interpretation 15. Moreover, postformation control need not be identical to what it was before the formation. For example, even if one brother's interest in the holding company LLC had been less than 50 percent, there still would not have been separately controlled businesses contributed, because the brother holding greater than 50 percent controlled the businesses both before and after their contribution to the LLC.

As for the third party's purchase, Formal Interpretation 15 provides that acquisitions of membership interests in an LLC are not reportable unless (1) a business is contributed to the LLC as consideration for LLC interests (resulting in a potentially reportable new LLC formation) or (2) 100 percent of the LLC is acquired (which is treated as the acquisition of all the assets of the LLC). In this scenario, the third party contributed only cash, and hence its acquisition of less than 100 percent of the membership interests in holding company LLC would also be nonreportable.

83 | Applicable provisions. Formal Interpretation 15, 801.90.

Issue. Do any of the following factual scenarios involve the requisite contribution, for a reportable LLC formation, of two preexisting separately controlled businesses coming under common control?

Facts.

1. X creates X-LLC, a single-member LLC, with $50 million cash. Y then contributes two businesses in exchange for a 90 percent interest in X-LLC.

2. A and B form LLC-1, with A contributing a business and B contributing only cash. Control is designed to be 50-50, but B has a right to a priority return on profits until a certain threshold is obtained, giving B a right to well over 50 percent of the profits for a period of time. During that time, for financial and business reasons, A contributes additional cash to LLC-1, and the ownership interests are adjusted so that each of A and B are entitled, as originally intended, to 50 percent of the assets of LLC-1 upon dissolution. A and B then agree to form a new LLC, LLC-2, and contribute the businesses held in LLC-1, with A contributing additional businesses and B contributing additional cash.

3. AB-Partnership, owned two-thirds by A and one-third by B, is converted into AB-LLC, with the same ownership. A also has a 51 percent interest in AC-LLC, in which the 49 percent interest is held by C. A then forms a new LLC with C ("ABC-LLC"), with A contributing its controlling interests in AB-LLC and AC-LLC, and C contributing its 49 percent interest in AC-LLC. C also contributes a sufficient amount of cash to purchase membership interests in ABC-LLC so that it and A both hold 50 percent.

4. A currently holds 60 percent of an existing LLC that is an operating business. B holds the other 40 percent. B will contribute a business to the LLC and as a result, the percentage ownership will change to B holding 60 percent and A holding 40 percent.

Analysis. Only the fourth situation satisfies the requirement for two preexisting separately controlled businesses coming under common control in one LLC.

In the first scenario, because only Y is contributing businesses it controls, there are no separately controlled businesses involved. Note that even if X had contributed two businesses to X-LLC in connection with its original formation, that original formation would have been nonreportable, because two or more different persons must participate in an LLC formation for it to be reportable; in this circumstance, however, Y's contribution in exchange for a controlling interest would have resulted in a potentially reportable LLC formation.

In the second scenario, all businesses contributed to LLC-2 were controlled by A prior to their contribution, so again there are no separately controlled businesses involved. The control adjustments made to LLC-1 prior to formation of LLC-2 were a critical factor, because otherwise B would have controlled the businesses contributed from LLC-1, which, combined with the businesses newly contributed by A, would have resulted in two preexisting separately controlled businesses being contributed. However, provided the PNO is satisfied that there are legitimate financial and business reasons for such adjustments, they will be respected and not made the subject of 801.90 avoidance inquiries.

The third scenario again involves preexisting businesses that were all controlled by one party to the LLC formation (here A), resulting in no reportable LLC formation. The conversion, in the first step, of a partnership to an LLC, with no change in ownership interests, would be nonreportable regardless of the number of businesses involved.

The fourth and last scenario would be treated by the PNO as the formation of a new LLC. Since A controlled the existing LLC prior to B's contribution of a business it controls, there are two previously separately controlled businesses being combined in the LLC. Since B will control the "new" LLC, it will file to acquire the assets of the existing LLC, but not the business it is contributing.

| 84 | **Applicable provision.** Formal Interpretation 15.

Issue. Is there a reportable LLC formation where two preexisting, separately controlled businesses are being contributed, but the only one worth in excess of $50 million is being contributed by the person who will control the LLC?

Facts. A and B form a new LLC, with each contributing cash and an exclusive IP license. The LLC will pay A more than $50 million in royalties under the exclusive IP license contributed by A, but only $40 million in royalties to B for the exclusive license granted by B. A will hold a 60 percent interest in the LLC, and B a 40 percent interest.

Analysis. Because A will hold the only controlling interest, and the only asset valued in excess of $50 million was controlled by A prior to its contribution, there is not a reportable formation under the facts described. Under Formal Interpretation 15 (*see* Appendix) each party taking a controlling interest is considered an acquiring person as to the assets contributed by the other, but at least one of these acquisitions needs to be reportable under the "size" thresholds for there to be a reportable LLC formation. In this example, A is acquiring control of assets worth less than $50 million; B is not acquiring control of any assets. It is irrelevant that A will control total assets valued in excess of $50 million as a result of the transaction. On the other hand, if A and B were holding joint control of the LLC, B would have to report as an acquiring person in connection with the assets being contributed by A.

| 85 | **Applicable provisions.** Formal Interpretation 15, 801.10, 802.30.

Issue. Does a majority member of an LLC have to file notification as both an acquiring and acquired person for its transfer of an exclusive technology license to the LLC?

Facts. Companies A and B intend to form a new LLC. Company A will acquire a 60 percent interest in the LLC and Company B will acquire the remaining 40 percent interest. The fair market value of A's and B's contributions of separate businesses are each valued at less than $50 million.

Contemporaneously with the formation of the LLC, but under a separate agreement, Company A also will enter into a licensing agreement with the LLC pursuant to which the LLC will receive an intellectual property license exclusively to use Company A's technology within a specified field of use. The LLC will pay Company A more than $50 million for the exclusive technology license.

Analysis. The transfer of the exclusive license to the LLC is viewed by the PNO as the contribution of an additional business to the LLC as part of the formation of the LLC. Because the only acquiring person in the formation is A (by virtue of its 60 percent controlling interest), the only assets being acquired are those of the business being contributed by B. Since they are valued at less than $50 million, no aspect of the formation is reportable.

Note that if A were contributing the exclusive license to a preexisting LLC in exchange for cash, A would not be exempt from reporting under Section 802.30 because it does not control the LLC "by reason of holdings of voting securities." A would have to file both as an acquiring and an acquired person. If, however, A were contributing the exclusive license to a preexisting LLC in exchange for additional interests in the LLC, the PNO would treat the transaction as a re-formation of the LLC, which is analyzed in the same way as the original LLC formation. *See* Formal Int. 15, at Appendix; *see also* Int. 83.

86 | Applicable provision. Formal Interpretation 15.

Issue. Does an acquiring person in connection with an LLC formation make a reportable acquisition by acquiring 100 percent of a partnership or another LLC that it already controls?

Facts. A and B are forming a new LLC that will be held 60 percent by A and 40 percent by B. A's and B's interests in two limited partnerships, jointly held by A and B, will be contributed to the formation of the LLC. LP1 is held 60 percent by A and LP2 is held 60 percent by B. The question presented was whether A would have to make two filings in the formation, because A is the controlling member in the formation of LLC, which will hold 100 percent of the partnership interests in LP1 and LP2. The concern was whether A must file as both an acquiring and acquired person in the acquisition of the assets of LP1, and as an acquiring person in the acquisition of the assets of LP2 from B.

Analysis. The PNO's position is that, based on the language in Formal Interpretation 15 (*see* Appendix) with respect to how to determine the acquiring person in an LLC formation, A need only file for the acquisition of the assets of LP2, which it did not control pre-formation. The relevant language of Formal Interpretation 15 states that "if 'A' and 'B' form a 60-40 LLC, the 60 percent member, 'A,' will be an acquiring person *with respect to the contributions of 'B.'*" Formal Int. 15, at Appendix (emphasis added). The PNO interprets this language to mean that in the context of an LLC formation, each acquiring person need only report on the acquisition of assets of those entities that it did not control prior to the formation. This is the case even though outside the LLC formation context a person acquiring 100 percent of a partnership that it already controls clearly makes a potentially reportable acquisition. Note also that if a third party, "C," held 10 percent of the interests in LP1 and LP2 both before and after the LLC formation, there would be no reportable acquisition, and hence no reportable formation, because A's acquisition of less than 100 percent of LP2 is nonreportable.

| 87 | **Applicable provisions.** 801.2(e), 801.30, 803.5(b).

Issue. Where a dissenting shareholder of an acquired person, against its wishes, receives stock of the acquiring person involved in a merger, is that acquisition potentially reportable?

Analysis. Although under state law the dissenting shareholder is forced to accept the terms of the merger and thus to surrender his or her shares in the acquired company, that shareholder nevertheless acquires voting securities that were not previously held. Under Section 801.2(e) that transaction is reportable if the other criteria of Section 7A are met. Such shareholder does not file as a Section 801.30 transaction but relies on the merger agreement (to which the person is not a party) for purposes of the non-Section 801.30 filing. For purposes of complying with the "good faith intention" portion of the affidavit requirements of Section 803.5(b), the dissenting shareholder need only assert that he has "the good faith intention to accept the stock as required by the operation of law." *See* Int. 262.

| 88 | **Applicable provision.** 801.4.

Issue. If the waiting period applicable to a secondary acquisition is scheduled to expire after that of the primary acquisition, can the acquiring person avoid delay in consummating the latter by placing in escrow the voting securities to be acquired in the secondary transaction?

Analysis. The PNO has indicated its willingness to permit the shares to be acquired in a secondary acquisition to be transferred into an escrow at the time of the consummation of the primary acquisition prior to the expiration of the waiting period for the secondary acquisition. In order for an escrow arrangement to be used without causing a violation of the Act, the escrow agreement must insulate the acquiring person from receiving beneficial ownership and must contain an unwind provision that allows the escrow agent to sell the voting securities to a third party should the secondary acquisition be challenged.

Under the Rules, the waiting period for a secondary acquisition may expire later than the waiting period for a primary acquisition if (1) the notifications for the two transactions are filed at different times; (2) the primary acquisition is entitled to a shorter waiting period than the secondary acquisition, e.g., if the primary acquisition is a cash tender offer; (3) requests for additional information are issued in the secondary but not the primary transaction; (4) such requests are issued in both transactions, but those that affect the running of the waiting period are complied with more quickly in the primary than in the secondary transaction; or (5) early termination is granted in the primary transaction before the waiting period is terminated or expires for the secondary transaction.

89 | Applicable provisions. 801.10, 801.90.

Issue. Should lease payments or the value of leased land be included in the acquisition price where the acquiring person will purchase operating assets (a plant and equipment) but lease the land upon which the plant and equipment reside?

Facts. Buyer is considering purchases of operating assets (primarily two manufacturing plants and equipment) from seller. The fair market value of the assets is approximately $40 million. The operating assets are located on land with a separate fair market value of approximately $20 million. Seller will convey the land and buildings to a third party ("Landlord") who will lease the land and buildings to the Buyer.

Buyer and Landlord propose to enter into a long-term lease of the land and buildings (anticipated to be 15 to 20 years – less than the estimated remaining economic life of the buildings) on "market terms." Landlord will retain title to the land and buildings throughout the lease term, be free to assign the lease to a third party, and there would be no covenant not to compete by either Landlord or Seller. Buyer will have an option to purchase the land and buildings at the end of the lease term (but not before) on negotiated arm's length terms. Buyer has a good faith, economic justification for structuring the transaction in this manner.

Analysis. The size-of-transaction is $40 million (the amount to be paid for the operating assets). The lease payments and the value of the land and buildings should not be included in calculating the size-of-transaction.

The specific facts of this scenario are important to the outcome because they indicate that Buyer is not acquiring beneficial ownership of the leased property from Landlord. *Cf.* Int. 4. If Buyer were acquiring beneficial ownership of both the leased property and the operating assets, the PNO would disregard the intermediate transaction with Landlord, and treat the entire transaction as reportable.

90 | Applicable provisions. 801.10, 801.90.

Issue. Under what circumstances will a two-step transaction be treated as a single transaction for HSR reporting purposes?

Facts. A currently holds less than 50 percent in an LLC. All the rest of the member interests are held by an unrelated party, B. A holds other business assets outside the LLC, the fair market value of which is less than $50 million. B will acquire A's outside assets through the LLC, without any change in the respective holdings of the LLC member interests by A and B.

For tax reasons, B would prefer to structure the acquisition in two steps, the second occurring immediately after the first. In the first step, A would sell the assets to the LLC in exchange for additional member interests, which would give A over 50 percent of all the member interests. In the second step, A would sell to B, for cash equal to half the value of the assets just transferred into the LLC, enough of A's member interests in the LLC to return A and B to the respective membership percentages they currently hold.

Analysis. The two steps would not be considered separately and, instead, would be considered part of a single transaction. Since the respective member interests of A and B would be exactly the same immediately after the transaction as they are now, the only acquisition that would need to be considered is the acquisition by B of the assets now held separately by A. In this instance, the fair market value of the assets being acquired from A is below the size-of-transaction threshold.

91 Applicable provision. 801.10.

Issue. How should an exclusive license agreement be valued?

Facts. A grants B an exclusive license to intellectual property, in return for an agreement by B to pay royalties to A over the life of the license. B is able to estimate the gross amount of the royalty payments that it reasonably expects to pay over the life of the license. B also is able to estimate the amount that it would be willing to pay today if it were to acquire a similar license on a fully paid-up basis.

Analysis. The grant of an exclusive license is considered to be the transfer of assets for HSR purposes. *See* Int. 29. The PNO's position is that the gross amount of future royalties due under the license agreement must be used for the valuation determination. The future royalties must be determined at face value, not discounted to present value. If the amount of future royalties is too speculative to estimate reasonably, the acquisition price is undetermined, and the value of the license is the current fair market value of a fully paid-up license. *See* Int. 101. Pursuant to Section 801.10(c)(3), the fair market value should be determined in good faith by the acquiring person's board of directors or equivalent body (or its delegee) within 60 calendar days prior to filing notification under the act, or if no filing is required, within 60 calendar days prior to consummation of the acquisition.

92 | Applicable provision. 801.10.

Issue. How does one value an acquisition of exclusive rights to intellectual property?

Facts. Corporation A acquires an exclusive license for certain intellectual property that is being developed by Corporation B. The purchase price is $10 million cash, in addition to which A will make milestone payments of $25 million in each of the first three years of development, provided certain developmental targets are reached. If the licensed product is eventually marketed by A, B will receive royalty payments based on a percentage of future sales. If the product is ultimately as successful as both companies hope, these future royalties may amount to hundreds of millions of dollars.

Analysis. The PNO treats the acquisition of exclusive rights to intellectual property as an acquisition of assets, and the value of assets being acquired is the fair market value of the assets, or if determined and greater than the fair market value, the acquisition price. *See* Section 801.10. In the typical contract for an exclusive license to intellectual property still under development, the acquisition price may be impossible to determine. The most that B is guaranteed to receive under the contractual arrangement described above is the initial payment of $10 million; however, it is entirely possible that B will receive hundreds of millions of dollars over the course of the agreement. Ordinarily, for HSR valuation purposes, future payments are counted at their full value (i.e., not discounted to present value or discounted for risk). However, if future payments are contingent on conditions outside the control of the parties, it may be impossible to calculate them with reasonable certainty. In this case, therefore, the value of the acquisition is the fair market value of all of the assets being received, as determined by the acquiring person in accordance with Section 801.10(c)(3).

According to Section 801.10(c)(3), the fair market valuation must be made in good faith by the board of directors (or equivalent body) of the ultimate parent of A, the acquiring party. The board may delegate that function to another person: the PNO will accept the chief financial officer of A, or any financial officer of A with direct responsibility for the proposed transaction, as a de facto board delegee. The determination must be made within 60 calendar days prior to the HSR filing, or if there is no HSR notification, within 60 calendar days prior to closing of the agreement.

The valuation must be made in good faith. The valuation need not be in accordance with GAAP; any reasonable basis for making the valuation is acceptable. The PNO has provided little guidance on how the valuation is to be performed, other than to say that the goal is to determine what a licensee would pay at present in cash for the assets being acquired, in an arm's length negotiation. Generally, the PNO will accept any calculation made on a commercially reasonable basis, so long as there is no evidence that the determination has been made in bad faith. Thus, it is entirely possible that this transaction will not be notifiable if the odds that the licensed product will be successfully developed and marketed are slim.

93 | Applicable provision. 801.10.

Issue. In what circumstances should the pay-off of the acquired person's existing debt be included in the acquisition price of a voting securities acquisition?

Facts. Company A is acquiring all of the stock of Company B. Individual C is the UPE of Company B. The determined purchase price of Company B's stock is $25 million. Company B has approximately $30 million of debt with unrelated third-party lenders, with respect to which Individual C has a personal loan guarantee. In connection with the acquisition of B's voting securities, A will pay off the debt to the third-party lenders.

Analysis. The PNO's general position with regard to voting securities is that the dollar value of the liabilities of the acquired person is not aggregated with the purchase price in calculating the size-of-transaction. Therefore the value of voting securities being acquired is $25 million, and no filing is required. *See* Ints. 97, 98.

94 | Applicable provision. 801.10.

Issue. How is the size-of-transaction calculated where all or part of the consideration is publicly traded voting securities of the acquiring person?

Analysis. The PNO has addressed the issue as follows:

If the target is nonpublicly traded: the size of transaction is the acquisition price, if determined, or the fair market value of the target's voting securities if the acquisition price is not determined.

The acquisition price is undetermined if: (1) the stock portion of the consideration will not be a fixed-ratio exchange or (2) the closing is more than 45 days in the future. In these two instances, the size-of-transaction will be the fair market value of the target's voting securities. This fair market valuation may be relied on for sixty days. If the transaction does not close and no HSR filing occurs within the 60-day period, another determination of the size-of-transaction must be made. If an HSR filing is made during the 60-day period in reliance upon the fair market valuation, the fair market valuation continues to be valid while the HSR filing is pending.

If the stock consideration is a fixed-ratio exchange and closing will be within 45 days, the size-of-transaction will be the acquisition price, since it can be determined. The acquisition price will be the sum of the cash component of the consideration (if any) and the market price of the stock component of the consideration (determined by analogy to 801.10(c)(1)). If for some reason, the transaction does not close within 45 days, another determination of the size-of-transaction must be made.

If the target is publicly traded: the size-of-transaction is the greater of the acquisition price, if determined, or the market price of the voting stock of the target; or if neither is determined, the fair market value of the target's voting securities.

If the consideration is not based on a fixed-ratio exchange, the acquisition price cannot be determined. If the transaction will close more than 45 days in the future, neither the acquisition price nor the market price of the target can be determined. In this situation, the size-of-transaction is the fair market value of the target's voting securities (presumably the current trading price) and may be relied on for sixty days.

If closing will occur within 45 days, the size-of-transaction is the greater of the acquisition price (the sum of the cash component of the consideration (if any) and the market price of the stock component of the consideration) or the market price of the voting stock of the target. Again, if for some reason, the transaction does not close within 45 days, another determination of the size-of-transaction must be made. *See* Int. 96.

| 95 | **Applicable provisions.** 801.10, 801.40.

Issue. How does one value voting securities being acquired in connection with the formation of a new joint venture corporation ("Newco") where the acquiring person will both contribute and sell assets to the venture?

Analysis. The PNO has advised that the value of the Newco voting securities being acquired by an acquiring person at the formation of Newco could be the fair market value of all assets transferred to the corporation by that acquiring person, whether designated as a contribution in exchange for voting securities or as assets being sold to the venture, less the cash received for the purchased assets.

In cases in which an acquiring person contributes assets to Newco in exchange for voting securities of Newco, the acquiring person values the shares of Newco voting securities it will acquire at fair market value. The fair market valuation must be made in accordance with Section 801.10(c). If the acquiring person contributes assets (or stock for that matter) to Newco at the time of Newco's formation in exchange for voting securities of Newco, and sells assets or stock to Newco at the time of Newco's formation in exchange for cash, the valuation test remains the same for the shares of Newco that the acquiring person will receive. See Int. 119 for the general rules used in valuing the voting securities being acquired in a corporate joint venture formation.

96 Applicable provisions. 801.10(a), 801.10(c).

Issue. How does one value voting securities acquired in a stock-for-stock transaction?

Facts. Company A intends to acquire 100 percent of the voting securities of Company B, a privately held company, in exchange for shares of Company A's voting securities. Company A's voting securities are traded on a national exchange and the number of shares to be provided to Company B shareholders will be calculated by determining that amount of Company A's stock equal to $100 million divided by the five-day average closing price of Company A's stock for the five days prior to consummation.

Analysis. Calculating the value of voting securities acquired in a transaction in which all or part of the consideration is voting securities of another issuer turns on whether the voting securities to be acquired are publicly traded or nonpublicly traded. If the voting securities to be acquired are publicly traded, the value of such securities is the greater of the acquisition price, if determined, or the market price of the stock. If the acquisition price is not determined, the value is the market price. See Section 801.10(a)(1). Market price is generally defined as the lowest closing quotation or, in an interdealer quotation system, the lowest closing bid price within 45 calendar days prior to the consummation of the transaction but not earlier than the day prior to the execution of the relevant agreement or letter of intent. See Section 801.10(c). If the acquisition price is not determined, and the closing is more than 45 days in the future, the value of the publicly traded voting securities to be acquired is fair market value. See Int. 100; Section 801.10(c)(3). If the voting securities to be acquired are not publicly traded, the value of such securities is the acquisition price, if determined, or the fair market value of the acquired stock if the acquisition price is not determined. See Section 801.10(a)(2).

In this situation, Company B is a privately held company whose stock is not listed on a national exchange. Under Section 801.10(a)(2), the stock of Company B being acquired by Company A is valued by using the acquisition price, if determined, or the fair market value of the stock. Because Company A's consideration for the Company B stock is subject to a five-day average formula, the acquisition price cannot be determined. Therefore, the value of the Company B stock is the fair market value.

Not only is the acquisition of 100 percent of the stock of Company B by Company A potentially reportable under the HSR Act, but also the acquisition of shares of Company A voting securities by each stockholder of Company B could be reportable. The Company A voting securities to be acquired by each Company B stockholder must be valued pursuant to Section 801.10(a)(1) at the greater of market price or acquisition price. Again, because the acquisition price is not determined, the Company A voting securities to be acquired by each Company B stockholder must be valued at market price, which, because it is traded on a national exchange, is the lowest closing price within 45 days of consummation. If closing is more than 45 days away, each stockholder of B must determine the fair market value of the shares of A voting securities that it will acquire.

This situation does not address valuation in a fixed-ratio stock-for-stock transaction (i.e., where each share of Company B voting securities is to be acquired for a fixed number of Company A voting securities). In such a case, the PNO advises that the acquisition price is determined by analogy to Section 801.10(c). The acquisition price for the Company B voting securities to be acquired by Company A is the market price of the Company A voting securities that will be used as consideration for the Company B shares or, if closing is more than 45 days away, the fair market value of the B voting securities to be acquired as determined by Company A's board or its delegee. The value of the A voting securities to be acquired by each B shareholder (assuming closing will occur within 45 days) would be the market price of the A voting securities. Otherwise, each B shareholder must determine the fair market value of the Company A voting securities it will acquire. *See* Int. 94.

| 97 | **Applicable provisions.** 801.10(a), 801.10(c)(2), 7A(a)(3)(B).

Issue. In the acquisition of voting securities, must the determination of the acquisition price include payments made by the acquiring person to restructure an existing loan to the acquired entity in such a way as to obtain cancellation of guarantees of the loan given by three individual shareholders of the acquired entity?

Facts. All of the voting securities of a corporation are being acquired for $47 million in cash. In addition, the acquiring person has agreed to make a $4 million partial prepayment of an outstanding $6.8 million loan obligation of the acquired corporation in exchange for the cancellation of personal guarantees of the loan issued by the natural person shareholders of the acquired corporation.

Analysis. Section 801.10(c)(2) requires that all consideration for voting securities be included in calculating the acquisition price of such securities. In this situation, the acquisition price equals $51 million (the sum of the cash purchase price of $47 million plus $4 million, which is cash paid to cancel the loan guarantees). The face value of the loan is not included in the acquisition price, nor is some calculation made of the value of the loan guarantee that was cancelled. The consideration given for the benefit of the shareholders for the voting securities in this case consists of total cash payment made for the voting securities.

This is a fairly unusual situation. As a general matter, when an acquiring person is paying off or assuming debt of the acquired entity at the closing, such actions are not added to the acquisition price of the voting securities being acquired. This is true even if the debt being paid off was debt owed to the target's selling shareholders. This reasoning applies equally to the express assumption of debt. *See* Int. 93. The effect is the same whether the entity is acquired with the debt outstanding and the acquiring person subsequently pays off the debt or if the debt is repaid at closing. By contrast, liabilities assumed by an acquiror in an *asset* acquisition must be separately included in the value of the transaction. *See* Int. 122.

98 | Applicable provisions. 801.10(a)(2)(i), 801.90.

Issue. How does one value a purchase of voting securities of seller's subsidiary, where buyer arranges for a third-party loan to seller's subsidiary the proceeds of which are used to retire an intracompany debt owed by the subsidiary to its parent?

Facts. The facts are as follows: (1) X, a subsidiary of seller A, owes its parent $21 million; (2) B purchases all of the stock of X from A for a stated purchase price of $45 million; (3) B arranges for an $11 million loan to subsidiary X from a third-party lender and guarantees the loan; and (4) subsidiary X pays the $11 million to its parent, A, which agrees to forgive the entire $21 million obligation owing from its subsidiary.

Analysis. The value of the voting securities will be $45 million. Normally an assumption of liabilities is required to be included in the acquisition price only where assets are being acquired, since preexisting liabilities would otherwise remain the responsibility of the seller of the assets after the sale. A purchaser of a majority of an issuer's stock automatically acquires the issuer's preexisting liabilities when it acquires control of the issuer, and the extent of those liabilities is presumably reflected in the acquisition price for the stock.

The parties determined, apparently through arm's length bargaining, that the value of X's stock was $45 million. That valuation presumably reflected X's outstanding debt to its parent and/or the new debt that it assumed in obtaining the bank loan to pay off the debt to its parent. There is no indication that the stock was deliberately undervalued, or that the third-party loan and the guarantee arrangements or the repayment of the debt were not bona fide. In the absence of some evidence that repayment of X's outstanding debt to its parent included disguised consideration for purchase of X's stock (which might constitute an avoidance pursuant to Section 801.90), there is no basis for questioning the acquisition price negotiated by the parties.

The fact that the purchaser arranges for (and guarantees) a loan to the purchased company, enabling it to repay an outstanding obligation to its former parent, does not affect the consideration paid for the stock of X. That the parent was willing to accept $11 million in full payment of a $21 million obligation makes it appear even less likely that the stated $45 million purchase price undervalued X's stock.

| 99 | **Applicable provisions.** 801.10(a), 801.10(c), 801.40.

Issues. How does one determine the acquisition price in a stock-for-stock transaction, where consideration for the acquisition of the stock of a newly formed corporation consists of a minority interest in a publicly traded company? How is the new corporation's size-of-person determined, for purposes of deciding whether formation of the corporation is itself reportable where the entire assets of the new corporation being formed by two or more shareholders will be minority publicly traded securities to be transferred by the parties forming the corporation?

Analysis. Formation of a corporation is potentially reportable under Section 801.40. To determine whether the formation is reportable, the parties must determine the value of the voting securities each will acquire at the formation of the new corporation and the new corporation's "size" under the size-of-person test. *See* Int. 95; Section 801.40(d). Section 801.10(a) prescribes how to value the voting securities of the new company to be acquired by the forming stockholders. Based on Section 801.10, the value of the shares of the newly formed corporation, which obviously were not publicly traded, would be the acquisition price, if determined. The acquisition price in this case is equal to the value of the traded minority shares being given as the consideration for the new shares. In similar situations, the PNO has stated that the value of the acquired shares is equal to the market price of the traded shares under Section 801.10(c)(1). *See* Int. 96.

In order to determine the size of the new corporation under Section 801.40(d), the forming parties must value all of the assets and minority voting securities that they agree to transfer to the new company. In this case, the parties forming the new corporation agree to contribute only minority voting securities of publicly traded corporations. The PNO instructs parties to use the fair market value of publicly traded securities as the measure of a newly formed entity's size-of-person under these circumstances. *See* Int. 96.

The parties should not use the Section 801.10(c)(1) market value or some other accounting value that the new company intends to use to value the minority shares contributed to the new corporation at the time of its formation. It is the PNO's view that Section 801.10 controls the determination of value only for purposes of size-of-transaction related issues, not for size-of-person issues. Note that if a controlling interest in the publicly traded corporation had been contributed to the new corporation at the time of its formation, the new corporation would inherit the financials of that corporation in determining its size-of-person.

| 100 | **Applicable provisions.** 801.10(a), 801.13(a), 801.10(c).

Issue. How is the value of open market purchases of voting securities determined?

Analysis. In an open market purchase of voting securities, the acquisition price of the securities "to be acquired" often will be determined, since the acquiring person usually will know the cost of the securities before purchasing. If the acquisition price has been determined, the value of the voting securities shall be the market price or the acquisition price, whichever is greater. Section 801.10(a)(1)(i). The SBP explains that, for example, where a person makes a tender offer at a price higher than market, the tender offer price best reflects the value of the transaction to the parties. However, "if the market price exceeds the acquisition price, the market price must be employed as the value for purposes of the act." 43 Fed. Reg. 33,450, 33,470 (July 31, 1978).

If the acquisition price is not determined for an open market purchase (e.g., if a buy order is placed without a fixed price), Section 801.10(a)(ii) states that the value of the voting securities shall be the market price as determined under Section 801.10(c)(1).

Note that the above discussion relates only to the valuation of voting securities that are to be acquired in the contemplated acquisition, and not to the value of any voting securities of the acquired issuer that have been previously acquired and currently held by the acquiring person. The latter are valued under Section 801.13(a)(2). *See* Int. 153 (concerning valuation of previously acquired shares in connection with open market purchases).

101 | Applicable provisions. 801.10(a), 801.10(b), 801.10(c).

Issue. Is there a determined acquisition price in a transaction in which a portion of the consideration is contingent on future events?

Analysis. If the consideration for a transaction includes contingent payments, the issue is whether the acquisition price can be "determined." It is the responsibility of the acquiring person to decide whether it can make a reasonable estimate of the acquisition price. When there is a reasonable basis for estimating the contingent portion of the acquisition price, and using that basis the acquiring person is able to state the total consideration to be paid, including both the cash portion at closing and the amount of the contingency, the acquisition price is determined. In some instances, for example, when earnouts are based on sales targets that approximate historical sales growth, or when the contingent portion of the consideration is a currency exchange rate, there would seem to be a reasonable basis for such estimation. In other circumstances, such as milestone payments subject to achieving various levels of Food and Drug Administration approval for a to-be-developed product, it could be highly speculative. If a reasonable estimate cannot be made, the acquisition price is not determined. However, the value of the contingency cannot be deemed to be zero merely because the amount of the future payment cannot reasonably be estimated. But if the future payment is unlikely, its value could approach zero.

Where the amount of the contingency is too speculative to be reasonably estimated, the acquisition price is not determined, and a fair market valuation by the board of the acquiring person would be used pursuant to Section 801.10(c)(3). *See* Int. 116. (A reasonable formulation of the fair market value is generally the amount a third-party buyer, in an arm's length transaction, would pay at present in cash for the stock (or assets) being acquired without any contingent payment.)

Note that applying formulas reflecting probability of receiving future payments does not render the acquisition price determined. For example, if a contract provides for a contingent payment of $100 million, it would be potentially reasonable for the acquiring person to estimate that it either would or would not be paid. However, simply adding $50 million to the acquisition price because there is a 50 percent probability of receiving a $100 million earnout is not appropriate.

| **102** | **Applicable provisions.** 801.10(b), 801.10(c), 801.2(d).

Issue. Is the acquisition of a membership interest in a nonprofit corporation a reportable event under the HSR Act?

Facts. B, a nonprofit corporation with more than $100 million in annual net sales or total assets, becomes the sole "member" of A, a nonprofit corporation having approximately $45 million in annual net sales or total assets, in exchange for a contribution of $2 million for capital improvements and the guarantee of $49 million of A's liabilities.

Analysis. While it can be argued that the acquisition of membership interests in a nonprofit entity that does not issue voting securities is not the acquisition of assets or voting securities under the HSR Act, the PNO's position is that any adjustment or restructuring of membership interests in nonprofit or nonstock corporations that has the effect of combining the business and operations of two or more previously existing separate entities is a merger or a consolidation within the meaning of Section 801.2(d), and thus reportable if the size-of-person and size-of-transaction tests of Section 7A(a) are met and no exemption applies. Although Section 801.2(d)(1)(i) defines such transactions as acquisitions of voting securities, the PNO views combinations of not-for-profits as asset acquisitions for purposes of resolving valuation issues and completing the HSR Notification and Report Form.

Because the PNO takes the position that such a transaction is treated as an acquisition by B of the assets of A, Section 801.10(b) controls as far as valuation is concerned. *See* Ints. 74, 79. Section 801.10(b) states that the value of assets to be acquired is the fair market value of the assets, or, if determined *and* greater than the fair market value, the acquisition price.

The acquisition price must include the value of all consideration for the assets to be acquired including the value of certain assumed liabilities. *See* Int. 122. In this case, there is an argument that the acquisition price has been determined as B will contribute $2 million plus the $49 million guarantee in return for becoming A's sole member. Even though it is earmarked for expenditure on subsequent capital improvements, the $2 million cash contribution is "consideration" paid by B in return for becoming A's sole member. The $49 million guarantee, however, should not be treated as an assumption of liabilities to be included in the "consideration," because the guarantee does not assure that anything will be paid by the guarantor or relieve the primary obligor of its legal duty to pay. There is no right to compel the guarantor to pay absent a default by the primary obligor. While the guarantee has a commercial value, it is likely to be substantially less than the value of a current assumption of the liability. *See* Int. 108. Thus, the "acquisition price" would be the $2 million contribution plus the value attributed to B's $49 million guarantee. This means that for HSR purposes, the size-of-transaction will be the fair market value of the assets of A or this "acquisition price" if it is greater than the fair market value and it can be determined by B. If the acquisition price cannot be "determined," the fair market value must be used to determine the size-of-transaction. The fair market value of A's assets must be determined by B's board of directors in accordance with Section 801.10(c)(3).

103 Applicable provisions. 801.10(b), 802.2.

Issue. How does one value the acquisition of a seller's interests as lessee in nonexempt property?

Analysis. The value of the lease interests being acquired would be the premium (if any) that the purchaser will pay to the seller with respect to the assignment of such interests. No other value, including the present value of the seller's rental obligations (which will be assumed by the purchaser), is relevant to the valuation of the lease interests.

The PNO's position is that the transfer of an existing lease is the transfer of an asset but that an existing lease has no value when it is transferred, unless the buyer pays a premium in order to acquire it (i.e., an amount greater than the periodic payments on the existing lease). Any lump sum paid by the buyer to the seller in connection with assumption of an existing lease is presumed to constitute a premium and must be included in the acquisition price. *See* Int. 104 for HSR analysis of a sublease as opposed to the HSR analysis of a lease acquisition which is discussed in this interpretation.

Note that if the real property subject to the lease would be exempt from acquisition under Section 802.2, the acquisition of the lease interest also is exempt and not valued even if a premium is paid. If, however, an acquisition of an exempt lease interest includes the acquisition of a nonexempt business, then the assets or voting securities of that nonexempt business would need to be separately valued for potential reportability.

104 | Applicable provision. 801.10(b).

Issue. Are subleases entered into between a buyer and seller potentially reportable asset acquisitions and, if so, how are such subleases valued?

Analysis. The PNO's position concerning subleases and assignments begins with the proposition that entering into a lease is generally not an asset acquisition and therefore is not reportable. Similarly, entering into a sublease is generally not regarded as an asset acquisition for the same reasons, and is therefore not reportable. (As is the case with entering into a lease, entering into a sublease would only be reportable if it constituted the present transfer of beneficial ownership of the underlying asset. *See* Int. 28.) The HSR analysis for entering into a sublease is not affected by whether the sublease payments to the sublessor exceed the payments by the lessee/sublessor to the original lessor.

The rights conferred by an *existing* lease, however, are an asset and transfer of such an asset may be reportable if the jurisdictional prerequisites of the Act are met. *See* Int. 103. Thus, the potential reportability of the transfer of these kinds of property interests is governed initially by whether the parties frame the transaction as an assignment or a sublease.

To determine whether an assignment of a lease is reportable, the value of that acquisition must be determined under Section 801.10(b). If no consideration is paid to the assignor (and the assignee thereafter simply makes the regular rental payments that otherwise would have been the responsibility of the assignor), the PNO regards the acquisition price as zero. If consideration is paid to the assignor for such an assignment, the consideration is the acquisition price valued according to normal HSR procedures. The acquisition price (if any) will be the premium paid by the assignee to assume the assignor's obligations on the existing lease. Note that the PNO has advised that, if the acquisition involves an existing lease for realty, the direct acquisition of which would be exempt, then such a lease acquisition also would be exempt even if the acquisition price or premium exceeds the $50 million threshold. *See* Int. 103. This would also apply to the assignment of such a lease.

105 | Applicable provision. 801.10(b).

Issue. How does one value outstanding purchase orders that are acquired as part of an acquisition of the assets of the purchaser?

Analysis. The PNO has advised that the only circumstances where a purchase order has any value for HSR purposes is where payments have been made by the purchaser, but goods have not been delivered. The obligation to make future payments to the supplier for goods not yet supplied is not a liability that needs to be added to the acquisition price. *See* Ints. 107, 121.

106 | Applicable provisions. 801.10(b), 801.10(c).

Issue. How should a buyer value assets to be acquired when the purchase price is less than $50 million and the buyer is not assuming any liabilities with respect to the purchased assets, but the assets were valued on the seller's most recently regularly prepared balance sheet at more than $50 million?

Analysis. The book value of assets does not itself have any bearing on the size-of-transaction calculation and does not necessarily have any bearing on fair market value. Section 801.10(b) provides that the value of assets to be acquired for determining the size-of-transaction shall be the fair market value of the assets, or, if determined and greater than the fair market value, the acquisition price.

Fair market value of assets to be acquired must always be determined in good faith by the acquiring person's board of directors (or individuals exercising similar functions if the acquiring person is not incorporated) or its delegee. *See* Section 801.10(c)(3). The value of those assets on the seller's most recent balance sheet may, or may not, bear any relevance to fair market value.

In this case, if the board reasonably determines that the fair market value of the assets is less than $50 million, no HSR filing is required because the purchase price also is less than $50 million.

| 107 | **Applicable provisions.** 801.10(b), 801.10(c)(2), 801.10(c)(3).

Issue. How does one value obligations for future payments to be made by a purchaser in connection with an asset purchase?

Analysis. The value of assets to be acquired in an asset acquisition is the greater of fair market value or acquisition price (if the acquisition price is determined). *See* Section 801.10(b). The PNO requires that, in calculating the "acquisition price," future payments of a fixed amount must be included at face value (excluding interest if interest is explicitly specified as such) and may not be discounted to present value. *See* 43 Fed. Reg. 33,450, 33,471 (July 31, 1978). In making a "fair market value determination" in an asset acquisition that includes future payments, it is not inappropriate to discount those future payments to net present value since the fair market value represents what a willing buyer would pay at present for the assets.

Editor's Note. A buyer's assumption of an obligation to pay a fixed amount in the future to the seller is not included in the acquisition price if that obligation represents payments under an executory contract with the seller (e.g., lease payments or an obligation to buy a stated quantity of goods in the future from the seller) for which the goods or services have not yet been received. See Ints. 105, 121. What has to be included in the acquisition price for acquiring an asset is any obligation to pay a fixed amount in the future, where no additional offsetting consideration (other than the discharge of the obligation itself) will be received for those payments.

108 Applicable provisions. 801.10(b), 801.10(c)(2).

Issue. How does one value loan guarantees in an asset acquisition?

Analysis. Where the acquiring person in an asset acquisition enters into a loan guarantee for debt owed by the seller rather than directly assuming the obligation for the loan from the seller, the value of the guarantee should be included in the acquisition price. A determination of the value of the guarantee must be made and included in the acquisition price. That value will reflect the likelihood that the payment will in fact be made. The face value of the loan is not included in the acquisition price, only the value of the guarantee.

109 | Applicable provisions. 801.10(b), 801.10(c).

Issue. Does one include, in the size-of-transaction, revenues to be received by a buyer as a collection agent for a seller on accounts receivable associated with a business being sold?

Facts. Buyer intends to acquire a business through the acquisition of certain tangible and intangible assets. Following the closing, Buyer plans to serve as a collection agent for the Seller and to attempt to collect Seller's receivables and remit the proceeds of what is collected to the Seller. If Buyer fails to collect and remit the amount of Seller's receivables shown on Seller's closing balance sheet within a specified period of time, Buyer would pay Seller an amount in cash equal to one-third of the shortfall. If Buyer later collects those slow-paying accounts it would be entitled to retain one-third of the amount collected for itself and would remit the other two-thirds to Seller.

Analysis. The PNO has advised that a bona fide collection arrangement is not considered a transfer of the underlying outstanding accounts receivable. Under a bona fide collection arrangement, the Buyer must function solely as a collection agent for the Seller and must not assume any of the benefits or risks normally associated with the transfer of beneficial ownership of the accounts receivable.

The key question raised is whether the arrangement with respect to receivables reflects either (1) acquisition of some or all of the receivables or (2) additional consideration for the other assets purchased. If the answer to both questions is negative, the value of the receivables is not included in the size-of-transaction calculation.

There is some question in this case, however, regarding whether Buyer was in fact the agent of Seller for purposes of collecting the receivables. The Buyer appeared to be partially guaranteeing collection of the Seller's receivables, because it agreed to pay the Seller one-third of the face value of all receivables remaining uncollected after a period of time (though the Buyer was apparently entitled thereafter to retain only one-third of any amount subsequently collected, an amount that would approximate the amount Buyer had paid the Seller earlier for these previously unsolicited accounts). Thus, it does not appear that the Buyer was necessarily purchasing any receivables.

In this example, if the amount of the contingent payment to Seller (less the amount subsequently recouped by Buyer from late pay accounts) could reasonably be been valued by the Buyer, it must be included in the acquisition price of the assets being purchased. If the contingent payment could not reasonably be valued, then the acquisition price of the assets was not "determined," and the Buyer would have to make a determination of the fair market value of the acquired assets. *See* Ints. 101, 107, 111, and 118.

110 | Applicable provision. 801.10(b).

Issue. How should a transaction be valued where one partner would obtain the interests in a partnership it does not already hold and as a result would hold 100 percent of the partnership interests?

Analysis. For HSR purposes, the acquiring partner is deemed to be purchasing all of the partnership's assets, not just the proportion of the assets represented by the partnership interests being purchased. When one partner acquires the interests in a partnership it does not already hold, so that it will hold 100 percent of such interests, the acquisition is analyzed as that partner's acquisition of 100 percent of the assets of the partnership. In this example, the PNO regards the acquisition price as not being "determined" within the meaning of Section 801.10(b). The reason is that the partner who is buying out the other partner(s) will presumably pay a purchase price that does not reflect 100 percent of the value of the partnership's assets. For example, one 50 percent partner could presumably purchase the other 50 percent partner's interest for approximately half of the value of the partnership.

On the other hand, if the person who will hold 100 percent of a partnership's assets after the transaction is not presently a partner in the partnership, the amount paid is viewed by the PNO as the acquisition price for 100 percent of the partnership's assets. Of course, any liabilities assumed by the purchaser must be added to the acquisition price.

Whether or not the acquisition price is determined, Section 801.10(b) requires a determination by the acquiring person of the fair market value of the assets being purchased. Thus, whatever the acquisition price might be, if the fair market value of *all* of the partnership's assets is greater, that will be the relevant value for the size-of-transaction test.

| **111** | **Applicable provisions.** 801.10(b), 801.10(c).

Issue. How are accounts receivable valued when the acquiring person agrees to purchase uncollected receivables after a defined time period?

Facts. Certain assets of B are to be acquired by A for $45 million. A does not want to buy B's accounts receivable, which B carries on its books at a value of $10 million. Accordingly, A and B agree that B's accounts receivable will not be sold to A at closing. Rather, following the closing, A will serve as collection agent for B's accounts receivable. The collection period will last from 90 to 180 days. At the end of the collection period, any uncollected accounts receivable will be purchased by A from B at book value.

Analysis. Section 801.10(b) states that the value of assets to be acquired should be the fair market value of the assets, or, if determined and greater than the fair market value, the acquisition price. If a reasonable basis exists, A should value the contingent payment that it may have to make at the conclusion of the collection period for B's uncollected receivables. This amount should be added to the $45 million to determine the acquisition price. *See* Int. 101. If a reasonable basis for valuation of the contingent payment does not exist, the acquisition price cannot be determined.

A should also make a good faith determination of the fair market value of 100 percent of the assets to be acquired under Section 801.10(c)(3), including any accounts receivable it expects to purchase later. *See* Ints. 101, 109. A must compare this fair market value to the acquisition price, if it is determined, and use the higher number for the value of the assets.

Editor's Note. *The acquiring person's good faith estimate of the value of the expected payment to be made for the uncollected accounts receivable is determinative when calculating the value of the assets to be acquired for purposes of Section 801.10(b). Thus, in this case, if A concludes in good faith that the contingent payment will be less than $5 million and that the fair market value of the assets to be acquired is less than $50 million, no HSR filing will be required. This is true even if the contingent payment ends up being larger than $5 million and the actual consideration paid (the combination of the $45 million for the initial assets and the amount paid for the uncollected accounts* *receivable) exceeds $50 million. No HSR filing is required at that point, either for the original deal or for the acquisition of the remaining uncollected accounts receivable. The PNO permits the acquiring person to use its original estimate as long as it was made in good faith.*

112 Applicable provisions. 801.10(b), 801.10(c)(3).

Issue. If the acquisition price in an asset acquisition is acknowledged by the purchaser to exceed $50 million, must a good faith determination of the fair market value of the assets nevertheless be made?

Analysis. Yes. The fair market value must be determined by the board of the UPE of the acquiring person (or individuals exercising similar functions in an unincorporated entity) or its delegee even if the acquisition price is clearly above the $50 million reporting threshold because the valuation will determine what fee must be paid. If the acquisition price is $500 million or more, it is not necessary to determine the fair market value of the assets to be acquired for purposes of determining the applicable HSR filing fee amount. *See* Int. 272.

113 | Applicable provisions. 801.10(b), 801.10(c)(3).

Issue. How is the acquisition price of assets calculated when the purchase agreement provides for the purchaser to assume an employment contract and certain contingent liabilities?

Analysis. If the payments due to the employee under the contract are for future services, the assumption of an employment contract is not included in the acquisition price. The assumption of the employment contract does not constitute part of the consideration for the asset purchase because the purchaser gains the benefits of the employee's service as well as assuming the obligation to pay for those services. If, however, the purchaser assumes debt owed to the employee for past services, the amount of the outstanding debt must be included. *See* Int. 32 (covenants not to compete).

The contingent liabilities must, however, be included in the acquisition price. The purchaser must attempt in good faith to value the contingency and to include that value in the acquisition price. If the acquisition price can be determined, the value of the assets to be acquired is the acquisition price, or fair market value, whichever is greater. If the acquisition price cannot be determined, fair market value must be used. *See* Ints. 101, 107, and 109.

114 | Applicable provisions. 801.10(c), 801.13(a).

Issue. In a series of acquisitions of voting securities traded on a national exchange, does the value of previously acquired voting securities fluctuate with the market, or is it fixed forever at the time those securities were acquired?

Analysis. The value of previously acquired voting securities must be redetermined whenever additional shares will be acquired, using the "market price" as calculated pursuant to Section 801.10(c). *See* Section 801.13(a). The acquiring person must revalue its holdings at least daily when making a series of acquisitions and may, but need not, do so more than once a day. *See* Int. 153.

| 115 | **Applicable provision.** 801.10(c).

Issue. To determine the "acquisition price" in an acquisition, is it necessary to include the consideration paid to an acquired person for recruitment services rendered by the acquired person for the acquiring person?

Facts. Company A proposes to acquire certain assets from Company B in an asset purchase agreement. The fair market value of such assets is substantially below $50 million. B presently employs a number of employees who have specialized knowledge and skills related to the assets being bought by A. A is unwilling to consummate its acquisition of the assets unless a specified minimum number of B's employees accept offers of employment made by A. A and B will enter into a recruitment agreement that will provide for B to use its best efforts to cooperate in A's recruiting efforts and to persuade B's employees to accept such offers of employment. A will pay B additional consideration for B's services under the recruitment agreement. The value of the consideration of the assets and the consideration paid to B under the recruitment agreement is more than $50 million.

Analysis. For purposes of applying the size-of-transaction test, the consideration paid to B under the recruitment agreement need not be aggregated with the consideration paid to B under the asset purchase agreement. Only the consideration paid for the assets acquired is considered part of the "acquisition price" for purposes of the size-of-transaction test. "The acquisition price shall include the value of all consideration for such ... *assets* to be acquired." Section 801.10(c)(2) (emphasis added).

116 | Applicable provisions. 801.10(c), Formal Interpretation 15.

Issue. When can parties rely upon a third-party fair market value determination if other reasonable ways to determine fair market value exist?

Facts. Company A and Company B intend to form a new LLC to combine their respective businesses. A and B will each acquire a 50 percent interest in the LLC. Both A and B will "control" the LLC and the two separately controlled businesses being contributed to the LLC. No purchase price has been established. A must make a fair market valuation of the assets B will contribute to the LLC and B must make a fair market valuation of the assets A will contribute to the LLC. The companies retained accountants to perform the preliminary valuations of their respective businesses. The accountants determined that each company's contribution is less than $50 million. There is, however, a reasonable method of deriving a fair market value for A's contribution that is greater than $50 million.

Analysis. Under the Rules, the board of directors of each acquiring person must decide in good faith on the fair market value of the assets it is acquiring. If the directors believe that the accountants' valuation best reflects the fair market value, they may use that calculation even if others could reasonably reach a different conclusion.

117 Applicable provision. 801.10(c).

Issue. Is the outstanding principal of a nonrecourse loan secured by a mortgage on nonexempt real property that is being acquired in an asset transaction included in the determination of the acquisition price?

Analysis. A nonrecourse loan is a loan that is secured by specific assets, usually the property, and that in the event of default or foreclosure, the lender has "no recourse" to any other assets of the borrower to make himself whole. The acquiring person would not be assuming liability for the loan personally but would make payments on the loan to avoid foreclosure. The PNO's position is that the principal amount of the loan must be included in the calculation of the acquisition price for the underlying nonexempt real property.

| **118** | **Applicable provisions.** 801.10(c)(2), 801.10(b).

Issue. May customer accounts payable be "netted" against customer accounts receivable in determining the value of an acquisition of all the assets of a business?

Facts. In an acquisition of the assets of a service business, the acquiring person sought to purchase for approximately $30 million the furniture, leaseholds, and rights to use the acquired person's name. Pursuant to a supplemental agreement, the purchaser agreed to acquire for no additional consideration to the seller the seller's current accounts, including approximately $30 million worth of accounts payable and approximately $30 million worth of accounts receivable.

Analysis. It is not appropriate to set off accounts payable against accounts receivable in this situation. Even though the buyer was apparently assuming the seller's obligation to pay those creditors in return for acquiring the receivables, the PNO would include the full amount of the accounts payable in concluding that the total consideration for the purchased assets was approximately $60 million. Because the acquisition price exceeded $50 million, the proposed transaction satisfies the size-of-transaction threshold test.

"Netting" the value of liabilities assumed against the value of assets received would run directly counter to Section 801.10(c)(2), which requires that the value of all consideration paid to the seller must be included in the acquisition price. Here, the buyer is paying $30 million and assuming the obligations represented by $30 million of outstanding accounts payable to acquire the assets (including the accounts receivable). Even though no additional consideration is paid for the accounts receivable, the acquisition price is $60 million.

The acquiring person has an obligation under Section 801.10(b) to make a fair market value determination of all of the assets being acquired without regard to liabilities. This is the value used for the size-of-transaction test, unless the acquisition price is determined and greater.

| **119** | **Applicable provisions.** 801.10(c)(2), 801.10(a)(2), 801.40(d)(2), 801.40(b).

Issue. In the formation of a corporate joint venture, where three companies will each contribute cash and also extend loans to the joint venture corporation, how do the forming companies determine the value of the new venture's voting securities that they will acquire?

Facts. Three companies plan to form a joint venture. Each of the three will contribute $45 million in cash and, in addition, each will extend or guarantee a loan of $10 million to the joint venture; in return, each will receive one-third of the joint venture's voting securities. Each forming shareholder is a $100 million person.

Analysis. The value of the joint venture voting securities to be acquired by each contributing stockholder is the acquisition price, if determined, or fair market value if the acquisition price is not determined. *See* Section 801.10(a)(2).

The PNO's position is that the value of the voting securities to be acquired by each of the three companies includes not only the $45 million contribution made by each, but also the value of any additional consideration contributed to the venture by each. (Note that the value of the voting securities to be acquired by each of the forming shareholders reflects the entire $45 million that each of them has agreed to contribute, regardless of when the contribution will be made.) The principal amounts of the loans should not be considered in valuing the securities, pursuant to Section 801.10(c)(2), if the loans were arm's length transactions, made at current interest rates, with the expectation of being repaid by the venture. If the loans were offered at favorable rates, however, the true value of the loans must be assessed and added to the cash contributions to determine the value of the voting securities being acquired.

The assumption implicit in the interpretation is that loans made to the venture at "normal" arm's length rates do not affect the value of the venture's securities, whereas loans made at favorable rates or under conditions of risk not normally acceptable would increase the value of those securities. Thus, the value of such favorable loans would be relevant not only to a determination of the value of the joint venture voting securities to be acquired by the contributing stockholders, but also to the fair market valuation of such shares. Similarly, the value of the venturer's guarantee of loans made to the joint venture needs to be assessed. If the guarantee adds value to the joint venture, this added value must be included in the fair market value determination.

The provision of Section 801.40(d)(2) that requires inclusion of the face value of loans made or guaranteed by any person contributing to the formation of the joint venture relates only to determining the assets of the joint venture for purposes of Section 801.40(b) and to determining whether any exemption applies. This section does not affect the valuation of the joint venture's voting securities for purposes of the size-of-transaction test.

120 **Applicable provision.** 801.10(c)(2).

Issue. When consideration for an acquisition of assets includes a promissory note bearing interest at a market rate, is it necessary to include interest payments under the note as part of the acquisition price?

Analysis. No. Interest does not constitute part of the acquisition price. Only the principal amount of the note (not discounted to net present value) need be included. This result is consistent with the SBP's treatment of installment contracts: "The value of an installment contract is the value of the total payments of principal to be made under the contract, but excluding interest." 43 Fed. Reg. 33,450, 33,471 (July 31, 1978).

121 | Applicable provision. 801.10(c)(2).

Issue. How does one determine the acquisition price in an acquisition of assets where the assets are composed of a portfolio of executory contracts and where the acquiring person will assume the seller's future performance obligations under the contracts, receiving a future income (i.e., payment) stream from the other parties to those contracts?

Analysis. The acquisition price is the consideration paid by the acquiring person to the acquired person, the premium paid to the acquired person, in connection with the assumption of the acquired person's obligations under the contracts. If the acquiring person assumes the performance obligations without the payment of any additional consideration, the acquisition price is zero. If services have not been performed, however, or only partially performed under the contracts, but the acquired person has received the payments under the contracts, the value of the services to be performed pursuant to such contracts by the acquiring person (to the extent that payments have been received) must be valued and treated as consideration received by the acquired person.

Special procedures are used by the PNO to determine the acquisition price for two specific kinds of acquisitions of executory contracts. Where a person acquires a portfolio of life insurance policies, it often *receives* a lump sum cash payment, representing the cash reserves (often required by regulatory authorities) that ensure the seller's ability to meet its eventual obligations under the policies being transferred. In this situation, the value of life insurance policies being acquired includes the excess value (if any) that the acquiring person pays to obtain the policies, plus the value (if any) of the "customer lists" comprised of the identities of the owners and named insureds on the policies. The excess value consists of the difference (if any) between the actuarially determined present value of the obligations to pay death benefits under the policies (i.e., the present value of the obligations assumed by the purchaser) and the cash reserves transferred by the seller to the purchaser to cover those obligations. Note, however, that indemnity reinsurance agreements, where the policies and reserves do not change hands, are not viewed as asset acquisitions.

A similar analysis has been used by the PNO for valuing demand deposits in connection with acquisitions of branch banks. A purchaser who assumes the obligation to pay out bank customer deposits on demand usually receives the cash deposits held by the bank. Those amounts are offset against each other and the excess amount (if any) paid by the purchaser is relevant to determining acquisition price. That excess amount either can be paid in cash to the seller, or the seller can transfer cash deposits or cash reserves that are less than the total amount of the obligations being acquired any separate value attributed to depositor lists also is included in the acquisition price. This analysis also is used in valuing an acquisition of a pension fund where both the obligation to make pension payments and the funds that back the obligation pass to the acquiring person.

| 122 | **Applicable provisions.** 801.10(c)(2), 801.10(c)(3).

Issue. When is an assumption of liabilities relevant to the value of a transaction and how is such an assumption valued?

Analysis. Where an acquired person's liability of determined amount is expressly assumed by an acquiring person as part of the consideration paid in an asset acquisition, the amount of the liability is included in the acquisition price at face value and cannot be discounted to present value.

Where a person acquires voting securities conferring control of an entity that has outstanding liabilities, the acquiring person is not treated as having separately assumed those liabilities for purposes of determining the size-of-transaction. (Obviously, the value of the acquired securities may be affected by the existence of these outstanding liabilities.) Thus, a person who acquires for $5 million all of the voting securities of a corporation having $50 million of outstanding indebtedness has made a $5 million (rather than a $55 million) acquisition.

In determining the value of assets being acquired, liabilities being assumed by the purchaser must be included in the acquisition price, but the fair market value of the underlying assets should normally be determined without regard to a mortgage or other liability to which the acquired asset is subject.

For example, if a $5 million building, subject to a preexisting $4 million mortgage, is being acquired for $1 million, the acquisition price of the interest in that building being acquired is only $1 million. If the purchaser is also assuming the mortgage (which would normally be the case), the $4 million liability must be included in the *acquisition price*, which is therefore $5 million. Thus, the liability is included (but not double-counted) in the acquisition price. In determining the *fair market value* of the assets being acquired, the building should be valued without regard to the mortgage (assuming that the acquiring person is acquiring the entire building).

123 Applicable provisions. 801.11, 801.40(d).

Issue. How is the size of an existing joint venture determined for size-of-person test purposes?

Analysis. For purposes of the size-of-person test, the size of an existing joint venture is determined under Section 801.11. Thus, its annual net sales will be shown on its last regularly prepared annual statement of income and expense, and its total assets will be as shown on its last regularly prepared balance sheet. These principles are subject to the other requirements of Section 801.11, which require that the annual net sales and total assets of each entity included within the joint venture be consolidated within the joint venture and that the financial statements utilized for the determination are prepared in accordance with the accounting principles normally used by the joint venture. Until regularly prepared documents are created, pro forma statements must be used.

Section 801.40(d) is used to determine the size of a joint venture only in connection with the transaction by which the joint venture is formed. In determining whether certain size-based exemptions apply to the formation of a joint venture or other corporation, one must calculate the newly formed entity's size under Section 801.40(d). At all times thereafter, the size of the venture is governed – as with any other person – by the provisions of Section 801.11.

124 Applicable provisions. 801.11, 801.40(d).

Issue. When a new corporation having two or more shareholders is formed for purposes of making an acquisition, are assets contributed to the newly formed corporation solely for use in making the acquisition counted in determining the new corporation's size-of-person?

Analysis. The question must be analyzed in two parts. First, the formation of the new corporation having two or more shareholders may be separately reportable under Section 801.40. For that purpose, Section 801.40(d) is used to measure the size of the newly formed corporation and requires inclusion of all assets that the corporation will obtain at the closing of the transaction by which it is formed. That rule also requires inclusion of any additional assets that either a person contributing to the formation of the corporation has agreed to transfer or for which agreements have been secured for the corporation to obtain at any time. Any amount of credit or any obligations of the corporation that any person contributing to the formation has agreed to extend or guarantee at any time also must be included. Thus, where a new corporation has, at the time of its formation, obtained any commitments for loans or other transfers of assets meeting the criteria of Section 801.40(d), the amounts of such loans or the value of those assets to be transferred must be included in its size-of-person.

With respect to the proposed acquisition by the new corporation after its formation, Section 801.11 is used to determine the acquiring entity's size-of-person. The new corporation's size-of-person is determined by reference to the total assets of the new corporation on its last regularly prepared balance sheet (if any) and by the annual net sales on the new corporation's last regularly prepared annual income statement (if any). If, however, the new corporation is controlled by one or more entities, the size-of-person is determined by looking at the most recent regularly prepared balance sheet and annual income statement of the new entity's ultimate parent entity/entities. If the new entity does not have a regularly prepared balance sheet, and is its own ultimate parent entity, Section 801.11(e) provides that cash loaned or contributed to or otherwise obtained by a newly formed entity for purposes of financing its acquisition of another entity is not included in the calculation of the newly formed entity's size-of-person in determining whether the acquisition is reportable. Only cash or cash-equivalent assets may be excluded under this rule. Therefore, any noncash assets to be used as consideration in the subsequent acquisition must be included in the new entity's size. Note that if the new corporation acquires the stock of the target company in several different transactions, it may exclude the value of the target stock it holds in calculating its size-of-person in making additional acquisitions of the target's stock.

Note also that if the anticipated acquisition by the newly formed entity is valued in excess of $200 million, both the statutory size-of-person test and therefore also Section 801.11(e) are inapplicable.

| 125 | **Applicable provisions.** 801.11(a), 801.11(b)(2), 801.11(e).

Issue. For purposes of determining if a person satisfies the size-of-person test, may the person rely on its regularly prepared financials for the prior fiscal year?

Facts. A person's present fiscal year will end before the scheduled closing date for a proposed acquisition, but new regularly prepared financials will not be available until after the closing.

Analysis. The person not only may rely upon the prior financials, it must do so. Even if the person knows that the forthcoming regularly prepared financials will show it to satisfy the size-of-person test, it must rely on its most recent, regularly prepared financials (which need not be audited), so long as they are not more than fifteen months old. Note that Section 801.11(b)(2) marks the fifteen-month period from the date of filing notification, if a filing is required, or the date of consummation, if no filing is required.

If new regularly prepared financials are completed shortly before the scheduled consummation and reveal that the size-of-person test is now satisfied, the person must file notification, even if the consummation date would be delayed as a result. If the person does not have financials regularly prepared within the past fifteen months, new pro forma financials must be prepared. The pro forma annual income statement must be based on the person's most recently completed fiscal or calendar year. The pro forma balance sheet would reflect assets that the person will have immediately prior to the anticipated closing. *See* Section 801.11(e).

Editor's Note. Even though when making a size-of-person determination the regularly prepared financials relied upon may not be older than fifteen months, the PNO permits the use of financial information up to eighteen months old to supply revenue information for Item 5 of the HSR form (as long as that is the most recent data available). See Int. 287.

| 126 | **Applicable provisions.** 801.11(a), 801.11(b)(2), 801.11(c)(2).

Issue. Should the results of an audit conducted in connection with an acquisition, but not finalized until after the closing, be considered in determining whether the acquired person satisfies the size-of-person test?

Facts. All of the voting securities of the target are being acquired at a purchase price (more than $50 million but less than $200 million) to be adjusted after the closing, depending on the outcome of a full audit, the results of which will not be available until after the closing. The last regularly prepared financial statements of the acquired person, prior to the anticipated audit date, show annual net sales and total assets of under $10 million.

Analysis. Audited statements that are not available at the time of closing cannot be used; but regularly prepared statements (even if unaudited) that are available before closing must be used. Thus in this fact situation, the audit results should not be used for determining either the size-of-person or whether any exemptions apply, since the closing will have been completed prior to their availability. This result is consistent with the PNO's position that events subsequent to the preparation of the last "regularly prepared" financial statements (other than the addition of new entities within the person) are disregarded until new regularly prepared financial statements are created. The results of such audits also cannot be used, for example, to justify withdrawing a previous filing where the company is subsequently shown not to satisfy the size-of-person test.

In any case, depending upon the circumstances, the audit results might not constitute "regularly prepared" financial statements pursuant to Section 801.11. If they are not prepared at the normal time and in the manner normally used by the person, they would not be regularly prepared and would not be used, even after the merger, to determine the person's size-of-person.

Note also the issue of when, during the process of preparation, financials become "regularly prepared." That is, when does a party become entitled or required to use those financials to determine its size under Section 801.11? The PNO has stated that one indication that financials are regularly prepared is that they are in some way relied on or used by management. Early drafts of financials that the party generally would not rely upon are not yet "regularly prepared." If, however, a final draft exists (for example, management-approved financials that have been supplied to the auditors), the PNO says those should be considered the most recent regularly prepared financials until the final version (e.g., the audited financials) are ready, even though it is still possible that figures in the final version will change.

| 127 | **Applicable provisions.** 801.11(a), 801.11(i)(2).

Issue. How are the annual net sales of a natural person determined?

Analysis. The SBP contains the following discussion on this subject: "The 'annual net sales' of a natural person will be the annual net sales of all entities (including partnerships) he or she controls, plus any annual net sales from proprietorships." 43 Fed. Reg. 33,450, 33,474 (July 31, 1978).

The PNO advises natural persons to include in their "annual net sales" on a pro forma annual income statement any income from investment assets (as defined in Section 801.1(i)(2)). Salary from employment or gain on the sale of a personal residence or personal property, however, should *not* be included. But natural persons must include any dividends that they receive from their holdings of securities and any distributions that they receive from partnerships.

A natural person also must include all of the "sales" of any partnership or any other entity that he or she "controls." Similarly, all of the assets of any "controlled" partnership or other entity must be included in the natural person's total assets. In addition, the value of the person's interests in any partnerships, corporations, or LLCs that are not controlled by him or her must be included in the total asset calculation.

| 128 | **Applicable provisions.** 801.11(b), 801.11(d), 801.1(i)(2).

Issue. For purposes of the size-of-person test, how does an individual value his or her interests in (1) a corporation that he or she controls, (2) a partnership in which the corporation that the person controls is the only general partner, and (3) a second corporation that is controlled by the partnership?

Analysis. Section 801.11(d) requires that an individual include in his or her size-of-person all "investment assets, voting securities and other income-producing property." See Section 801.1(i)(2) for the definition of "investment assets." The PNO has stated that an individual who controls a corporation must include within his or her size-of-person all of the assets of that corporation, as shown on its last regularly prepared balance sheet, and all of the annual sales on the corporation's income statement, rather than the value of the individual's holdings in the corporation. *See* Int. 127.

There is not enough information supplied to determine whether the individual controls the partnership. If the partnership is controlled by the first corporation or by the natural person, all of the assets and sales of the partnership, as well as all of the assets and sales of the second corporation, would have to be included in the calculation of the individual's total assets and sales. "Control" of a partnership is determined by Section 801.1(b) ("having the right to 50 percent or more of the profits of the entity, or having the right in the event of dissolution to 50 percent or more of the assets of the entity"). Under current interpretations, merely being a general partner of a partnership does not, alone, constitute "control" of a partnership for HSR purposes.

Moreover, if the partnership is not controlled by the first corporation or by the natural person, the partnership interest is considered "income producing property" and is treated the same way as a minority stock interest is treated, i.e., only the value at which it is carried on the first corporation's financial statements is included.

If the partnership is its own UPE, its assets and sales are not attributable to the individual. Nor would the assets or sales of any entity controlled by the partnership (in this case, the second corporation) be attributed to the individual, unless the corporate general partner or the individual controls the partnership.

| 129 | **Applicable provision.** 801.11(b)(1).

Issue. Must an acquisition of assets or voting securities by a person be included in calculating that person's size-of-person if the acquisition took place after the preparation of the person's most recent regularly prepared financial statements and before the close of the next fiscal year?

Analysis. Ordinarily, the last regularly prepared financials determine a person's size-of-person, regardless of any subsequent events. There is, however, an exception to this rule. Section 801.11(b)(1) requires that the annual net sales and total assets of a person shown on its most recent financials must include the annual net sales and total assets of each entity included within that person and, if necessary, must be revised to do so. The PNO has interpreted this provision to require a person to recompute its annual net sales and total assets in the event that the person has acquired control of any additional entities since the last regularly prepared financials were issued. The restated financials will then be used to determine the size-of-person.

Acquisitions of voting securities, provided that they result in an acquisition of control of an entity, will always affect the size-of-person determination in subsequent transactions. The total assets and annual net sales of the newly acquired entity must be consolidated in the person's restated financials and included in the size-of-person calculation.

The PNO's position is that asset acquisitions may trigger Section 801.11(b)(1) when the person acquires all or substantially all of the assets of an entity. For example, a person, with under $100 million in annual net sales and total assets reported on its last regularly prepared financials, acquires substantially all of the assets of another unrelated entity before the close of the next fiscal year. Under these facts, the PNO position is that the person would have to include the most recent year's annual net sales and the assets of the newly acquired company with its own annual net sales and total assets in determining whether its size-of-person exceeds $100 million in subsequent transactions. The acquisition of all or substantially all of the assets of another entity is treated as an acquisition of the entity. If the acquisition is of less than all or substantially all of the unrelated entity's assets, the acquired assets (and the most recent year's annual net sales attributable to such assets) would not be included in determining size-of-person.

Editor's Note. *The PNO permits downward adjustments to a person's most recent financial statements to reflect divestitures occurring after the time they were prepared.* See *Ints. 131, 138.*

130 | Applicable provisions. 801.11(b)(1), 801.11(d), 801.11(e).

Issue. How must a person reflect on its financial statements the annual net sales and total assets of all entities that it controls?

Analysis. Section 801.11(b)(1) requires restatement of a person's existing financial statements if the annual net sales and total assets of all entities controlled by that person are not consolidated therein. Any such restatement should include only the "nonduplicative" assets and sales of the controlled entities. It is not necessarily required that such adjustments be consistent with GAAP; however, the resulting restatements must be prepared in accordance with the accounting principles normally used by the person. In fact, the SBP states that mandatory use of GAAP was specifically rejected. 43 Fed. Reg. 33,450, 33,473 (July 31, 1978).

Where a person has no financial statements, pro forma statements must be prepared. Such pro forma financials should similarly reflect only "nonduplicative" assets and sales. Section 801.11(d) allows certain assets to be excluded from either preexisting or pro forma financials of a natural person. Moreover, for any pro forma financials prepared by an acquiring person which is its own UPE and has no regularly prepared financials for purposes of the size-of-person test, Section 801.11(e) allows the exclusion of any cash that will be used by that person as consideration (and incidental expenses) in the acquisition.

131 Applicable provision. 801.11(b)(1).

Issue. In calculating the size-of-person, is it necessary to include the assets of an unconsolidated subsidiary, all of the voting securities of which will be distributed prior to the acquisition?

Facts. X intends to acquire all of the voting securities of A for more than $50 million but less than $200 million. A has an 80 percent owned subsidiary, B. A will distribute the voting securities of B to A's present shareholders before X's acquisition of A. A and B maintain separate financial statements, and A's most recent regularly prepared balance sheet and annual statement of income and expense do not include the assets or sales of B.

Analysis. The PNO indicated that the sales and assets of B should not be considered in determining A's size-of-person, because the sales and assets of B are not currently consolidated on A's financial statements and at the time of the acquisition B will no longer be a controlled entity within person A. The PNO interprets Section 801.11(b)(1) to require that the annual net sales and total assets of the person, as reflected on its last regularly prepared financial statements, be recalculated only to include the annual net sales and total assets of an unconsolidated entity "included within the person" at the time of the acquisition.

| 132 | **Applicable provision.** 801.11(b)(2).

Issue. Should the value of intangible assets, such as an exclusive license, which do not appear on an entity's last regularly prepared balance sheet be included in the calculation of the size-of-person?

Analysis. There is no requirement to restate a regularly prepared balance sheet to include the omitted assets, so long as those assets are intentionally omitted from the entity's regularly prepared balance sheets. Section 801.11(b)(2), as well as the SBP, make clear that reliance on the figures included and set forth in the last regularly prepared balance sheet is permissible so long as the balance sheet relied upon was prepared in accordance with accounting principles normally used by such person. The "accounting principles" referred to need not be "generally accepted accounting principles," a requirement specifically deleted from draft versions of Section 801.11(b)(2). 43 Fed. Reg. 33,450, 33,473 (July 31, 1978). However, if assets were mistakenly omitted from the regularly prepared balance sheet, and the mistake is found, the balance sheet must be corrected and restated to include the omitted assets.

133 | Applicable provision. 801.11(c).

Issue. The regularly prepared financials of an acquired person state separately "net sales," "intercompany sales," and "total sales." Which of these figures should be used in determining annual net sales for purposes of the size-of-person test?

Analysis. Section 801.11(c) specifies that annual net sales are to be "as stated on the last regularly prepared annual statement of income and expense," but the Rules do not identify what specific entry from those financials must be relied upon. The PNO has advised that where there are a number of line item entries on the specified financials with respect to sales, one may, *in certain circumstances,* exercise some discretion as to which figure to use. For example, advertising agencies often directly purchase advertising time or space with media outlets for their clients. At a later time, the client makes one payment to the agency that covers the cost of the advertising as well as the agency fee. The PNO has stated that in this situation, the advertising agency can break down the client payments to exclude the pass-through advertising cost and include only its fee in the calculation of annual net sales. The PNO has made clear, however, that the breakdown must appear as line item entries on the face of the financial statements.

Also, if the annual income statement expressly subtracts intercompany sales from total sales and discloses a net sales item, it is permissible to refer to the net sales item that does not include intercompany sales to determine whether the size-of-person test is satisfied. If, however, there is only an entry on the annual income statement for total sales, and intercompany sales are not expressly subtracted from this entry, the total sales entry must be used to determine if the size-of-person test is satisfied without subtracting intercompany transfers.

| 134 | **Applicable provision.** 801.11(c).

Issue. If a natural person who does not normally prepare balance sheets and annual statements of income and expense knows that he or she satisfies the size-of-person test, must that person prepare a set of financial statements prior to filing notification in order to file notification in connection with an acquisition?

Analysis. No. The PNO has stated that the individual may concede that the Act applies to him or her and need not prepare a set of financial statements to prove it. The SBP to Section 801.11(c) (43 Fed. Reg. 33,450, 33,474 (July 31, 1978)) requires that if no regularly prepared statements of income and expenses exist, "statements must be prepared if necessary to determine whether the act applies." Where a person concedes that the Act applies, the PNO does not require preparation of financial statements to verify that fact. In such circumstances, however, the natural person must state, in the filing, that the size-of-person test is satisfied.

135 | Applicable provisions. 801.11(c), 801.11(e).

Issue. May a company that has been in existence only six months use a regularly prepared six-month statement of income to determine its net sales for purpose of the size-of-person test?

Analysis. Yes. In this situation, the person's "annual" net sales for size-of-person purposes are its actual sales for the six-month period reflected on the income statement. *See* 801.11(c). The PNO has stated that year-long projections of sales need not be calculated, even though to do so would result in the company's satisfying the size-of-person test. A person normally does not satisfy the size-of-person test until it has regularly prepared a balance sheet showing total assets of $10 million or more or an annual statement of income and expense showing net sales of $10 million or more. If a newly formed entity has a regularly prepared income statement, this statement is to be relied on, no matter how many months of operations it covers, until the next year's income statement is prepared.

On the other hand, if a newly formed entity has never created a regularly prepared balance sheet, it must prepare a pro forma balance sheet in order to determine its size-of-person. *See* 801.11(e). But a newly formed entity is never required to create a pro forma income statement. (The Rules only require the creation of pro forma balance sheets, not pro forma income statements, for entities without regularly prepared financial statements.) Thus, assuming that a newly formed entity does not control another entity that has a regularly prepared annual statement of income for the last year, until that newly formed entity has prepared such an income statement, it does not have annual net sales for determining size-of-person.

136 Applicable provision. 801.11(c).

Issue. How do insurance companies determine annual net sales and total assets for purposes of the size-of-person test?

Analysis. Many insurance companies report their operations to state insurance authorities on forms developed by the National Association of Insurance Commissioners (NAIC). A life insurance company that used the format of the NAIC "Annual Statement Blank for Life and Accident and Health Insurance (Form 1)" for its last regularly prepared annual report of operations should refer to "total net premiums written" as its "annual net sales" for purposes of Section 801.11(c)(1).

Title insurance companies that report annual operations on "NAIC Annual Statement Blank for Title Insurance (Form 9)" and casualty insurers that report on "NAIC Annual Statement Blank for Fire and Casualty Insurance (Form 2)" should use "net premiums written" for their "annual net sales." A title insurer that files asset balance sheets under the format of the "NAIC Annual Statement Blank for Title Insurance (Form 9)" may use "admitted value" on its most recent Form 9 for its "total assets" under Section 801.11(c)(2), whether or not those figures are calculated in accordance with GAAP. Alternatively, it may simply use its last regularly prepared balance sheet.

| 137 | **Applicable provisions.** 801.11(c), 801.11(e).

Issue. In calculating the total assets of a newly formed acquiring person, may reliance be placed on a balance sheet, prepared in connection with the transaction, that is reasonably believed to portray the financial condition of the acquiring person accurately?

Analysis. No. Such a document may not be relied upon. Although there is no requirement under the Act that financial statements relied upon to determine the size-of-person be audited, balance sheets used for HSR size-of-person purposes must be regularly prepared. *See* Section 801.11(c). The PNO has consistently stated that a special purpose balance sheet (e.g., a balance sheet prepared for a bank in a loan transaction setting) is not "regularly prepared," and these special purpose balance sheets cannot be used as proxies for pro forma balance sheets for the size-of-person test. Therefore, in this situation, a pro forma balance sheet must be created in accordance with Section 801.11(e) to determine the size-of-person. *See* Int. 141.

138 Applicable provision. 801.11(c)(1).

Issue. Must income from discontinued operations or a completed divestiture, separately stated on an entity's last regularly prepared annual statement of income and expense, be included for purposes of the size-of-person test? If such assets are separately stated on the entity's last regularly prepared balance sheet, must they be included in the entity's total assets?

Analysis. According to the PNO, revenues from "discontinued" operations or a divested asset may be excluded only under certain circumstances. If the financial statements expressly state that the operations will be discontinued and they have, in fact, been discontinued, the income from the discontinued operations may be excluded. This is also applicable to excluding such assets from the total balance sheet assets. In such circumstances the fact that the operations will be discontinued must be included on the face of the financial statements. For divestitures, the potential divestiture and its value must be stated with specificity on the financial statements, and the asset must have been divested.

139 | Applicable provision. 801.11(c)(2).

Issue. Where an asset shown on a regularly prepared balance sheet has an offsetting liability specifically related to the asset and shown on the balance sheet, can the net value of the asset be used for determining the size-of-person?

Analysis. The PNO position is that, once assets are listed on a balance sheet, there is little flexibility in the total asset calculation. Virtually without exception, such asset/liability entries cannot be netted, and the full value of the asset therefore must be included in determining the size-of-person. The SBP explicitly states that liabilities are to be disregarded when determining a person's total assets (except for depreciation under certain circumstances).

Note, however, that if an asset is specifically identified on the balance sheet as a fiduciary asset (i.e., a trust account held on behalf of a client) then it may be excluded.

| **140** | **Applicable provisions.** 801.11(c)(2), 801.11(d), 801.40(d).

Issue. What accounting principles should be used by a person that does not have regularly prepared financials and is required to prepare a pro forma balance sheet in order to determine whether the person will satisfy the size-of-person test?

Analysis. Where a person does not already have regularly prepared financials and needs to determine whether the size-of-person test is satisfied, it must prepare a pro forma balance sheet generally reflecting, among other things, the fair market value or the acquisition cost of all assets. Note that a natural person need not prepare financial statements if he or she knows that they exceed the size-of-person threshold. *See* Int. 134.

When a natural person or any entity that does not have a regularly prepared balance sheet is required to prepare a pro forma balance sheet, the assets to be reflected frequently have not been acquired recently, and the PNO does not require a present fair market valuation. Rather, any proper accounting practice is acceptable. Generally, an individual will reflect assets at acquisition value, even though that value may be substantially below current market value. A natural person may exclude certain noninvestment assets pursuant to Section 801.11(d).

Note that in connection with determining the "size" of a newly formed corporate joint venture under Section 801.40, the longstanding PNO position is that fair market value must be used for contributions to the newly formed entity in connection with analyzing the reportability of the formation of the venture.

141 Applicable provisions. 801.11(c)(2), 801.11(e).

Issue. Is a person's pro forma balance sheet, prepared at the time of its formation in order to determine its size, a "last regularly prepared balance sheet" which may be relied upon in connection with subsequent transactions?

Analysis. No. The PNO's position is that a person cannot rely on a previously prepared pro forma balance sheet for later acquisitions. Until a person regularly prepares a balance sheet in the ordinary course of its business, it does not have a "last regularly prepared balance sheet." Such a person must prepare a new pro forma balance sheet for purposes of the size-of-person test prior to any postformation acquisitions, and it must reflect the person's total assets as of the closing of the contemplated transaction. When a person contemplating an acquisition, however, prepares a balance sheet in order to determine its size-of-person at that time, it need not include (1) anticipated additional infusions of cash planned after closing of the transaction in question or (2) the proceeds of loans where cash will be used as consideration for the contemplated acquisition. *See* Section 801.11(e); Int. 137.

142 | Applicable provisions. 801.11(c)(2), 801.11(e).

Issue. Are assets, including cash, reflected on a regularly prepared balance sheet that are used as consideration for a proposed acquisition included for purposes of determining the acquiring person's size-of-person?

Analysis. Yes. Assets, including cash, shown on an entity's most recent, regularly prepared balance sheet are counted toward that entity's size-of-person, regardless of whether any of such assets are to be used in making a proposed acquisition. Conversely, assets obtained since, and not shown on, the most recent balance sheet are not counted unless the person purchases all or substantially all of the assets of an entity. *See* Int. 129.

Editor's Note. When an entity has a regularly prepared balance sheet, Section 801.11(c)(2) applies. If no regularly prepared balance sheet exists, see Section 801.11(e). Where there is no regularly prepared balance sheet and the entity is not controlled by an entity with a regularly prepared balance sheet, cash to be used as consideration for a proposed acquisition would not count toward the entity's size-of-person. See Int. 147.

143 | Applicable provision. 801.11(c)(2).

Issue. Is a balance sheet that is regularly prepared each year for purposes of determining a company's contributions to an employee profit-sharing plan, a "last regularly prepared" balance sheet within the meaning of Section 801.11(c)(2)?

Analysis. Yes. If a balance sheet is annually prepared in accordance with the accounting procedures normally used by that company, it can qualify as the company's "last regularly prepared" balance sheet. The statements prepared in connection with the company's profit-sharing plan contributions are the "last regularly prepared" balance sheets only until the next regular annual statements or other regularly prepared balance sheets (if any) are prepared.

144 Applicable provision. 801.11(c)(2).

Issue. In a balance sheet with a two-column format showing a company's assets according to both (1) GAAP and (2) "market" value, which should be used for the size-of-person test?

Analysis. The PNO does not require a company to use GAAP. As long as the two-column balance sheet is the format regularly utilized by the company, the PNO's present position is that the company should use the higher of the two columns of the balance sheet in determining its size-of-person under the Act.

145 | Applicable provision. 801.11(e).

Issue and Facts. Three parties (none of them $100 million persons) form an unincorporated joint venture in which they are equal partners. At the time of formation, two of the three contribute cash to the venture and the third contributes assets valued in excess of $50 million. Simultaneously with its formation, the venture uses the contributed cash to purchase more than $50 million but less than $200 million of additional assets from an unrelated seller whose size exceeds $100 million. Does the newly formed acquiring person satisfy the size-of-person test?

Analysis. The asset acquisition is reportable. A newly formed entity contemplating an acquisition must create a pro forma balance sheet for purposes of determining its size-of-person under Section 801.11. Since the newly formed venture is not controlled by another entity, it is the acquiring person, and its size is determined by preparation of a pro forma balance sheet. The seller of the assets being purchased by the venture satisfies the $100 million size-of-person test; thus, the purchase of more than $50 million but less than $200 million worth of assets is reportable if the venture satisfies the $10 million size-of-person test.

The cash contributed by the two venturers can be excluded from the venture's pro forma balance sheet under Section 801.11(e) (assuming that all of the cash is to be used as consideration in the acquisition of additional assets), but the assets contributed by the third venturer must be included. The venture, therefore, satisfies the $10 million size-of-person test, and the transaction is reportable. *See* Int. 146.

146 | Applicable provision. 801.11(e).

Issue. Does a newly formed partnership satisfy the size-of-person test when it uses cash contributed to it at the time of its formation by the partners to buy assets from one of the partners or to buy assets from a third party?

Facts. Three parties form an unincorporated joint venture in which they are equal partners. Each contributes only cash to the venture. The joint venture subsequently uses the cash to acquire two collections of assets (each worth more than $50 million but less than $200 million) from one of the venturers and from a $100 million seller. At the time of these acquisitions, the joint venture does not have regularly prepared financial statements. Does the newly formed acquiring person satisfy the size-of-person test?

Analysis. Application of Section 801.11(e) differs where cash is being used by a newly formed entity to purchase assets (or stock) from two different sellers. In this case, the *cash* contributed to the venture for purposes of making the second acquisition would be included on the venture's pro forma balance sheet for purposes of determining its size prior to making the first acquisition and the $10 million size-of-person test would be satisfied. If the venturer selling assets to the venture were a $100 million person, the size-of-person test will be met.

The same analysis must be performed for the second acquisition (i.e., contributed cash to be used in making the second acquisition is excluded from the pro forma balance sheet that determines the venture's size for purposes of the second acquisition). Since the venture would be a $10 million person, both parties will meet the size-of-person test in the venture's acquisition of assets from the $100 million seller. *See* Int. 145.

147 | Applicable provisions. 801.11(e), 801.40(d), 801.11(c)(2).

Issue. When a person is required to prepare a pro forma balance sheet to determine whether the size-of-person test is satisfied, how does the Section 801.11(e) pass-through rule affect that balance sheet?

Analysis. The pass-through provision of Section 801.11(e)(1)(ii) applies only to acquiring persons, not to acquired persons. (The pro forma balance sheet of an acquired person must include all assets held by the person at the time of the acquisition or determined in accordance with Section 801.40(d), if that subsection applies. *See* Section 801.11(e)(2).) Section 801.11(e)(1) is available only if the acquiring person does not have a regularly prepared balance sheet as identified in Section 801.11(c)(2), which is subject to the nonduplicative consolidation requirements of Section 801.11(b). Note that the existence of a regularly prepared balance sheet for any entity within the acquiring person precludes the applicability of Section 801.11(e). (In such case, a pro forma balance sheet must be prepared for the entire entity including the balance sheet assets of the entity with the balance sheet. The 801.11(e) rule may not be used in this instance.)

Section 801.11(e) provides that the pro forma balance sheet of an acquiring person that does not have a regularly prepared balance sheet will include all assets of that person and any entities that it controls at the time of the acquisition, except that specified assets are to be excluded: (1) all cash and cash equivalents that will be used as consideration in an acquisition of assets from or voting securities issued by one or more entities within a single acquired person; (2) all cash to be used to pay legal, accounting, and other fees and expenses in connection with the acquisition; and (3) all securities (voting and nonvoting) issued by (but not assets of) one or more entities within the acquired person. *See* Section 801.11(e)(1).

Where a person contemplates multiple (e.g., open market) acquisitions of the stock of a single issuer, Section 801.11(e) provides that the person may exclude from its pro forma balance sheet not only funds to be used for such acquisitions but also the stock of that person already purchased. Thus, new pro forma balance sheets prepared during the course of such multiple purchases continue to exclude the stock already acquired as well as cash for additional purchases of shares of the same person. The justification for this rule is that if a single large purchase of the person's stock would not be reportable, there is no reason to treat a series of smaller transactions differently.

Conversely, all noncash assets (all tangible and intangible assets including minority interests of persons other than the one whose stock is being purchased) must be included in the purchasing entity's pro forma balance sheet. Cash to be used to acquire voting securities or assets of any other person would also be included in the purchaser's pro forma balance sheet.

Of course, if the purchaser creates a regularly prepared balance sheet in the course of its open market purchases, its size-of-person is thereafter governed by Section 801.11(c)(2). Therefore, although there is no requirement under the Rules that a regularly prepared balance sheet be prepared before closing, if such a balance sheet is prepared, a filing will be required if that balance sheet reflects assets, even including cash to be used for the purpose of the acquisition, which meet the size-of-person test.

148 | Applicable provisions. 801.11(e), 801.40.

Issue. Is a newly formed entity that is its own UPE and does not have a regularly prepared balance sheet required to include in the assets shown on its pro forma balance sheet the value of contractual rights to receive loans or guarantees to determine whether an acquisition by the new entity must be reported?

Analysis. Other than in connection with the formation of a new corporation by two or more persons subject to Section 801.40, at which time the assets of the new corporation must include the full amount of any loan to be made or guaranteed by a contributor to the new entity's formation, loans and guarantees are typically included only to the extent that they have already been drawn upon by the new entity. *See* Ints. 124, 184. Section 801.11(e), however, requires inclusion of the proceeds drawn upon only if not used to buy voting securities or assets of the acquired person or to pay incidental expenses relating to that acquisition.

In addition, the contractual right to receive a loan or guarantee may be considered an asset if the loan is to be made at a below-market rate, in which case the market value of the contractual right for the loan or guarantee must be included in determining the size of the new corporation.

| 149 | **Applicable provision.** 801.11(e).

Issue. When an acquisition (with a value of more than $50 million but less than $200 million) is to be made by a newly formed partnership that has less than $10 million of assets other than cash to be used in making the acquisition, is the size-of-person test satisfied?

Analysis. The acquiring person's last regularly prepared balance sheet determines that person's size, but if no such balance sheet exists, the person must prepare one. Thus, if the partnership is the UPE of the acquiring person, the assets of the partnership and all entities controlled by it will determine whether the size-of-person test is satisfied. Section 801.11(e) provides that cash to be contributed to a newly formed entity (not having a regularly prepared balance sheet and not controlled by another person) and used in making an acquisition need not be counted toward the size-of-person test.

Of course, where the newly formed entity is a corporation or LLC, the question of whether its formation is separately reportable must be analyzed under Section 801.40 and Formal Interpretation 15 respectively (*see* Appendix). Section 801.11(e) is applicable to acquisitions by newly formed entities of all types, not just to newly formed partnerships. *See* Int. 124. The PNO also has concluded that neither a formation balance sheet nor a preacquisition pro forma combined balance sheet is considered a regularly prepared balance sheet. *See* Int. 141.

If the proposed transaction is valued at greater than $200 million, the size-of-person test is eliminated and the transaction would be reportable unless an exemption applied. *See* Section 7A(a).

150 | Applicable provisions. 801.13, 801.90, 7A(a)(2).

Issue. When are multiple acquisitions by the same person aggregated for purposes of determining their reportability?

Analysis. If a person makes two (or more) acquisitions of stock of the same issuer, all voting securities of the issuer that will be held by the acquiring person after the consummation of the second (or each) acquisition are deemed voting securities held as a result of the second (or that) acquisition.

An acquiring person must aggregate two separate acquisitions of assets from the same person, or from entities controlled by the same person, for purposes of the size-of-transaction test if the agreement or letter of intent for the second acquisition is signed within 180 days following the first acquisition and no HSR notification was made for the first acquisition. If aggregation results in a filing obligation, the acquired person must file for both the previously sold and the to-be-sold assets and should note this in the filing. Section 801.13(b)(2). Note that the PNO takes the position that aggregation is appropriate in certain circumstances that do not strictly comport with the above-described facts, if the circumstances suggest that the parties may be employing a device for avoidance. *See* Int. 192; Section 801.90.

The dollar value of asset acquisitions from two or more "related" persons (e.g., from two separate partnerships having some or all of the same partners but not under common control for HSR purposes) are not aggregated. Similarly, for purposes of the size-of-person test in Section 7A(a)(2), the annual net sales and total assets of multiple sellers (or multiple buyers) are aggregated only to the extent that any of such sellers (or buyers) are commonly controlled.

| 151 | **Applicable provisions.** 801.13, 801.14, 801.15, 802.10.

Issue. Do stock or assets of a person that were acquired in an exempt transaction constitute stock or assets "held as a result of the acquisition," for purposes of determining the reportability of a later acquisition of stock or assets of the same acquired person?

Analysis. Section 801.15 provides that stock or assets will not be "held as a result an acquisition" if the acquisition of the assets or shares was exempt (or would have been exempt had the Act and the Rules been in effect) under certain specified exemptions. Later purchases of nonexempt assets or stock of the issuer need not be aggregated with the exempt stock or assets for purposes of the size-of-transaction test if the first purchase is exempt pursuant to one of the exemptions listed in Section 801.15(a). The value of the assets and shares acquired in such exempt acquisitions will not be counted in determining the value of the assets and shares held in the second acquisition. Not every exemption is covered by this rule. For example, if the first purchase was exempt pursuant to Section 802.10 (the stock dividends and split exemption) such stock would be held as a result of the second acquisition, since Section 801.15(a) accords no special treatment for such purchases.

Section 801.15(b) provides that assets or stock exempt when acquired under other exemptions will not be "held" as a result of a subsequent acquisition unless "the limitations contained in Section 7(A)(c)(9) or those sections do not apply or as a result of the acquisition would be exceeded . . . ." *See* Section 801.15, Examples 4-8; *see also* Int. 206.

| **152** | **Applicable provisions.** 801.13(a), 801.32, 810.10, 802.31, 801.15(a).

Issue. If a person holds both common stock and convertible preferred stock (with no present rights to vote for directors) of the same issuer, how is the common stock valued when the convertible preferred stock is subsequently converted into common stock of the same issuer?

Analysis. Any common stock held at the time of the conversion of the preferred stock is deemed under Section 801.13(a)(1) to be voting securities held as a result of the acquisition. (In this case, pursuant to Section 801.32 the conversion is the potentially reportable acquisition.) Under Section 801.13(a)(2), common stock held prior to the conversion is valued at market price, if publicly traded. See Sections 801.10(c)(1) and 801.10(c)(3).

This interpretation appears to be a relatively straightforward application of Section 801.13(a); however, the facts in this instance were rather unusual. Company A sold its subsidiary S to Company B in exchange for 2,500,000 shares of common stock and 150,000 shares of convertible preferred stock of Company C convertible one to one for common shares. The sale of S was not reportable because B did not meet the size-of-person test.

The contract assigned a dollar value to the S stock and the C stock; however, because of a separate agreement between A and C protecting the price at which A could resell the C stock, the C common stock was valued at $20 per share, approximately 40 percent above the market price of $14 per share. The convertible preferred stock of C was not publicly traded. Consequently, the value of the voting securities of C acquired by A was exactly $50 million, making the acquisition nonreportable. The value attributed to the convertible preferred stock was not included in determining the value of the voting securities to be held as a result of the original acquisition of common stock because the acquisition of convertible voting securities is exempt pursuant to Section 802.31, and Section 801.15(a) does not require that the value of that exempt purchase be aggregated.

Had B converted the convertible preferred stock prior to selling to A, A's acquisition of C's stock would have been reportable (the acquisition price would have exceeded $50 million). See Section 801.10(a). But B did not convert because of the parties' need to close quickly.

A always intended to convert the preferred stock as soon as possible and intended to file an appropriate HSR notification prior to the conversion. But when A considered converting two weeks later, the application of Section 801.13(a) indicated that the value of the voting securities to be held as a result of the acquisition was less than $50 million. The PNO confirmed that the market price approach of Section 801.13(a) was correct despite the fact that application of the higher acquisition price would have triggered a filing.

Interpretations Relating to Part 801 189

153 | Applicable provisions. 801.13(a), 801.10.

Issue. How are open market purchases of voting securities of the same issuer over a period of time valued for purposes of subsequent purchases?

Analysis. As a person makes open market purchases, each purchase requires a new determination of whether a notification threshold will be crossed. For each purchase, the acquiring person must revalue the voting securities of the acquired issuer that it already holds, and add the value of the additional shares that it intends to purchase. If the resulting value exceeds $50 million, the particular purchase that would exceed the threshold is subject to notification and waiting period requirements. A similar computation is used with respect to higher thresholds.

An acquiring person would value the voting securities it already holds in the acquired issuer pursuant to Section 801.10(c)(1), if the securities are publicly traded, or pursuant to Section 801.10(c)(3), if the securities are not publicly traded. An acquiring person would add to this amount the value of voting securities it intends to acquire of the same acquired person pursuant to the valuation instructions in Section 801.10. *See* Section 801.13(a); Int. 100.

With respect to publicly traded shares, the effect of these interpretations in a market in which the price of the particular stock is rising could be to permit, without notification, accumulation of shares with a current market value of greater than $50 million. The reason is that the market price – the lowest closing quotation in the previous forty-five-day period – will generally be lower than the acquisition price for shares currently being purchased. Since each purchase results in revaluation of previously acquired shares, additional shares could be purchased without exceeding the next notification threshold.

If, on the other hand, the market price of the shares were generally declining over the forty-five-day period prior to contemplated open market purchases, market price and acquisition price would likely be similar, or perhaps identical. The acquisition price might even fall below the lowest closing bid price during the previous forty-five days, in which case "market price" would exceed it. In these situations the revaluation of previously acquired shares might not permit accumulations of shares with current value in excess of $50 million.

The PNO position is that an acquiring person must revalue its holdings at least daily under the forty-five-day rule and may, but need not, do so more than once a day if making multiple open market purchases on the same day. Thus, the reportability of all purchases is determined with reference to the value of the purchaser's holdings through the previous day (or holdings even through the current day if the acquiring person elects to revalue more than once during the day), regardless of whether the person plans one or several additional open market purchases. This permits an acquiring person to determine the exact number of additional shares that may be purchased without reporting.

154 | Applicable provisions. 801.13(b)(2)(ii), 801.90.

Issue. Is the purchase of substantially all of the assets of an entity, transferred to the purchaser at two separate closings ten months apart, aggregated for purposes of the size-of-transaction test under Section 801.13(b)(2)(ii)?

Analysis. Section 801.13(b)(2)(ii) requires aggregation of an asset acquisition with a separate, earlier acquisition of assets from the same person if the previous acquisition was made within 180 days preceding the signing of the later agreement and no filing was made for the previous acquisition. Where a single agreement covers two acquisitions more than six months apart, or where a second agreement is signed prior to consummation of the first acquisition, a literal reading of the rule would not require aggregation. In either scenario, the acquiring person would not have "acquired" assets from the acquired person within 180 days prior to signing the agreement for the second acquisition.

The PNO's position, however, is that as long as there is one agreement (even if there are separate contracts and separate closings), the parties must file for the whole transaction even if the closings occur more than six months apart. Thus, the parties cannot structure separate closings to avoid aggregation under Section 801.13(b)(2). *See* Section 801.90. The PNO takes the position that the HSR filing in such a case must be made for the whole transaction, and the waiting period must expire, prior to closing any part of the transaction. *See* Int. 254.

On the other hand, if a second agreement for the acquisition of assets is entered into prior to the closing of a previous asset acquisition, as long as the two agreements are separate (not raising Section 801.90 issues, *see* Int. 192), no aggregation would be required for the second asset acquisition. The PNO regards the intent of Section 801.13 to be clear, although separate agreements between the same parties (such as described above) may warrant close scrutiny under Section 801.90.

155 | Applicable provision. 801.13(b)(2)(ii).

Issue. Is aggregation of two asset acquisitions within a 180-day period required under Section 801.13(b)(2)(ii) when an acquiring person first acquires assets from an unincorporated joint venture with two ultimate parent entities, and later acquires assets directly from one of those ultimate parent entities?

Analysis. Yes. Aggregation is required under Section 801.13(b)(2)(ii) whenever the acquired person is the same in multiple asset transactions if one closes less than 180 days before the agreement for the second acquisition is executed. The existence of an additional acquired person in the first transaction does not eliminate the aggregation requirement of Section 801.13. The aggregation hinges on there being a common UPE.

There is no aggregation when an acquiring person is making two separate acquisitions, one a $1.1 million asset acquisition from a corporation controlled by a single individual, and the second, a $49 million asset acquisition from a partnership in which another corporation controlled by the same individual was a general partner. Aggregation is not required in this case unless the individual controls the partnership.

156 | Applicable provisions. 801.13(b)(2)(ii), 801.13(a), 801.14.

Issue. If, within 180 days after an asset purchase, the same acquiring person purchases all of the voting securities of the selling entity, is aggregation of the two transactions required?

Analysis. The PNO's position is that aggregation is not required, even if the combined value of the two transactions exceeds $50 million and the value of each alone is less than $50 million. The second example following Section 801.14 is similar to this situation.

Aggregation is not required because assets acquired from a person are not "assets of the acquired person which the acquiring person would hold as a result of the acquisition," within the meaning of Section 801.14(b), unless the asset aggregation rule of Section 801.13(b)(2)(ii) applies. That provision is triggered only where two acquisitions of assets from the same person occur within a stated period of time. Here, one acquisition was of assets, but the second was of voting securities, and Section 801.13(b)(2)(ii) is therefore inapplicable.

Editor's Note. Aggregation of two separate acquisitions from the same acquired party may be required, depending on timing and a number of other factors, if: (1) both transactions involve acquisitions of assets (see Section 801.13(b)(2)(ii); Int. 150), (2) both transactions involve acquisitions of voting securities (see Section 801.13(a); Int. 150), and (3) the first involves an acquisition of voting securities and the second involves an acquisition of assets. See Section 801.14, Example 1; Int. 157. Only where the first transaction involves an acquisition of assets and the second involves an acquisition of voting securities is aggregation not required. See Section 801.14, Example 2.

| 157 | **Applicable provisions.** 801.14, 802.21, 801.13(a)(3).

Issue. Where an acquiring person acquires less than 50 percent of the voting securities of a person and, either simultaneously or thereafter, purchases assets of the same person, are the values of the two transactions aggregated for purposes of the size-of-transaction test?

Analysis. Yes. Example 1 following Section 801.14 describes such a situation and concludes that, to determine the size of the transaction, the value of the assets to be acquired must be added to the value of the acquired person's held voting securities. The only exception of course, is where an HSR filing had been made for the previous acquisition of the voting securities and the waiting period had expired, or the acquisition was exempt pursuant to Section 802.21. In that case no aggregation is required because the voting securities are not "held" as set forth in Section 801.13(a)(3).

When an acquiring person has previously purchased, and still holds, less than 50 percent of the voting securities of one subsidiary and thereafter wishes to purchase any assets from a different subsidiary of the same parent, aggregation is required. An acquisition of 50 percent or more of the voting securities of an entity, however, results in a transfer of control of that issuer to the acquiring person. Thereafter, the acquiring person does not hold any voting securities of the acquired person. Instead, it holds voting securities of an entity included within (i.e., controlled by) itself. Thus, any subsequent acquisitions of assets by the acquiring person from the same acquired person are analyzed separately from the prior transaction. The PNO has stated, however, that if the controlling stock interest and assets are being acquired in a single transaction the value of the two would be aggregated under Section 801.14 for purposes of the size-of-transaction test. *See* Int. 158.

There is a different result, however, if assets are acquired prior to the acquisition of voting securities from the same person. If an asset acquisition precedes a voting securities transaction, no aggregation is required. *See* Ints. 151, 156.

| 158 | **Applicable provisions.** 801.14, 801.13(a), 7A(a)(2), 801.2(b).

Issue. Is an acquisition of control of separate subsidiaries of the same parent in the same transaction aggregated for purposes of the size-of-transaction test?

Analysis. Yes. The "acquired person" is the UPE of the acquired subsidiaries plus all entities included within it; hence, the aggregate value of voting securities of the acquired person to be held as a result of the acquisition for purposes of the $50 million size-of-transaction test, is determined by aggregating the value of the stock of each of the subsidiaries being acquired.

There has been confusion over the interaction between Sections 801.13(a) and 801.14(a) as they relate to the size-of-transaction test. The starting point in the analysis is Section 7A(a)(2), which states that the Act will apply if "as a result of such acquisition the acquiring person would hold an aggregate amount of the voting securities and assets of the acquired person . . . (B)(i) in excess of $50,000,000 . . . ."

In determining the value of voting securities and assets held "as a result of such acquisition," Section 801.14 specifies that it is the sum of the value of all voting securities and all assets of the "acquired person" that the "acquiring person would hold as a result of the acquisition," determined in accordance with Section 801.13. With regard to voting securities, "all voting securities of the *issuer* which will be held by the acquiring person after the consummation of an acquisition shall be deemed voting securities *held as a result of the acquisition.*" Section 801.13(a) (emphasis added).

In view of the reference to voting securities of the *issuer* in Section 801.13(a), some have interpreted the rule as not requiring aggregation of shares of different issuers even if under common control. But the PNO has focused on the reference to voting securities and assets of the acquired *person* in Sections 801.2(b) and 801.14 to conclude that the simultaneous acquisition of the stock of separate issuers within the same person must be aggregated for purposes of the size-of-transaction test.

By contrast, when controlling interests in two subsidiaries are purchased in clearly separate transactions, absent a purpose to avoid reporting, the PNO takes the position that after the acquiring person controls the first subsidiary, it no longer holds voting securities of the acquired person. Thus, unless a single transaction includes two separate purchases, notification is not required for the second purchase unless it meets the size-of-transaction test on a stand-alone basis.

| 159 | **Applicable provisions.** 801.20(c), 801.1(h), 7A(a), 7A(c), 802.21.

Issue. Where an issuer makes a tender offer for its own shares, a shareholder who does not tender will, to the extent the issuer's tender offer is successful, increase its percentage holdings of the issuer's shares. Are there any circumstances under which the shareholder may have a reporting obligation in this situation?

Analysis. No, unless the shareholder was instrumental in causing the tender offer to occur. *See* Int. 190. Absent the shareholder causing the tender offer to occur, a filing is only required if an "acquisition" takes place. An example of this situation is set forth in the SBP for Section 801.20(c):

> [I]f a person acquired less than 15 percent of the shares of an issuer, and thereafter the issuer purchased enough of its own stock so that the originally purchased shares constituted more than 15 percent of the shares then outstanding, no notification would be required, because the increase in percentage holdings did not result from an acquisition by the person whose holdings met or exceeded a notification threshold.

43 Fed. Reg. 33,450, 33,482 (July 31, 1978).

The 15 percent threshold referenced in the SBP has been changed. *See* Section 801.1(h). However, the principle is still accurate. No HSR filing is required unless there is either an acquisition by an *acquiring* person or somehow the shareholder who crosses a threshold without an acquisition was instrumental in causing the issuer to take the action that caused the shareholder to cross a threshold. Any subsequent "acquisitions" by the shareholder may be reportable. Section 801.20(c) states that *acquisitions* meeting the criteria of Section 7A(a) (and not otherwise exempted by Section 7A(c) or Section 802.21) are reportable even though "[t]he acquiring person's holdings initially may have met or exceeded a notification threshold by reason of . . . events other than acquisitions."

160 Applicable provisions. 801.21, 801.13(b), 7A(a)(2).

Issue. In an acquisition of all of the assets of an entity, is cash held by that entity included, for purposes of the size-of-transaction test, in the value of the assets to be acquired?

Analysis. No. Section 801.21 states that, for purposes of Sections 801.13(b), 801.1(h)(1), and 7A(a)(2), cash shall not be considered an asset of the person from which it is acquired. Section 801.21, however, does not apply when valuing voting securities. In those cases, the cash held by the person whose voting securities are being acquired may not be excluded in valuing the voting securities.

| **161** | Applicable provisions.   801.21, 7A(a)(2), 801.1(h)(1), 801.13(b).

Issue. Is the acquisition of cash equivalents in an asset transaction a potentially reportable transaction?

Analysis. No. Section 801.21(a) provides that for purposes of determining the aggregate total amount of assets under Sections 7A(a)(2), 801.1(h)(1), and Section 801.13(b), cash shall not be considered an asset of the person from which it is acquired. The PNO has taken the position that it will treat "cash equivalents" (as that term is defined below) like cash for purposes of this rule. Cash equivalents are not defined in the Rules or the SBP, but the PNO considers such things as demand deposits, certificates of deposit, notes, treasury bills, and travelers checks to be cash equivalents.

In one case, Corporation A, a publicly held investment company registered under the Investment Company Act of 1940, intended to purchase all of the assets of Corporation B, another registered investment company. The value of Corporation B's assets exceeded $50 million, but consisted mainly of cash and cash equivalents; the value of Corporation B's other assets was well below $50 million. Notification was not required because, under Section 801.21, the cash and cash equivalents were not considered to be assets of B for purposes of calculating the size-of-transaction test, and the remaining assets standing alone did not meet the test.

| 162 | **Applicable provisions.**   801.21, 802.1, 7A(c)(1), 7A(c)(2), Formal Interpretation 9.

Issue. Is the acquisition of accounts receivable a potentially reportable transaction?

Analysis. The FTC issued a formal interpretation on March 20, 1980, stating that accounts receivable are not treated as "exempt assets when acquired" and are not covered by Section 801.21. *See* Formal Int. 9, at Appendix. The PNO has also taken the position that accounts receivable are not "other obligations" under Section 7A(c)(2).

The stated rationale for treating accounts receivable differently from cash is that an acquisition of accounts receivable can, under very special circumstances, have competitive consequences. Formal Interpretation 9 cites *United States v. Household Finance Corp.,* 602 F.2d 1255 (7th Cir. 1979), as the reason for the change of FTC policy. In that case, the DOJ successfully challenged a merger of two consumer finance companies, the assets of which were predominantly accounts receivable.

Normally, however, accounts receivable are not productive assets, the transfer of which may have competitive consequences. Thus, the PNO position is that acquisitions of accounts receivable may be exempt under Section 7A(c)(1) and Section 802.1 (the "ordinary course of business exemptions") if the requirements of these provisions are met and an operating unit is not being acquired. *See* Int. 7.

| **163** | **Applicable provisions.** 801.21, 7A(a)(2), 801.1(h)(1), 801.13(b).

Issue. Would A have to file to report its transfer to B of securities of issuer X, an entity not controlled by A?

Analysis. No. Section 801.21 states: "For purposes . . . of . . . Section 7A(a)(2) and §§ 801.1(h)(1) and 801.13(b): . . . (b) Neither voting or nonvoting securities . . . shall be considered assets of another person from which they are acquired." Accordingly, no notification is required by A. B and X, however, must comply with the requirements of the Act as acquiring and acquired persons respectively. *See* Section 801.21, Examples 1 and 2. Not only are the voting securities issued by X not *assets* of A (because of Section 801.21), they are also not *voting securities* of A since A does not control X.

| **164** | **Applicable provisions.** 801.30, 801.1(f)(3).

Issue. If nonvoting securities automatically attain voting rights at the time of an IPO, does this constitute a potentially reportable conversion? Or is this a nonreportable "automatic maturation of inchoate rights," such as when omitted dividends cause preferred stock to attain voting rights?

Analysis. The PNO has now taken the position that if the securities were acquired *prior* to the point in time when the issuer is in its "quiet period" (the period during which the securities laws require the issuer to refrain from any promotion of its securities) the subsequent automatic "conversion" to voting stock at the time of the IPO would not be a reportable conversion. If the securities are acquired at any time *during* the time the issuer is deemed to be in its "quiet period" or "in registration," then a filing must be made and the waiting period observed prior to the IPO and the automatic conversion if the jurisdictional tests of the Act are otherwise satisfied and no exemption applies.

For purposes of this HSR analysis, the PNO takes the position that an issuer is deemed to be in its "quiet period" when it reaches an understanding with a broker dealer to start the IPO process. This is before a registration statement is filed and encompasses the period of time during which the prospectus is prepared. The "organization meeting" is a good proxy for when a company begins its "quiet period" under this definition.

| 165 | **Applicable provision.** 801.30.

Issue. Where Company B grants Company A a contractual option to acquire all of the voting securities of a subsidiary of Company B, would the subsequent acquisition be governed by the procedures of Section 801.30?

Analysis. No. This scenario is not literally among the types of "nonconsensual" transactions listed in Section 801.30(a). Specifically, the "option" here is not within the terms of Section 801.30(a)(7), which requires, among other things, that the option or warrant be the subject of a currently effective registration statement filed with the SEC. Thus, exercise of the option described above would be subject to non-Section 801.30 HSR procedures and waiting periods if the jurisdictional tests of the Act are otherwise satisfied and no exemption applies. In such a case, Company A would have to notify Company B in advance of its intended exercise of the option, so that Company B could prepare its filing before the waiting period starts.

166 | Applicable provisions. 801.30, 803.5.

Issue. Company A makes a proposal to Company B that the two entities be merged. Company A simultaneously files notification with the enforcement agencies. Because it is not clear whether the proposal will be accepted or resisted (and a letter of intent has not therefore been signed), Company A designates its notification as a Section 801.30 filing, sends Company B a Section 803.5(a) notice, and attaches a Section 803.5(a) affidavit to its filing. Is Company A's notification valid? Does it start the running of the waiting period?

Analysis. The PNO would not accept such a filing as a Section 801.30 transaction without some additional statement that Company A intended to make open market or other purchases meeting a reporting threshold. An affidavit stating an intention to acquire shares of an issuer and thereby cross a notification threshold will be sufficient for purposes of both Section 801.30 and Section 803.5(a) if the purchaser will acquire shares of the issuer through open market purchases, privately negotiated purchases with holders of the issuer's shares, or other types of purchases described in Section 801.30. Under such circumstances, the acquiring person's filing will start the waiting period.

167 Applicable provisions. 801.30(b)(2), 803.5(a), 802.51.

Issue. Where a tender offer is made but is contingent upon the approval of the management of the target, and the acquiring person files notification, must the acquired person complete its filing within the time period specified in Section 801.30(b)(2)?

Analysis. Yes. The offeror expressed a good faith intention to make the acquisition, publicly announced the tender offer, and properly notified the acquired person under Section 803.5(a)(1). Its filing therefore complied with the Rules and was accepted by the PNO. A timely notification filing by the acquired person is therefore required by Section 801.30(b)(2). *See* Ints. 261, 262.

Editor's Note. The implication of this interpretation is that even if the target's management rejects the tender offer, the acquiror's filing is still valid and serves to start the waiting period.

| **168** | **Applicable provisions.** 801.33, 803.2(a), 802.51.

Issue. May a tender offeror, who has accepted a majority of the target's tendered shares for payment, withdraw an HSR filing previously made by the target in connection with a proposed disposition of certain of the target's assets in a transaction with another party?

Facts. Company A, a Canadian issuer, was the object of a hostile tender offer by Company B. HSR notifications were filed. As a defense against the tender offer, Company A agreed to sell its "crown jewel" division to Company C, and both A and C filed Notification and Report Forms with respect to that disposition. Before the HSR waiting period applicable to this transaction expired, the HSR waiting period applicable to the tender offer expired. More than 50 percent of the voting securities of Company A had been tendered, but not actually paid for. Canadian law creates a contractual obligation on the part of the offeror to pay for all shares tendered prior to expiration, but allows six days between expiration of the tender offer and payment for the shares.

Analysis. In a case involving a hostile tender offer under Canadian law, the PNO concluded that after expiration of the offer, the offeror had beneficial ownership of voting securities that had been tendered and accepted for payment, even though payment had not been made. *See* Section 801.33. Because more than 50 percent of the voting securities of the target had been tendered and accepted for payment, the PNO determined that the offeror controlled the target and could withdraw the target's HSR filing related to the proposed disposition.

Because Section 803.2(a) requires notification to be filed by the preacquisition UPE (or by an entity included within the UPE and authorized by the UPE to file on its behalf), a change in the identity of the UPE (resulting from acceptance for payment of half or more of its shares) prior to expiration of a waiting period relating to a previous filing by the issuer permits (but does not require) the new UPE to withdraw the previous filing as unauthorized. Withdrawal of the notification prevents the underlying transaction from being lawfully consummated. Note that if the new UPE desired to proceed with the sale to Company C, no new filing would have been required if the new UPE did not withdraw the earlier filing. *See* Int. 265.

169 | Applicable provision. 801.40.

Issue. Is the conversion of a 50/50 partnership into a corporation reportable?

Facts. Corporations A and B are equal partners in Partnership X. The partners wish, by a two-step procedure, to convert Partnership X into a corporation but retain the equal ownership interests. Each corporation will first form a wholly owned subsidiary to which its respective partnership interests will be transferred. The two subsidiaries will then be merged, and the parent corporations will exchange the respective interests in the merging subsidiaries for 50 percent of the stock of the resulting corporation.

Analysis. The PNO views the conversion of a partnership (or an LLC for that matter) to a corporation as a formation of a new corporation subject to Section 801.40 analysis. Newco will inherit the annual sales and total assets of the partnership as its size-of-person. If the size-of-person test of 801.40(c) is satisfied and a former partner acquires voting securities of the new corporation valued in excess of $50 million but less than $200 million, the formation will be reportable. (If a former partner acquires voting securities of the new corporation valued in excess of $200 million, the size-of-person test does not apply and the formation will be reportable unless an exemption applies. *See* Section 801.40(b).)

| 170 | **Applicable provisions.** 801.40, 801.1(f).

Issue. Is the formation of an unincorporated joint venture ever reportable?

Analysis. Yes. The formation of certain LLCs is reportable even though they are not corporations and even though the SBP for Section 801.40 provides:

> since the rule [Section 801.40] applies only to the formation of corporations, the formation of entities other than corporations is, by virtue of this rule, not brought within the coverage of the act and need not be preceded by compliance with the act's requirements.

43 Fed. Reg. 33,450, 33,485 (July 31, 1978).

The FTC issued Formal Interpretation 15, effective as of March 1, 1999, which describes the circumstances under which the formation of an LLC is reportable. The Formal Interpretation has been modified twice, and the most current version, dated March 23, 2001, is included in the Appendix. The Formal Interpretation provides generally that formation of an LLC may be reportable if two or more preexisting, separately controlled businesses will be contributed to the new LLC and at least one member will control the company. Size-of-person and size-of-transaction tests of Section 7A(a) are applied to determine if a filing is required. *See* Int. 81.

Editor's Note. *It is also possible that an unincorporated joint venture could be reportable under Section 801.40 if the interests in the joint venture are deemed to be "voting securities." "Voting security" is defined in Section 801.1(f) to mean "any securit[y] which at present or upon conversion entitle[s] the owner or holder thereof to vote for the election of directors of the issuer, or at an entity included within the same person as the issuer, or, with respect to unincorporated entities, individuals exercising similar functions." See, e.g., Int. 71.*

Thus, if the interests in the entity entitle the holder to vote for the election of individuals with functions similar to directors, the interests may be deemed to be voting securities, and Section 801.40 would apply to the formation. The PNO has found that formations of certain business trusts are potentially reportable under this analysis. Formations of foreign entities (including foreign LLCs) may also come within this analysis. See Int. 177.

| 171 | **Applicable provisions.** 801.40, 803.10(a)(2).

Issue. Could the acquisition of voting securities of a new corporation be analyzed under Section 801.40 even after its incorporation?

Analysis. Yes, under certain circumstances. The reporting requirements of the Act and the Rules relating to formations of new corporations do not focus specifically on the technical incorporation of a new corporation, but on the acquisition of voting securities by two or more acquiring persons during the organization of the venture. Thus, if a contributor's acquisition of voting securities occurs sometime after the date of incorporation, that acquisition nevertheless may be analyzed under Section 801.40. Under the PNO's interpretation of Section 801.40, the formation analysis is a continuum, and the corporation will not be deemed formed until all contributors identified as those participating in the formation of a new corporation have, in fact, contributed and received their interest in the corporation.

In one case, A and B agreed in principle to pursue the acquisition of another corporation, "Target." A formed a wholly owned subsidiary, Newco, and purchased its stock for $50,000 cash plus a commitment to contribute an additional $450,000. B was later to purchase an equal amount of stock of Newco for $500,000, but only if the acquisition of Target could be arranged. At that time, members of the management group of Target would also purchase 10 percent of Newco. The PNO advised that the formation of Newco should be analyzed under Section 801.40 with A, B and the management group regarded as contributing to the formation, rather than as the acquisition of shares of A's subsidiary, Newco, by B and the management group.

In a second case, Section 801.40 was applied to the formation of a wholly owned corporate subsidiary, which was created to serve as the acquisition vehicle for a leveraged buyout. After its formation, the subsidiary would enter into loan agreements with various institutional lenders, which would acquire less than $50 million (and less than 50 percent) of the subsidiary's stock in return for loans exceeding $25 million. The PNO took the position that the intended stock purchase arrangements with lenders rendered this transaction the reportable formation of a joint venture or other corporation within the meaning of Section 801.40. There were three stated reasons for this conclusion. First, agreements with the institutional lenders had apparently been arranged prior to formation of the subsidiary. Second, the loan-stock purchase transactions were to take place shortly after formation of the subsidiary. Third, the acquisitions by the lenders appeared to be part of an overall plan to infuse capital into the subsidiary for purposes of financing its leveraged buyout.

The PNO came to the opposite conclusion, however, in a third case where two members of a management group formed a corporation and sold shares some four months later to different members of the management group and others, where there was no commitment at the time of the original transaction for others to purchase shares in the new corporation.

In yet another case, the PNO concluded that Section 801.40 was inapplicable to a corporation's formation of a wholly owned subsidiary whose shares it intended to make available in a public offering. In this case, the PNO treated the formation as exempt under Section 802.30, but noted that later purchases in the public offering would be subject to the Act if the size-of-person test (if applicable: *see* Section 7A(a)) and the size-of-transaction test were met.

Whether a transaction is regarded as part of the formation of a new corporation to be analyzed under Section 801.40, or as a simple acquisition of voting securities in an existing corporation, can determine the reportability of the acquisition of voting securities. Another complication of the Section 801.40 analysis is that, under Section 803.10(a)(2), no waiting period for an acquisition subject to Section 801.40 starts to run until after filings are received from all persons contributing to the formation that are required to file. *See* Int. 274.

172 Applicable provisions. 801.40, 801.10(a), 801.90, 7A(c)(10).

Issue. Would the commitment of joint venturers to contribute equal amounts of additional capital in the future be considered in determining the value of the voting securities acquired in the formation of the joint venture corporation?

Analysis. Yes, unless the commitment is contingent. If the commitment is not conditional, the fair market value of each joint venturer's shares should reflect the value of the full amount of the commitments. Committed and unconditional future contributions of the joint venturers to the joint venture must be included within the assets of the joint venture for Section 801.40(d) purposes. The acquisition price of the shares, which should determine their value (Section 801.10(a)(2)(i)), is the value of all consideration being given for the shares, which would include the contractual obligation to make any future contributions. 43 Fed. Reg. 33,450, 33,471 (July 31, 1978). *See* Int. 119.

On the other hand, if the commitment is conditional, it will not affect the value of voting securities acquired or the size of the Newco in the formation of the joint venture. For example, A, B, and C form a joint venture, Newco. Each contributes $10 million initially and agrees, upon the satisfaction of certain conditions, to contribute an additional $41 million in the future. In exchange A, B, and C each receive 33.3 percent of Newco voting securities. Since the additional contributions to capital are not certain, the fair market value of the Newco stock acquired by each of A, B, and C is less than $50 million and no reporting is required for the formation of the joint venture. Furthermore, no filing is required subsequently if the conditions are met and A, B, and C make the anticipated capital contributions. Such contributions would not be acquisitions of voting securities subject to the Act's requirements, or, if voting securities were then issued, the percentage interests of the shareholders would not be increased, and those acquisitions would be exempt under Section 7A(c)(10).

Instead of agreeing to contribute additional amounts in the future, if, for some "non-HSR avoidance reason," the shareholders agree to purchase additional shares in equal amounts at a point in the future, the value of the shares acquired at the formation of the joint venture would then reflect only the capital initially contributed. The shareholders' percentage interests would not increase as a result of those subsequent acquisitions and those transactions would be exempt under

Section 7A(c)(10). If, however, there is no legitimate business purpose for delaying the purchase of the additional shares, and one person's aggregate purchases exceed $50 million, this structure might be regarded as a device for avoidance under Section 801.90.

| 173 | **Applicable provisions.** 801.40, 803.10.

Issue. Would co-venturers, who file in connection with a Section 801.40 formation, have to amend their filings if before the actual formation of the corporation one of the co-venturers drops out of the venture and is replaced by another investing party?

Analysis. Maybe. If the new investor, previously unidentified, is making a reportable acquisition of more than $50 million of voting securities of the new corporation and such acquisition satisfies the size-of-person test (if applicable) and is not otherwise exempt. The co-venturers who had already filed would have to amend their filings to include the new investor and all would have to wait for the expiration or termination of a new waiting period. The PNO does not require a new filing fee for the amended transaction (other than from the new venturer). Of course, the waiting period for the formation does not begin to run until all parties of the joint venture file notification or amend their earlier notifications.

Also, the venturer that filed and then dropped out will not be refunded its filing fee.

| 174 | **Applicable provisions.** 801.40, 802.51, 802.52.

Issue. Do the Section 802.51(a) and Section 802.52 exemptions apply to acquisitions subject to Section 801.40?

Facts. A letter to the PNO sought guidance on a transaction involving the formation of a corporate joint venture by a U.S. person and a development company controlled by a foreign government. The joint venture was to be organized under the laws of the foreign country and was not to have any assets within the United States.

Analysis. The PNO concluded that the transaction was not reportable, even though the size-of-person (under Section 801.40(c) and (d)) and size-of-transaction tests were satisfied, because the acquisition by the U.S. person was exempt under Section 802.51(a) and the acquisition by the foreign development company was exempt under Section 802.52. The PNO reached this conclusion even though it was anticipated that the joint venture would in the future have sales in the United States in excess of $50 million. Speculative future sales in or into the United States are irrelevant to a Section 802.51 analysis.

| 175 | **Applicable provisions.** 801.40, 801.2(d).

Issue. Is the formation of a joint venture corporation, as an acquisition vehicle in a subsequent merger or consolidation, covered by Section 801.40?

Analysis. No. The PNO's position is that Section 801.40 does not cover a multishareholder corporation formed in connection with an anticipated merger or consolidation; rather, the formation is governed by Section 801.2(d). According to the SBP, the parenthetical phrase "(except . . . in connection with mergers and consolidations)" is intended to remove such formations from the scope of Section 801.40 as they are unlikely to raise competitive concerns separate and apart from the merger or consolidation itself which is subject to 801.2(d). In contrast, a multishareholder corporation formed as an acquisition vehicle other than in connection with a merger or consolidation, and "true" joint ventures where multiple venturers contribute assets to a new corporation, are within the scope of Section 801.40. *See* Int. 251.

| 176 | **Applicable provisions.** 801.40, 802.51(a).

Issue. Is notification required in connection with the formation of a foreign corporate joint venture, where at least one shareholder will hold voting securities of the venture valued in excess of $50 million?

Analysis. Yes, provided the special size-of-person tests in Section 801.40(c) are met and unless otherwise exempt. Section 801.40(d) states the size-of-transaction test applicable to joint ventures at the time of their formation. Note the size criteria in Section 801.40 are stated on a worldwide basis and without regard to the nationality of the joint venture corporation or the contribution shareholders. The dollar value of the securities to be purchased, as stated above, satisfies the size-of-transaction test. Thus, the contemplated joint venture is reportable unless it is otherwise exempt under another provision of the regulations. For example, the transaction may satisfy the requirements set forth in Section 802.51(a) (acquisitions of voting securities of a foreign issuer), and therefore be exempt from the Act's reporting requirements. *See* Int. 174.

| 177 | **Applicable provisions.** 801.40, 801.1(f), Formal Interpretation 15, Items 6(b) and 6(c).

Issue. Does Formal Interpretation 15 (*see* Appendix) which describes the circumstances under which the formation of an LLC and the acquisition of interests in an existing LLC are reportable, apply to foreign LLCs?

Analysis. No. The PNO's position is that Formal Interpretation 15 does not apply to foreign entities. The PNO understands that the laws of some countries permit the existence of entities called "limited liability companies" that appear to have substantially different characteristics than U.S. LLCs. The PNO concluded that they would not apply the Formal Interpretation 15 analysis to these foreign LLCs, but rather would apply a "voting securities" analysis to determine if the ownership interests in a given situation constitute voting securities under Section 801.1(f). If the interests are determined to be voting securities, the 801.40 analysis will apply. If they are not determined to be voting securities, the formation will be treated like the formation of a partnership. This means that a foreign LLC (or any foreign entity for that matter) will either be treated for HSR purposes as a corporation or a partnership. The LLC rules will not apply.

The PNO's "voting securities" analysis focuses on the definition of voting securities in Section 801.1(f). The questions are: does the entity have a board of directors (or individuals exercising similar functions), who is on the board, and does the interest hold get to vote for the election of this board? So, for example, if the foreign entity does not have a board of directors or the equivalent governing body, it would be treated like a partnership. Furthermore, the PNO takes the position that even if a foreign entity does have a board of directors or the equivalent governing body, it still would be treated like a partnership so long as the board of directors or the equivalent governing body consists solely of (1) directors, officers, or employees of the foreign entity's owners or of other entities under common control with the foreign entity's owners and (2) officers of the foreign entity. However, if a foreign entity has a board of directors or the equivalent governing body and even one owner of that foreign entity elects or selects a third party to sit on that board, the foreign entity would be treated like a corporation.

Whether a particular foreign entity would be deemed a partnership or corporation for HSR purposes could impact whether the formation of that entity would be reportable or whether an acquiring person's subsequent acquisition of interests in that entity would be reportable. The formation of corporations by two or more persons would be reportable if thresholds are satisfied and no exemption applies, whereas the formation of partnerships are never reportable. Also, the acquisition of voting securities of a corporation would be reportable if thresholds are satisfied and no exemption applies, whereas the acquisition of interests in a partnership would not be reportable if the acquiring person would not hold 100 percent of the interests of the partnership as a result. Moreover, to complete Items 6(b) and 6(c) of the filing, it is necessary to determine whether a foreign entity in which the acquiring person (or issuer whose stock is being acquired) owns interests would be deemed a corporation or partnership for HSR purposes. Items 6(b) and 6(c) seek information about corporations, and not partnerships, in which the acquiring person (or issuer whose stock is being acquired) owns interests.

Editor's Note. *Formation of U.S. LLCs (and other transactions involving U.S. LLCs) are always analyzed under Formal Interpretation 15, even if it has a board of directors or an equivalent governing body. See* Ints. 81 *through* 86. *The PNO does not apply a "voting securities" analysis to a U.S. LLC.*

| 178 | **Applicable provision.** 801.40(a).

Issue. Are lenders who provide financing to a newly formed entity without receiving any securities of that entity contributing to its formation and therefore deemed to be acquiring persons under Section 801.40(a)?

Analysis. The PNO confirmed that a lender who provides financing to a newly formed entity without receiving any of its securities is not "contributing to the formation" of that entity within the meaning of Section 801.40(a). The lender is also not an *acquiring* person under that section. *See also* Int. 179. Furthermore, the amount of any financing that such a lender would provide is not included in the joint venture corporation's size under Section 801.40(d).

| 179 | **Applicable provisions.**   801.40(c), 801.40(d), 801.1(f), 801.2(a).

Issue. Is a party who will make loans or guarantee obligations of a newly formed corporate joint venture and who will acquire nonvoting options, warrants, or other nonvoting convertible securities of the venture an "acquiring person" and/or a "person contributing to the formation" of the venture, such that the value of its loan or guarantee must be included among the venture's assets under Section 801.40(d)?

Analysis. A lender who provides financing to a newly formed entity and who receives, as a result, a convertible security of that new entity that is not presently entitled to vote for the election of directors (e.g., convertible debentures) is considered an acquiring person under Section 801.40 and Section 801.2(a), because it will hold voting securities, as defined by Sections 801.1(f)(1) and (2).

A lender who is taking convertible voting securities in exchange for its loan is counted as an acquiring person in the size-of-person test in Section 801.40(c), but the value of its loan is not counted toward the total assets of the joint venture in Section 801.40(d). Conversely, if the lender is taking securities with a present right to vote for directors in exchange for its loan, it is deemed to be both an acquiring person and a contributor to the formation. Therefore, it is counted as an acquiring person for purposes of Section 801.40(c) *and* the amount of the loan is counted toward the total assets of the joint venture in Section 801.40(d).

The PNO has concluded that being a contributor is not synonymous with being an acquiring person pursuant to Section 801.2(a). One may be deemed a contributor either (1) by contributing assets (including cash) in exchange for voting securities (whether or not presently entitled to vote) or (2) by receiving securities presently entitled to vote (whether or not contributing assets to the venture).

180   Applicable provisions. 801.40(c), 801.40(d).

Issue. How is the size of a to-be-formed corporate joint venture determined where its assets will consist exclusively of a majority of the stock of a preexisting corporation?

Analysis. Under Sections 801.40(c) and (d), the size of a corporate joint venture includes all *assets* being contributed by the venturers. Where those assets consist of a minority stock interest in another corporation, the size of the joint venture normally would be the fair market value of the assets (i.e., the stock) being transferred to the venture. Where a controlling interest in an issuer is being transferred to the joint venture, 100 percent of the assets of the issuer (as stated on its last regularly prepared balance sheet) should be included when calculating the size of the joint venture. The value of the assets of an issuer that the joint venture will control need not be stepped up to fair market value.

| **181** | **Applicable provisions.** 801.40(d), 801.11(e).

Issue. Are voting securities that a newly formed corporation has a contractual commitment to acquire included within its assets at formation under Section 801.40(d)?

Analysis. The PNO has advised that voting securities and other assets to be acquired from a person that is not a contributor to the formation of the joint venture are not included in the assets of the new venture under Section 801.40(d). The acquisition of those voting securities and other assets should be separately analyzed as an acquisition by the newly formed entity. In that analysis, Section 801.11(e) would frequently be available to limit the size of the new corporation, assuming it was its own UPE, and had not, prior to that acquisition, regularly prepared financial statements. If this is the case, and the size-of-transaction of the assets or voting security acquisition contemplated by the new corporation did not exceed $200 million, the acquisition may not be reportable.

The PNO also has said that assets (including cash) and voting securities that the newly formed corporation has a contract to acquire from a contributor to the formation of the joint venture clearly are included in the assets of the corporation pursuant to Section 801.40(d)(1) when they will be received as capital contributions. Assets or voting securities that the newly formed corporation has contracted at arm's length to buy from a person contributing to the formation generally will not affect the new company's total assets. The language of Section 801.40(d)(1) says that the newly formed corporation's assets will include "[a]ll assets which any person contributing to the formation of the joint venture or other corporation has agreed to transfer . . . at any time . . . ." But, if the joint venture is paying fair value for those assets or voting securities to be acquired, inclusion of the value of the assets or voting securities in determining the newly formed corporation's total assets pursuant to Section 801.40(d) would involve double counting.

| 182 | **Applicable provisions.** 801.40(d), 801.11(e).

Issue. May forming shareholders' contributions of capital to a newly formed corporation, to be used in making an acquisition by that corporation, be excluded when determining the newly formed corporation's size-of-person?

Analysis. Whenever a new corporation is formed and then it subsequently makes an acquisition there are two different transactions that must be analyzed and the size-of-person determined in two different contexts. For purposes of determining the size-of-person in the formation transaction, contributions of capital by the forming shareholders are considered. *See* Section 801.40. However, when the new company is involved in subsequent transactions, if it is its own UPE and does not have a regularly prepared balance sheet, in accordance with Section 801.11(e), contributions in the form of cash may be excluded from the newly formed corporation's pro forma balance sheet created to determine its size and thus the reportability of its intended acquisition. *See* Int. 124.

183 | Applicable provision. 801.40(d).

Issue. If at the time of its formation by two or more persons, a new corporation will acquire assets with service contracts providing for a future income stream in exchange for future services, is the future income stream includable as an asset of the joint venture for HSR reporting purposes?

Facts. Four joint venture partners seek to dissolve their partnership and form a new joint venture in corporate form, apparently transferring all the assets of the partnership to the corporation. The partnership has "present assets" valued at substantially less than $10 million but also has service contracts requiring future performance by the partnership and providing for a future income stream to the partnership.

Analysis. The present assets of the joint venture valued at well below $10 million will be included as assets of the new corporation. In addition, the PNO counsels that the service contracts already entered into, with performance to occur in the future, would also be considered an asset of the joint venture and valued at fair market value. The fair market value of the service contracts and the other "assets" would be aggregated to determine the total value of the assets transferred to the corporation for HSR reporting purposes. In the facts presented one cannot determine the appropriate value of the contracts, but as described in detail in Ints. 4, 103, and 104, in valuing a contract that is transferred one looks not at the income stream but at the premium (if any) paid for the contract.

| 184 | **Applicable provisions.** 801.40(d), 801.11(e)(1)(ii).

Issue. Are assets or cash to be used by a newly formed joint venture to acquire another entity considered assets of the joint venture for purposes of applying the size-of-person test in connection with the formation of the venture?

Analysis. Assets or cash *contributed* to a corporation newly formed by two or more persons (hereafter "Newco") are included in Newco's assets under Section 801.40(d) regardless of the purpose for which they will be used. Funds *borrowed* by the venture for purposes of making an acquisition may or may not have to be included in the venture's assets. Loans to the joint venture made or guaranteed by a venturer are included in the venture's assets provided the venturer acquires voting securities in the formation. Loans from third parties that are not guaranteed by a venturer that is acquiring voting securities are not included. Section 801.11(e)(1)(ii) (which excludes cash held by the corporation for certain acquisitions and expenses) is inapplicable to formation calculations under Section 801.40(d).

185 Applicable provision. 801.90.

Issue. Does introducing additional steps to a transaction, which arguably results in the transaction being nonreportable, constitute a transaction or device for avoidance?

Facts. A wishes to acquire all of the assets of BSUB valued at $80 million. BSUB is a wholly owned subsidiary of B, which has four 25 percent shareholders. The shareholders of B create a new shell corporation, C, in which each also holds a 25 percent interest. Assets of BSUB valued at $40 million are then transferred to C in a nonreportable transaction. A subsequently acquires all of the assets of BSUB and C for $40 million each. Because C and BSUB are within separate acquired persons, the acquisitions are not aggregated and neither acquisition meets the size-of-transaction test.

Analysis. The PNO views this as a transaction or device for avoidance and the parties would be deemed to be in violation of the Act under Section 801.90. There appears to be no reason to create the extra steps other than to avoid an HSR filing requirement. Consequently, PNO would look through to the substance of the transaction, which is A acquiring $80 million of assets originally held by BSUB, a reportable transaction for which notification should have been filed.

186 | Applicable provisions. 801.90, 801.15(b), 802.51.

Issue. Can the transfer of assets from a U.S. to a foreign subsidiary constitute a transaction or device for avoidance?

Facts. A, a foreign person, wishes to purchase a wholly owned U.S. subsidiary of B, valued at $60 million. B proposes to create a new wholly owned foreign subsidiary into which it will transfer certain of the U.S. subsidiary's assets, valued at $20 million. The assets to be transferred accounted for less than $50 million of sales in or into the United States. A will then acquire 100 percent of the voting securities of both subsidiaries.

Analysis. The PNO views this as a transaction or device for avoidance. Since the acquisition of the foreign subsidiary will be exempt under Section 802.51 (the transferred assets had less than $50 million in sales in the most recent fiscal year), it will not be held as a result of the acquisition and its value is not included in the size-of-transaction. *See* Section 801.15(b). Therefore, the size-of-transaction includes only the value of the U.S. issuer, which A has determined to be less than $50 million. Absent any compelling reason to transfer the assets to the new foreign subsidiary, the PNO would view this as a transaction or device for avoidance. Therefore, the substance of the transaction is A acquiring the U.S. subsidiary, which is valued in excess of $50 million. The parties should accordingly file.

187 Applicable provisions. 801.90, 801.11(b), 801.11(c), 801.11(e).

Issue. Is there any requirement that a newly created entity develop a regularly prepared balance sheet within any particular period of time? May it rely indefinitely upon pro forma balance sheets that reflect assets insufficient to meet the size-of-person test?

Analysis. The Rules do not specify any time period within which a newly created entity must develop its first regularly prepared financial statements. The prudent course would be to analyze this issue under Section 801.90. A newly created entity would thus have no obligation to develop and rely upon regularly prepared financial statements within any particular time period. On the other hand, the failure to develop such financials solely in order to avoid a notification obligation may be a device for avoidance. Thus, the longer the period during which pro forma financials are relied upon, the greater may be the need to justify the delay. The issue of whether delay is a device for avoidance, raising a Section 801.90 problem, would likely be analyzed in terms of reasonableness, taking all relevant facts into account.

Relevant to the analysis of the reasonableness of a delay would be facts relating to the business of the newly created entity. An entity, for example, set up on a calendar year basis might be requested to justify its failure to prepare financials within a reasonable time after close of the calendar year.

Because of the operation of Section 801.11(e), there may be an incentive for a newly created entity to rely on the use of pro forma financials for as long as possible, since funds contributed or borrowed for the purpose of acquiring the stock of a single issuer, and any such stock purchased, may be excluded from such balance sheets. The newly created entity's first regularly prepared balance sheet will presumably reflect both the borrowed or contributed funds and the stock purchased, and the entity's assets may thus exceed the $10 million (or even $100 million) threshold.

Section 801.11(b)'s requirement that a person rely on its most recent regularly prepared financial statements prepared no more than fifteen months prior to filing or consummation suggests the possibility of a requirement to prepare the first such financials within that period. The PNO, however, infers no such requirement. The reason for the fifteen-month period was to facilitate inclusion of the net sales from the person's most recently completed fiscal year, and the PNO has not read

Section 801.11(b) to require the preparation of financials within, or even after, fifteen months. This does not create a problem for evaluating the size-of-person because pro forma financials must be current as of the closing of any transaction that requires their preparation.

188 | Applicable provisions. 801.90, 7A(c)(3).

Issue. Is acquiring 50 percent or more of an issuer for less than $50 million, when the buyer's intent is to acquire 100 percent, a transaction or device for avoidance?

Facts. A intends to acquire 100 percent of the voting securities of B pursuant to a tender offer and merger agreement. As a first step it agrees that the controlling shareholder will tender all of its shares for $40 million. A will then one week later merge with B in consideration of $30 million to be paid to the remaining shareholders, which will be exempt under Section 7A(c)(3) of the Act. The agreement states no reason for the one week lag between steps.

Analysis. The PNO views this as a transaction or device for avoidance. A has an agreement with B and its controlling shareholder that will result in A acquiring B in its entirety. There is no purpose to making a tender offer for the controlling shareholders' voting stock one week before acquiring the remainder of the voting securities other than to avoid an HSR filing. The PNO would look through this arrangement and deem A to be acquiring 100 percent of the voting securities of B, valued at $70 million and requiring a filing. *See* Int. 254.

189 | Applicable provision. 801.90.

Issue. Is a change in a UPE, prior to a transaction closing, a potential transaction or device for avoidance?

Facts. A will acquire 100 percent of the voting securities of B through its wholly owned subsidiary ASUB for less than $200 million. A is a $100 million person and B is a $10 million person. Prior to the transaction closing, A intends to sell 30 percent of its interest in ASUB to each of two affiliated companies not within A's person, making ASUB its own UPE. ASUB is not a $100 million person on its own, therefore its acquisition of B is not reportable.

Analysis. The PNO views this as a potential transaction or device for avoidance. If A's sale of voting securities of ASUB to the two affiliates is determined to be a sham (e.g., beneficial ownership did not transfer) or if A were to re-acquire the shares of ASUB shortly after its acquisition of B, the transaction would be deemed to be a transaction or device for avoidance.

190 Applicable provisions. 801.90, 802.30.

Issue. Can an issuer's redemption of its own voting stock be viewed as a potential transaction or device for avoidance?

Facts. A, B, and C each currently hold one-third of the voting securities of corporation X. A enters into an agreement with B, C, and X in which A will contribute $100 million to X, which X will use to redeem all of the voting stock held by B and C. As a result, A will now hold 100 percent of the voting securities of X, valued in excess of $50 million. A did not file notification prior to the redemption on the basis that it had not made an acquisition, since its increase in holdings in X was the result of the redemption by X of its own stock, an event that is exempt under Section 802.30.

Analysis. The PNO views this as a potential transaction or device for avoidance. If the redemption had occurred without any active participation by A, there may have been justification for not filing notification. Since A is deemed to be instrumental in causing the redemption to occur, the PNO would look through the redemption to the substance of the transaction, which is A acquiring a reportable amount of X voting securities. *See* Int. 159.

| 191 | **Applicable provision.** 801.90.

Issue. When can the formation of a partnership be viewed as a potential transaction or device for avoidance subject to Section 801.90?

Facts. A and B form a partnership into which A will contribute $100 million in cash and B will contribute a factory valued at $100 million. A will have a 90 percent interest in the partnership with B holding the remaining 10 percent interest. In addition, $90 million of the cash in the partnership will transfer to B on closing. There is also an option granted to A that will allow it to cause the partnership to redeem B's 10 percent interest at the end of one year for $10 million in cash.

Analysis. The PNO views this as a potential transaction or device for avoidance. The partnership appears to have been created as a transient structure to accomplish the acquisition of the factory by A without filing notification. The cash flowing back out of the partnership to B also does not seem to be a bona fide equalization payment. The PNO would view the partnership as a sham and would require A to file for the acquisition of more than $50 million in assets from B. If, on the other hand, the arrangement was permanent (no option and no intent to acquire the rest of the partnership interests) and there was a sound business justification for the arrangement, this may be permissible as a bona fide equalization payment. *See* Int. 27.

Editor's Note. *The PNO generally employs a two-step analysis to determine whether a structure is a potential transaction or device for avoidance. First, the PNO assesses whether the transaction has been structured to avoid a filing obligation. Second, it identifies the substance of the transaction. If the substance of the transaction is reportable under the Act and the Rules, the device for avoidance may be disregarded and the failure to file treated as a violation.*

Applying the two-step analysis here does not necessarily lead to the PNO's position. The substance of the resulting structure is the formation of a partnership owned 90 percent by A and 10 percent by B. The capital contributions of the parties after taking into account the $90 million payment to B roughly correspond to the 90/10 relationship. Since the formation of a bona fide partnership is outside the coverage of the Act, one may well argue that this transaction should not be subject to Section 801.90, since the substance of the transaction would not *otherwise be reportable under the Act. Further, if A were to ever redeem B's remaining 10 percent interest, the redemption would cause A to hold 100 percent of the partnership interests, and A would be potentially subject to notification requirements under the Act at that time. The fact that an option exists to allow A to redeem B's interest does not necessarily lead to the conclusion that A intends to exercise the option.*

The "two-step analysis" described above may be difficult to apply in practice as it is difficult to isolate specific scenarios that would likely cause the agencies to allege a Section 801.90 violation. Conversely the following structures or decisions would be unlikely to raise Section 801.90 concerns:

1. *All things being equal, two parties decide to form a joint venture as a partnership rather than a corporation;*

2. *Two parties decide to form a partnership where one party holds 99 percent of the partnership interests and one party holds 1 percent of the partnership interests. However, the majority holder has no present intention of acquiring the remaining 1 percent;*

3. *A party chooses to buy a subset of a seller's assets valued under Section 801.10 at $49.9 million; and*

4. *Given a choice, a party chooses to acquire convertible securities rather than securities with present voting rights.*

192 | Applicable provisions. 801.90, 801.13(b).

Issue. Is entering into two contracts for asset acquisitions from the same acquired person within 180 days a device for avoidance?

Facts. A and B enter into an agreement under which A will acquire assets from B valued at $40 million. Sixty days later, for legitimate business reasons, the parties enter into another agreement for A to acquire from B an additional $20 million in assets, which had not been anticipated at the time of the first agreement. The acquisition of assets that are the subject of the first agreement has not yet been consummated.

Analysis. Under Section 801.13(b)(2)(i), the second set of assets would not be aggregated with the first and no filing would be required. *See* Int. 154. Multiple asset acquisitions may be aggregated for purposes of "size-of-transaction" analysis where an agreement to purchase a second set of assets from the same acquired person is entered into within 180 days of the acquisition of a prior set of assets, and notification was not required for the first set. In the instant example, however, the acquiring person has not yet acquired the first set of assets. Thus, aggregation would not be required, and each acquisition would be treated separately. Further, the PNO would not view this as a potential transaction or device for avoidance as long as (1) there were legitimate business reasons to have two separate agreements and (2) the second acquisition was not anticipated at the time of the first agreement.

This example assumes that the PNO or other administrative body charged with determining compliance under the Act has agreed that the business reasons underlying the need to have two separate agreements were "legitimate" and not pretextual. Parties to transactions should be aware that the PNO may carefully scrutinize any transaction and assess the legitimacy of any asserted business justification for a particular transaction's structure.

193 | Applicable provision. 801.90.

Issue. Is the choice of type of legal entity to be used in the formation of a joint venture relevant to the PNO's consideration of whether a given structure is a transaction or device for avoidance?

Facts. A, B, and C wish to form a joint venture to combine their respective businesses. Each will hold a one-third interest in the joint venture valued in the aggregate at $900 million. As there is some urgency to consummate the venture, the parties choose to create the joint venture in the form of an LLC (which, under Formal Interpretation 15 (*see* Appendix) would not be reportable since no person will control the venture) as opposed to a corporation (which would require the parties to file).

Analysis. The PNO does not view this as a potential transaction or device for avoidance even though not having to observe the HSR waiting period was the principal consideration in the choice of an LLC over a corporation. Parties are under no obligation to structure a transaction in a manner that necessarily triggers notification obligations. As long as this transaction results in a legitimate LLC and is not a sham, there would be no reason to treat this as a transaction or device for avoidance.

194 | Applicable provisions. 801.90, 801.11(c)(2).

Issue. Would delaying closing of a transaction until the size-of-person test is no longer satisfied be viewed as a transaction or device for avoidance?

Facts. A is planning to acquire in excess of $50 million (but less than $200 million) in assets from B, a $100 million person. A's most recent regularly prepared balance sheet shows $11 million in assets and its most recent annual statement of income shows $9 million in sales. A has prepared a draft of its next regularly prepared balance sheet that will be available to management for use in two months. That balance sheet will show $9 million in assets. A and B are currently scheduled to close in 30 days, but choose to delay the closing until A's next balance sheet is available.

Analysis. The PNO does not view this as a potential transaction or device for avoidance. The size-of-person test is a bright line test applied at the time of closing. Section 801.11(c)(2) indicates that where a person has a regularly prepared balance sheet, that person's total assets are as stated on such balance sheet. Postponing the closing date until a new regularly prepared balance sheet is available that would cause the transaction to fail the size-of-person test would not result in a violation of Section 801.90.

195 | Applicable provisions. 801.90, 801.11(b), 7A(a)(2).

Issue. Would a Section 801.90 problem arise where, shortly before it is to be acquired for more than $50 million (but less than $200 million) by a $100 million corporation, a $10 million corporation, aware of the size-of-person thresholds of the Act, declares an extraordinary (and accelerated) dividend that reduces its size below $10 million on its next regularly prepared balance sheet, which is prepared by the time of closing?

Analysis. The PNO does not view this as a potential transaction or device for avoidance. Section 7A(a)(2) of the Act establishes bright line size-of-person tests. Section 801.11(b)(2) instructs that the sales and assets of a person are to be determined by referring to clearly identified financial statements and further provide that those financial statements are to be prepared "in accordance with the accounting principles normally used by such person . . . ." If the financial statements have been regularly prepared in accordance with the person's normal accounting practices and show that the person does not satisfy the relevant size-of-person test, the transaction would not be reportable.

Editor's Note. *The PNO may look behind the financials based upon Section 801.90's proscription against devices for avoidance when certain factors indicate that the financial statements do not accurately reflect the person's size. But, so long as the dividend was actually distributed, the balance sheet would presumably accurately reflect the person's size. Thus, there should be no reason to implicate Section 801.90 on these facts.*

196 | Applicable provisions. 801.90, 801.1(b).

Issue. Would the following transaction, under which a seller wishes to sell certain assets to related purchasers, be treated as a single transaction or two separate transactions?

Facts. A seller wishes to transfer a plant and certain inventory to two related purchasers. The combined value of the plant and the inventory to be transferred exceeds $50 million. But the plant and the inventory are each separately valued at less than $50 million. The purchasers are separate corporations that are not controlled by any other entity. They are "related" in that they are jointly operated; both have the same chief executive officer and the same shareholders. One corporation is a manufacturer/wholesaler and the other is a retailer and they are not under common control as defined by the Rules. The transactions are negotiated at the same time by the same people.

Analysis. The PNO has taken the position that the transactions are separate. Consequently, neither transaction would satisfy the size-of-transaction test, since neither transaction would be valued in excess of $50 million. The PNO cited two factors for its position: (1) the structure of the purchasing corporations and the relationship between them predated contemplation of the transactions and were not created for purposes of avoiding HSR reporting obligations, and (2) there appeared to be a valid business reason for transferring the plant to the purchaser corporation engaged in manufacturing and the inventory to the purchaser engaged in retailing.

Editor's Note. The Rules establish several bright line tests for control of an entity under the Act. Applied to the facts presented, these tests result in each purchasing entity being part of a different person. The Rules do not require aggregation of acquisitions by entities under common de facto control when the control tests in the Rules are not satisfied. A detailed review of the application of Section 801.90 and many of the legal and policy issues it raises is contained in Malcolm R. Pfunder, Transactions or Devices for Avoidance of Premerger Notification Obligations: Toward an Administrable and Enforceable Interpretation of 16 C.F.R. § 801.90, *58 ANTITRUST L.J. 1031 (1990).*

INTERPRETATIONS RELATING TO PART 802 OF THE RULES

197 | Applicable provisions. 802.1, 802.4, 802.5.

Issue. Is the acquisition of real property by a REIT a reportable transaction?

Analysis. The acquisition of real property by a REIT is exempt. The longstanding position of the PNO is that a purchase by a REIT of any type of realty is exempt, no matter who the seller is or whether the realty would otherwise be exempted. A REIT is in the business of buying, owning, leasing, and selling real property, so any acquisition of real property by a REIT is in the ordinary course of the REIT's business and therefore exempt under Section 802.1. The SBP states that the "acquisition of all of the assets of a REIT by another REIT is currently an exempt transaction, even though the acquired REIT may hold certain non-real estate assets, and new Section 802.5 does not supersede this exemption." 61 Fed. Reg. 13,666, 13,683 (Mar. 28, 1996).

Note also that a REIT may acquire voting securities of another REIT regardless of the holdings of the acquired REIT without a reporting obligation. A non-REIT, however, acquiring voting securities of a REIT, must determine if the REIT has sufficient nonexempt assets to render the Section 802.4 exemption unavailable.

The so-called "REIT exemption" described above also may apply to an acquisition by an entity that intends to, but has not yet, qualified as a REIT. In one example, Purchaser, a recently formed corporation, intended to qualify as a REIT for federal income tax purposes, but was unable to make the federal tax election as a REIT until it had completed its first tax year. Nevertheless, a wholly owned subsidiary of Purchaser intended to purchase real property assets prior to Purchaser's federal tax election. Despite not having taken the requisite federal tax election, Purchaser had taken all appropriate steps to qualify as a REIT: the requisite REIT provisions were included in the corporation's articles of incorporation, it filed a registration statement with the SEC that states that it will be operated so as to qualify as a REIT, and it sought and received a tax opinion stating that it would qualify as a REIT. There was no reason to believe that it would not qualify as a REIT. In this circumstance, the PNO's position was that the ordinary course exemption for acquisitions of realty by REITs applied to its subsidiary's purchase.

| 198 | **Applicable provisions.** 802.1(a), 802.1(d).

Issue. Is the exemption provided by Section 802.1(d) available for the acquisition of goods that once may have qualified as an operating unit under Section 802.1(a), but have not been in operation for a significant period of time?

Facts. A purchaser intends to acquire assets that had been used by the seller to convert coal into natural gas, but had not been used by the seller in twenty years. The buyer intends to use the assets for the conversion of natural gas into electricity, and would need to make a substantial capital investment in order to do so.

Analysis. Although Section 802.1 is available to acquisitions of goods and realty in the ordinary course of business, it is not available where such goods and realty comprise an operating unit. The PNO's position, however, is that this transaction is eligible for the exemption provided by Section 802.1(d) for acquisitions of used durable goods transferred in the ordinary course of business. The PNO apparently found that the assets described were not an operating unit because: (1) the assets were not operating at the time of the purchase, had not been in operation for some time, and had generated no revenue in the preceding several years; (2) the assets could not be used without a substantial infusion of capital; and (3) the use to which the assets would be put by the purchaser was different than the seller's use – one converted coal to natural gas and the other intended to convert natural gas to electricity.

| 199 | **Applicable provisions.** 802.1(a), 802.1(d)(4), 802.4.

Issue. May the sale of voting securities of an issuer whose only asset is a computer system that solely provided internal management and administrative support be exempt as a sale of goods in the ordinary course?

Facts. The seller intends to transfer a computer system to a shell subsidiary, and the purchaser intends to acquire the voting securities of the subsidiary. The computer system had been used only for internal purposes, but did provide services to a previously sold subsidiary of the seller, at cost, for a startup period after its sale.

Analysis. The PNO's position is that the sale of the computer system would be reportable. If the acquisition of the computer system was structured simply as an asset acquisition, the transaction would be exempt under Section 802.1(d)(4) as the sale of used durable goods that had been used by the seller "*solely* to provide management and administrative support services for its business operations" (emphasis added). The sale of the stock of an entity that holds those same assets, however, would be reportable. While Section 802.1(d) is usually inapplicable to acquisitions of operating units, the SBP states that "[t]he transfer of goods that solely provide internal management and administrative support services does not constitute the acquisition of an operating unit." 61 Fed. Reg. 13,666, 13,673 (Mar. 28, 1996). The use of the computer system by the previously owned entity for a short time after its sale to a third party would not defeat the exemption because the computer services were used by the sold entity while it was part of the seller, and apparently were necessary to integrate the sold entity with its third-party purchaser. Since the arrangement was "at cost" for a short time frame the PNO did not view the arrangement as a sale of computer services to a third party. Therefore the "solely" requirement of Section 802.1(d)(4) would not be defeated.

Here, however, the relevant transaction is an acquisition of voting securities. While Section 802.4 exempts acquisitions of voting securities of issuers that hold certain assets, the direct acquisition of which would be exempt under specified rules or provisions of the Act, Section 802.1 is not included in Section 802.4. The PNO interprets Section 802.4 strictly and has not extended the exemption to cover an acquisition that would be exempt pursuant to Section 802.1 had it been structured as an asset acquisition. Consequently, this transaction is reportable under the Act.

200 | Applicable provisions. 802.2(c), 7A(c)(1).

Issue. Is the purchase of raw timberland exempt as an acquisition of unproductive real property?

Facts. The acquiring company agreed to buy 230,000 acres of raw timberland from the acquired company for a price of $85 million (in cash or like timberland). The timberland includes no income-producing manufacturing facilities, and the timberland is being purchased solely for the purpose of maintaining an inventory of raw timber to be used in the ordinary course of purchaser's business operations. Timber is the purchaser's primary raw material for its manufacturing operations, and the purchaser makes regular purchases of raw timberland in accordance with its business needs.

Analysis. The acquisition of unproductive real property, such as raw timberland, is exempt pursuant to Section 802.2(c). The inclusion of any assets in the transfer that are not considered unproductive under Section 802.2(c), however, must be analyzed as a separate potentially reportable acquisition. Any property that abuts nonexempt productive property also being acquired in the same transaction will be considered productive property and not exempt unless the property is physically separated from the productive property. *See* Section 802.2(c)(2)(iii). Physical separation of the productive and unproductive real property by a fence or road built by a common owner would not be sufficient to allow separate treatment of the unproductive real property. The productive and unproductive property must be separated by another legally distinct parcel of real property. *See* Int. 202.

201 | Applicable provision. 802.2(c).

Issue. May a former manufacturing plant be "unproductive real property," the acquisition of which is exempt from HSR filing requirements?

Facts. The property was originally used as a manufacturing plant. But prior to the sale, seller removed all machinery and other equipment specific to the manufacturing operations, and now intends to sell the stripped-down factory.

Analysis. The PNO's position is that the stripped-down factory qualifies as "unproductive real property," the acquisition of which is exempt under Section 802.2(c). Section 802.2(c)(i) defines "unproductive real property" as "any real property, including raw land, structures or other improvements (but excluding equipment) . . . that has not generated total revenues in excess of $5 million during the thirty-six (36) months preceding the acquisition." To the extent the factory generated revenues in the preceding thirty-six months, the PNO apparently attributed such revenues not to the factory structure and raw land but to the machinery and other equipment that had been removed. Thus, the remaining property would be "unproductive." The sale of the plant's equipment and machinery to a third party may be separately reportable if all of the jurisdictional tests are met and an exemption is not otherwise available.

| 202 | **Applicable provision.** 802.2(c).

Issue. Must one aggregate the revenue from several distinct parcels of timberland in determining whether the revenue limits of the exemption for unproductive real property under Section 802.2(c) have been exceeded?

Facts. The seller, a paper company, intends to sell several different parcels of timber to the purchaser. The seller has harvested trees on the parcels to produce pulp for its papermaking business.

Analysis. Section 802.2(c)(1) exempts the sale of unproductive real property that has not generated total revenues in excess of $5 million during the thirty-six month period preceding the acquisition. The revenues of different parcels need not be aggregated if they are not contiguous. To qualify as separate parcels, however, there must be distinct, physical separation between parcels. If any to-be-sold parcels abut, the sales of abutting parcels must be aggregated. *See* Int. 200.

| 203 | **Applicable provisions.** 802.2(c)(1), 802.2(c)(2)(ii).

Issue. May real property that previously contained productive assets be considered unproductive real property where the productive assets have been demolished and/or diminished significantly in terms of productive revenue?

Facts. Buyer plans to purchase forty-eight acres of urban real property for development. Sometime prior to the sale, the property contained railroad tracks, warehouses and parking lots. However, the railroad tracks have been removed and the warehouses have been demolished. The parking lots have been leased to a third party, but lease payments to the seller have aggregated less than $300,000 over the previous three years, and a de minimis amount in the previous twelve months. The railroad tracks have not generated any revenues in the previous three years.

Analysis. The acquisition of the parcel was determined to be exempt as an acquisition of unproductive real property under Section 802.2(c)(1) because it had not generated revenues in excess of $5 million in the preceding thirty-six months. Section 802.2(c)(2)(ii) denies an exemption for "non-manufacturing facilities that were in operation at any time during the twelve (12) months preceding the acquisition." Although the parking lots had generated nominal revenue in the twelve months prior to the sale, the PNO apparently viewed the vacant land and blacktop parking lots as insufficiently "improved" to constitute a "non-manufacturing facility" under Section 802.2(c)(2)(ii).

204 | Applicable provisions. 802.2(d), 802.2(e), 802.5.

Issue. Does the exemption for transfers of residential property apply to transfers of (a) timeshare facilities or (b) trailer parks where the trailers themselves were owned and would continue to be owned by the residents, not the trailer park owner/manager?

Analysis. The PNO's position is that the acquisition of timeshare facilities is exempt under either (1) Section 802.2(d) as an acquisition of "residential properties" or (2) Section 802.2(e) as an acquisition of a hotel. The units are owned by individuals and are used as secondary residences therefore triggering Section 802.2(d). Alternatively, although the ownership structure is different, the PNO reasoned that *use* of the timeshare resembles hotel residency and hotel acquisitions are explicitly exempt under Section 802.2(e). The trailer park property is also residential, and therefore its acquisition is exempt under Section 802.2(d). An alternative exemption might also be available in certain circumstances under Section 802.5, which exempts investment real property assets. This exemption would be available only if (a) the seller has been leasing its parcels of real estate to the trailer home owners, and (b) the buyer intends to continue to lease to those (or similar) trailer home owners. Any goodwill associated with the residential property being sold is an exempt asset so long as it is associated only with the exempt realty assets. If the residential property being sold includes nonexempt assets, such as, for example, a property management business that manages property other than the residential property being sold, then the total value of the related goodwill would have to be allocated between the exempt and nonexempt assets and added to the value of the nonexempt assets to determine whether the size-of-transaction test is satisfied.

205 | Applicable provision. 802.2(d).

Issue. Does an acquisition of an assisted living facility qualify as an acquisition of exempt residential property?

Facts. A seller intends to transfer a facility that houses seniors who live independently. The residents, however, also receive varying degrees of medical assistance, up to and including nursing care.

Analysis. An acquisition of a nursing home is not exempt as an acquisition of "residential property." The transfer of a "senior residence" where the residents truly live independently and are not provided with medical services would be exempt under Section 802.2(d) as a transfer of residential property. But where some or all of the facility's residents are provided special medical services, including nursing care, from the facility's assets, the buyer must determine the fair market value of the assets attributed to medical care and must file if the fair market value of the medical assets exceeds the HSR size-of-transaction threshold.

| 206 | **Applicable provisions.** 802.2, 802.4, 801.15.

Issue. Must one aggregate previous exempt acquisitions from the same ultimate parent (although not the same issuer) in determining whether the Section 802.4(a) threshold for nonexempt holdings has been exceeded?

Facts. Company A purchased minority shares of a subsidiary of Company B (Sub B-1) for more than $50 million, but determined that the acquisition was exempt under Section 802.4 since Sub B-1's assets consisted of realty the direct acquisition of which would be exempt under Section 802.2. Later, Company A acquired minority shares of Sub B-2 (another subsidiary of Company B) for less than $50 million. Sub B-2 held nonexempt realty assets (as determined under Section 802.2) valued in excess of $50 million.

Analysis. The PNO determined that Company A held the shares of Sub B-1 for purposes of analyzing the acquisition of the Sub B-2 shares. Section 801.15 governs whether an acquiring person must aggregate prior exempt acquisitions with the subject acquisition for purposes of determining whether the size-of-transaction test is satisfied. Section 802.4 is listed in Section 801.15(b) as one of the categories of prior acquisitions that need not be aggregated with the current acquisition as long as the limitations set forth for prior exemption are not exceeded as a result of the current acquisition. If such limitations would be exceeded, the prior acquisition must be aggregated with the current acquisition. Thus, Company A must determine if the limitation in Section 802.4 ($50 million in nonexempt assets) is being exceeded as a result of the subsequent acquisition of Sub B-2 stock. Because that limitation would be exceeded in this case, the Sub B-1 stock is deemed to be held as a result of the acquisition and must be aggregated with the Sub B-2 stock acquired for purposes of the size-of-transaction threshold for the Sub B-2 acquisition. Section 802.4(b) states specifically that, for purposes of this exemption, "issuer" means a single issuer or two or more issuers controlled by the same acquired person.

207 Applicable provisions. 802.2(e), 802.4.

Issue. Where a purchaser intends to acquire an entity that owns three hotels, one with a casino and two without casinos, may the parties exclude the hotels without casinos in determining whether the size-of-transaction test is satisfied?

Facts. Purchaser intends to buy all of the voting securities of a seller whose assets consist of a hotel with a casino, and two other hotels without casinos. The fair market value of the hotel with the casino is below the HSR minimum transaction size. The value of the seller's voting securities, however, is above the minimum transaction size.

Analysis. The PNO's position is that the transaction is exempt under Section 802.4. Section 802.4 exempts the acquisition of voting securities of an issuer whose assets, together with those of all entities it controls, consist of assets the direct acquisition of which would be exempt under Section 802.2, where the fair market value of the remaining nonexempt assets of the issuer does not exceed $50 million. Here, the hotel with the casino is a nonexempt asset, while the hotels without casinos are exempt assets under Section 802.2(e). Accordingly, because the value of the nonexempt asset (the hotel with the casino) is less than $50 million, the transaction is exempt from reporting obligations under Section 802.4.

208 | Applicable provisions. 802.2(e), 802.5.

Issue. Is the acquisition of a hotel/casino exempt under Section 802.2(e) or Section 802.5 where the current owner leases the casino portion of the hotel to a third party to operate?

Facts. The current owner of the hotel leases the casino areas of the hotel to a third party (unaffiliated with the purchaser) that owns all of the gambling equipment and holds the gaming license to operate such casino rooms from state authorities. The purchaser of the hotel/casino intends to continue the same arrangement with the third party.

Analysis. The PNO's position is that the acquisition is exempt under Section 802.5, which exempts acquisitions of investment rental property assets. Under Section 802.5(b), investment rental property assets are real property assets "that will not be rented to entities included within the acquiring person except for the sole purpose of maintaining, managing or supervising the operation of the real property, and will be held solely for rental or investment purposes." Because the purchaser will continue to lease the casino area to the same person for the operation of the gambling activities in the hotel, the terms of Section 802.5 would be met. Hotels with casinos are specifically *not* exempt assets under Section 802.2(e)(2). But, here, the PNO takes the position that because the acquisition of the casino is itself exempt, it will permit the parties to use the Section 802.3(e)(1) exemption for the hotel. If the buyer were to hold the casino in a manner other than for rental or investment purposes, the transaction would not be exempt.

209 | Applicable provisions. 802.2(e), 802.4, 802.50, 802.51.

Issue. Is the acquisition by a foreign person of 100 percent of the voting securities of a foreign issuer exempt from notification requirements where the acquired foreign issuer has two assets: (1) a manufacturing plant located outside the United States, valued at $60 million, with no sales in or into the United States; and (2) a hotel in the United States valued at $60 million?

Analysis. The transaction is reportable. On its own, an acquisition by a foreign person of the stock of a foreign issuer that only holds a foreign manufacturing facility with no sales in or into the United States would be exempt under Section 802.51(b). Further, on its own, an acquisition of a hotel would be exempt under Section 802.2(e), and the acquisition of voting securities of an issuer that holds only a hotel would also be exempt under Section 802.4. However, in this case, the foreign issuer's holdings include the hotel, an asset within the United States having an aggregate value greater than $50 million (thereby taking the transaction outside the limits of Section 802.51), as well as the foreign manufacturing plant, an asset having an aggregate value greater than $50 million, that does not qualify for the Section 802.4 exemption.

Section 802.4, which provides an exemption for the acquisition of voting securities of an entity that holds assets, the direct acquisition of which would be exempt, specifically delineates the categories of assets that are treated as exempt for purposes of that exemption. Significantly, Section 802.4 does not include Section 802.50 or Section 802.51 in its list of relevant exemptions. Thus, Section 802.4 does not exempt the acquisition of voting securities of issuers with foreign assets valued in excess of $50 million even if the direct acquisition of those assets would be exempt. Notwithstanding that the direct acquisition of the foreign manufacturing facilities would be exempt under Section 802.50 and the acquisition of the voting securities of the foreign issuer would be exempt under Section 802.51, but for its ownership of the U.S. hotel, the PNO's position is that the acquisition by a foreign person of voting securities of a foreign issuer is not exempt where the acquired issuer holds more than $50 million of assets in the United States even if the direct acquisition of such assets would be exempt under Section 802.2(e) because Section 802.51 does not distinguish between exempt and nonexempt U.S. assets. *See also* Ints. 213, 243.

Editor's Note. *Because Section 802.4 does not reference all rules that could exempt the direct acquisition of assets, there may be circumstances, such as the hypothetical discussed here, where a transaction may be reportable if structured as an acquisition of voting securities but nonreportable if structured as an asset acquisition.* See also *Int. 213*.

| 210 | **Applicable provisions.** 802.2(e), 802.2(f).

Issue. Is the transfer of two hotels, including restaurants, a golf course with a pro shop and restaurant, and a campground exempt from notification?

Analysis. Whether the transaction is exempt would depend upon the value of the campground and its facilities. The acquisition of the hotels is exempt under Section 802.2(e). This exemption would apply to the acquisition of the hotels and hotel "improvements such as golf, swimming, tennis, restaurant, health club or parking facilities." The golf course also is independently exempt under the Section 802.2(f) exemption for recreational land "used primarily as a golf course or swimming or tennis club facility, and assets incidental to the ownership of such property." The acquisition of the campground and its related facilities, however, is not exempt, and that portion of the transaction must be separately valued by the purchaser to determine whether it meets the size-of-transaction test.

211 | Applicable provision. 802.3.

Issue. Is the exemption for certain acquisitions of carbon-based mineral reserves under Section 802.3 available for the acquisition of methane gas reserves and related long-term sale contracts?

Facts. The purchaser intends to acquire methane gas reserves and rights to such reserves. The methane gas was generated by coal deposits. The purchaser would also acquire long-term contracts to sell the processed methane to third party resellers.

Analysis. The sale is exempt as long as the value of the exempt category of assets (methane reserves and associated production assets) is less than $500 million. Section 802.3(a) exempts "[a]n acquisition of reserves of oil, natural gas, shale or tar sands, or rights to reserves of oil, natural gas, shale or tar sands together with associated exploration or production assets" but only if their value does not exceed $500 million. Section 802.3(c) defines "associated exploration or production assets." The PNO has determined that the definition is broad enough to include the long-term sale contracts as long as those contracts are being acquired by the purchaser in connection with its acquisition of the methane gas reserves. A transfer of the sale contracts alone would not be exempted by Section 802.3, and would be reportable if the jurisdictional tests were met and no other exemptions were available. Note that the long-term contracts may not have any value unless a premium is being paid for their acquisition. *See* Int. 183. The PNO has provided similar advice with respect to methane gas reserves generated by landfills.

| 212 | **Applicable provisions.** 802.4, 802.3(a), 7A(c)(2).

Issue. Where an acquiring person acquires an issuer that holds cash, and the cash was generated solely from the sale of exempt assets or the operation of an exempt business, may the value of the cash be excluded from the value of the nonexempt assets?

Analysis. Section 802.4 exempts the acquisition of voting securities of an issuer if the acquired issuer and all the entities that it controls do not hold nonexempt assets valued in excess of $50 million. The PNO has determined that cash is an exempt asset under Section 802.4 if it has a close nexus to assets exempted by the sections referenced in Section 802.4. The PNO has determined that cash was an exempt asset in the following circumstances:

1. Where a person acquires the voting stock of a petroleum company, the cash and accounts receivable from the sale of the crude oil or natural gas produced from the reserves now being sold is considered to constitute "associated exploration or production assets" within the meaning of Section 802.3(c). Therefore, their value counts toward the $500 million limit of the exemption. *See* Section 802.3(a); and

2. Where a person acquires an issuer that has cash on hand and the right to receive future cash payments from a minority interest it holds in a trust, and that trust holds only mortgage loans and mortgages, the cash derived from the issuer's interest in the mortgage business is an exempt asset. *See* Section 7A(c)(2).

Cash from other sources (for example the sale of a nonexempt asset) is not an exempt asset under Section 802.4 and would be included in determining whether the issuer has sufficient nonexempt assets to require a filing.

Editor's Note. *The PNO applies the principle underlying this interpretation to other assets that are closely related to an exempt business, e.g., receivables, prepaid taxes.*

213 | Applicable provisions. 802.4, 802.51.

Issue. Is an acquisition of all of the voting securities of a U.S. issuer exempt under Section 802.4 where the issuer's only asset is 100 percent of the voting securities of a foreign issuer whose direct acquisition would be exempt under Section 802.51?

Analysis. Section 802.51 exempts the acquisition of voting securities of a foreign issuer if it does not have at least a certain level of contact with the United States (assets in the United States valued in excess of $50 million, or sales in or into the United States of over $50 million in its last fiscal year). Section 802.4 exempts the acquisition of voting securities of the issuer if the direct acquisition of the issuer's assets would be exempt, but only if the acquisition of such assets would be exempt under Section 7A(c)(2) of the Act (relating to bonds, mortgages, and certain other nonvoting securities or instruments), Section 802.2 (relating to certain acquisitions of real property assets), Section 802.3 (relating to certain acquisitions of carbon-based mineral reserves), or Section 802.5 (relating to certain acquisitions of investment real property assets). Because Section 802.51 is not included in Section 802.4, the above described acquisition would not be exempted by Section 802.4. *See also* Int. 209.

| 214 | **Applicable provisions.** 802.4, 801.4.

Issue. In an acquisition of all of the voting securities of an issuer, how are the acquired issuer's noncontrolling interests in various types of entities treated in determining whether the $50 million limitation for nonexempt assets has been exceeded under Section 802.4 when acquiring voting stock of the primary issuer?

Analysis. The PNO's position is that the value of noncontrolling interests in other entities should not be included when valuing nonexempt assets for purposes of Section 802.4. Any noncontrolling interest in a corporation would be analyzed separately as a "secondary acquisition" (defined under Section 801.4) and would be separately reportable if it met the statutory thresholds on its own. Any interest in a noncorporate entity whose indirect acquisition resulted in the acquiring person holding 100 percent of that entity also would be separately reportable if it satisfied the jurisdictional thresholds.

| 215 | **Applicable provisions.** 802.4(c), 801.10(c)(3), 802.50, 802.51.

Issue. Where the purchaser is acquiring a voting stock interest in the acquired person but does not have access to the acquired person's books and records, how may it make the determination whether the issuer has sufficient nonexempt assets to require a filing?

Analysis. Section 802.4 exempts the acquisition of voting securities of an issuer if the acquired issuer and all the entities that it controls do not hold nonexempt assets greater than the minimum transaction size. The acquiring person's board of directors, or its designee, must determine the fair market value of the nonexempt assets in order to determine whether there are sufficient nonexempt assets to exceed the $50 million limitation in Section 802.4. In doing so, the PNO has advised that the acquiring person may designate the acquired person's board of directors as the entity to which the fair market value determination has been delegated under Section 801.10(c)(3).

If the purchaser has a relationship with the seller that would make such an arrangement impossible (i.e., a hostile tender offer), it should file notification and advise the PNO of the situation. The PNO will make the determination once the seller's filing is received. If the transaction is deemed to be nonreportable, the parties will be notified and the filing fee will be refunded. The same procedure should be used if a purchaser is unable to determine whether an acquisition is exempt under Section 802.50 or 802.51.

216 | Applicable provision. 802.5.

Issue. Is the acquisition of a realty management company by a REIT a reportable transaction?

Analysis. If the realty management company manages only property presently held by the REIT (or only property to be acquired by the REIT together with the acquisition of the realty management company), then the purchase of such management assets or voting securities are exempt from reporting as incidental to the real property held or being acquired. If the management activities involve (in whole or in part) realty not held (or to be held) by the acquiring REIT, Section 802.5 will not exempt that portion of the voting securities or assets that is devoted to the management of third party realty, and such assets or voting securities must be separately valued to determine if the size-of-transaction test is satisfied.

217 | Applicable provision. 802.5.

Issue. How is the Section 802.5 exemption applied for acquisitions of investment rental property where a portion of the property is currently used by the seller, rather than rented or leased to third parties?

Facts. Purchaser intends to purchase from seller four transmission towers (each with a fair market value of $20 million) for total purchase price of $80 million. Purchaser plans to lease all of the space on the towers to unaffiliated third parties for transmission of broadcast signals. Seller currently leases one-half of the capacity on each of the towers to third parties, but uses the remaining tower capacity for its own transmission purposes.

Analysis. Where a portion of the assets involved in a transaction are currently used by the seller (or when the buyer intends to use a portion of the assets itself), the PNO applies a two-prong analysis to determine what percentage of the assets will qualify for the investment rental property exemption set forth in Section 802.5.

The first prong of the analysis focuses on the current use of the assets. The PNO's position is that only that portion of the assets that currently meets the definition of investment rental property in the hands of the seller is eligible for the exemption. Section 802.5 sets out four examples of "investment rental property": "(1) Property currently rented, (2) Property held for rent but not currently rented, (3) Common areas on the property, and (4) Assets incidental to the ownership of property, which may include cash, prepaid taxes or insurance, rental receivables and the like." In the facts set forth above, only half the towers' capacity is eligible for the Section 802.5 exemption. Therefore, the other half (which we will assume for simplicity has a fair market value of $40 million) will not qualify for the Section 802.5 exemption.

The second prong of the analysis focuses on the intended use of the assets by the buyer. Section 802.5(b) states: "'Investment rental property assets' means real property that will not be rented to entities included within the acquiring person . . . and will be held solely for rental or investment purposes." Thus, if the buyer intends to use some or all of the acquired assets for itself, that portion of the assets will not qualify as "investment rental property assets" under the second prong of the analysis. Since the buyer is going to lease all of the capacity on the towers it is acquiring from the seller to third parties unaffiliated with the buyer, one hundred percent of the assets will qualify under the second prong.

Only the smaller of the percentage of assets under the two prongs of the analysis will qualify for the Section 802.5 exemption. Since one-half of the tower assets are eligible for the Section 802.5 exemption under the first prong, and all of the assets qualify under prong two, one-half of the assets will qualify for the exemption and the other half (with a fair market value of $40 million) will not. Since the value of the nonexempt portion of the assets is less than the $50 million size-of-transaction threshold, no HSR filing will be required. (Note that because the seller is unaffiliated with the buyer, it would not affect the analysis if the buyer leased space back to the seller.)

The HSR outcome does not change if the facts are changed so that the buyer will lease only half of the tower capacity and use the rest for itself. In that case, one-half of the assets qualified for the exemption under the first prong and one-half qualifies under the second prong. Thus, one-half of the assets will qualify for the exemption and the nonexempt portion of the transaction still has a fair market value of only $40 million.

If, however, the buyer decides to use three-quarters of the towers' capacity for itself and lease out only one-quarter, an HSR filing will be required (assuming other HSR thresholds are met and no other HSR exemption applies). Although one-half of the transmission towers' value is eligible for the Section 802.5 exemption under the first prong, only one quarter (or $20 million of value) is eligible for the Section 802.5 exemption under the second prong. Since only the smaller amount under the two prongs of the analysis qualifies for the exemption, only assets with a fair market value of $20 million will be eligible for the exemption. This leaves $60 million worth of assets not eligible for the exemption, and this amount exceeds the HSR size-of-transaction threshold.

Finally, if we assume the buyer intended to use all of the tower capacity itself instead of leasing the tower space to third parties, none of the assets would qualify for the Section 802.5 exemption under the second prong of the test and whatever the percentage calculated under the first prong, none of the assets will qualify for the exemption. Similarly, if the seller were currently using all of the tower capacity itself instead of just half, none of the assets would qualify for the Section 802.5 exemption under the first prong of the test and whatever the buyer's intent, none of the assets will qualify for the exemption.

Note that the PNO does not require that the exact same portion of a single asset qualify as the "investment rental property" asset in the hands of both the buyer and the seller. For example, if the seller currently leases one-half of the capacity of a transmission tower to third parties and the buyer also plans to lease one-half of the capacity of the tower to third parties, the PNO will not insist that the one-half to be leased by the buyer be the exact same portion as that leased by the seller to qualify for the exemption. The PNO will just use percentages. However, if there are separately identifiable assets, the PNO will do the analysis independently for each asset. So, for example, if there are two separate transmission towers involved in the transaction and seller currently uses tower A, and leases tower B, while buyer plans to use tower B and lease tower A, when you work through the two prongs of the analysis for each of the assets separately, neither asset will qualify for the Section 802.5 exemption.

Editor's Note. *The application of this rule seems overly complicated. A focus on the buyer's intent alone would probably permit the agencies to receive notice of all necessary transactions.*

218 | Applicable provisions. 802.5, 802.2(h).

Issue. Is the Section 802.5 exemption available when one mini-warehouse business buys another?

Facts. The buyer and seller are both in the business of leasing "mini-warehouse" space to consumers for temporary storage. Seller would exit the business as a result of the sale. Buyer intends to continue to rent space to existing and future customers of the mini-warehouse business.

Analysis. The transaction met all of the criteria of Section 802.5, which exempts acquisitions of investment rental property and is, therefore, exempt. The acquired property was held for rent (and currently rented) and will be rented by the buyer to persons or entities not included within the buyer's ultimate parent. Unlike Section 802.2(h), the Section 802.5 exemption is available even when all of an operating unit is acquired.

219 Applicable provisions. 802.21, 801.90, 801.1(h).

Issue. After expiration of a fifteen-day waiting period for a cash tender offer, may the offeror immediately take advantage of the provisions of Section 802.21 and purchase shares other than through a tender offer (e.g., on the open market) up to the next Section 801.1(h) reporting threshold above that for which the tender offer notification was filed?

Analysis. The offeror may make such acquisitions. Once the cash tender offer waiting period has expired, purchases by any mechanism up to the next notification threshold can be made without any additional filing or waiting period. There is some risk of a Section 801.90 violation, however, if a transaction is structured as a tender offer merely to get a fifteen-day waiting period but the acquiring person has no actual intention of making the acquisition in that manner.

Editor's Note. Given the significant obligations imposed by the U.S. securities laws in the cash tender offer context, as well as the requirement of the Act that a cash tender offer be publicly announced, it seems unlikely that an acquiring person would actually engage in a specious cash tender offer merely to gain the benefit of a shorter waiting period.

220 | Applicable provisions. 802.21, 803.7.

Issue. May an acquiring person refile for the same notification threshold that it has previously crossed and obtain the Section 802.21 five-year exemption from refiling requirements, running from the expiration or termination of the refiled HSR, even if the acquiring person does not in fact make an additional acquisition within the next twelve months?

Facts. Where a company's savings plan filed notification as an acquiring person five years ago for its acquisition of $200 million of the issuer's outstanding voting securities, and the $100 million threshold was crossed within one year thereafter, may it now obtain another five-year exemption by filing notification for the same $100 million threshold, even if its holdings of the issuer's voting securities already exceed that threshold?

Analysis. The PNO confirmed that the acquiring person may renew its five-year Section 802.21 exemption by filing notification for the $100 million threshold. Under Section 802.21, having once reached that level of holdings, an acquiring person may refile for the same $100 million threshold to obtain the ability to recross the $100 million threshold for another five years, regardless of whether it expects to cross that threshold again within the next twelve months. The Section 802.21 five-year exemption applies to the new notification if either (1) the threshold for which notification is filed is reached or exceeded (without reaching the next threshold) within twelve months thereafter or (2) that threshold has already been reached or exceeded at the time the new notification is filed.

Section 803.7 in effect causes an acquiring person's notification to "expire" one year after the end of the waiting period, if during that time the person does not "meet or exceed the notification threshold with respect to which the notification was filed." In this case the acquiring person was concerned that, in renewing its notification after the five-year exemption provided in Section 802.21, it might be required to file notification at the next higher (i.e., $500 million) threshold and reach that level within the next twelve months, or else have to file notifications annually until it did so. The PNO said that Section 803.7 does not impose such a requirement.

Interpretations Relating to Part 802 271

221 | Applicable provision. 802.21(b).

Issue. Does the Section 802.21 transition rule, which reconciles the pre-2001 notification thresholds with the thresholds established in 2001, exempt the following transaction?

Facts. A filing for an acquisition of voting securities of B indicated that it intended to exceed the 25 percent notification threshold. The waiting period expired on July 1, 1999. In the year following expiration of the waiting period, A acquired 20 percent of B's voting securities, valued at $75 million. In December of 2003, A intends to acquire additional voting stock of B that will result in it holding 24 percent of the voting securities of B, valued at $110 million.

Analysis. A will not be required to make a filing in connection with its December 2003 acquisition. Under Section 802.21(b), A has five years from the expiration of the original waiting period (until July 1, 2004) to acquire up to the next highest notification threshold, above that which it met or exceeded during the year following expiration of the waiting period, without refiling, even if in doing so it exceeds one or more of the notification thresholds established in 2001. In this instance, A exceeded the 15 percent notification threshold in the first year (note that the fact that it indicated the 25 percent notification threshold in it filing is irrelevant to this analysis as it will be deemed to have crossed the highest relevant threshold that it in fact crossed within one year of HSR clearance). Thus, it has five years from the end of the waiting period to acquire up to 25 percent of B's voting securities (the next highest notification threshold under the pre-2001 rules) without triggering notification requirements, even though in doing so it will exceed the $50 million and $100 million notification thresholds established in 2001. If A intends to acquire additional shares of B that will result in it meeting or exceeding 25 percent, it must file notification at the appropriate dollar notification threshold (under the thresholds established in 2001), even if the five-year period has not expired, prior to making the acquisition.

222 | Applicable provision. 802.21(b).

Issue. Does the Section 802.21 transition rule, which reconciles the pre-2001 notification thresholds with the thresholds established in 2001, exempt the following transaction?

Facts. A filed notification for an acquisition of voting securities of B indicating that it intended to exceed the 25 percent notification threshold. The waiting period expired on February 28, 1997. In the year following expiration of the waiting period, A acquired 26 percent of B's voting securities, valued at $125 million. In December of 2003, A will acquire additional voting stock of B that will result in it holding 27 percent of the voting securities of B, valued at $130 million.

Analysis. A will be required to make a filing in connection with its December 2003 acquisition. Since the five-year period following expiration of the waiting period will have expired, the Section 802.21(b) exemption will no longer be available. The Section 802.21(a) exemption will also not be available. Notwithstanding the fact that A currently holds sufficient voting securities of B to exceed the $100 million notification threshold, since A has never filed to exceed the $100 million notification threshold (under the thresholds established in 2001) it cannot acquire any additional stock of B without a filing. Therefore, A must file notification at the $100 million notification threshold and observe a waiting period prior to making the December 2003 acquisition.

Interpretations Relating to Part 802 273

| 223 | **Applicable provisions.** 802.21, 801.4, 802.10, 7A(c)(3), 7A(c)(10), 802.30, 801.1(b), 801.1(c).

Issue. Whether another HSR filing must be made when an acquiring person purchases directly the voting securities of an acquired person that previously was the subject of a secondary acquisition filing by the acquiring person.

Facts. Three years earlier, the acquiring person, Company X, had filed to acquire 50 percent of the voting securities of Company A. Because the sole asset of Company A was 49.9 percent of the voting securities of Company B, Company X also filed, at the 25 percent threshold, for a secondary acquisition of the B shares held by A. Both A and B filed as acquired persons, the waiting periods expired, and the transaction consummated. As part of a restructuring, Company X now proposed to sell its 50 percent interest in A to A's other 50 percent shareholder, Company Y, in exchange for a direct 25 percent interest in B, currently held by Company Y.

Analysis. The PNO indicated that the sale by Company X of the 50 percent interest in A was exempt as an intraperson transaction under Section 7A(c)(3), (although not under Section 802.30), since Company Y already held 50 percent of the voting securities of A, although not under Section 802.30) and that the acquisition of the direct 25 percent interest in B was exempt under Section 802.21. Under Section 802.21, an acquisition of voting securities of an issuer is exempt if: (1) notification was filed with respect to an earlier acquisition of voting securities of the same issuer, (2) the new acquisition occurs within five years of the expiration or termination of the earlier waiting period, and (3) the acquisition will not increase the holdings of the acquiring person to meet or exceed the next notification threshold. Here, because Company X previously had filed notification for the secondary acquisition of B stock, the direct acquisition of the additional voting securities of B was an acquisition of securities "of the same issuer." Thus, as long as the transaction was completed within five years of the expiration of the waiting period for the earlier filing, and Company X did not meet or exceed the 50 percent threshold as a result of the acquisition, the transaction would be exempt from notification.

The PNO opined that the direct acquisition of B stock also would be exempt under Section 7A(c)(10) and Section 802.10. Under this reasoning, the shares of A, conferring control over the voting of 49.9 percent of B's securities, would be exchanged for shares of B conferring only 25 percent of the voting power of B (therefore not yielding an increase in the acquiring person's per cent share of outstanding voting securities of the issuer B). Having stated that Section 802.10 is not confined exclusively to stock splits and *pro rata* stock dividends, the PNO confirmed the application of Section 802.10 under these facts, since the acquiring person is deemed to hold the shares of B held by A pursuant to Sections 801.1(b) and (c), and because an entity holds the shares held by an entity that it controls.

224 | Applicable provisions. 802.23, 801.30, 803.5, 7A(e)(2), Item 6.

Issue. When a filing is made for a nontender offer transaction, otherwise subject to Section 801.30, and the acquiring person thereafter makes a cash tender offer during the waiting period, what steps must be taken to get tender offer treatment?

Analysis. In this situation, where the only change in the transaction is a switch from a standard Section 801.30 transaction to a Section 801.30 cash tender offer, the PNO will allow, though does not require, the acquiring party to amend its original filing, but it will be subject to a new fifteen-day waiting period, commencing upon the filing by the acquiring person of the amended notification. If an amended filing of this type is authorized by the PNO, no new filing fee is required. The PNO, however, requires (1) a new affidavit attesting that the acquired person has received notice of the tender offer pursuant to Section 803.5(b), (2) a revised description of the acquisition, (3) any new Item 4(c) documents, (4) any newly prepared financials, and (5) a new certification page.

When a Second Request is issued in a nontender offer Section 801.30 transaction, the target company must comply with a request issued to it in order to restart the waiting period. Section 7A(e)(2). In some instances of hostile open-market purchases, once a Second Request is issued, the acquiring person determines that, due to the target's refusal to comply with the request on an expeditious basis, it is necessary to make a tender offer in order to get the waiting period running again. In the context of a cash tender offer, only the acquiring person must comply with a Second Request to restart the waiting period. The PNO requires that the acquiring person make a new or amended filing and observe a new initial waiting period (fifteen days in the case of a cash tender offer) to get tender offer treatment. In addition, the acquired party must amend its filing to reflect any changes in its original filing as a result of the amended transaction. An additional filing fee is not required of either party. But this procedure also allows the agency to revise the original Second Request before reissuing it.

Editor's Note. Although the PNO requires the acquiring person to amend certain items on the form, there is no obligation to amend revenue disclosure if a more recent year's revenue becomes available since the original notification was submitted. Moreover, there is no obligation to update the Item 6 disclosure with respect to subsidiary lists, significant shareholders, or minority holdings.

225 | Applicable provision. 802.23.

Issue. Does Section 802.23, which provides an exemption from filing a new notification in certain circumstances where a tender offer is amended or renewed, apply where, following notification by the acquiring person with respect to a tender offer but prior to expiration of the waiting period, the parties agree to a friendly merger and the tender offer is suspended?

Analysis. Section 802.23 does not apply to this situation since the transaction does not involve an "amended or renewed" tender offer. Consequently, both the acquiring and acquired persons must amend their original filings to reflect the new structure of the proposed transaction. The PNO requires the acquiring person to file (1) a new affidavit that states the changed terms of the transaction, (2) a new description of the acquisition, (3) any new Item 4(c) documents, (4) any newly prepared financials, and (5) a new certification page. In addition, the acquired person under the original filing must amend its filing to reflect any changes in its original filing as a result of the amended transaction. The new (thirty day) waiting period commences when the amended filings have been received from both parties.

Significantly, if in the above question the waiting period had already expired following receipt of notifications with respect to the original tender offer, no new filing or amendment would be required. *See* Int. 265.

Editor's Note. *Although the PNO requires the acquiring person to amend certain items on the form, there is no obligation to amend revenue disclosures if a more recent year's revenue becomes available since the original notification was submitted. Moreover, there is no obligation to update the Item 6 disclosure with respect to subsidiary lists, significant shareholders or minority holdings.*

| 226 | **Applicable provision.** 802.30.

Issue. Is an entity's acquisition of assets from one of its two ultimate parent entities exempt as an intraperson transaction?

Analysis. Because the acquiring entity has two ultimate parents, this transaction involves two distinct acquisitions by two distinct acquiring persons, each of which must be analyzed separately. If an ultimate parent of the acquiring entity controls the acquiring entity as a result of the holding of voting securities, such an acquisition would be exempt pursuant to Section 802.30 as to an ultimate parent that is both the buyer and the seller; the same acquisition, however, may be reportable by the ultimate parent of the acquiring entity that is not the seller. Thus, even where two shareholders each hold 50 percent of the voting securities of an issuer, the intraperson transaction exemption may nevertheless not be available to all aspects of the transaction.

An entity may have more than one ultimate parent for several reasons. A corporation may have two shareholders with equal voting rights or one shareholder who has 50 percent or more of the corporation's voting securities and another person who has the contractual power presently to designate 50 percent or more of the corporation's directors. Partnership and LLC interests also may be divided so that more than one person is deemed to have control. The intraperson transaction exemption of Section 802.30 is available only where control is the result of holdings of voting securities. Therefore, the intraperson exemption is not available for transactions between a partnership and a controlling partner, between an LLC and a controlling member, or between a corporation, and a person who controls that corporation by virtue of a contractual power to elect or appoint 50 percent or more of the board (unless the contractual power is embodied in the voting securities). *See* Int. 228.

227 Applicable provisions. 802.30, 801.40.

Issue. Is the formation of a wholly owned subsidiary by a corporation that has two equal shareholders reportable under Section 801.40 or exempt under Section 802.30?

Facts and Analysis. A corporation with two 50 percent shareholders has two ultimate parent entities. Its formation of a wholly owned subsidiary is the formation of a new corporation subject to analysis under Section 801.40. Typically, the formation of a new, wholly owned subsidiary is exempt from reporting pursuant to the intraperson exemption of Section 802.30. The PNO's position is that the formation of a wholly owned subsidiary by a corporation with two 50 percent shareholders also is an exempt transaction under Section 802.30 so long as any assets being contributed to the new subsidiary come from the jointly held corporation and are not contributed directly from the two equal shareholders to the subsidiary. On the other hand, if assets are being contributed to the new subsidiary by the parents, then the formation of the new subsidiary may be reportable under Section 801.40 under the theory that one parent may be obtaining control of assets of the other parent that it did not previously hold.

228 | Applicable provisions. 802.30, 801.1(c)(3).

Issue. Is the acquisition by X, the principal shareholder of company A, of voting securities of A's wholly owned subsidiary B, exempt pursuant to Section 802.30 where some of X's interest in A is held by a trust?

Facts. X held 33 percent of the voting securities of A. X was also co-trustee of a trust that held 21 percent of the voting securities of A. The trust instrument gave X the power to vote the A stock.

Analysis. Section 802.30 requires that the acquiring and acquired persons be the same person "by reason of holdings of voting securities." If (1) X is the settlor of the trust in which certain of the A shares are held, and either the trust is revocable or X as settlor holds a reversionary interest in the trust, or (2) X has the power to remove and replace at least half of the trustees (whether or not X is the settlor), then X is viewed by the PNO as holding the shares of the trust. Under those circumstances, X would control A by reason of holding of voting securities, and its acquisition of shares of B would be exempt under 802.30. If, however, neither of these conditions applies, then the trust (and not X) holds the 21 percent interest. *See* Section 801.1(c)(3) (the trust and not the trustee holds the corpus of a trust). Thus, X does would not control A by reason of holding of voting securities for HSR purposes and the Section 802.30 exemption would not apply.

229 | Applicable provisions. 802.30, 7A(c)(3).

Issue. Is a corporation's pro rata distribution of the stock of a subsidiary to its two ultimate parent entities exempt under Section 802.30 as an intraperson transaction?

Facts. Corporation X, the voting securities of which are 50 percent owned by A and 50 percent owned by B, distributes 50 percent of the stock of a new wholly owned subsidiary to A and 50 percent to B.

Analysis. Each of A and B is an acquiring person when it receives the subsidiary's voting securities. Since X has two ultimate parent entities, however, there are two acquired persons, A and B. Section 802.30 is not applicable because the distribution of the subsidiary's voting securities is separated into two transactions: an acquisition by A and an acquisition by B. As a whole, there is a complete identity of acquiring and acquired persons involved in this transaction, i.e., A and B are acquiring persons and acquired persons. However, the PNO analyzes this and other transactions on a step-by-step basis rather than on an aggregate basis. It would analyze the acquisition by A and the acquisition by B as separate transactions. Because, as to each transaction, the acquiring and acquired persons are not identical, the exemption under Section 802.30 is not available.

The acquisitions would, however, be exempt under Section 7A(c)(3), which exempts "acquisitions of voting securities of an issuer at least 50 per centum of the voting securities of which are owned by the acquiring person prior to such acquisition." Here, each of A and B are deemed to control X, and, therefore, the new subsidiary of X. (See Int. 227 regarding the possible reportability of the formation of the new subsidiary if the parents, rather than the jointly controlled subsidiary, are contributing assets to the new subsidiary.) *See also* Int. 232.

| 230 | **Applicable provisions.** 802.30, 801.1(c)(3).

Issue. Is the redemption of shares held by one of two shareholders of a corporation, coupled with a transfer of certain of the corporation's assets to that shareholder, exempt under Section 802.30?

Facts. Corporation A has 99 shares of Class A Common Stock, 50 of which are held by B and 49 of which are held by C. Corporation A creates a new wholly owned subsidiary D and transfers certain assets to it. Corporation A is then essentially split up by redeeming 38 of B's shares, and Subsidiary D's shares are transferred to B as consideration for the redemption. As a result, C obtains control of what remains of Corporation A (without making an acquisition), and B obtains control of D and retains a minority interest in Corporation A.

Analysis. If the steps were specified to occur in this order, the PNO would analyze this complex transaction on a step-by-step basis and treat it as three separate transactions. First, the creation of the wholly owned subsidiary D, and the transfer of assets to it would be exempt under Section 802.30, since B is both the acquired and acquiring person through its holding of more than 50 percent of A's voting securities. Second, the redemption of a portion of B's holdings in A would be exempt because the issuer was acquiring its own shares. *See* Section 802.30, Example 4. Section 802.30, however, does not exempt the acquisition of D voting securities by B, since the redemption occurs before the transfer of D shares to B as consideration for the redemption, and B no longer controls A (the parent of D) at the time it acquires the shares of D, and that acquisition may be subject to notification requirements (under which B is the acquiring person and C, the new ultimate parent of A and D, is the acquired person).

C, the minority shareholder of Corporation A, ends up with control of that issuer (without the assets previously transferred to Subsidiary D), even though technically it has not made an acquisition of voting securities. On the other hand, if C is instrumental in causing the redemption to occur, a filing is required. *See* Int. 190.

Note that if the steps are to occur simultaneously, the PNO will analyze the transaction in all possible sequences. If one or more filings are required under different sequences, the parties may choose the sequence that will minimize the number of filings they are required to make as long as at least one filing is made.

231 | Applicable provisions. 802.30, 801.1(f).

Issue. Is the merger of Corporation A with Corporation B an exempt intraperson transaction where X controls both merging parties, but X's control of Corporation A results from an adverse financial development that triggers voting rights in theretofore nonvoting preferred, allowing X to elect a majority of Corporation A's Board of Directors?

Facts. X was a minority shareholder in Corporation A and also held that corporation's nonvoting preferred stock. In the event of certain adverse events, such as operating losses or a prolonged failure to pay dividends, X's preferred stock acquired voting rights, enabling X to elect 50 percent or more of Corporation A's Board of Directors. X also controlled Corporation B by virtue of holdings of voting securities. Subsequent to the triggering of X's voting rights in Corporation A, Corporation A intends to merge with Corporation B.

Analysis. The merger of Corporation A and B is an exempt intraperson transaction under Section 802.30.

According to the SBP, when events occur that allow X to elect a majority of Corporation A's Board of Directors (without the acquisition of any additional shares), X has not engaged in a reportable event. 43 Fed. Reg. 33,450, 33,463 (July 31, 1978). During the time that these conditions remained in effect, X had the ability to elect 50 percent or more of Corporation A's Board of Directors. Thus, a merger between Corporation A and Corporation B, which X also controlled by virtue of holding of voting securities, would be an exempt intraperson transaction.

The applicability of Section 802.30 is dependent upon the fact that X controls Corporation A by reason of holding of preferred shares that, because of certain events, acquired voting rights and are, therefore, "voting securities." This exemption would not be applicable where X's control arose from a contractual right to designate 50 percent or more of the issuer's Board of Directors.

| 232 | **Applicable provisions.** 802.30, 7A(c)(3).

Issue. In the dissolution of a corporate joint venture having two venturers with equal interests, may one venturer purchase the shares of the other without triggering notification? Alternatively, may the venture, without reporting, redeem the shares of one venturer by transferring one-half of the venture's assets to that venturer as consideration?

Analysis. Section 802.30, the intraperson exemption, applies only where the acquiring and acquired persons are the *same* person. The acquiring and acquired person must be the same person as to the entire transaction. Neither the "acquisition-of-stock" transaction in the first question nor the "acquisition-of-assets" transaction in the second question would be exempt under Section 802.30 because the acquired entity is included within two different acquired persons. The acquisition of shares of the venture by either shareholder from the other, however, would be exempt under Section 7A(c)(3), since the acquiring person would already hold at least 50 percent of the issuer. *See* Int. 229. (But, the 7A(c)(3) exemption does not apply to acquisitions of assets so the "acquisition-of-asset" transaction would not be exempt under either exemption.)

Note that the dissolution of a partnership or LLC would not be exempt. Because those structures do not issue voting securities, neither Section 7A(c)(3) nor Section 802.30 would apply. An acquisition that would result in an entity holding all of the interests in a partnership or all the membership interests in an LLC would be deemed to be an acquisition of all the assets of the entity, and, on that basis, potentially reportable. *See* Ints. 73, 82, and 233.

| 233 | **Applicable provision.** 802.30.

Issue. Is Section 802.30 applicable to the dissolution of a partnership?

Analysis. Because a partnership does not issue voting securities, Section 802.30 would not apply. If one partner buys out all of the interests of the other partner(s), (whether that partner controlled the partnership prior to the buy-out or not), the acquiring partner is deemed to have acquired all of the assets of the partnership, which will be reportable if the jurisdictional tests are satisfied. Likewise, if a partnership is dissolved and assets distributed to the partners, each partner has a potentially reportable acquisition of assets, even a controlling partner. *See* Int. 232.

| **234** | **Applicable provisions.** 802.30, 7A(c)(10), Formal Interpretation 15.

Issue. Can the Section 802.30 "intraperson" exemption apply to acquisitions of entities already controlled through an LLC or partnership?

Facts. A, an individual, proposes to purchase all of the voting securities of C. A already controls C by virtue of holding 51 percent of the membership interests in B-LLC, which holds 100 percent of C's voting securities.

Analysis. A cannot take advantage of the "intraperson" exemption because A's control of C at present is not as a result of holdings of voting securities. The acquisition is, however, exempt under Section 7A(c)(10) of the Act, because A will not be increasing, directly or indirectly, the percentage of shares held in C as a result of the proposed acquisition.

The Section 802.30 intraperson exemption would apply, however, if A held 100 percent of the membership interests in an intermediate LLC or 100 percent of the partnership interests in an intermediate partnership. In this circumstance, the PNO has indicated that A can "look through" the LLC or partnership to treat the holdings of that entity as if directly held, rather than held through the LLC or partnership. Thus, if the facts presented in this situation involved A holding 100 percent of B-LLC, A would have been able to use the Section 802.30 intraperson exemption as well.

| 235 | **Applicable provisions.** 802.50, 802.51, 802.3.

Issue. What constitutes "sales in or into the United States" within the meaning of Sections 802.50 and 802.51?

Facts. A foreign producer of natural gas desired to discontinue its operations and sell its mineral leases. The leases had a value in excess of $500 million. (The "carbon-based mineral reserves" exemption of 802.3 applies to assets located outside the United States, but the size of this transaction was too large for the exemption to apply.) An agency of the provincial government in the foreign country purchased all natural gas produced within the province, then resold the gas into the United States and elsewhere at prices that it set. Because of the location of the foreign producer's operations, virtually all of its gas was in fact ultimately sold into the United States, but the foreign producer had no control over those decisions and no ability to influence the location of the ultimate sale or the price that it received.

Analysis. Under these circumstances, the PNO told the potential purchaser of the mineral leases that the sales of natural gas would not be deemed "in or into the United States." *See* Ints. 236, 237.

236 | Applicable provision. 802.50(a).

Issue. What constitutes "sales in or into the United States" for purposes of Section 802.50(a)?

Facts. A seeks to acquire assets located in Hong Kong that generated approximately $62 million in sales to U.S. customers. The Hong Kong seller uses a commission agent located in New York to call on prospective customers. Representatives of the customers then travel to Hong Kong to view the products and negotiate prices and quantities. Purchase orders and letters of credit are then received by the Hong Kong company. The finished products are delivered to the U.S. customers in Hong Kong, Bangkok, or Taiwan, at which time title and risk of loss passes to the customer. The customer is responsible for transporting the goods and clearing customs.

Analysis. These sales were not "in or into the United States," because most of the indicia of beneficial ownership passed to the buyer outside the United States, and because the seller cannot control the ultimate destination of its products.

Interpretations Relating to Part 802 289

237 | Applicable provision. 802.50(a).

Issue. What constitutes "sales in or into the United States" for purposes of Section 802.50(a)?

Facts. A manufacturer in Japan sells its products to an unrelated Japanese trading company that is in the business of purchasing goods in Japan and shipping those products to the United States for resale.

Analysis. The Japanese manufacturer that sells its products to this trading company is not selling goods "in or into the United States" even though the trading company resells all of its purchases in the United States, and the manufacturer knows with certainty that its products will be resold in the United States. The indicia of beneficial ownership pass outside the United States, and the manufacturer has no control over the destination of its products.

The PNO has indicated that determining "sales in or into the United States" can often be a difficult issue. Other factors might be relevant to determining whether specified transactions involved the sale of goods "in or into the United States," other than where risk of loss and legal title passes. If goods specifically designed for the U.S. market (e.g., automobiles equipped to safety specifications required for import into the United States) are manufactured abroad and then sold and transferred outside the United States to a buyer who imports the goods and resells them with the United States, the initial sale by the foreign manufacturer might be deemed a sale in or into the United States.

Another issue addressed by the PNO concerns determining sales in or into the United States by foreign telecommunications companies, i.e., foreign telephone companies and communication satellite providers. Generally, the foreign telecommunications companies provide services outside the United States. The companies will derive sales in "or into the United States," however, if they own switching or relay stations in the United States, and charge customers in the United States a fee to transfer calls abroad.

Editor's Note. As noted, determining what constitutes *"sales in or into the United States"* can sometimes be difficult. A few principles can be gleaned from Ints. 235, 236 and 237. Generally, even if a foreign producer knows that all of its products will ultimately be sold in or into the United States, if it sells to an intermediary outside the United States, *and the intermediary is not obligated to sell the products into the United States, the sales will probably **not** constitute sales in or into the United States. See Int. 235. One exception to this general rule seems to be a situation where the product is designed in such a way that it can only be sold in the United States. In this case, even if the goods that are manufactured outside the United States are sold to an intermediary outside the United States, they will probably constitute U.S. sales because they can only be sold in the United States. This is the example in this interpretation (Int. 237) relating to automobiles equipped to pass safety inspections required for import into the United States. Interpretation 236 seems to stand for the idea that if the "sale" actually took place outside the United States (the buyer traveled outside the United States to negotiate the deal and the products are delivered to the U.S. customers outside of the United States), beneficial ownership of the product passed to the customer outside of the United States and the transaction will not be considered a U.S. sale.*

238 | Applicable provisions. 802.50, 801.15.

Issue. To what extent are asset acquisitions of both foreign and U.S. assets aggregated for purposes of determining whether notification is required?

Facts. X, a U.S. company, intends to acquire all of Y's assets and the size-of-person and commerce tests are met. Y's assets consist of:

1. One U.S. plant, valued at $10 million that generated $10 million in revenues in the most recent fiscal year;

2. One foreign plant, valued at $20 million, which had no sales into the United States in the most recent fiscal year; and

3. Another foreign plant, valued at $40 million, which had $45 million in sales into the United States in the most recent fiscal year.

Analysis. Section 802.50(a) provides that "[t]he acquisition of assets located outside the United States shall be exempt from the requirements of the act unless the foreign assets the acquiring person would hold as a result of the acquisition generated sales in or into the U.S. exceeding $50 million during the acquired person's most recent fiscal year."

The combined sales into the United States of the two foreign plants total $45 million and, therefore, do not exceed the limitation of Section 802.50(a) and are exempt under that section.

Section 801.15(b) states that assets, the acquisition of which is exempt under Section 802.50(a), will not be held as a result of the acquisition unless the limitation in that section, i.e., $50 million in sales into the United States derived from foreign assets, would be exceeded as a result of the acquisition. Because the only other component of the transaction is the acquisition of assets located in the United States, the U.S. sales attributable to those assets would not be aggregated with the sales into the United States of the foreign assets. Therefore, the limitation in Section 802.50(a) is not exceeded, and the foreign assets are not held as a result of the acquisition.

Because the assets held as a result of the acquisition (only the U.S. plant) are valued at only $10 million, the size-of-transaction test is not satisfied and the transaction is not reportable.

| 239 | **Applicable provision.** 802.50(a).

Issue. How is the phrase "assets located outside the United States" in Section 802.50(a) applied to movable assets?

Facts. Cruise ships, for example, frequently call on U.S. ports and sell tickets almost exclusively in the United States, even though they are foreign owned and foreign registered.

Analysis. The PNO requires a full factual analysis of the varying locations and uses of a movable asset, in this case cruise ships, to determine whether the assets should be viewed as "located outside the United States." The PNO looks not only to where the assets are generally located and who owns the assets, but also to the source of the revenues generated by the movable assets. In the case of cruise ships that frequently call on U.S. ports and for which tickets are sold almost exclusively in the United States, the assets would be viewed as "located in the United States." The PNO may take this view despite the fact that (1) the ownership and registry of the ships are foreign, (2) the captain and most of the crew are foreign, and (3) the ships may be located outside U.S. territory a majority of the time. This type of analysis applies to other movable assets, such as movable drilling rigs and platforms.

In the case of movable or intangible assets, the source of the revenues generated by the assets may be critical in determining where the assets are located for the purposes of Section 802.50(a), and the source of the revenues for the most recent fiscal year may give the best indication as to where the assets have competitive significance.

240 | Applicable provision. 802.51.

Issue. How is aggregation of sales in or into the United States and assets located in the United States handled when there are foreign and U.S. issuers being acquired from the same person in a single transaction?

Facts. A, a foreign person, intends to acquire 100 percent of the voting securities of four wholly owned subsidiaries of B, a foreign holding company with no other assets, for an aggregate purchase price of $60 million. The parties have allocated $15 million of the purchase price to each subsidiary. Three of the subsidiaries (W, X, and Y) are foreign and one (Z) is a U.S. issuer. None of the foreign subsidiaries has assets located in the United States. W has no sales in or into the United States. X and Y each had sales of $30 million into the United States in their most recent fiscal years.

Analysis. To determine the applicability of the exemption provided by Section 802.51, the sales into the United States of X and Y are aggregated. Because the aggregate sales of these two subsidiaries exceed $50 million, the acquisition of X and Y is not exempt under Section 802.51 and potentially subject to notification obligations. Given that W had no sales into the United States, however, its sales and assets are not included in the aggregation among the foreign subsidiaries, and its value is, therefore, not included in the size-of-transaction. The resultant $45 million acquisition (including the $15 million attributable to the acquisition of Z, which is not exempt) is nonreportable, as it fails to satisfy the size-of-transaction jurisdictional test. If W had any sales into the United States, those sales would have been included in the aggregation required under Section 802.51(b)(3) and none of W, X, or Y would have been exempted, making the size-of-transaction $60 million and the transaction subject to reporting. If the acquisition instead had been of 100 percent of the voting securities of B, the size-of-transaction would have been $60 million regardless of whether W had any sales into the United States.

| 241 | **Applicable provisions.** 802.51(a), 802.51(b), 801.40(d).

Issue. Is the formation of a joint venture exempt under Section 802.51(a) where each of the U.S. venturers is purchasing shares of a foreign corporation holding no assets located in the United States?

Facts. Several U.S. companies were among the parties forming a foreign joint venture corporation. The venturers had made aggregate commitments for future capital funding in excess of $10 million to the new corporation.

Analysis. The PNO agreed that the Section 802.51(a) exemption would apply. The foreign corporation has no assets located in the United States, other than arguably investment assets (the capitalization commitments). Because the joint venture corporation is newly formed, it has no U.S. sales.

Editor's Note. *Had the venturers, in the aggregate, committed to contribute assets located in the United States with a fair market value in excess of $50 million (other than investment assets, voting securities, or extensions of credit or guarantees), then reporting obligations might be required under Section 801.40 even though the venture is formed as a non-U.S. venture. Note that for purposes of 802.51(a) and (b), the "assets located in the U.S." must be valued at fair market value. See SBP, 67 Fed. Reg. 11,898, 11,900 (Mar. 18, 2002).*

| 242 | **Applicable provision.** 802.51(a).

Issue. Is the acquisition by a U.S. person of voting securities of a foreign issuer exempt pursuant to Section 802.51(a) where the target has divested all assets accounting for U.S. sales?

Facts. The foreign issuer had U.S. sales in excess of $50 million during its most recent fiscal year, but it has since sold the division that accounted for nearly all of its U.S. sales.

Analysis. The PNO advised that the acquisition would be exempt under Section 802.51(a) because the U.S. person would not hold, as a result of the acquisition, voting securities of an issuer that *presently* has annual sales in or into the United States in the most recent fiscal year in excess of $50 million, as the issuer has since disposed of the operations from which U.S. sales were derived.

| 243 | **Applicable provisions.** 802.51(b)(1), 802.2(d), 802.4, 7A(c)(1).

Issue. Is the acquisition by a foreign person of more than 50 percent of the voting securities of a foreign issuer exempt under the asset-value threshold of Section 802.51(b)(1) where the acquired issuer has $1.1 billion in U.S. assets, which consist entirely of office buildings and residential properties, the direct acquisition of which would be exempt under Section 802.2(d)?

Analysis. The transaction is not exempt under Section 802.51(b)(1), but may be exempt under Section 802.4, depending upon what other assets the foreign issuer holds. Section 802.51(b)(1) exempts the acquisition of control of a foreign issuer by a foreign person only if the foreign issuer does not have U.S. assets, other than investment assets, valued at $50 million or more. The PNO has refused to extend the exclusion for "investment assets" to cover all assets the direct acquisition of which would be exempt. The acquisition may, however, be exempt under Section 802.4, because the direct acquisition of all the U.S. assets (the office buildings and residential property) would be exempt under Section 802.2(d), assuming the foreign issuer does not have in excess of $50 million in other nonexempt assets. Note that the Section 802.50(a) exemption is not included in the list of exemptions qualifying under the 802.4 exemption. *See* Ints. 209, 213.

244 | Applicable provisions. 802.51(b)(1), 801.4.

Issue. Is the value of minority holdings of voting securities of a U.S. issuer held abroad included in the determination of the value of "assets located in the United States" for purposes of the asset-value threshold of Section 802.51(b)(1)?

Facts. A foreign corporation seeks to acquire all the outstanding voting securities of a foreign issuer, which held voting securities of a number of U.S. issuers. None of the foreign issuer's holdings constitute controlling interests, and their acquisition would not confer control of any U.S. issuer. The securities themselves are held outside the United States and have an aggregate value in excess of $50 million.

Analysis. The PNO's position is that these securities are not germane to the determination of the asset-value threshold under Section 802.51(b)(1). The issue of whether these securities are assets located in or outside the United States is irrelevant to application of the Section 802.51(b) exemption. The acquisition of voting securities of a foreign issuer by a foreign person is exempt under that provision unless it confers control of:

> [An] issuer (including all entities controlled by the issuer) [that] holds assets located in the United States (other than investment assets, *voting or nonvoting securities of another person*, and assets included pursuant to § 801.40(d)(2) of this chapter) having an aggregate total value of over $50 million; or made aggregate sales in or into the United States of over $50 million in its most recent fiscal year.

Section 802.51(b) (emphasis added).

The acquisition of the voting securities of each of the U.S. issuers must be separately analyzed to determine if any specific acquisition is reportable as a secondary acquisition pursuant to Section 801.4.

245 | Applicable provisions. 802.51(b)(1), 801.4.

Issue. Does Section 802.51(b)(1) exempt a foreign person's secondary as well as primary acquisition of voting securities from a foreign issuer?

Analysis. Section 802.51(b) may apply to either a primary or a secondary acquisition. The exemption is applied separately to the primary and secondary acquisitions that are taking place.

A foreign person's secondary acquisition, which is always an acquisition of a minority position, can never be reportable unless the acquiring person already holds stock of the secondary issuer. The reason is that Section 802.51(b)(1) exempts any foreign person's acquisition of the stock of a foreign issuer that does not confer control of that issuer. Unless the acquiring person already holds shares of the issuer, the acquisition of a minority interest cannot confer control of the issuer, and a filing would not be required. Even if the acquiror did hold shares of the issuer and the acquisition did confer control of that issuer, the transaction would nevertheless be exempt unless the issuer held U.S. assets valued in excess of $50 million or made sales in or into the U.S. in excess of $50 million in the most recent fiscal year.

246 | Applicable provision. 802.51.

Issue. Can an acquisition of less than 50 percent of the voting securities of a foreign issuer by a foreign person ever be reportable?

Facts. A, a foreign person, is acquiring 40 percent of the voting securities of B, a foreign issuer. In connection with the acquisition, A is entering into a shareholders agreement that will give it the contractual right to designate 3 of the 6 directors of B. A does not own any voting securities of B prior to this transaction.

Analysis. In this situation the Section 802.51(b) exemption applies and no HSR filing is required. Section 802.51(b) states "[t]he acquisition of voting securities of a foreign issuer by a foreign person shall be exempt from the requirements of the act unless *the acquisition will confer control* of the issuer . . . ." Section 802.51(b) (emphasis added). The PNO has taken the position that the above highlighted phrase means that control of the issuer must be conferred by the acquisition of voting securities of the issuer. Therefore, no acquisition by a foreign person as a result of which such person would hold less than 50 percent of the voting securities of a foreign issuer can be reportable regardless of any ancillary agreements entered into at the time of the acquisition that confer control through means other than the holding of voting securities.

If A already held voting securities of B that combined with the additional voting securities that are being acquired total 50 percent or more of B's voting securities, the acquisition would "confer control" and further analysis would have to be done to see if the other Section 802.51(b) exemption would be met.

| 247 | **Applicable provisions.** 802.63, 7A(c)(2).

Issue. May a debt holder of a company in bankruptcy rely on the exemption of Section 802.63 in a foreclosure of a secured obligation, an acquisition in partial or complete satisfaction of a secured or unsecured obligation, or an exchange of a debt security for assets or voting securities of the debtor?

Analysis. In many cases a debt holder in this situation will be able to rely on the exemption of Section 802.63 for these sorts of transactions. However, when a debtor's obligations or other creditor claims are acquired after the debtor company's impending bankruptcy is announced, the debt or claim holder is not viewed by the PNO as a "creditor in a bona fide credit transaction" and is, therefore, not able to make use of the exemption.

As an initial matter, any acquisition from a company of debt that carries no present voting rights, no matter at what stage, may be done without any filing requirement. *See* Section 7A(c)(2). Furthermore, normally a creditor may foreclose on collateral or negotiate the acquisition of receivables or other assets of a debtor in connection with a bona fide debt work-out without making a filing using the Section 802.63 exemption. This exemption is conditioned, however, on the debtor and original creditor having previously entered into a "bona fide credit transaction," and that original transaction must have been "entered into in the ordinary course of the creditor's business." Taken together, these two conditions mean that the debt obligation must have arisen from a transaction in which the debtor borrowed from the original creditor or purchased on credit extended by the original creditor in the ordinary course of the creditor's business. Once a debtor-creditor relationship has been created in this fashion, even if the debtor's obligation is subsequently transferred to a different creditor, any subsequent foreclosure or acquisition in lieu of foreclosure that satisfies or discharges the debt obligation in whole or in part is generally exempt.

An exception to this exemption (known as the "Vulture Fund" exception to Section 802.63) arises where an intention to initiate bankruptcy proceedings by or against the debtor is publicly announced and the obligations of the debtor or other creditor claims are acquired thereafter by a person that subsequently seeks to foreclose on collateral or acquire other assets (or securities) of the debtor in satisfaction of the acquired obligations. Where a debtor's obligations or other creditor claims are acquired after its impending bankruptcy is announced, the debt or claim holder is not viewed by the PNO as a "creditor in a bona fide credit transaction" and is, therefore, not able to make use of the exemption. This interpretation applies to a foreclosure of a secured obligation, to an acquisition in partial or complete satisfaction of a secured or unsecured obligation, or to the exchange of a debt security for assets or voting securities of the debtor, or indeed of any issuer.

Editor's Note. *While an acquisition by a creditor to create or discharge a bona fide debt in whole or in part is unlikely to have anticompetitive implications, the theory underlying the exception appears to be that acquisitions of claims or of debt previously issued by an entity that is now or soon will be in bankruptcy are more likely to be used as a vehicle for gaining control of the bankrupt debtor than just for obtaining repayment of the debt. Such a transaction may or may not have anticompetitive implications but the thought is that it is sufficiently indistinguishable from any other acquisition of assets or voting securities to warrant premerger notification and potential scrutiny by the antitrust enforcement agencies.*

248 | Applicable provisions. 802.63, 801.1(c)(1).

Issue. Upon dissolution of an equipment leasing arrangement, must the lessee file notification to purchase all of the equipment from the lessor?

Facts. Under an equipment leasing arrangement entered into to finance an acquisition of equipment, the lessor investment bank acquired the equipment and leased it back to the lessee for a period of eighteen years. Now that the lease term has run, the lessee intends to acquire the equipment.

Analysis. This transaction is not exempt under Section 802.63 which relates to certain acquisitions by creditors and insurers. That exemption applies to situations where (among other things) a creditor acquires an asset in **establishing** lease financing, but does not apply where the lessee is acquiring the leased assets at the end of the lease.

Unless there is some argument to be made that beneficial ownership of the leased equipment was with the lessee already, the purchase of the equipment by the lessee from the lessor would be reportable if the jurisdictional tests were met and no other exemption applied. Beneficial ownership of the equipment might be with the "lessee" if the "lease" was actually an installment sale. *See* Int. 4. For example, if the "lease" included an option to acquire the equipment for a nominal amount (below fair market value) at the end of the lease term, the PNO might conclude that beneficial ownership went directly to the "lessee" at the beginning of the "lease," and remained there for the duration of the "lease." In that event, the "lessee" might have had a filing obligation for an acquisition of the equipment at the beginning of the lease (assuming the jurisdictional thresholds were met and no other exemption applied), but would not have to file to acquire the asset at the end of the lease (since it already had beneficial ownership).

INTERPRETATIONS RELATING TO PART 803 OF THE RULES

249 | Applicable provision. 803 generally.

Issue. Where filings have been made for an acquisition by Company A of all outstanding voting securities of Company B and the parties, during the waiting period, amend their letter of intent to provide for a nonreportable sale of a plant by Company B to a third party prior to the stock acquisition, is amendment of the previous filings required?

Analysis. The PNO has taken the position that amendment of the pending filings is not required in this particular circumstance. The PNO requests, however, that the agencies be notified of the change by letter and that the resulting changes in the information supplied on the previous HSR filings be indicated. A specific determination has been made that such a letter would not be treated as an amendment to the pending filings and that the waiting period would not be affected.

The PNO advises parties to include assets in the original filing even if they are not expected to be part of the final transaction because their later elimination will not affect the filing or waiting period. On the other hand, if assets are not included in the original filing (because the parties assumed they would not be included in the final transaction), the PNO will require the parties to amend or refile their forms if the excluded assets eventually become a part of the transaction, and a new waiting period would run from the submission of the new or amended filings.

Editor's Note. A transaction that has been amended to include the transfer of fewer assets, or a smaller company, should only cause the actual transaction to have less of a competitive impact than the notified transaction. Thus, ordinarily the PNO would not require an amendment to the HSR, particularly where the changes have been made for reasons unrelated to potential competition issues. In some circumstances, however, parties have attempted to change the terms of an acquisition specifically in response to concerns raised by the antitrust enforcement agencies. This may raise a question as to whether the amended transaction is a new transaction requiring a new notification. See FTC v. Libbey, Inc., 211 F. Supp. 2d 34 (D.D.C. May 20, 2002). As of the date of publication, the agencies had not delineated clear guidelines as to when such changes to a transaction would give rise to new filing obligations.

250 Applicable provision. 803 generally.

Issue. Where a contemplated transaction (1) does not, under its terms, meet the Act's jurisdictional tests or (2) is covered by an exemption, but the parties anticipate that prior to consummation the tests are likely to be satisfied or the exemption may no longer apply, may they file in advance, in order to avoid having to file and wait at a later time?

Analysis. The PNO has indicated that it will accept filings with respect to transactions not meeting the Act's jurisdictional tests where those tests are likely to be satisfied prior to consummation. For example, the PNO has permitted an acquiring person in a tender offer to file notification where the tender offer price for the shares to be purchased was less than $50 million. The apparent rationale was that in a hostile tender offer, or where the possibility of a competing tender offer is contemplated, the original offeror might wish to increase either the number of shares it offers to purchase or the price it is willing to pay. A premerger notification requirement might thereby be triggered, and the intervening bidders might gain a timing advantage over the original offeror who had not yet filed notification. In anticipation of that situation, the PNO accepted the anticipatory filing.

Similarly, the PNO will accept filings when the size-of-person requirement is not satisfied at the time of filing but the parties believe that a new regularly prepared balance sheet will satisfy the size-of-person test. The PNO cautions that the parties should represent on the form that they are filing in anticipation of a new balance sheet that is expected to satisfy the size-of-person test.

In both situations described above, the FTC will not return the filing fee if the size-of-person or size-of-transaction thresholds are not actually satisfied.

251 Applicable provisions. 803 generally, 801.40.

Issue. Where two companies are forming a 50/50 joint venture corporation, which will then serve as an acquisition vehicle, is the formation of the subsidiary corporation potentially reportable and, if so, may they file for both acquisitions (i.e., acquisitions of the stock of both the joint venture corporation and the target) on one notification form?

Analysis. Generally, as long as the size criteria of Section 801.40(c) are met, the formation of an acquisition vehicle in a corporate form by two or more persons is itself reportable under Section 801.40. (The exception is when the acquisition's vehicle is formed as part of a subsequent merger or consolidation. *See* Int. 175.)

To avoid the burden of preparing an additional filing, the parties may each complete a form covering both acquisitions. This could result in a concurrent waiting period with respect to this two-step transaction, but only if the acquired person files at the same time as the joint venture partners. The PNO will, however, require two filing fees from each acquiring person—one for each reported acquisition.

The PNO recommends that the parties clearly represent that they are each making a filing for both steps of the transaction. The form should be completely clear on what is being addressed in each item on the form (especially Item 7) so that the reviewer can differentiate between the two steps of the transaction.

| 252 | **Applicable provisions.** 803 generally, 7A(b)(l)(B), 803.5(b).

Issue. What are the applicable waiting periods in a two-step transaction involving a cash tender offer and subsequent merger?

Analysis. If the tender offer is for 50 percent or more of the issuer's outstanding voting securities, the only waiting period will be the fifteen-day waiting period applicable to the cash tender offer. Once that waiting period has expired, any purchases, whether made pursuant to the cash tender offer or not, will be covered by that filing. *See* Ints. 225, 265.

When a filing is made on a two-step transaction for a tender offer of less than 50 percent and both steps are clearly identified, the PNO assigns two transaction numbers and starts two separate waiting periods - fifteen days for the cash tender offer and thirty days for the merger. This is advantageous for the parties because if, for any reason, the cash tender offer is dropped prior to expiration (or termination) of the waiting period, the thirty-day waiting period applicable to the merger already may be running. Of course, the waiting period applicable to the merger will have only begun when both the acquiring and acquired person have made a filing, and both parties have submitted the appropriate Section 803.5(b) affidavits. In this case, only a single filing fee is payable because the acquiring and acquired person are the same in each step of the two-step transaction. The amount of the fee is based on the value of the entire two-step transaction.

Interpretations Relating to Part 803 309

| 253 | **Applicable provisions.** 803 generally, 803.10, Items 4(a), 4(b) and 4(c).

Issue. In a non-Section 801.30 transaction, does the formal withdrawal of a filing by one of the parties during the waiting period mean that the transaction cannot be consummated until a new notification is filed and a new waiting period satisfied?

Analysis. If there is a formal withdrawal by one of the parties, the transaction cannot be consummated unless the parties comply ab initio with the Act. The FTC will not return the original filing fee and requires a new fee as well as new forms from all parties required to file if the transaction is revived.

The PNO, however, has adopted a procedure whereby an acquiring person is allowed to withdraw and refile its HSR filing one time, provided that the transaction is substantively unchanged from the original filing. If the acquiring person notifies the PNO of its intention to withdraw and refile, and does in fact refile within two business days of the withdrawal, no new filing fee is required but the parties receive a new waiting period. In this situation (where the acquiring person is going to refile within two business days of its withdrawal) the acquired person does not refile, only the acquiring person. This procedure is sometimes utilized to attempt to avoid the need for the issuance of a Second Request. Refiling and restarting the waiting period allows the parties additional time to respond to, and hopefully assuage competitive concerns that the reviewing agencies may still harbor with respect to the notified transaction at the end of an initial waiting period. The refiling party cannot simply resubmit the original filing, but must conduct a new search for Item 4 documents, update Items 4(a), 4(b) and 4(c), and provide a new certification. *See* Int. 267.

| 254 | **Applicable provision.** 803 generally.

Issue. May a person who has filed notification purchase voting securities of the acquired person during the waiting period provided that such purchases do not result in the holder's crossing of a notification threshold prior to expiration of the waiting period?

Analysis. The PNO confirmed that such purchases are permitted under the Act so long as any such acquisition does not confer control of the acquired issuer. For example, an acquiring person that currently holds no voting securities of the acquired person, may acquire up to $50 million in voting securities during the pendency of the waiting period so long as the percentage of voting securities held remains below 50 percent. The PNO will not permit acquisitions of voting securities of the target of 50 percent or more prior to termination of the waiting period because at that point the acquiring person will be deemed to have acquired beneficial ownership of the target and will be deemed in violation of the Act. *See* Int. 188.

The PNO does not permit partial purchases of assets in an asset transaction during the waiting period. For example, if an acquiring person has filed to acquire assets valued at $100 million, the acquiring person may not acquire (or otherwise take beneficial ownership of) any of the assets prior to clearance under the HSR process. Even if the $100 million deal is structured so that there are two separate agreements, one of which involves assets valued at less than $50 million, the parties must wait for clearance on both deals before closing either one. Only if there are two transactions that are separate would the parties be able to close one involving assets valued at less than $50 million. *See* Ints. 150, 154.

255 | Applicable provisions. 803 generally, 7A(g)(2).

Issue. How are notification and waiting period requirements affected by Section 363(b) of the Bankruptcy Code, relating to sales by a trustee in bankruptcy?

Facts. Section 363(b)(1) of the Bankruptcy Code, 11 U.S.C. § 363(b)(1) 2000, states: "The trustee, after notice and a hearing, may use, sell or lease, other than in the ordinary course of business, property of the estate."

In 1994, a new subsection (2) was added to Section 363(b) of the Code:

> (2) If notification is required under subsection (a) of Section 7A of the Clayton Act in the case of a transaction under this subsection, then—
>
> (A) notwithstanding subsection (a) of such section, the notification required by each subsection to be given by the debtor shall be given by the trustee; and
>
> (B) notwithstanding subsection (b) of such section, the required waiting period shall end on the 15th day after the date of the receipt, by the Federal Trade Commission and the Assistant Attorney General in charge of the Antitrust Division of the Department of Justice, of the notification required under such subsection (a), unless such waiting period is extended . . . .

The amendment affects all proceedings in which the bankruptcy petition was filed on or after October 22, 1994.

Analysis. The PNO interprets Section 363(b)(2)(A) of the Bankruptcy Code to require the trustee to file notification on behalf of the acquired person in reportable transactions involving the sale of property from a debtor's estate (the trustee executes the affidavit and certification, not the acquired person). It should be noted that if a company is a debtor-in-possession ("DIP") under Chapter 11 of the Bankruptcy Code, it has all the powers of a trustee. In that case, the company, as a DIP, will file the notification and an officer of the DIP company will execute the affidavit and certification. For purposes of the size-of-person test, the bankrupt debtor is the UPE, and the relevant annual net sales and total assets are those of the debtor, including any entities controlled by the debtor. (If one or more subsidiaries have filed for bankruptcy but the parent has not, each subsidiary in bankruptcy is considered to be its own UPE.) The acquired person's affidavit should state that it has the good faith intent to consummate the sale to the acquiring person contingent on bankruptcy court approval.

Section 363(b)(2) does not eliminate the filing obligation of the acquiring person, and the shortened fifteen-day waiting period only commences when notifications are received from both the acquiring person and the acquired person. (The fifteen-day waiting period applies whether the transaction involves assets or voting securities.) If a Second Request is issued, only the acquiring person is required to comply with the Second Request to restart the waiting period. Also, the second waiting period will expire ten calendar days after the acquiring person's compliance with the Second Request.

In order to accommodate the Section 803.5 affidavit requirements in a bankruptcy context, the PNO will accept filings prior to the existence of a letter of intent, agreement in principle, or contract, where the parties attest to a good faith intention to proceed with the proposed transaction upon approval by the bankruptcy court and supply a copy of the bankruptcy court's order setting forth procedures for the sale. Because bankruptcy court approval is required and the debtor in possession or the trustee may be aware that more than one person is interested in bidding, frequently an executed agreement cannot be obtained before the bankruptcy hearing. In this situation, the PNO will accept filings from multiple potential acquiring persons for the same assets, where each makes the representation of a good faith intention to purchase, subject to bankruptcy court approval.

One court has ruled that any action under Section 7A(g)(2) seeking an order requiring compliance with the Act and extension of the waiting period must be sought in the bankruptcy court (or the district court supervising the bankruptcy proceedings). *See In re Financial News Network, Inc.*, Case No. 91 B10891-FGC (Bankr. S.D.N.Y. Apr. 3, 1991), *aff'd*, 1991-1 Trade Cas. (CCH) ¶ 69,410 (S.D.N.Y. Apr. 18, 1991).

Editor's Note. *The PNO also applies the fifteen-day waiting period to foreign bankruptcies, despite the fact that the statute technically applies only to acquisitions covered by 11 U.S.C. § 363(b).*

256 Applicable provisions. 803.2(d), Form Item 5.

Issue. Does the Section 803.2(d) requirement that interplant transfers be included in dollar revenues reported on the notification form extend to revenues received by a UPE from its subsidiaries for management services?

Analysis. Interplant transfers of manufactured products must be included in dollar revenues reported on the notification form, but Section 803.2(d) applies only to manufactured products and not to other industries (e.g., oil and gas transfers, professional services). Thus, intercompany service revenue is not disclosed in Item 5. In this case, revenues received by an ultimate parent for management services rendered to its subsidiaries need not be reported.

If a subsidiary was being sold and the facts were reversed such that subsidiary's only revenues were for management services provided to the ultimate parent, because intercompany service revenue is not disclosed in Item 5, the subsidiary would report no income in Item 5. It would be helpful in this situation if there were a footnote included in the form explaining why no revenue is reported.

| 257 | **Applicable provision.** 803.3.

Issue. Are there circumstances under which parties may be allowed to avoid disclosure of certain of their holdings in the context of filing notification without having to comply with the requirements of Section 803.3?

Analysis. The PNO has allowed nonprofit religious organizations to avoid disclosing on their notification forms the existence and size of their noncommercial assets and revenues even though the parties may technically have been able to do so, where such disclosure was clearly irrelevant to any antitrust analysis of a reportable transaction, or where satisfactory assurances to that effect were obtained. The parties were not required to submit a reason for noncompliance pursuant to Section 803.3.

Where a religious organization is transferring assets or stock and provides all necessary information concerning the assets or issuer, the seller has been permitted to avoid disclosure of its other noncommercial assets or operations and the revenues derived therefrom. Similarly, acquirors that are religious orders or religious organizations that provide all relevant information concerning their commercial properties and operations in all types of businesses related to proposed purchases have been permitted to avoid disclosure or description of noncommercial assets and operations. Such purchasers are required to specify in their notifications the areas with respect to which all required information has been supplied.

Editor's Note. On one occasion, the PNO allowed a foreign corporation held directly by an agency of a foreign government to exclude certain nonpublic subsidiaries, limiting the information it provided to its publicly listed subsidiaries and those subsidiaries in a direct line with the acquiring entity. Because a foreign government was involved in the transaction, considerations of comity may have influenced the PNO's position. The foreign corporation had argued that it would be too burdensome to produce information for each of its thousands of nonpublic subsidiaries. It did, however, certify that none of those entities was engaged in the same line of business in the United States as the filing parties.

| **258** | **Applicable provisions.** 803.3, 801.12(b)(3), Form Item 6(b).

Issue. Where a company does not know the identity of its five percent shareholders (because, for example, its securities are issued in bearer form or held in street name), what are its obligations with respect to completion of Item 6(b) of the form, which requires a listing of such shareholders?

Analysis. A publicly traded U.S. corporation may rely on filings by its five percent shareholders with the SEC unless the information in the filings is known by the corporation to be inaccurate or outdated. Thus, ordinarily, a publicly traded corporation would have notice of its five percent shareholders.

The issue could arise, however, for nonpublicly traded companies and foreign companies. Where a reporting person has a reasonable basis for believing that a particular person has knowledge concerning the identity of five percent shareholders, the reporting person is obligated to request that person to disclose such information. If the person refuses to divulge this information, the reporting person should so indicate in a statement of reasons for noncompliance under Section 803.3. Ordinarily, the PNO will regard this as sufficient, particularly as to outside directors or other persons over whom the reporting person has little or no control. The refusal of a corporate officer to divulge such information might raise a question of noncompliance, even if a Section 803.3 statement is provided.

259 | Applicable provisions. 803.5, 803.6.

Issue. Will the FTC accept a filing that does not bear a notarized seal on the affidavit and certification?

Analysis. The PNO has stated that the language provided in 28 U.S.C. § 1746 relating to unsworn declarations under penalty of perjury may be used instead of notarization for both the affidavit and certification.

In locations where notaries are not required to use a seal, the PNO will accept notarized filings without a seal, provided that the certification complies with applicable state or foreign law.

260 Applicable provisions. 803.5, 803.6.

Issue. May a facsimile version of the Section 803.5 affidavit or Section 803.6 certification be filed with a notification form?

Analysis. A facsimile version of the affidavit or certification may be filed with a notification form, so long as the required originals are supplied to the PNO as soon as possible thereafter. The waiting period will begin at the time the completed notification form with faxed affidavit and certification is received.

261 Applicable provision. 803.5(a).

Issue. May a tender offeror file notification with respect to a conditional tender offer?

Analysis. A tender offer, the consummation of which is conditioned upon the happening of certain events, may be the basis of a notification, provided the offeror attests to its good faith intention to proceed with a reportable acquisition if those conditions are subsequently satisfied or waived. *See* Ints. 167, 262.

| 262 | **Applicable provision.** 803.5.

Issue. How can the parties to a contingent purchase arrangement (such as a stock option offered to a friendly third party by the target of a hostile tender offer or a "crown jewel" option to purchase specified assets) attest to their "good faith intention" to complete the transaction, as required by Section 803.5?

Analysis. There are a number of situations in which parties involved in a tender offer, or parties defending against a tender offer, may enter into option agreements that contemplate a purchase of assets or voting securities in the event of certain contingencies. For example, in a "lock-up" agreement, a target might grant an option to purchase a block of unissued common stock or treasury stock. Such an option might be used to assure that the optionee is able to purchase a specified minimum number of the target's shares. Alternatively, the purpose of the option might be to discourage a tender offer by another party, since the optionee would have the ability to purchase a sizable block of the target's stock as a defensive measure.

Similar arrangements are sometimes made with respect to asset purchases. A third party might, for example, be granted the option to purchase a particular collection of assets of a target company known to be attractive to a potential hostile tender offeror. This is sometimes referred to as a "crown jewel" purchase option.

The question arises whether these kinds of agreements represent "hypothetical" transactions, as to which premerger notification not only is not required but also is not permissible. Section 803.5(b) requires that, in non-Section 801.30 transactions, the filing persons attest to their good faith intentions to complete the transaction. Parties to the kinds of transactions described above may be unwilling—or indeed unable—to attest to such intentions at the time such agreements are entered into.

This in turn has implications for the timing of certain defensive measures in a tender offer context. If, for example, the parties to one of these option arrangements are unable to file premerger notifications until their intention to exercise the option to complete the transaction has "ripened" they may be at a disadvantage by reason of their inability to complete the contemplated transaction until after expiration of a thirty-day waiting period. By then the value of the option may be nil.

The PNO has taken a very broad view of what constitutes a good faith intention and generally will not question an affidavit that states a contingent intention. For example, an affidavit might say that X intends, subject to satisfaction of certain conditions set forth therein (e.g., existence of a competing tender offer), to exercise the option described in the offer to purchase. *See* Ints. 167, 261; *cf.* Int. 263.

| 263 | **Applicable provisions.** 803.5(a), 801.1(h), Form Items 2(d)(i) and 3(c).

Issue. Where an acquiring person knows the percentage of voting securities of an issuer that it wishes to acquire in a tender offer but is unable to determine what the acquisition price will be, and therefore cannot complete Items 2(d)(i) or 3(c) on the Form, may it nevertheless file notification? If so, what information must be provided in the notice letter supplied to the issuer and in the public statement of intention to make a tender offer pursuant to Sections 803.5(a)(1) and (2)?

Analysis. Notification may be filed under these circumstances. The letter supplied to the issuer, however, must state the Section 801.1(h) dollar or percentage threshold intended to be crossed by the acquisition. Thus, the acquiring person must in good faith estimate the value of the acquisition for purposes of determining the appropriate filing fee. The valuation should be based on the value of the greatest amount of voting securities the acquiring person is prepared to hold as a result of the tender offer. The public announcement of the intention to make the tender offer need not contain any information concerning either the number of shares to be purchased or the acquisition price.

| **264** | **Applicable provisions.** 803.5(a), 803.7, 801.1(h), 801.30.

Issue. In the affidavit required by Section 803.5(a), how specific must the acquiring person be in stating the Section 801.1(h) threshold that it intends to cross as a result of the proposed acquisition?

Analysis. Section 803.5(a) requires that the notice in a Section 801.30 transaction identify the specific classes of voting securities of the issuer sought to be acquired and, if known, the number of securities of each such class that would be *held* (not acquired) by the acquiring person as a result of the acquisition. If the number of shares is not known, the acquiring person must identify the specific notification threshold that it intends to meet or exceed. Once it has done so, the acquiring person also may designate a higher threshold for additional voting securities that it may hold in the one-year period provided by Section 803.7 following expiration of the waiting period. Such additional acquisitions will then be covered by the notification.

In drafting the notice letter and description of the transaction, it is important to note that the PNO does not accept a filing based solely on an acquiring person's statement that it "may exceed" a reporting threshold or that it may acquire "up to" a specific number or percentage of shares. A clear statement is required that the acquiring person intends to hold shares that meet or exceed a notification threshold that the person specifies. The person may then indicate that one or more additional thresholds may be crossed. See examples following Section 803.5(a)(2).

265 Applicable provisions. 803.7, 802.23, 801.1(h), 803 generally.

Issue. When must the parties to a transaction refile or amend their HSR notifications?

Analysis. New filings are not required in many situations in which the structure of the transaction is changed prior to consummation. On the other hand, new notifications will generally be required if significant new information would be revealed by new filings or if such a change may affect the enforcement agencies' antitrust analysis.

For example, the PNO has given the following guidance:

1. A company need not refile or amend if it substitutes one subsidiary for another as the acquisition vehicle (i.e., acquiring entity). If such a change is contemplated at the time of the original filings, it is recommended that the company note this possibility in its initial notification.

2. Beyond the provisions of Section 802.23 (related to amended or renewed tender offers), the PNO does not require an amendment or refiling for a change in the acquisition price, so long as the same Section 801.1(h) threshold level applies to the revised transaction.

3. Refiling *is* required if the ultimate parent entity of any acquiring person changes, unless the new ultimate parent entity was within the original ultimate parent entity. Note that the PNO does permit "filings-in-the-alternative" if the acquiring person thinks it may be acquired prior to the transaction for which it is filing. For example, if B (which as of the date of the filing is its own UPE) is filing to acquire C, but know that it, B, may be acquired by A prior to closing on C, B may explain this in its notification and provide information in the form in the alternative for B as UPE and A as UPE. A would have to submit a separate certification to certify the accuracy of A's information. A and B would have to submit statements that in the event a Second Request is issued to A or B in connection with B's acquisition of C, that A and B understand and agree that the extended waiting period will not begin to run until the issuing agency receives a response that substantially complies with the Second Request. A and B would also have to agree

that a statement that they are unable to comply with the Second Requests because A does not currently own B is not an adequate statement of reasons for noncompliance under Section 7A of the Clayton Act and Section 803.3 of the Rules.

If the UPE of the acquired person changes, no new filing or amendment is required if the acquisition is of assets or of an entity within the person, other than the UPE. Refiling *is* required if the filing was for the acquisition of the UPE, that UPE changes, the new UPE is not an entity that was controlled by the old UPE at the time of filing, and the new UPE is to be acquired.

4. A new filing or amendment is not required where a tender offeror decides after the waiting period expires to acquire shares through means other than a tender offer, provided that these acquisitions do not cross a new Section 801.1(h) threshold. *See* Int. 225.

Section 803.7 explicitly permits the acquiring person, within one year following the expiration of a waiting period, to increase its holdings up to "the notification threshold with respect to which the notification was filed," without refiling. There is no requirement in Section 803.7 that the *form* of the transaction be the same as that indicated in the initial filings.

A difficult issue arises where a tender offeror decides within a short time after its initial filing to acquire voting securities by means other than a tender offer. If the new acquisition is not a tender offer, a thirty-day waiting period would have been required and Section 802.23 does not apply. The PNO takes the position, based upon Section 803.7, that if the change occurs after the fifteen-day waiting period has expired, the new transaction can be completed without waiting thirty days after the initial filing. If the tender offer is dropped during the fifteen-day waiting period and replaced by a reportable nontender offer transaction, however, both parties must amend their filings, and a new thirty-day waiting period will begin to run upon notification by both the acquiring and the acquired person. *See* Int. 225.

Identifying a situation where a proposed transaction is restructured in a manner that alters its reporting obligations may be difficult. (Note the exception highlighted in Int. 267 regarding removal of assets after the reviewing agencies have raised objections to a proposed acquisition.) Generally, if the assets actually being acquired are among the assets identified in the original filing, no new filing will be required. Moreover, if a filing is made to acquire 50 percent or more of the voting securities of an issuer, the PNO specifically has said that the acquiring person can acquire all or any part of the stock of the issuer or any entity controlled by that entity within one year; the PNO also has stated that where notification has been filed to acquire 50 percent or more of an issuer's voting securities, that acquiring person can acquire all of the assets of the issuer and the entities it controls once the waiting period has expired. Similarly, where a filing is made to acquire all of the assets of a person or an entity, the acquiring person can acquire all of the voting securities or any part of the assets of that person or entity. The PNO also has determined that one who files to acquire 50 percent or more of the voting securities of an issuer may buy less than all of the assets of that issuer and its controlled entities on the basis of Section 803.7. In all cases where there is a significant change in the form of the transaction, the PNO advises parties to consult with it before proceeding to close the revised acquisition.

| 266 | **Applicable provisions.** 803.7, 802.21, 801.30.

Issue. What is the effect of withdrawing a filing after the waiting period has expired?

Analysis. The PNO's position is that withdrawing a filing after the waiting period has expired negates Section 803.7 such that the transaction cannot subsequently be completed without filing again and observing a new waiting period. Even after early termination or the expiration of the waiting period, if before closing the filing is withdrawn, the transaction cannot be closed without a re-filing. Thus, the one year period in Section 803.7 within which the parties must consummate a notified transaction would no longer apply once the filing has been withdrawn. In a non-Section 801.30 transaction, withdrawal by either the acquiring or acquired person nullifies the effect of the filing. In a Section 801.30 transaction only the acquiring person may effectively withdraw the filing.

The PNO believes the withdrawal of notification also affects the Section 802.21 analysis. Once the filing has been withdrawn, it is as if the filing was never made, and the parties can no longer rely on Section 803.7 or Section 802.21.

Editor's Note. In many, if not most, cases, parties do not withdraw their filings after the waiting period has expired even if the transaction falls apart. There is generally no advantage to a withdrawal, and if the deal does come together again and closes within a year of the termination of the HSR waiting period, no new filing would be required. One case where a withdrawal may make sense is where a target wanted to assure itself that the acquiring company could not acquire target's stock exceeding an HSR threshold without refiling.

| 267 | **Applicable provisions.** 803.10, Items 4(a), 4(b) and 4(c).

Issue. In what situations must a filing be withdrawn prior to the expiration of the initial waiting period?

Analysis. In situations where the enforcement agencies have raised antitrust objections to a proposed transaction and the parties have agreed to abandon the transaction prior to issuance of an injunction, the FTC and the DOJ have required the parties to withdraw their filings. In other cases, where parties have restructured transactions to eliminate "offending" assets from the purchase, the agencies have required that the acquired person withdraw its original filing and make an amended filing reflecting the revised transaction. In this situation, a new filing fee is generally not required.

In certain situations parties may decide voluntarily to withdraw and resubmit their filings, thereby initiating a new thirty-day waiting period. This process grants the agencies additional time to review the transaction and may help the parties avoid the issuance of a Second Request. The PNO will not require an additional filing fee for a withdrawn and resubmitted filing under the following circumstances:

1. The proposed acquisition does not change in any material way, i.e., if an asset deal, the exact same assets are the subject of the resubmission and, if a voting securities deal, the same issuer's shares are being acquired and the filing is for the same notification threshold;

2. The resubmitted notification is recertified, and the submission, specifically as it relates to Items 4(a), 4(b) and 4(c), is updated to the date of the resubmission; and

3. The resubmitted notification is refiled prior to the close of the second business day after withdrawal.

The PNO will assign the same HSR identification number to the transaction, and the new waiting period will commence on the day the notification is resubmitted. Withdrawal and resubmission during the initial waiting period, without the requirement to pay an additional fee, will only be permitted once. The withdrawal and resubmission may only be done by the acquiring person. *See* Int. 253.

268 | Applicable provisions. 803.10(a)(2), 801.40, Item 3(a).

Issue. When does the waiting period relating to the formation of a joint venture corporation, reportable pursuant to Section 801.40, commence?

Analysis. Section 803.10(a)(2) provides that the waiting period does not commence until "all persons contributing to the formation of the joint venture or other corporation that are required" to file for the acquisition of voting securities of the new company have filed. Even if filings have been made by one or more acquiring persons relating to their acquisition of shares of the new company, and that waiting period has expired, if another acquiring person is subsequently added that will be required to file in connection with the formation transaction, the waiting period previously observed is a nullity and a new waiting period will have to be observed for all acquiring persons. Those persons who had previously filed will not be required to refile forms; however, if adding the new acquiring person results in the need to make changes to a form already submitted (e.g., in the responses to Item 5(d) and/or Item 7), then each acquiring person must submit replacement pages and new certifications for the previous filing.

Note that it is difficult for the PNO to determine from the face of the form which acquiring persons contributing to the formation of the venture are required to file. Consequently, it is difficult for the PNO to know when all required filings have been received and when the waiting period has begun. The FTC encourages, but does not require, the filing person to identify all forming persons and indicate, in the Item 3(a) Description of the Acquisition, which persons are required to file notification.

When requests for additional information are issued in connection with the formation of a joint venture subject to Section 801.40, the additional waiting period does not begin to run until all of the acquiring persons to whom requests have been issued substantially comply with the requests.

269 | Applicable provisions. 803.11, 801.30.

Issue. When will early termination of the waiting period be granted?

Analysis. If early termination of the waiting period is requested by either party to a transaction on their form, it is granted after both agencies determine that they will not take any further action during the waiting period. Depending on the volume of transactions at any given time and whether any possible antitrust concern is raised by a particular filing, early termination is often granted within two weeks for non-Section 801.30 transactions. Early termination of the waiting period for Section 801.30 filings will not be granted until the acquired person makes its filing.

In situations where there are no antitrust concerns (or any initial questions are quickly resolved), the agencies have been cooperative in helping parties cope with significant timing exigencies. Where the reasons are truly compelling, the agencies have been able to work together with the parties to grant early termination in a matter of days. For instance, the PNO has worked with parties to expedite early termination where, absent such assistance, the acquired person would suffer material financial harms such as an inability to meet payroll. Conversely, the PNO has found certain claims to be less than sufficiently compelling to justify extraordinary measures. The PNO has generally found claims such as (1) a need to close quickly for accounting purposes, (2) a need to meet a publicly announced closing date, or (3) an assertion that "the deal may fall through" to be insufficient reasons for expediting grants of early termination. The PNO's position is that it is incumbent on the filing person to present any extraordinary exigency in its filing.

Parties should note that grants of early termination are not confidential, and that the agencies may grant early termination if one party to a transaction requests it even if the other party does not. After the parties are notified by phone (the PNO considers messages left with assistants or secretaries of the HSR contact person and voicemail messages as constituting notification), the FTC "publishes" notice of early terminations (1) in the Federal Register, (2) on a recorded telephone system message, (3) by hard copy (available from the FTC public reference room), and (4) on the FTC's Web site (www.ftc.gov). This public notice only identifies (1) the acquiring person, (2) the acquired person, (3) the acquired entity, and (4) the date of the grant of early termination. Publication is not made until the day after the parties are notified. *See* Int. 23.

270 | Applicable provision. 803.30.

Issues. May a person obtain an informal interpretation regarding an HSR question from the PNO? If a person has obtained an informal interpretation from the FTC, must it also confirm the advice given with the DOJ?

Analysis. A person can request informal, nonbinding interpretations from the PNO and, under Section 803.30, the "[FTC] staff may consider requests for formal or informal interpretations as to the obligations under the act and these rules of any party to an acquisition." Parties may contact the PNO, which will respond to phone calls, e-mails, and requests for meetings. All PNO responses will be made orally. The PNO does not give informal interpretations in writing or by return e-mail.

Informal interpretations given by the PNO, including advice given orally in response to a telephone inquiry, should not be confirmed through discussions with the staff of the DOJ. The PNO will, however, consult with the DOJ on issues relevant to the DOJ, such as a pending DOJ investigation.

Parties can confirm advice given orally by sending a letter outlining the facts presented and conclusion reached. These letters are subject to FOIA and a redacted version may be made public. However, letters can be written in a way that describes the facts and issues generically without identifying the parties or the transaction.

| 271 | **Applicable provisions.** 803.1(a); Form generally.

Issue. Will the FTC accept filings submitted on forms generated by the filing person's word processing system rather than those submitted on the FTC's preprinted Form?

Analysis. Different formats tracking the FTC's preprinted Form as closely as practicable can be used as long as the information requested is provided in the same sequence as the preprinted Form. The FTC has made the Form available for downloading from the FTC's Web site (www.ftc.gov) in multiple formats.

INTERPRETATIONS RELATING TO THE NOTIFICATION AND REPORT FORM

| 272 | **Applicable provisions.**   Form generally, Item 2(d)(iii), 801.10(c)(3).

Issue. Where the acquisition price in an asset acquisition exceeds $50 million, does Item 2(b)(i) or any other Form item, require a determination of the fair market value of the assets by the filing person's board of directors, in accordance with Section 801.10(c)(3)?

Analysis. Where the acquisition price in an asset acquisition exceeds $50 million, and the other criteria of Section 7A are met, the transaction is reportable. Item 2(d)(iii) requests that the reporting person give the total value of the assets to be held as a result of the transaction. The SBP (43 Fed. Reg. 33,450, 33,471 (July 31, 1978)) states that, if the parties are certain that the transaction is reportable a fair market value determination is not required. But amendments to the Act now require that a filing fee be paid based on the amount of assets held as a result of the acquisition. Thus, a fair market valuation will be necessary to determine the appropriate filing fee. *See* Int. 112. Item 2(e) also now requires acquiring persons to identify the person responsible for making the fair market value determination when one is required by the Rules.

| 273 | **Applicable provisions.** Item 2(a), 801.2(e).

Issue. Does Form Item 2(a) require filing persons to list as "acquiring persons" former shareholders in a corporation being merged into another, who acquire voting securities of the surviving corporation in return for surrendering their shares of the acquired issuer?

Analysis. The PNO's position is that Item 2(a) seeks to identify only those persons who, as a result of the transaction, will hold securities of the *acquired issuer*. *See* SBP, 43 Fed. Reg. 33,450, 33,521, 33,522-23 (July 31, 1978). Thus, this item does not require a list of those persons who will hold securities of the *acquiring person* as a result of the transaction, and the extent of their previous ownership of the acquired issuer seems irrelevant.

If the acquisition of voting securities of the acquiring person is separately reportable under Section 801.2(e), separate filings will need to be made, and the identities of these individuals and the extent of their holdings shown in those filings.

274 Applicable provisions. Items 3 and 5(d), 801.40, 803.3.

Issue and Facts. Corporation A and an individual are forming a new corporation (Newco) to purchase all the stock of Corporation B. Corporation A will own 80 percent and the individual will own 20 percent of Newco. Corporation A does not know the individual's total assets, and because the value of Newco stock held by A will be less than $200 million, the formation of Newco is reportable by Corporation A under Section 801.40(c) only if the individual has total assets of $10 million or more. (The individual's acquisition of Newco shares is nonreportable because it has a value less than $50 million.) Newco's acquisition of Corporation B is reportable in any case. How should Corporation A complete the relevant items on the notification form(s)?

Analysis. The PNO prefers that Corporation A file two notification forms, one notification form for the formation of Newco and one for the acquisition of Corporation B. The PNO, however, will accept one notification form for both the formation and the acquisition so long as the filing person separates the responses (e.g., the Item 3 responses) for each of the separate transactions.

If Corporation A has no reason to believe that the individual has sufficient assets to satisfy Section 801.40(c), it may fully describe all contemplated transactions in response to Item 3 and not respond separately to Item 5(d). If, on the other hand, Corporation A has reason to believe that the individual has total assets of $10 million or more, it should complete Item 5(d) with whatever information it has available, as well as Item 3 as indicated above. Whenever a person does not have information required to be provided by one or more items of the form, he must include a Section 803.3 statement of reasons for noncompliance.

The PNO cautions that a party to a transaction has an affirmative obligation to determine whether another party to the transaction meets a jurisdictional test that would require an HSR filing. This could be accomplished by a representation in the agreements relating to the possible HSR reportability of the transaction.

This issue takes on added significance in light of the filing fee requirement. If the other venturer meets the size-of-person test, then A is required to pay two filing fees, one for the formation of Newco under Section 801.40 and one for Newco's acquisition of B. The PNO must make its own determination of reportability. Thus, it would seek to determine whether the investor is a $10 million person. If A had filed on the assumption that the other venturer was a $10 million person (i.e., paid two filing fees), and the PNO determines that the Section 801.40 transaction was not reportable, the filing fee related to the Section 801.40 transaction would be returned. If the PNO determines that the other venturer was a $10 million person and A has not filed on the Section 801.40 transaction, then A would be in violation if it were to proceed with the transaction without filing and waiting.

275 Applicable provision. Item 4(b).

Issue. How does a natural person respond to Item 4(b) if he or she does not have a regularly prepared balance sheet or comparable document, but the entities controlled by such person do have such documents?

Analysis. Submission of the balance sheets of the unconsolidated U.S. issuers controlled by the natural person will constitute substantial compliance. The natural person need not create a balance sheet for purposes of satisfying Item 4(b), but should state that it does not have responsive financial statements of its own. If, however, the submitted balance sheets do not satisfy the size-of-person test, the natural person should submit a statement with the filing stating that the natural person meets the size-of-person test.

276 | Applicable provisions. Items 4(b) and 5.

Issue. How should a reporting person respond to Form Items 4(b) and 5 with respect to recent acquisitions of assets? Must revenues attributable to such assets be included in responses to Item 5 for the period prior to their acquisition? Must annual reports and annual audit reports be provided for entities all the assets of which have been previously acquired by the reporting person?

Analysis. Item 5(a) instructs reporting persons to include "the total dollar revenues for 1997 for all *entities* included within the person filing notification at the time this Notification and Report Form is prepared (even if such *entities* have become included within the person since 1997)." Item 5(a) (emphasis added). Conversely, dollar revenues attributable to assets sold to the reporting person by entities that that person did not acquire and does not control need not be included. However, while the language of Item 5 does not currently require revenue information relating to assets previously acquired by reporting persons, the PNO requests that the relevant base year revenues be supplied where possible.

If, however, all or substantially all of the assets of an operating business have been acquired, the PNO presumes, for the purposes of Item 5, that the person has acquired an entity. The PNO considers acquiring all or substantially all of the assets of an entity tantamount to acquiring 50 percent or more of the voting securities of an entity. Thus, the person must include the relevant revenue information from the acquired entity with the later filing.

With respect to Item 4(b), the instructions require disclosure of financial statements of the reporting person and "each unconsolidated United States *issuer*." Item 4(b) (emphasis added). Unless the acquiring person in fact acquired 50 percent or more of the voting securities or otherwise acquired control of an issuer as opposed to merely acquiring substantially all of the assets Item 4(b) should not be read to require disclosure of the financial statements of that entity.

Also note that because Item 4(b) is limited to unconsolidated U.S. issuers, the Form does not require disclosure of financial statements for unconsolidated U.S. partnerships or LLCs.

Editor's Note. *The "base year" currently used in the form is 1997. This base year changes after the Census Bureau issues its Economic Census*

Report and its numerical list for the data it collects every five years. The 2002 reports will probably be issued sometime in 2004 or 2005 at which time the FTC will most likely change the form to require 2002 data as the base year.

277 | Applicable provision. Item 4(c).

Issue. How does the PNO interpret the requirements of Item 4(c)?

Analysis. The FTC has taken an expansive view of the scope of Item 4(c). Item 4(c) calls for:

> all studies, surveys, analyses and reports which were prepared by or for any officer(s) or director(s) . . . for the purpose of evaluating or analyzing the acquisition with respect to market shares, competition, competitors, markets, [and] potential for sales growth or expansion into product or geographic markets . . . .

Content, not form, determines whether a document is responsive to Item 4(c). Accordingly, the following are examples of the type of documents that would qualify as Item 4(c) materials if they contain 4(c) content: overhead slides used in presentations, e-mail, recordings of presentations or meetings, handwritten notes on index cards or the back of an envelope, a spreadsheet showing how market shares may be impacted by the transaction, a map with different colors representing the regions covered by different competitors, bullet points explaining the competitive benefits the acquisition will provide, and a memo detailing the products or research and development that a party may discontinue post-closing. Of course, the foregoing list is not exhaustive but simply illustrative.

If the FTC or DOJ determines that the person filing should have submitted a document in response to Item 4(c), the agency can impose civil penalties (currently up to $11,000 per day per party for noncompliance) and/or restart the waiting period. For instance, in 1999, an entity settled charges that it failed to provide certain Item 4(c) documents with the Notification and Report Form it filed for a proposed acquisition – paying nearly $3 million in fines. *See United States v. Blackstone Capital Partners II Merchant Banking Fund L.P.*, 1999-1 Trade Cas. (CCH) ¶ 72,484 (D.D.C. 1999) (Enf. Action F). *See also United States v. The Hearst Trust*, 2001-2 Trade Cas. (CCH) ¶ 73,451 (D.D.C. 2001) (Enf. Action D). The FTC discovered those documents after the expiration of the waiting period. The FTC settled that matter for 100 percent of the potential civil penalty ($4 million).

Editor's Note. *Item 4(c) is perhaps the most sensitive item on the Form. The Editors recommend that practitioners educate themselves on the myriad intricacies of Item 4(c) (that are far too numerous to cover in detail in this publication). Many excellent articles on the topic have been published over the years. Recent articles on Item 4(c) include William J. Baer & Deborah Feinstein,* Item 4(c): The Next Step in HSR Reform, *16-SPG ANTITRUST 43 (2002); and Marian R. Bruno, Brian C. Mohr, Bruce J. Prager,* Some Practical Guidance for the HSR Practitioner: Locating and Identifying Item 4(c) Documents, *16-SPG ANTITRUST 46 (2002).*

| 278 | **Applicable provision.** Item 4(c).

Issue. What kinds of market studies prepared for a prospective acquiror by outside consultants must be submitted in response to Item 4(c)?

Analysis. Documents prepared for any officers or directors of the acquiror by outside consultants, such as investment banking firms or acquisition consultants, that analyze the acquisition candidate and are otherwise within the specifications of Item 4(c), must be submitted.

It is possible to argue, however, that a document prepared by an investment banker or other consultant for a director or officer, which is directed primarily at an overall assessment of the market involved might not be responsive to Item 4(c) on the grounds that it was not prepared for the purpose of evaluating or analyzing the acquisition. The PNO interprets Item 4(c) as requiring submission of offering memoranda and other documents prepared by an investment banker or any other person (including agents of the target company or its owner) for the purpose of soliciting expressions of interest from prospective purchasers of the subject company. The seller must always submit these documents as 4(c) documents, and the purchaser must also submit these documents if it has received them.

| 279 | **Applicable provisions.** Item 4(c), 803.3(d).

Issue. Must documents prepared by an attorney that otherwise qualify as Item 4(c) materials be submitted with the Notification and Report Form?

Analysis. The person filing notification may, where appropriate, withhold documents on the basis of the attorney-client or work product privilege, but must assert the privilege and provide a Section 803.3 statement of reasons for noncompliance (setting forth all facts relied on in support of the assertion of privilege). Submission of a privileged document in response to Item 4(c) may waive the privilege.

| 280 | **Applicable provision.** Item 4(c).

Issue. Who is included in the scope of document production responsive to Item 4(c) of the Notification and Report Form?

Analysis. The PNO requires submission of any document with 4(c) content prepared by or for any officer or director of the acquired person or acquiring person or of any entity within that person (or in the case of unincorporated entities, individuals exercising similar functions). For purposes of Item 4(c), officers are limited to those positions designated by the bylaws or articles of incorporation or appointed by the board of directors (or to individuals designated in a similar way by an unincorporated entity).

281 | Applicable provision. Item 5.

Issue. Does a domestic wholesaler of computer monitors report manufacturing revenues in Item 5 if the wholesaler sells monitors that are produced for that wholesaler by either an affiliated or independent company in Japan pursuant to a contractual arrangement?

Analysis. The wholesaler does not report manufacturing revenues in Item 5. Consistent with the treatment by the Bureau of Census, revenues from any U.S. sale of a product produced outside the United States should be regarded as either retail or wholesale (i.e., nonmanufacturing) revenues for purposes of Item 5 reporting, regardless of the relationship between the foreign manufacturing entity and the U.S. wholesaler. Indeed, sales of products manufactured by the reporting person in its own plants located outside the United States should not be shown as manufacturing revenues, regardless of where or to whom they are sold. *See* Int. 1.

| 282 | **Applicable provisions.** Item 5, 803.2.

Issue. May a natural person that is a large investor with significant investment revenue limit its Item 5 revenue response to the entities that he or she controls?

Analysis. The PNO's current position is that a natural person must provide information relating to his or her own investment income in responding to Item 5. Under the PNO position, a natural person's investment revenues must be listed in response to Item 5 under the appropriate NAICS code for an investor. A natural person does not include wages or salary in its Item 5 responses. Revenues of entities controlled by a natural person are listed under the NAICS codes applicable to the entities' activities.

Under Section 803.2, when a natural person (or any person), files as an acquired person, the response for purposes of Items 5 to 8 need only relate to the assets being acquired and each entity whose voting securities are being acquired.

283 | Applicable provision. Item 5.

Issue. How does a reporting person in an acquisition of voting securities respond to Item 5 where the issuer has fewer lines of business at the time of acquisition (due to divestiture, sale, spin-off, etc.) than it had in the base year?

Analysis. If the divested assets did not constitute an entity, the base year revenues attributable to those assets should be reported in Item 5(a). If manufacturing revenues were attributable to the assets, they should be reported in Item 5(b)(i) and the 10-digit NAICS code should be shown as deleted in Item 5(b)(ii).

If more than 50 percent of the voting securities of a subsidiary or substantially all of the assets of an entity have been divested since the base year, the entity is no longer within the person filing notification. In this case, no revenues attributable to that entity are reported in the base year or the most recent year. If manufacturing revenues were derived from such an entity, the NAICS codes are not shown as deleted in Item 5(b)(ii).

Note that the PNO's position with regard to transferred or divested lines of business does not apply to lines of business that have been shelved or shut down. The PNO requires full information on lines of business that have been shut down but remain a part of the acquired issuer.

284 Applicable provisions. Items 5, 7, 803.2(b).

Issue. Where an acquired person is selling some but not all of the assets generating revenues within a particular NAICS Code, should the acquired person respond to Items 5 and 7 with respect to all of its assets in that NAICS Code, or only those assets being sold?

Analysis. The acquired person should limit its responses to those particular assets being acquired in the transaction subject to notification. Section 803.2(b)(1)(ii) instructs acquired persons in asset acquisitions to respond to Items 5 through 8 "only with respect to the assets to be acquired."

For example, if an acquired person is selling six of its ten widget wholesaling establishments, its Item 5 responses must include only those wholesaling revenues derived from the six establishments being sold. Similarly, in response to Item 7(c)(iii), the acquired person must list only those states in which the customers of the six establishments being acquired are located.

285 Applicable provision. Item 5(a).

Issue. When a reporting person's fiscal year differs from the calendar year, which fiscal year revenues should be reported for the base year?

Analysis. The filing person should use the fiscal year that includes the most calendar months in the base year. If the fiscal year ends June 30, so that each fiscal year contains six months of the base year, the PNO advises that one should report revenues from the most recent fiscal year. For example, if the base year is 1997 and the company's fiscal year ends on June 30 of each year, the PNO requests that the company provide information for the year ended June 30, 1998 for the base year.

| 286 | **Applicable provisions.** Items 5(a), 7(c).

Issue. How does a manufacturer that also wholesales its own products respond to Item 5(a) and to the subparts of Item 7(c)?

Analysis. The answer depends upon whether the manufacturer performs its wholesaling functions at its manufacturing plant(s) or at separate wholesale branches or offices. The Census Bureau defines wholesale trade to include "sales offices and sales branches (but not retail stores) maintained by manufacturing . . . enterprises apart from their plants . . . for the purposes of marketing their products." *See* OFFICE OF MANAGEMENT AND BUDGET, NORTH AMERICAN INDUSTRY CLASSIFICATION SYSTEM 507 (2002), *available at* www.census.gov/epcd/naics02/def/NDEF42.HTM#N42.

Thus, if a manufacturer engages in wholesaling functions at its plant, it should respond to Item 5(a) using the NAICS Codes for manufacturing rather than wholesaling, and it should respond to Item 7(c)(i) rather than 7(c)(iii). If it conducts its wholesaling operations in establishments apart from its manufacturing plants, it should report its manufacturing revenues under Items 5(a), 5(b)(i) and 5(b)(iii) and separately, the revenues from its wholesale branches should be classified under wholesale trade NAICS Codes (sector 42) for Items 5(a) and 5(c). If there is an Item 7(a) overlap, responses may be necessary to both Items 7(c)(i) and 7(c)(iii). In such instances, there may be intracompany revenue attributable to the transfer of the goods from the manufacturing operations to the distribution operations that should be disclosed. It may benefit the reporting person to put the PNO on notice of this issue by including a footnote to the PNO that states that the wholesaling revenues may be overstated due to internal or intracompany transfers.

287 Applicable provisions. Items 5(b)(ii) and (iii), 5(c).

Issue. Where a reporting person's financial statements (and the NAICS breakdown of that financial data) are not usually available until six months after the close of its fiscal year, and the statements for its most recent fiscal year will not be available until shortly after a date on which it wishes to file notification, may it respond to Items 5(b)(ii), 5(b)(iii), and 5(c) using data from the previous year's financial statements, even though that data will be approximately eighteen months out of date?

Analysis. A reporting person may provide revenue information that is up to eighteen months out of date, so long as such revenue data constitute revenues of the latest year that is reasonably available. For example, where the reporting person's financial statements and NAICS data for calendar year 2000 would not be ready until mid-2001, and the reporting person intended to file its Notification and Report Form in May 2001, the PNO stated that the reporting person should answer Items 5(b)(ii), (iii), and 5(c) based on calendar year 1999 revenues, as shown on the reporting person's June 2000 financial statements.

Alternatively, the instructions for Items 5(b)(iii) and 5(c) state that, if such data have not been compiled for the most recent year, estimates may be provided if a statement describing the method of estimation is furnished. However, as noted above, estimates are not required if the actual data supplied are not more than eighteen months old. If the actual data is more than eighteen months old then the filing person must make estimates for the most recent year.

Note that whatever year's revenues are supplied in response to Items 5(b)(iii) and 5(c), they must reflect the revenues earned in that year by all of the relevant entities owned by the filing person at the time its notification is filed. Thus, for example, the acquiring person supplying calendar year 1999 revenues in the above example must provide such revenues for all entities owned by the person in May of 2001, when it makes its filings.

Editor's Note. Even though the PNO permits the parties to use financial information up to eighteen months old for purposes of supplying information for Item 5 of the HSR form (as long as that is the most recent data available); the parties must use regularly prepared financials no older than fifteen months for purposes of calculating the size-of-person. See Int. 125; Section 801.11(b)(2).

288 Applicable provision. Item 5(b)(ii).

Issue. When preparing a Notification and Report Form for a manufacturing company organized after the base year, should Item 5(b)(ii), Products Added or Deleted, be completed?

Analysis. All products of the manufacturing company that did not exist in the base year should be listed in Item 5(b)(ii) along with the year in which they were added and the current year revenues of each product, even if the "addition" arises from the company's formation. This question arises because, under the circumstances described above, there will be no response to Items 5(a) and 5(b)(i), as the company did not exist in the base year.

| 289 | **Applicable provisions.** Item 5(d), 803.2(c)(1).

Issue. In responding to Item 5(d) must a U.S. corporation filing with respect to the formation of a joint venture or other corporation describe the contributions of a foreign joint venturer consisting solely of assets located outside the United States to which no U.S. sales were attributable?

Analysis. The PNO's position is that under these circumstances Item 5(d) does not require the reporting party to submit information concerning contributions to the joint venture of assets located outside the United States to which no U.S. sales were attributable. Section 803.2(c)(1) states in pertinent part that "[i]n response to items 5, 7 and 8 ... [i]nformation shall be supplied only with respect to operations conducted within the United States." Thus, the foreign assets being contributed to the venture by the foreign party would not have to be described by the U.S. venturer.

290 | Applicable provision. Item 6, Formal Interpretation 15.

Issue. If the person filing notification is a partnership, how does it respond to Item 6 of the Form?

Analysis. In response to Item 6(a), a partnership must list all entities with assets of $10 million or more that it controls as well as all entities with assets of $10 million or more controlled by such entities, within the meaning of Section 801.1(b).

However, under Item 6(b) a partnership or LLC will generally response "none," because it has no shareholders. A partnership, whether general or limited, is not regarded as issuing voting securities. *See* Int. 73. Similarly, LLCs do not issue voting securities. *See* Formal Int. 15, at Appendix. Thus, the partners or members are not "shareholders" for purposes of Item 6(b). If, however, the partnership or LLC controls a corporation, it must provide the shareholder information of the controlled entity as required by Item 6(b).

The partnership must disclose under Item 6(c) those corporations in which it holds 5 percent or more of the outstanding voting securities, although issuers with total assets of less than $10 million may be omitted.

291 | Applicable provisions. Items 7, 8, 801.40.

Issue. How does a person acquiring voting securities in the formation of a joint venture or other corporation respond to Items 7 and 8?

Analysis. A person acquiring voting securities in the formation of a joint venture or other corporation reportable under Section 801.40 must, for purposes of responding to Item 7, examine the NAICS industry codes in which either (1) any other acquiring person (whether required to file or not) derived U.S. revenues, or (2) the joint venture plans (without time limit) to derive U.S. revenues. *See* SBP, 43 Fed. Reg. 33,450, 33,532 (July 31, 1978). If there is an overlap with any of the six-digit industries in which the reporting person derived revenues in the most recent year, then that person must respond to the applicable subsections of Item 7(c).

NAICS overlaps between venturers are not material to Item 8 disclosure obligations. Thus, the acquiring person need consider only the six-digit NAICS industry codes in which the joint venture or other corporation reasonably can be expected to derive U.S. dollar revenues of $1 million or more annually. The reporting person must provide certain information with respect to its previous acquisitions of entities that derived revenues in any of the same six-digit industries, subject to certain limitations recited in the instructions to Item 8 and in Section 803.2.

| 292 | **Applicable provision.** Item 7(c)(iv).

Issue. In responding to Item 7(c)(iv), does a reporting person list as "establishment[s] from which dollar revenues were derived" (1) locations in which the person holds only a security interest, (2) locations owned by companies in which the person holds less than a 50 percent interest, (3) locations owned by limited partnerships in which the person is a general partner but does not have a majority equity interest, (4) locations that are managed but not owned by the person, or (5) locations that are leased by the person?

Analysis. Item 7(c)(iv) requires a reporting person who derives revenues in any of the same six-digit NAICS Code industries in which any other person that is a party to the acquisition also derived dollar revenues in the most recent year to list "each establishment from which dollar revenues were derived in the most recent year." The PNO has stated that the types of locations listed in (1)-(4) above are not considered "establishments" in response to Item 7(c)(iv), but that leased property is considered to be an establishment for Item 7(c) purposes as there is no requirement that the location be owned by the person deriving revenues from it.

ENFORCEMENT ACTIONS DEALING WITH THE HART-SCOTT-RODINO ACT

INTRODUCTION

Under Section 7A(g)(1) of the HSR Act, any person who fails to comply with the HSR Act's notification and waiting requirements is liable for a civil penalty of up to $11,000 for each day the violation continues.[1] To date, no HSR Act civil penalty case has been litigated; all have settled, either simultaneously with the filing of the complaint or before trial.

Section 7A(g)(1) requires that such penalty be recovered in a civil action brought by the United States. Although the Attorney General is responsible for all litigation in which the United States is a party (28 U.S.C. § 516), either the DOJ or the FTC can investigate these cases. On August 2, 1991, the DOJ and the FTC entered into a Memorandum of Agreement whereby FTC attorneys can be appointed as Special Attorneys, pursuant to 28 U.S.C. §§ 515, 543, to prosecute civil penalty actions on behalf of the United States under 15 U.S.C. § 18a(g)(1) for violation of the Act's premerger notification and waiting requirements. *See* 4 Trade Reg. Rep. (CCH) ¶ 9853, at 17,356 (Aug. 2, 1991). Therefore, since 1991, FTC attorneys, acting as Special Attorneys for the United States, have routinely filed HSR violation cases on behalf of the United States that were the product of an FTC staff investigation.

The following summaries provide a description of each HSR violation case filed since the inception of the Act. These descriptions are based on publicly available information, including court filings and press releases issued by the respective agency upon the filing of the complaint. Generally, when complaints have been filed contemporaneously with settlement papers, the complaint, public statements from the agencies, and competitive impact statements that are filed in instances in which the complaint seeks injunctive relief (in the case of DOJ actions that are filed when the HSR civil penalty action also involves Sherman Act violations), have contained detailed descriptions of the challenged conduct and possible defenses claimed by the parties. In other instances,

---

[1] Effective November 20, 1996, the dollar amounts specified in civil monetary penalty provisions within the FTC's jurisdiction were adjusted for inflation in accordance with the Debt Collection Improvement Act of 1996, Pub. L. No. 104-134 (Apr. 26, 1996). The adjustment included, in part, an increase from $10,000 to $11,000 for each day during which a person in violation of the Act under Section 7A (g)(1), 15 U.S.C. § 18a(g)(1). 61 Fed. Reg. 54,548 (Oct. 21, 1996), corrected at 61 Fed. Reg. 55,840 (Oct. 29, 1996).

for example when a complaint initiating litigation is filed by the agency and settled at some later time, the complaints tend to have more limited information on the nature of the challenged conduct and the theories of violation.

A **Enforcement action.** United States v. Smithfield Foods, Inc., Case No. 1:03CV00434 (D.D.C. filed Feb. 28, 2003).

Applicable provisions. 7A(a), 7A(c)(9), 7A(g), 802.9.

Issues. Failure to file; investment-only exemption.

Brief statement of the facts alleged. The complaint alleged that Smithfield, the nation's largest hog producer and pork packer, twice failed to file an HSR Notification and Report Form before acquiring voting securities in its chief competitor, IBP, Inc., in an amount exceeding the notification threshold. Smithfield allegedly began acquiring IBP voting securities on May 19, 1998 through a wholly owned subsidiary, SF Investments, Inc. Smithfield made an additional purchase on June 26, 1998, which purportedly resulted in Smithfield holding over the then $15 million notification threshold. Smithfield continued to acquire IBP securities through June 29, 1998. On October 1, 1998, Smithfield began to liquidate its holdings of IBP and, on that date, the value of its holdings fell below $15 million. On June 30, 1999, Smithfield again began acquiring IBP voting securities and its holdings exceeded the then $15 million filing threshold with an acquisition on December 8, 1999. Smithfield continued to acquire IBP securities through September 11, 2000. On January 5, 2001, Smithfield began liquidating its IBP holdings (which were purported to be worth over $100 million) and, by January 12, 2001, the value of Smithfield's holdings again fell below $15 million.

Action taken. The DOJ filed a complaint on February 28, 2003, alleging that Smithfield's acquisitions on June 26, 1998 and December 8, 1999 each required the filing of a Notification and Report Form under the Act. The DOJ complaint alleged that the transactions were not covered by the solely for investment exemption because, at the time of both acquisitions, Smithfield also was considering and taking steps toward combining with IBP. The DOJ is seeking the maximum daily penalty of $11,000 for each day Smithfield was in violation of the Act, for a total civil penalty of $5.478 million. As of this edition's printing, the matter remains pending in litigation. For additional information, see www.usdoj.gov/opa/pr/2003/February/03_at_125.htm.

B **Enforcement action.** United States v. Gemstar-TV Guide International, Inc. and TV Guide, Inc., Case No. 1:03CV00198 (D.D.C. filed Feb. 6, 2003).

Applicable provisions. 7A(a), 7A(g), 801.1(c), 801.2(a).

Issues. Gun-jumping; premature exercise of control; agreement to act jointly; beneficial ownership.

Brief statement of the facts alleged. Gemstar International Group, Ltd. and TV Guide, Inc. were competitors developing and selling interactive television program guides ("IPGs") to providers of packaged subscription television services. In mid-1999 Gemstar and TV Guide entered into joint venture discussions that, by August, had become merger discussions. In October 1999, the parties entered into an agreement to merge and thereafter filed HSR Notification and Report Forms. The applicable waiting period expired without DOJ enforcement action and the merger was consummated in July 2000. The complaint alleges that, prior to the expiration of the HSR waiting period, the parties began conducting their business jointly and merging most of their IPG decision-making processes, including agreeing to "slow roll" pending negotiations with certain customers, agreeing to the prices and material terms that TV Guide would offer customers before consummating the merger, allocating markets and customers between them, transferring control over important assets, and acting jointly on numerous business decisions.

Action taken. On February 6, 2003, the DOJ filed a complaint alleging that these and other activities amounted to "gun-jumping," i.e., a transfer of unlawful control over the business and an agreement to act jointly, which amounted to a "de facto acquisition" prior to closing in violation of the Act. The complaint also alleged that these activities amounted to unlawful agreements among competitors in violation of Section 1 of the Sherman Act. In a proposed final judgment filed simultaneously with the complaint, Gemstar and TV Guide agreed to settle these allegations, with Gemstar-TV Guide (the merged entity) agreeing to pay $5,676,000 in civil penalties for violating the HSR Act, the maximum civil penalty allowable ($11,000 per day per defendant). At the time, this civil penalty was the highest ever paid in an HSR violation case.

The proposed final judgment also prohibits the defendants from entering into any agreement to combine, merge, or transfer, in whole or in part, any operational or decision-making control over the marketing or distribution of any to-be-acquired product, service, or technology, in any future acquisition or merger before expiration of the HSR waiting period in any reportable transactions. The proposed final judgment also prohibits the defendants from entering into various agreements with a competitor between the beginning of negotiations until the consummation or abandonment of certain specified types of transactions involving that competitor. Finally, the proposed final judgment also required the defendants to permit certain customers, who had signed agreements with the defendants during the period of the illegal conduct, to terminate those agreements without penalty. For additional information, see www.usdoj.gov/opa/pr/2003/February/03_at_073.htm.

C **Enforcement action.** United States v. Computer Associates International, Inc., 2002-2 Trade Cas. (CCH) ¶ 73,883 (D.D.C. 2002).

Applicable provisions. 7A(a), 7A(g), 801.1(c), 801.2(a).

Issues. Gun-jumping; premature exercise of control; beneficial ownership.

Brief statement of the facts alleged. Computer Associates and Platinum agreed to merge in 1999 and notified the transaction. Under the merger agreement, Platinum allegedly agreed to limit discounts and other terms offered to customers during the period prior to closing, and to obtain approval from Computer Associates before providing discounts of more than 20 percent to its customers. Computer Associates also installed one of its employees at Platinum's headquarters during the HSR waiting period to review and approve customer contracts, and to undertake other activities related to the management of Platinum.

Action taken. In September 2001, the DOJ filed a complaint against Computer Associates and Platinum alleging that these and other activities amounted to an exercise by Computer Associates of unlawful control over Platinum's business prior to closing in violation of the Act, and collusion among competitors, in violation of Section 1 of the Sherman Act. The complaint alleged that the parties were in continuous violation of the Act for a period of fifty-eight days, and sought the maximum civil penalty from each party of $638,000, for a total civil penalty of $1.276 million.

The parties agreed to settle the charges in April 2002, prior to trial, by each agreeing to pay a total civil penalty of $638,000 for the alleged HSR violation. In addition, Computer Associates entered into an order prohibiting it from agreeing on prices, approving or rejecting proposed customer contracts, and exchanging prospective bid information with all future merger partners. The decree permits certain agreements and conduct, including the use of a provision that requires the to-be-acquired person to operate its business in the ordinary course, use of material adverse change provisions, which give the acquiring person certain rights in the event there is a material adverse change in the to-be-acquired person's business, and certain information exchanges for due diligence purposes if appropriate competitive safeguards are employed.

In a separate action, prior to the expiration of the HSR waiting period, the DOJ filed a complaint and final judgment in May of 1999 settling charges that the merger violated Section 7 of the Clayton Act. Both firms competed head-to-head in multiple computer software markets. Computer Associates agreed to divest certain Platinum products and related assets. For additional information, see www.usdoj.gov/atr/public/press_releases/2002/ 11029.pdf.

D **Enforcement action.** United States v. The Hearst Trust, 2001-2 Trade Cas. (CCH) ¶ 73,451 (D.D.C. 2001); FTC v. The Hearst Trust, Case No. 1:01CV00734 (D.D.C. settlement order filed Dec. 14, 2001).

Applicable provisions. 7A(d), 7A(g), Item 4(c).

Issue. Failure to file 4(c) documents.

Brief statement of the facts alleged. In January 1998, Hearst (composed of The Hearst Trust, The Hearst Corporation, and First DataBank, Inc.) acquired Medi-Span, Inc. and Medi-Span International. The parties notified the transaction in December 1997 and the applicable waiting period expired. During a subsequent investigation to determine whether the acquisition violated Section 7 of the Clayton Act and Section 5 of the FTC Act, FTC staff discovered certain documents that were not submitted by Hearst as Item 4(c) documents with its original Notification and Report Form. The omitted documents included high-level corporate analyses of the acquisition and its competitive effects and documents that went to the Hearst Board of Directors. Hearst amended its notification in August 2001 and included the documents that were not submitted in the original notification, as well as a list of documents responsive to Item 4(c) but withheld on grounds of privilege.

Action taken. In April 2001, the FTC filed a complaint alleging that Hearst's acquisition of Medi-Span violated Section 7 of the Clayton Act and Section 5 of the FTC Act, and that Hearst's failure to provide the 4(c) documents in its original notification violated the Act. The complaint sought divestiture of the acquired business and equitable relief, including disgorgement of unlawful monopoly gains.

In October 2001, at the request of the FTC, the DOJ filed a complaint seeking civil penalties for the HSR violation and a proposed final judgment whereby Hearst agreed to pay a civil penalty of $4 million. At the time, this civil penalty represented the largest amount ever paid by a single company for a violation of the Act.

In December 2001, prior to trial, Hearst agreed to settle charges that its acquisition of Medi-Span violated Section 7 of the Clayton Act and Section 5 of the FTC Act. The company agreed to divest the acquired business to an FTC-approved buyer and to pay $19 million as disgorgement of unlawful profits obtained by Hearst during the time that it operated the acquired business. This was the first disgorgement ordered in a merger case. For additional information, see www.ftc.gov/opa/2001/10/hearst.htm and www.ftc.gov/opa/2001/12/hearst.htm.

E **Enforcement action.** United States v. Input/Output, Inc., 1999-1 Trade Cas. (CCH) ¶ 72,528 (D.D.C. 1999).

Applicable provisions. 7A(a), 7A(g).

Issue. Gun-jumping; beneficial ownership.

Brief statement of the facts alleged. Input/Output, Inc. and DigiCOURSE executed an Agreement and Plan of Merger in September 1998 pursuant to which Input/Output was to acquire 100 percent of the voting securities of DigiCOURSE, a subsidiary of The Laitram Corporation. The parties filed their Notification and Report Forms on October 14, 1998. After the parties executed the merger agreement but prior to expiration of the waiting period, the complaint alleges that Input/Output began to exercise operational control over DigiCOURSE's business. For example, Input/Output allegedly assigned DigiCOURSE officers to positions and titles within Input/Output, provided the officers with offices at Input/Output's facilities, and gave them new business cards bearing their new titles that the officers distributed to DigiCOURSE's customers. Input/Output also authorized DigiCOURSE's President to travel overseas to resolve a commercial dispute between Input/Output and one of its customers and sought his comments on a contemplated acquisition by Input/Output. On November 3, 1998, both parties took steps to halt the alleged activities. The waiting period expired on November 13, 1998.

Action taken. In April 1999, FTC attorneys, acting as Special Attorneys to the U.S. Attorney General, filed a complaint alleging that the actions of the parties constituted a transfer of beneficial ownership of DigiCOURSE to Input/Output prior to the expiration of the applicable waiting period, in violation of the Act. The complaint alleged that the parties were in continuous violation of the Act during the period beginning on or about October 10, 1998, and ending on November 3, 1998, when they took steps to halt the premature consummation of the transaction. At the same time, a final judgment was filed whereby Input/Output and Laitram (DigiCOURSE's parent) agreed to settle these charges whereby each agreed to pay a civil penalty of $225,000, for a total civil penalty of $450,000. For additional information, see www.ftc.gov/opa/1999/04/input.htm.

F **Enforcement action.** United States v. Blackstone Capital Partners II Merchant Banking Fund L.P., 1999-1 Trade Cas. (CCH) ¶ 72,484 (D.D.C. 1999).

Applicable provisions. 7A(d), 7A(g), 803.6(a), Item 4(c).

Issue. Failure to file 4(c) documents; individual liability.

Brief statement of the facts alleged. Under a 1996 acquisition agreement, Blackstone and The Loewen Group agreed jointly to acquire Prime Succession, Inc. Blackstone filed its Notification and Report Form in October 1996. Early termination of the waiting period was granted in May 1997 and the transaction closed. (Loewen failed to notify the Prime transaction prior to closing the transaction and was the subject of a separate action charging that its failure to file violated the Act. *See* Enforcement Action G.)

In October 1996, Loewen notified another transaction. Included in Loewen's filing was a copy of a document addressed to Blackstone that allegedly should have been submitted as an Item 4(c) document by Blackstone with its filing in the Prime transaction. This document identified Loewen and Prime as operators of cemeteries and funeral homes, and described an agreement between Blackstone and Loewen by which Loewen was likely to obtain complete ownership of Prime.

Action taken. In March 1999, FTC attorneys, acting as Special Attorneys to the U.S. Attorney General, filed a complaint alleging that Blackstone's failure to provide this document was a violation of the Act. Simultaneously, a final judgment was entered whereby Blackstone agreed to pay a civil penalty of $2.785 million, the maximum civil penalty allowable. Howard Lipson, the general partner of Blackstone who certified the completeness of the filing, also individually agreed to pay a civil penalty of $50,000.

The FTC press release noted that this was the first case to impose HSR civil penalties individually on a company official in addition to the company itself. According to the press release, Mr. Lipson was the author of the subject document, had a copy of the document in his own files, and knew the document contained detailed competitive information. Nevertheless, Mr. Lipson certified Blackstone's filing as "true, correct and complete," even though he failed to provide the subject document. "Given all those circumstances, the agencies concluded that

Mr. Lipson 'knew or should have known' that the filing was inaccurate. Accordingly, it is appropriate that Mr. Lipson pay a penalty for what was at a minimum his reckless disregard for his obligations under the HSR Act." (FTC Press Release, Mar. 30, 1999.) For additional information, see www.ftc.gov/opa/1999/03/blackst.htm.

G **Enforcement action.** United States v. Loewen Group, Inc., 1998-1 Trade Cas. (CCH) ¶ 72,151 (D.D.C. 1998).

Applicable provisions. 7A(a), 7A(g).

Issue. Failure to file.

Brief statement of the facts alleged. Loewen, a Kentucky based owner and operator of funeral homes and cemeteries, and its parent company, agreed to a leveraged buyout of Prime Succession, Inc. through a joint acquisition with Blackstone Capital Partners II Merchant Banking Fund L.P. Under a May 29, 1996 agreement, Loewen was to contribute $60 million toward the leveraged buyout of Prime: $10 million for voting securities and $50 million for nonvoting securities. The FTC alleged that Loewen reviewed the planned leveraged buyout of Prime and concluded that the step involving Loewen's planned acquisition of $10 million of Prime voting securities would not be subject to the notification and waiting period requirements of the Act. On June 14, 1996, Loewen paid a $20 million down payment on its purchase of Prime securities. The complaint, however, alleges that before the leveraged buyout of Prime was undertaken, its structure was changed. As a result, on August 26, 1996, Loewen paid a total of $78 million, including $16 million for 24 percent of Prime's voting securities, a price that made the transaction reportable under the Act (under the HSR Act's former $15 million threshold).

Loewen did not file its notification form until October 1996, after the acquisition was consummated. FTC issued a Second Request; the waiting period ultimately terminated in May 1997. The PNO discovered Loewen's failure to file timely when it reviewed a filing by Loewen in connection with another transaction.

Action taken. In March 1999, FTC attorneys, acting as Special Attorneys to the U.S. Attorney General, filed a complaint alleging that Loewen's failure to file was a violation of the Act. The complaint alleged that Loewen was in violation of the Act from August 26, 1996 until May 13, 1997, when the waiting period for the transaction expired. Simultaneously, a final judgment was entered whereby Loewen agreed to pay a civil penalty of $500,000. (See also Enforcement Action F regarding a separate action filed against Blackstone for its violation of the Act related to the same transaction.) For additional information, see www.ftc.gov/opa/1998/03/loewen.htm.

H **Enforcement action.** United States v. Mahle GmbH, 1997-2 Trade Cas. (CCH) ¶ 71,868 (D.D.C. 1997).

Applicable provisions. 7A(a), 7A(g).

Issue. Failure to file.

Brief statement of the facts alleged. In June of 1996, Mahle GmbH, a German piston manufacturer, acquired 50.1 percent of the voting securities of Metal Leve, S.A., a Brazilian competitor, for approximately $40 million without filing a premerger notification report (the old $15 million notification threshold applied). The complaint alleged that the parties knew of their HSR obligations and had considered the tradeoffs between the costs of compliance and the risks of noncompliance. The parties did not notify the transaction until July of 1996, nearly a month after the acquisition was consummated.

Action taken. In June 1997, FTC attorneys, acting as Special Attorneys to the U.S. Attorney General, filed a complaint alleging that the parties' failure to satisfy the notification and filing requirements with regard to this transaction was a violation of the Act. The complaint alleged that the parties were in violation of the Act from June 26, 1996 through at least March 20, 1997, when Mahle filed an application with the FTC for approval to divest the acquired business. Simultaneously, a final judgment was also filed whereby Mahle and Metal Leve each agreed to pay a civil penalty of $2,801,000 for a total of $5,602,000, the maximum civil penalty allowable. At the time of the filing, this was the largest amount ever imposed as a civil penalty for a violation of the Act.

In a separate action, the FTC issued an administrative complaint and a proposed consent order in February 1997, alleging that Mahle's acquisition violated Section 7 of the Clayton Act and Section 5 of the FTC Act. The consent order required Mahle to divest the acquired business. The FTC made the complaint and consent order final in June 1997 and approved Mahle's March 20, 1997 application for approval of divestiture of the acquired business. For additional information, see www.ftc.gov/opa/1997/97/mmlcivp4.htm.

I Enforcement action. United States v. Figgie International Inc., 1997-1 Trade Cas. (CCH) ¶ 71,766 (D.D.C. 1997).

Applicable provisions. 7A(a), 7A(g), 801.1(h).

Issue. Failure to file.

Brief statement of the facts alleged. In July 1988, Mr. Figgie purchased voting securities of Figgie International which, when combined with the voting shares previously held by him, brought the value of his holdings above the $15 million threshold but not above 15 percent, which at the time was the next highest notification threshold. Then, in December 1988, Mr. Figgie purchased restricted voting securities of Figgie International that gave him the right to vote the shares and to receive any dividends attributable to the shares. Under the terms of Figgie International's 1988 restricted stock purchase plan, Mr. Figgie was not entitled to sell or dispose of any voting securities until all restrictions were automatically lifted in July 1993. At the time he purchased the shares under the 1988 restricted plan, Mr. Figgie acquired beneficial ownership of those voting securities. Mr. Figgie held the restricted voting securities at the time he purchased them according to Figgie International's restricted stock purchase plan and thus held 13.3 percent of the outstanding voting securities of Figgie International. Mr. Figgie allegedly acquired 100,000 additional shares of Figgie International stock in August 1992, giving him over 15.2 percent of the company's outstanding voting securities. Neither Mr. Figgie nor Figgie International filed the required HSR notification in connection with the August 1992 acquisition until October 13, 1993.

Action taken. In February 1997, FTC attorneys, acting as Special Attorneys to the U.S. Attorney General, filed a complaint alleging that the failure to notify and obey the applicable waiting periods for the August 1992 transaction prior to consummation violated the Act. Simultaneously, a final judgment was entered whereby Mr. Figgie and Figgie International each agreed to pay a civil penalty of $75,000, for a total penalty of $150,000. For additional information, see www.ftc.gov/opa/1997/02/figgie-7.htm.

J **Enforcement action.** United States v. Foodmaker, Inc., 1996-2 Trade Cas. (CCH) ¶ 71,555 (D.D.C. 1996).

Applicable provisions. 7A(a), 7A(g).

Issue. Failure to file.

Brief statement of the facts alleged. In October of 1992, Chi-Chi's, Inc., a wholly owned subsidiary of Foodmaker, Incorporated, acquired Consul, Inc., operator of 26 Chi-Chi's franchises in the United States and Canada, without notifying the transaction under the Act. At the time of the acquisition, Consul had initiated bankruptcy proceedings, submitting a reorganization plan to the court. Chi-Chi's had submitted an alternative plan under which it proposed to acquire 100 percent of Consul's voting securities. The bankruptcy court approved Chi-Chi's alternative plan in October 1992. Chi-Chi's completed the acquisition, valued at $12.7 million, on October 23, 1992. (Under former Section 802.20, notification was required for change of control acquisitions of voting securities where the acquired person had annual net sales or total assets of $25 million or more.) It was not until January 26, 1994, upon notification by the PNO of its obligation to file, that Foodmaker filed the required notification.

Action taken. In August 1996, FTC attorneys, acting as Special Attorneys to the U.S. Attorney General, filed a complaint alleging that Foodmaker's failure to file a Notification and Report Form violated the Act. The complaint alleged that Chi-Chi's knew that filing was required before it could acquire Consul's voting securities, yet it determined to proceed with the transaction without making the filing. In addition, the complaint alleged that Foodmaker, as parent company of Chi-Chi's, was responsible for the filing and had approved the acquisition and authorized the expenditure. Simultaneously, a final judgment also was entered whereby Foodmaker agreed to pay a civil penalty of $1.45 million. The ten-day waiting period to which this particular deal was subject expired on Feb. 5, 1994. Therefore, the complaint alleged that Foodmaker was in continuous violation of the HSR Act from Oct. 23, 1992 until Feb. 5, 1994. The civil penalty Foodmaker agreed to pay to settle the charges in this case represented virtually the maximum amount the company could pay without violating outstanding loan commitments, which could have put the company into default. For additional information, see www.ftc.gov/opa/1996/08/foodmake.htm.

K **Enforcement action.** United States v. Titan Wheel International, Inc., 1996-1 Trade Cas. (CCH) ¶ 71,406 (D.D.C. 1996).

Applicable provisions. 7A(a), 7A(g), 801.1(c)(1).

Issues. Gun-jumping; beneficial ownership.

Brief statement of the facts alleged. Titan Wheel International, Inc., and Pirelli Armstrong Tire Corporation entered into an asset purchase agreement that, effective July 17, 1994, gave Titan Wheel control of the Pirelli Armstrong Des Moines plant and other assets. Titan Wheel purportedly took control of more than $15 million of Pirelli assets including the inventory, machinery, equipment, and customer and supplier lists before the companies filed their notifications. The purchase agreement in the acquisition was subsequently amended and control of the plant returned to Pirelli Armstrong. During this time, the parties did make the requisite HSR filings and the waiting period was terminated early, after control of the plant was returned to Pirelli.

Action taken. In May 1996, FTC attorneys, acting as Special Attorneys to the U.S. Attorney General, filed a complaint alleging that Titan Wheel's control of the assets prior to filing and waiting until the expiration of the HSR waiting period constituted a violation of the HSR Act. The complaint alleged that Titan Wheel was in continuous violation of the Act for a period of thirteen days. A final judgment was also filed simultaneously with the complaint whereby Titan Wheel agreed to pay a civil penalty of $130,000, the maximum civil penalty allowable. For additional information, see www.ftc.gov/opa/1996/05/titan.htm.

L **Enforcement action.** United States v. Automatic Data Processing, Inc., 1996-1 Trade Cas. (CCH) ¶ 71,361 (D.D.C. 1996).

Applicable provisions. 7A(d), Item 4(c).

Issue. Failure to file 4(c) documents.

Brief statement of the facts alleged. In 1994, Automatic Data Processing ("ADP") agreed to acquire certain assets from AutoInfo, Inc. The complaint alleged that ADP did not submit any documents that were responsive to Item 4(c) in its filing, made on Dec. 7, 1994. The initial thirty-day waiting period for that filing expired without either the FTC or the DOJ taking any action to challenge the transaction. The transaction was completed in April 1995. After the transaction was publicly announced, the FTC received complaints expressing concern that the acquisition would harm competition for computer information and communications services in the automotive recycled parts and automobile insurance industries in the United States. The FTC subsequently reopened its investigation, and issued a subpoena for documents from ADP in order to investigate the transaction's competitive effects. In response to the subpoena, ADP submitted several documents that allegedly should have been included in the filing as Item 4(c) documents. The documents included a marketing plan that explained how the acquisition would enable ADP to "monopolize" the relevant market. ADP ultimately submitted the missing documents when it resubmitted its Notification and Report Form in January 1996.

Action taken. In March 1996, FTC attorneys, acting as Special Attorneys to the U.S. Attorney General, filed a complaint alleging that ADP's failure to provide the documents in its filing violated the Act. The complaint alleged that ADP was in violation of the Act from April 1, 1995, at least until it refiled its notification on January 23, 1996, at which time it submitted additional documents in response to Item 4(c). Simultaneously with the complaint, a final judgment was also filed whereby ADP agreed to pay a civil penalty of $2.97 million. At the time of filing of the final judgment, this was the largest HSR civil penalty ever imposed involving the failure to submit Item 4(c) documents.

In a separate action, the FTC filed an administrative complaint in November 1996, alleging that ADP's acquisition of AutoInfo violated Section 7 of the Clayton Act and Section 5 of the FTC Act. In June 1997, prior to trial, ADP settled those charges by entering into a consent agreement whereby ADP agreed to divest the assets it acquired in the transaction. For additional information, see www.ftc.gov/opa/1996/9603/adpauto.htm.

| ***M*** | **Enforcement action.** United States v. Sara Lee Corp., 1996-1 Trade Cas. (CCH) ¶ 71,301 (D.D.C. 1996).

Applicable provisions. 7A(a), 7A(g), 801.10, 801.90.

Issues. Failure to file; fair market value; avoidance device.

Brief statement of the facts alleged. In 1991, Sara Lee Corporation acquired Reckitt & Colman plc's shoe care products business for approximately $25.8 million. Despite valuing the U.S. assets being acquired substantially more than the U.K. assets, Sara Lee split the $25.8 million purchase price into two separate contracts, one of which valued U.S. assets at $13.1 million, and another that valued U.K. assets at $12.7 million. Sara Lee did not notify the transactions prior to closing. Subsequent to closing, the FTC began an investigation of whether the transaction violated Section 7 of the Clayton Act and Section 5 of the FTC Act. During that investigation, the FTC determined that the fair market value of the U.S. assets acquired actually exceeded the then $15 million threshold of the Act, and, therefore, the parties should have filed prior to acquiring the U.S. assets. Sara Lee did not file the required notification until August 1994.

Action taken. In February 1996, FTC attorneys, acting as Special Attorneys to the U.S. Attorney General, filed a complaint alleging that Sara Lee's failure to file violated the Act. The complaint alleged that the Sara Lee subsidiary that made the acquisition sought to undertake the acquisition without notifying the transaction because of concern that the FTC or the DOJ would challenge the acquisition and that Sara Lee was in violation of the Act from the date of closing until it belatedly filed its Notification and Report Form and that waiting period expired. Simultaneously, a final judgment was filed whereby Sara Lee agreed to pay a civil penalty of $3.1 million. At the time, this was the largest civil penalty ever imposed for a violation of the Act.

In a separate action, the FTC filed an administrative complaint alleging that Sara Lee's acquisition violated Section 7 of the Clayton Act and Section 5 of the FTC Act by creating a virtual monopoly in the shoe care products business. Sara Lee agreed to resolve those charges in June 1994 by agreeing to divest several brands of shoe care products. For additional information, see www.ftc.gov/opa/1996/02/sara.htm.

N **Enforcement action.** United States v. Farley, 1995-1 Trade Cas. (CCH) ¶ 70,883 (N.D. Ill. 1995).

Applicable provisions. 7A(a), 7A(c)(9), 7A(g), 802.9.

Issues. Failure to file; investment-only exemption.

Brief statement of the facts alleged. William Farley, majority shareholder of Farley, Inc. ("Farley") began to acquire stock in West Point-Pepperell, Inc., in March 1988, and acquired in excess of the then $15 million threshold of the Act. Farley did not file its notification, however, until two months later when Farley filed for a planned cash tender offer for the remaining outstanding shares of West Point, wherein it acquired a controlling interest.

Action taken. In February 1992, FTC attorneys, acting as Special Attorneys to the U.S. Attorney General, filed a complaint alleging that Farley's failure to file violated the Act. Farley defended the failure to file, claiming that its acquisition was made "solely for purposes of investment" and therefore was exempt from the filing requirements under Section 802.9. The FTC, however, claimed that the exemption did not apply because Farley was considering the possibility of acquiring control of West Point at the time of the initial purchase of West Point stock. The complaint alleged that Farley was in violation of the Act for a period of 91 days, from March 24 through June 22, 1988.

In January 1995, Farley agreed to settle these charges prior to trial and a final judgment was entered whereby Farley agreed to pay a civil penalty of $425,000. For additional information, see www.ftc.gov/opa/predawn/F95/farley-westpt2.htm.

O   **Enforcement action.** United States v. Pennzoil Co., 1994-2 Trade Cas. (CCH) ¶ 70,760 (D.D.C. 1994).

Applicable provisions. 7A(a), 7A(c)(9), 7A(g), 802.9.

Issues. Failure to file; investment-only exemption.

Brief statement of the facts alleged. The complaint alleged that Pennzoil Co. acquired more than $15 million in Chevron Corp. voting securities without filing notification under the HSR Act, and that Pennzoil later acquired additional Chevron stock. As a result of the acquisitions, Pennzoil held approximately 8.9 percent of Chevron stock valued at $2.1 billion. Pennzoil did not file its notification under the Act until approximately 10 months after the acquisition.

Action taken. In September 1994, FTC attorneys, acting as Special Attorneys to the U.S. Attorney General, filed a complaint alleging that Pennzoil's failure to file violated the Act. The FTC concluded that Pennzoil's acquisition was not exempt under the "solely for purposes of investment" exemption of Section 802.9. The complaint alleged that while Pennzoil was acquiring Chevron voting securities, members of Pennzoil's senior management were anticipating membership on Chevron's Board of Directors and participation in the formulation of basic business decisions by the company. In addition, the FTC press release announcing the complaint noted that in promulgating the "solely for investment" exemption in 1978, the FTC and the DOJ noted that companies acquiring securities of competing firms would not normally qualify for the exemption. The complaint alleged that Pennzoil and Chevron were competitors in the oil and gas business. Simultaneously with the filing of the complaint, a final judgment was filed whereby Pennzoil agreed to pay a civil penalty of $2.6 million. For additional information, see www.ftc.gov/opa/predawn/F95/pennzoil-chevr.htm.

| P | **Enforcement action.** United States v. Anova Holding AG, 1993-2 Trade Cas. (CCH) ¶ 70,383 (D.D.C. 1993).

Applicable provisions. 7A(a), 7A(g), 802.51.

Issues. Failure to file promptly after discovery of inadvertent failure to file.

Brief statement of the facts alleged. Stephan Schmidheiny, a Swiss businessman, acquired, in separate transactions, two Swiss firms that do business in the United States. Schmidheiny acquired control of Landis & Gyr AG in January 1988, and of Wild Leitz Holding AG in June 1989, both without filing the required notifications. In August 1989, the complaint alleged that Schmidheiny notified the FTC that he had discovered the violations, but then did not submit filings for the transactions until February 4, 1991, more than seventeen months after the failure to file was purportedly discovered.

Action taken. In September 1993, FTC attorneys, acting as Special Attorneys to the U.S. Attorney General, filed a complaint alleging that Schmidheiny's failure to file violated the Act. Simultaneously with the filing of the complaint, a final judgment was filed whereby Schmidheiny agreed to settle charges that his failure to file violated the Act. Schmidheiny and his firms agreed to pay a total civil penalty of $414,650. For additional information, see www.ftc.gov/opa/predawn/F93/schmidhei8.htm.

$\boxed{Q}$ Enforcement action. United States v. Honickman, 1992-2 Trade Cas. (CCH) ¶ 70,018 (D.D.C. 1992).

Applicable provisions. 7A(a), 7A(g), 801.90.

Issues. Failure to file; avoidance device.

Brief statement of the facts alleged. Harold A. Honickman was a major bottler of Pepsi-Cola and Canada Dry in the New York City metropolitan area. In 1987, Honickman allegedly attempted to evade the HSR Act's notification obligations by using multiple business entities to acquire Seven-Up Brooklyn Bottling Company. Allegedly, Seven-Up Brooklyn was sold to L.I. Acquisition Co., Melville Beverage Partners LP, Berriman Cozine Corp., and R.C. Acquisition Co. Honickman's interest in the first three entities gave him control of Seven-Up Brooklyn assets that, in the aggregate were valued in excess of the then $15 million notification threshold. Honickman was given the contractual right to manage virtually all the acquiring entities and provided the money to make each of the purchases. His partners in each of the acquisition vehicles were either his children or close business associates. Honickman never filed a Notification and Report Form for any of these acquisitions.

Action taken. In October 1992, FTC attorneys, acting as Special Attorneys to the U.S. Attorney General, filed a complaint alleging that Honickman's failure to file violated the Act. According to the complaint, Honickman was in violation of the Act for a period of nearly one-and-a-half years. Simultaneously with the filing of the complaint, a final judgment was filed whereby Honickman agreed to pay a civil penalty of $1.976 million. For additional information, see www.ftc.gov/opa/predawn/F93/honickman2.htm.

| R | **Enforcement action.** United States v. Beazer plc, 1992-2 Trade Cas. (CCH) ¶ 69,923 (D.D.C. 1992).

Applicable provisions. 7A(a), 7A(g), 801.90.

Issues. Failure to file; avoidance device.

Brief statement of the facts alleged. In 1987, Beazer plc, a U.K. construction company, began acquiring voting securities in Koppers, Inc., a U.S.-based construction company. Beazer formed a partnership as a device to avoid complying with the Act. Beazer allegedly made the acquisition pursuant to a plan to acquire all of Koppers' voting securities in a series of acquisitions through several entities, while delaying filing under the Act. In September 1987, Beazer began purchasing Koppers' securities through a wholly owned U.S. subsidiary called Bright Aggregates, Inc., formed specifically for that purpose. Beazer stopped purchasing Koppers' stock through Bright when the value of the acquired stock equaled approximately $14 million. In October 1987, Bright, together with SL-Merger Inc., and Speedward Limited (subsidiaries of Shearson Lehman Brothers Holding, Inc. and National Westminster Bank PLC, respectively), allegedly began purchasing stock through a newly formed general partnership called BNS Partners. The partnership was structured so that no one partner held more than a 49 percent interest, but the partnership agreement gave Beazer the right to purchase the interests of Shearson and National Westminster at some later date and Beazer could be required to buy the remaining shares if called upon to do so by the other partners. Beazer had the sole authority to operate the partnerships. Beazer then formed BNS Inc., structured among partners Bright, SL-Merger and Speedward in the same proportions as BNS Partners, to file a cash tender offer for all of the remaining outstanding Koppers voting securities. BNS Inc. made the cash tender offer on March 3, 1988. It was then that Beazer filed the required premerger notification forms. Beazer became the sole owner of Koppers on January 20, 1989, when it purchased the Koppers interests owned by SL-Merger and Speedward.

Action taken. In August 1992, FTC attorneys, acting as Special Attorneys to the U.S. Attorney General, filed a complaint alleging that Beazer's failure to file violated the Act. According to the complaint, Beazer was in violation of the Act for a period of 152 days.

Simultaneously with the filing of the complaint, a final judgment was filed whereby Beazer agreed to settle charges that its failure to file violated the Act. Beazer agreed to pay a civil penalty of $760,000.

In a separate action, on March 18, 1988, the DOJ filed a complaint alleging that the proposed acquisition of Koppers by BNS Inc. would violate Section 7 of the Clayton Act by substantially lessening competition in the southern California aggregates market. A consent judgment was entered requiring BNS Inc. to divest any interest it acquired in Koppers' southern California aggregates plant. For additional information, see www.ftc.gov/opa/predawn/F93/beazer-pl6.htm.

|S| **Enforcement action.** United States v. Atlantic Richfield Co., 1992-1 Trade Cas. (CCH) ¶ 69,695 (D.D.C. 1992).

Applicable provisions. 7A(a), 7A(g), 801.1(c)(1).

Issues. Gun-jumping; beneficial ownership.

Brief statement of the facts alleged. U.F. Genetics entered into a contract with Atlantic Richfield Company ("ARCO") on December 29, 1986 to acquire ARCO Seed for $18 million. On the same day, U.F. Genetics allegedly paid $9.18 million into an escrow account and $8.82 million in cash and notes to ARCO. U.F. Genetics received 49 percent of the voting securities of ARCO Seed and the right to vote the remaining 51 percent, while the share certificates for that 51 percent were placed into an escrow account. The parties filed their required notifications one day later, on December 30, 1986, reporting U.F. Genetics' intention to acquire the remaining 51 percent of the voting securities.

Action taken. In December 1991, FTC attorneys, acting as Special Attorneys to the U.S. Attorney General, filed a complaint alleging that U.F. Genetics took premature control of ARCO Seed's business in violation of the Act. The complaint alleged that U.F. Genetics' acquisition of 49 percent of the voting securities with the permanent right to vote the remaining 51 percent placed in escrow amounted to the acquisition of beneficial ownership of 100 percent of the voting securities. According to the complaint, ARCO and U.F. Genetics were in violation of the Act from December 29, 1986 through January 29, 1987, the day on which the HSR waiting period expired.

In February 1992, prior to trial, ARCO entered into a settlement by agreeing to pay a civil penalty of $290,000. In April 1992, prior to trial, U.F. Genetics also settled by agreeing to pay a civil penalty of $150,000. U.F. Genetics had previously agreed to settle these charges in November 1989, but the company then filed for bankruptcy protection. FTC attorneys filed a claim in the Bankruptcy Court for a penalty of $150,000 but U.F. Genetics objected, claiming that the previous settlement agreement was not binding. U.F. Genetics subsequently agreed to withdraw its objections to the FTC's claim and pay the civil penalty. The FTC simultaneously agreed to subordinate its claim to the claims of certain other creditors. For additional information, see www.ftc.gov/opa/

predawn/F93/arco-ufge7.htm and www.ftc.gov/opa/predawn/F93/ufgenetic3.htm.

| T | **Enforcement action.** United States v. General Cinema Corp., 1991-2 Trade Cas. (CCH) ¶ 69,681 (D.D.C. 1992).

Applicable provisions. 7A(a), 7A(g), 7A(c)(9), 802.9.

Issues. Failure to file; investment-only exemption.

Brief statement of the facts alleged. General Cinema Corp. acquired stock in Cadbury Schweppes plc in September 1986 and accumulated Schweppes' holdings that exceeded the then $15 million threshold. General Cinema defended its failure to file a Notification and Report Form based upon the "solely for investment purposes" exemption.

Action taken. In January 1991, FTC attorneys filed a complaint alleging that General Cinema's failure to file prior to consummating the transaction violated the Act. The FTC concluded that General Cinema did not acquire the stock solely for investment purposes, because General Cinema at the time of the acquisitions was considering ways to participate in the formulation, determination, or direction of the basic business decisions of Cadbury Schweppes, in which case the investment exemption does not apply. The complaint alleged that General Cinema was in violation of the Act from September 11, 1986, until February 25, 1987, a total of 168 days.

In January 1992, prior to trial, General Cinema agreed to settle the charges and a final judgment was entered whereby General Cinema agreed to pay a civil penalty of $950,000 (out of a maximum possible civil penalty of $1.68 million). For additional information, see www.ftc.gov/opa/predawn/F93/generalci3.htm.

U **Enforcement action.** United States v. Cox Enterprises, Inc., 1991-2 Trade Cas. ¶ 69,540 (N.D. Ga. 1991).

Applicable provisions. 7A(a), 7A(g), 7A(c)(9), 802.9.

Issues. Failure to file; investment-only exemption.

Brief statement of the facts alleged. Cox Enterprises purchased 2.25 million shares of stock of Knight-Ridder, Inc., between January and November 1986 for $101 million. Both companies owned newspapers and television and radio stations in various locations. Cox began selling shares of Knight-Ridder on January 16, 1987 and reduced its holdings to less than $15 million by January 28, 1987. Cox did not file a Notification and Report Form for its purchases of Knight-Ridder over $15 million, claiming that its acquisitions were made solely for purposes of investment and therefore were exempt from the Act under Section 802.9.

Action taken. On March 18, 1991, the DOJ filed a complaint in the U.S. District Court for the Northern District of Georgia, charging that Cox violated the Act for the 367 days that it held Knight-Ridder securities valued in excess of the notification threshold without filing a Notification and Report Form. The DOJ claimed that the solely for investment exemption did not apply to the Cox acquisition and sought a civil penalty of $3.67 million. Prior to trial, Cox agreed to settle the charges and a final judgment was entered whereby Cox agreed to pay a civil penalty of $1.75 million. For additional information, see *Government Says Cox Purchase Lacked Federal OK,* Associated Press, March 8, 1991, *available at* 1991 WL 6175680.

$\boxed{V}$ **Enforcement action.** United States v. Aero Limited Partnership, 1991-1 Trade Cas. ¶ 69,451 (D.D.C. 1991).

Applicable provisions. 7A(a), 7A(g); 7A(c)(9), 802.9.

Issues. Failure to file; investment-only exemption.

Brief statement of the facts alleged. Aero, the parent corporation of Trans World Airlines, acquired voting securities of USAir in 1986 and 1987 that were in excess of $15 million. Aero did not file a Notification and Report Form claiming that the acquisitions were made solely for purposes of investment and were, therefore, exempt from the requirements of the Act under Section 802.9.

Action taken. In May 1991, the DOJ filed a complaint alleging that Aero violated the Act by failing to file a Notification and Report Form prior to acquiring the USAir shares. The complaint alleged that the acquisitions were not made solely for purposes of investment within the meaning of the Act. The complaint alleged that Aero was in violation of the Act for a period of 224 days. Simultaneously with the complaint, a final judgment was filed whereby Aero agreed to pay a civil penalty of $1.125 million. For additional information, see *TWA Agrees to $1.1 Million Penalty for USAir Stock Buy,* Associated Press, May 30, 1991, *available at* 1991 WL 6188380.

W **Enforcement action.** United States v. Atlantic Richfield Co., 1991-1 Trade Cas. (CCH) ¶ 69,318 (D.D.C. 1991).

Applicable provisions. 7A(a), 7A(g), 801.1(c)(1).

Issues. Gun-jumping; beneficial ownership.

Brief statement of the facts alleged. The Atlantic Richfield Co., and its majority-owned subsidiary, ARCO Chemical Co. (collectively, "ARCO"), entered into an agreement with Union Carbide Corp. to purchase Union Carbide's urethane polyol and propylene glycol assets and operations. The complaint alleged that Union Carbide transferred those assets and operations to ARCO on September 27, 1989, when Union Carbide received the full agreed-upon purchase price under the parties' acquisition agreement and ceded the benefits and risks of ownership to ARCO. Union Carbide thereafter continued to operate those assets and operations, but only as a caretaker for ARCO. Only later did the parties file their Notification and Report Form.

Action taken. In January 1991, the DOJ filed a complaint alleging that ARCO's and Union Carbide's failure to file prior to undertaking the transaction violated the Act. The complaint alleged that beneficial ownership transferred from Union Carbide to ARCO because the parties effectively passed all benefits and risks of ownership to ARCO, thereby eliminating Union Carbide as an independent competitor. Under a final judgment filed contemporaneously with the complaint, ARCO and Union Carbide each agreed to pay a civil penalty of $1 million (for a total civil penalty of $2 million).

In a separate action, in 1990, the FTC filed a preliminary injunction action to rescind the transaction, alleging that the transaction violated Section 7 of the Clayton Act and Section 5 of the FTC Act. In September of 1990, the parties entered into a consent agreement to resolve those charges and agreed to divest certain assets and other relief. For additional information, see www.ftc.gov/opa/predawn/F93/arcoucc.htm.

X **Enforcement action.** United States v. Equity Group Holdings, 1991-1 Trade Cas. (CCH) ¶ 69,320 (D.D.C. 1991).

Applicable provisions. 7A(a), 7A(g), 801.90.

Issues. Failure to file; avoidance device.

Brief statement of the facts alleged. Equity Group Holdings, a partnership equally controlled by two brothers, Steven M. Rales and Mitchell P. Rales, acquired stock in Interco Inc. From May 2 through May 24, 1988, Equity Group bought Interco stock. On May 18, the partnership had purchased more than $15 million of the stock, and it continued acquiring stock until May 24. On May 24, 1988, the Rales brothers, through two corporations, and two associates formed a limited partnership (City Capital Associates Limited Partnership) in which the Rales brothers each owned 49 percent of the limited partnership interests. City Capital then continued to acquire Interco shares. Notifications were not filed until November 1988, when City Capital reported its intention to acquire up to 100 percent of Interco's stock.

Action taken. In January 1991, the DOJ filed a complaint alleging that Equity Group's failure to file violated the Act. The complaint alleged that the use of the two corporations as 49 percent partners in the partnership to make these acquisitions was an avoidance device under Section 801.90. The FTC found that the substance of the transaction was a purchase by an entity in which Equity Group had a 98 percent interest. The complaint alleged that Equity Group was in continuous violation of the Act from May 18 through November 25, 1988. Simultaneously with the filing of the complaint, a final judgment was filed whereby Equity Group agreed to pay a civil penalty of $850,000. For additional information, see www.ftc.gov/opa/predawn/F93/rales.txt.

Y **Enforcement action.** United States v. Service Corp. International, 1991-1 Trade Cas. (CCH) ¶ 69,289 (D.D.C. 1991).

Applicable provisions. 7A(a), 7A(g), 801.90.

Issues. Failure to file; acquisition through an agent; avoidance device.

Brief statement of the facts alleged. On December 30, 1986, Service Corp. International's ("SCI") acquired all of the voting securities of Centurion National Group, Inc. ("CNG") for more than $15 million, but did not file its Notification and Report Form until January 27, 1987. (The waiting period expired on February 26, 1987.) SCI acquired the Centurion shares through an agent. At the time of the alleged acquisition, SCI and CNG were both in the funeral and cemetery services industry.

Action taken. In January 1991, the DOJ filed a complaint alleging that SCI's failure to file violated the HSR Act. The complaint alleged that SCI was in continuous violation of the Act for a period of 59 days. Simultaneously with the filing of the complaint, a final judgment was filed whereby SCI agreed to pay a civil penalty of $500,000.

Z Enforcement action. United States v. Reliance Group Holdings, Inc., 1990-2 Trade Cas. (CCH) ¶ 69,248 (D.D.C. 1990).

Applicable provisions. 7A(a), 7A(g), 802.9.

Issues. Failure to file; investment-only exemption.

Brief statement of the facts alleged. Reliance Group Holdings began acquiring voting stock in Spectra-Physics, Inc. in November 1985. As a result of acquiring additional shares in August 1986, Reliance held Spectra-Physics voting stock valued in excess of the then $15 million threshold. Reliance continued buying Spectra-Physics' securities through December 1986. In January 1987, Reliance filed its Notification and Report Form stating an intention to acquire between 15 percent and 25 percent of Spectra-Physics, but withdrew the notification in February 1987. On July 1, 1987, Reliance sold all of its interest in Spectra-Physics.

Action taken. In October 1990, the DOJ filed a complaint alleging that Reliance's failure to file violated the Act. The complaint alleged that the acquisitions at issue were not made solely for the purposes of investment within the meaning of the Act. The complaint alleged that Reliance remained in violation of the filing requirements of the Act from August 27, 1986, to at least February 15, 1987, when the waiting period would have expired had Reliance not withdrawn its filing. In a final judgment filed simultaneously with the complaint, Reliance agreed to pay a civil penalty of $550,000. For additional information, see www.ftc.gov/opa/predawn/F93/rel.group7.txt.

| AA | **Enforcement action.** United States v. Baker Hughes Inc., 1990-1 Trade Cas. (CCH) ¶ 68,976 (D.D.C. 1990).

Applicable provisions. 7A(d), 7A(g), Item 4(c).

Issue. Failure to produce 4(c) documents.

Brief statement of the facts alleged. In May 1989, Oy Tampella AB (Tampella) and Baker Hughes filed Notification and Report Forms relating to a proposed acquisition by Tampella of certain assets of Baker Hughes (the asset acquisition). This transaction was subsequently restructured and the parties filed revised Notification and Report Forms on July 24, 1989. Early termination of the waiting period for this asset acquisition was granted on July 25 and the parties consummated this transaction on July 31, 1989.

Subsequently, Tampella and Baker Hughes entered into another transaction whereby a Tampella subsidiary would acquire all of the voting securities of Eimco Secoma S.A. (Eimco), a subsidiary of Baker Hughes (the Eimco transaction). During the course of the DOJ's investigation of the proposed Eimco transaction, Tampella submitted a business plan that was prepared for officers of Tampella and that evaluated and analyzed the prior asset acquisition with respect to market shares, competition, competitors, markets, and the potential for sales growth or expansion into product or geographic markets. Tampella failed to include this document in response to Item 4(c) of its Notification and Report Form filed for the asset acquisition. Tampella provided the document to the DOJ on October 6, 1989, and to the FTC on November 27, 1989.

Action taken. In December 1989, the DOJ filed a complaint seeking an injunction to block the proposed Eimco transaction as violating Section 7 of the Clayton Act. The complaint also alleged that Tampella's failure to produce the subject document in response to Item 4(c) in its filing for the asset acquisition was a violation of the Act. The complaint sought the maximum civil penalty for each day that Tampella was in violation of the Act.

In March 1990, prior to trial on the merits of the allegations concerning the HSR violation, Tampella agreed to settle these charges and a final judgment was entered whereby Tampella agreed to pay a civil penalty of $275,000. This was the first case to impose HSR civil penalties on a company for failing to submit Item 4(c) documents.

With respect to the allegations concerning the Eimco transaction, on February 21, 1990, after two days of hearings, the district court denied the request for a permanent injunction and dismissed that portion of the complaint. The U.S. Court of Appeals affirmed that dismissal in July 1990. *See United States v. Baker Hughes, Inc.*, 1990-1 Trade Cas. (CCH) ¶ 68,930 (D.D.C. 1990), *aff'd,* 1990-1 Trade Cas. (CCH) ¶ 69,084 (D.C. Cir. 1990).

| BB | **Enforcement action.**   United States v. Tengelmann Warenhandelsgesellschaft, 1989-1 Trade Cas. (CCH) ¶ 68,623 (D.D.C. 1989).

Applicable provisions. 7A(a), 7A(g), 801.90.

Issues. Failure to file; avoidance device.

Brief statement of the facts alleged. The Great Atlantic & Pacific Tea Co. Inc. ("A&P") acquired over half of the voting securities of Waldbaum Inc. in 1986 for an acquisition price in excess of the notification threshold. A&P did not notify the transaction, having structured the transaction through a general partnership comprised of A&P and five members of the Waldbaum family.

Action taken. In June 1989, the DOJ filed a complaint alleging that A&P's failure to file violated the Act. This was the first case brought dealing with the so-called "partnership loophole." According to the complaint, the partnership used here was an avoidance structure "created for the purpose of avoiding the obligation to comply with the notification and waiting period requirements of the Act. The substance of the transaction . . . was that of an acquisition by defendants of Waldbaum's." In a final judgment filed simultaneously with the complaint, A&P agreed to settle charges that its acquisition violated the Act and agreed to pay a $3 million civil penalty, at that time the largest civil penalty ever assessed for an HSR violation. Subsequently, in 1987, the agencies addressed the "partnership loophole" by amending the definition of "control" as it applies to partnerships. *See* 52 Fed. Reg. 20,058 (May 29, 1987). For additional information, see www.ftc.gov/opa/predawn/F89/aandp.txt.

CC **Enforcement action.** FTC v. Illinois Cereal Mills, Inc., 691 F. Supp. 1131 (N.D. Ill. 1988), *aff'd sub nom.* FTC v. Elders Grain, Inc. 868 F.2d 901 (7th Cir. 1989).

Applicable provisions. 7A(a), 7A(g), 801.9, 801.13(b)(2)(ii).

Issues. Failure to file; avoidance device.

Brief statement of the facts alleged. On June 5, 1988, Illinois Cereal acquired Lincoln Grain Company's assets from its parent Elders Grain Inc. The parties did not file Notification and Report Forms. The parties structured the transaction so that Illinois Cereal would pay Lincoln $14 million, for its dry corn mill assets and 90 rail cars, and Elders $100,000 for an option to purchase a grain elevator connected to the mill. The option permitted Illinois Cereal to purchase the grain elevator for $6 million within five years of the transaction. Illinois Cereal also leased a portion of the grain elevator for $250,000 per year plus handling charges.

Action taken. On June 6, 1988, after learning of the transaction, the FTC filed a complaint seeking a temporary restraining order. The complaint alleged that the transaction violated Section 7 of the Clayton Act and Section 5 of the FTC Act. The FTC sought either rescission or the appointment of a receiver to operate and manage the assets pending the outcome of litigation.

The FTC later moved to amend the complaint to claim that the transaction also violated the Act because the actual value of the transaction was over $15 million and the parties had structured it so as to avoid a premerger filing (leases in which certain indicia of ownership are transferred and that operate as effective asset acquisitions may be deemed constructive transfers of beneficial ownership by the agencies. *See* Int. 4. The district court denied the motion to amend the complaint, because it would have required additional discovery and result in a delay of the hearing.

The district court ultimately granted the FTC's request for rescission. The Seventh Circuit affirmed this decision on January 30, 1989. The parties rescinded their transaction on March 14, 1989 and entered into a consent decree with the FTC. Pursuant to the decree, for a ten-year period Illinois Cereal was required to provide 30 days advance notice to the FTC and receive prior approval for all purchases of industrial corn milling assets from a single seller worth $500,000 or more. For additional information, see www.ftc.gov/opa/predawn/F89/illgrain.txt.

DD **Enforcement action.** United States v. Lonrho PLC, 1988-2 Trade Cas. ¶ 68,232 (D.D.C. 1988).

Applicable provisions. 7A(a), 7A(g).

Issue. Failure to file.

Brief statement of the facts alleged. In October 1986, Lonrho, Inc., a wholly owned subsidiary of Lonrho PLC, acquired 40 percent of the voting securities of Diamond A Cattle Company for an amount in excess of $15 million. The parties did not file Notification and Report Forms prior to consummating the transaction. In November 1986, the parties filed these forms stating that on October 21, 1986, Lonrho had purchased 50 percent of the voting securities of Diamond A. The waiting period related to that filing expired on December 27, 1986.

Action taken. In July 1988, the DOJ filed a complaint alleging that the parties' failure to file prior to consummating the second acquisition violated the HSR Act. The complaint named Lonrho, Diamond A, and Robert O. Anderson, Diamond A's UPE. The complaint alleged that the parties were in continuous violation of the Act for the period October 21, 1986, through December 27, 1986. Simultaneously with the filing of the complaint, a final judgment was also filed whereby Lonrho and Diamond A each agreed to settle all charges by paying a civil penalty of $122,000 (for a total civil penalty of $244,000).

Editor's Note. This was the first case to impose an HSR Act civil penalty on an acquired (in addition to an acquiring) person.

EE **Enforcement action.** United States v. Roscoe Moss Co., 1988-1 Trade Cas. (CCH) ¶ 68,040 (D.D.C. 1988).

Applicable provisions. 7A(a), 7A(g).

Issue. Failure to file.

Brief statement of the facts alleged. Roscoe Moss Co. began to acquire stock in the San Jose Water Co. on November 22, 1977. The complaint alleged that on December 1, 1984, Moss acquired additional stock that caused the value of its holdings to exceed $15 million. Moss continued to acquire additional voting securities of San Jose Water Co. during the period from December 1984 through February 12, 1986. Moss filed a Notification and Report Form on February 24, 1986, stating its intention to acquire at least 25 percent of SJW Corp., which was formed in 1985 and held the stock of its wholly owned subsidiary, San Jose Water Co.

Action taken. In May 1988, the DOJ filed a complaint alleging that Moss' failure to file violated the Act. The complaint also named Roscoe Moss Jr., of Flintridge, Calif., the company's majority stockowner. In a final judgment filed simultaneously with the complaint, the defendants agreed to pay $500,000 in civil penalties. For additional information, see www.ftc.gov/opa/predawn/F88/moss.txt.

| FF | **Enforcement action.** United States v. Wickes Cos., 1988-1 Trade Cas. (CCH) ¶ 67,966 (D.D.C. 1988).

Applicable provisions. 7A(a), 7A(g), 801.90.

Issues. Failure to file; acquisition through an agent; avoidance device.

Brief statement of the facts alleged. The complaint charged that Wickes Companies, Inc. acquired stock in Owens-Corning Fiberglass Corp. through an agent, Bear Stearns, in an amount beyond the then $15 million filing threshold. Wickes eventually filed a Notification and Report Form, but not within the time frame established by the Act.

Action taken. In March 1988, the DOJ filed a complaint alleging that Wickes' failure to file violated the Act. In a final judgment filed contemporaneously with the complaint, Wickes agreed to settle charges that its acquisition violated the Act and agreed to pay a civil penalty of $300,000.

This was the first case filed concerning the use of an investment banking firm as an agent in a stock acquisition to avoid filing under the Act. Shortly thereafter, complaints making similar allegations that persons were using brokerage firms as agents in order to avoid filing requirements were filed against Donald Trump, First City Financial Corp. Ltd. and Roxboro Investments (1979) Ltd. *See* Int. 49 (for a more detailed description of such put-call arrangements); *see also* Enforcement Actions GG and HH (for other actions filed at about this same time containing similar allegations). For additional information, see www.ftc.gov/opa/predawn/F88/wickes.txt.

GG **Enforcement action.** United States v. Trump, 1988-1 Trade Cas. (CCH) ¶ 67,968 (D.D.C. 1988).

Applicable provisions. 7A(a), 7A(g), 801.90.

Issues. Failure to file; acquisition through an agent; avoidance device.

Brief statement of the facts alleged. Donald Trump allegedly made indirect acquisitions in amounts exceeding the Act's notification thresholds in two separate gaming companies, Holiday Corporation and Bally Manufacturing Corporation, through an agent, Bear Stearns & Company. Trump eventually filed notifications, but not within the time period required by the Act.

Action taken. On April 5, 1988, the DOJ filed a complaint charging that Donald Trump, despite having made the acquisitions through an investment bank, held beneficial ownership of the stock acquired in Holiday and Bally and violated the notification requirements of the Act. In a final judgment filed contemporaneously with the complaint, Trump settled the charges by agreeing to pay a civil penalty of $750,000. *See* Int. 49 (for a more detailed description of such put-call arrangements); *see also* Enforcement Actions FF and HH (for other actions filed at about this same time containing similar allegations). For additional information, see www.ftc.gov/opa/predawn/F88/trump.txt.

HH **Enforcement action.** United States v. First City Financial Corp., 1988-1 Trade Cas. (CCH) ¶ 67,967 (D.D.C. 1988).

Applicable provisions. 7A(a), 7A(g), 801.90.

Issues. Failure to file; acquisition through an agent; avoidance device.

Brief statement of the facts alleged. First City allegedly made an indirect acquisition in an amount exceeding the Act's notification threshold in Ashland Oil Inc. in 1986 through Bear Stearns & Company. First City eventually filed a notification, but not within the time period required by the Act.

Action taken. On April 1, 1988, the DOJ filed a complaint charging that First City, despite having made the acquisitions through an investment bank, held beneficial ownership of the stock acquired in Ashland Oil and violated the notification requirements of the Act. In a final judgment filed contemporaneously with the complaint, First City settled the charges by agreeing to pay a civil penalty of $400,000. *See* Int. 49 (for a more detailed description of such put-call arrangements); *see also* Enforcement Actions FF and GG (for other actions filed at about this same time containing similar allegations). For additional information, see www.ftc.gov/opa/predawn/F88/firstcity.txt.

II **Enforcement action.** United States v. Bell Resources Ltd., 1986-2 Trade Cas. (CCH) ¶ 67,321 (S.D.N.Y. 1986), 51 Fed. Reg. 11,489 (Apr. 3, 1986).

Applicable provisions. 7A(a), 7A(g), 7A(c)(9), 802.9.

Issues. Failure to file; investment-only exemption.

Brief statement of the facts alleged. On September 27, 1984, Weeks Petroleum Ltd., a subsidiary of Bell Resources Ltd., began purchasing shares of Asarco Inc. By November 21, 1984, Weeks had purchased over $15 million worth of Asarco stock. Weeks continued purchasing Asarco stock until November 28, 1984. Weeks claimed that these transactions were exempt from the filing requirements of the Act under the "solely for purposes of investment" exemption. On March 8, 1985, Weeks filed a Notification and Report Form for its intended purchase of 25 percent of Asarco. The waiting period for that filing expired on April 7, 1985.

Action taken. In August 1985, the DOJ filed a complaint against Weeks, its parent Bell Resources, and the Chairman of the Board of Bell Resources, alleging that an HSR filing should have been made in November 1984, before Weeks crossed the $15 million threshold. The complaint alleged that the parties were in violation of the Act from November 21, 1984 through April 7, 1985. The complaint stated that these acquisitions were not made solely for purposes of investment and therefore did not qualify for the exemption.

Prior to trial, in March 1986, a proposed final judgment was filed whereby Weeks agreed to pay a civil penalty of $450,000. For additional information, see www.ftc.gov/opa/predawn/F86/weekspet.htm.

JJ **Enforcement action.** United States v. Coastal Corp., 1985-1 Trade Cas. (CCH) ¶ 66,425 (D.D.C. 1984).

Applicable provisions. 7A(a), 7A(g), 802.9.

Issues. Failure to file; investment-only exemption.

Brief statement of the facts alleged. On January 19, 1984, Coastal, a natural gas pipeline company, purchased 75,500 shares of Houston Natural Gas Corporation ("HNG"). At the time, Coastal already owned over $15 million worth of HNG's voting securities. Coastal did not file a Notification and Report Form at the time of this purchase. Coastal contended that the acquisition was solely for purposes of investment and therefore exempt from filing under Section 802.9. The FTC claimed that it had reason to believe that Coastal's intent included the possibility of acquiring control of HNG. Subsequent to Coastal's January 19 purchase, Coastal on January 27, 1984, had publicly announced a tender offer to acquire HNG stock and filed a notification.

Action taken. On August 30, 1984, the DOJ filed a complaint alleging that Coastal had failed to file a Notification and Report Form in violation of the Act. Simultaneously with the filing of the complaint, a final judgment was also filed whereby Coastal agreed to settle the charges by agreeing to pay a civil penalty of $230,000, the maximum allowable civil penalty. By separate agreement with the FTC, Coastal also divested the 75,500 shares of HNG securities that it had purchased.

APPENDIX: FORMAL INTERPRETATIONS

Formal Interpretation 1

Cite. 6 Trade Reg. Rep. (CCH) ¶ 42,475, at 42,601 (Aug. 25, 1978) (with inquiry letters and additional information as found at www.ftc.gov/bc/hsr/frmlintrps/fi01.htm).

Text. [COVINGTON & BURLINGTON LETTERHEAD]
888 Sixteenth Street, N.W.
Washington, D.C. 20006

August 15, 1978

Malcolm R. Pfunder, Esq.
Associate Director, Premerger
Notification and Screening
Federal Trade Commission
Pennsylvania Avenue at 16th Street
Washington, D.C. 20580

Dear Mr. Pfunder:

I write to record my understanding, based upon our telephone conversation of August 14, that it is the staff's position that so long as companies will be filing premerger notification reports as to a merger or acquisition under the requirements of the Hart-Scott-Rodino Act, they need not also file letters of notification and reports as to such merger or acquisition under the Commission's existing notification requirements. I refer, of course, to transactions which are agreed on in principle before the effectiveness of the new regulations but which will not be consummated until after effectiveness. This interpretation sensibly avoids unnecessary and duplicative filings.

Sincerely,

[Signature]
Edwin M. Zimmerman

Dear Mr. Zimmerman:

Your letter of August 15 gives me the opportunity to explain a couple of points which have been the subject of numerous telephone and letter inquiries over the past few weeks. I have taken the liberty of putting your letter and my response on the public record, in order to clarify the relationship between the Commission's existing premerger notification program and the new program which is to be implemented under Section 7A of the Clayton Act, as added by Section 201 of the Hart-Scott-Rodino Antitrust Improvements Act of 1976.

The existing program, in its present form, dates back to 1974 (39 Federal Register 35717, October 3, 1974). That program required that certain mergers or acquisitions be reported to the Commission by filing of a letter of notification and one or more "Special Reports." In most situations covered by that program, each of the parties to a merger or acquisition was required to file a Special Report within ten days after reaching an agreement or understanding in principle to merge or to acquire assets or stock.

The Commission has recently amended its existing program to eliminate these requirements for any company (1) that files notification under Section 7A of the Clayton Act or (2) that is exempt from filing requirements under Section 7A or the rules implementing that section (43 Federal Register 28046, June 28, 1978). That amendment becomes effective on the effective date of the new premerger notification rules, which were published on July 31 (43 Federal Register 33450) and become effective on September 5, 1978 (*see* 43 Federal Register 34443). Promulgation of the new rules raises the question posed by your letter: must companies which are covered by and will be reporting under the new rules also file Special Reports under the existing program where an agreement or understanding in principle to merge or acquire is reached more than ten days prior to September 5, 1978?

Your letter of August 15 correctly summarizes the staff's position. While the existing program technically requires the filing of a Special Report in this situation, that filing would in our view unnecessarily duplicate the requirements of the new program. Reporting under the existing program is thus no longer required of any person who files under the new program. The only transactions which must still be reported under the Commission's 1974 program are (1) those which will be fully consummated before September 5, 1978 (because they will not be subject to the requirements of Section 7A), and (2) those which will be consummated on or after September 5,1978, are subject to the reporting requirements of Section 7A and the new premerger notification rules, and are not reported under the new program. In other words, on and after September 5, 1978, the existing premerger notification requirements will continue to apply only to those persons who are parties to transactions covered by the Hart-Scott-Rodino program but who, for whatever reason, decline to comply with the requirements of the new program.

Thank you for your inquiry.

Sincerely yours,

[Signature]
Malcolm R. Pfunder
Associate Director for Premerger Notification

Formal Interpretation 2

Cite. 6 Trade Reg. Rep. (CCH) ¶ 42,475, at 42,601 (Sept. 26, 1978) (with inquiry letters and additional information as found at www.ftc.gov/bc/hsr/frmlintrps/fi02.htm).

Text.
FEDERAL TRADE COMMISSION
WASHINGTON. D. C. 20580
BUREAU OF COMPETITION
September 26, 1978

Mr. Laurence T. Sorkin
Cahill, Gordon & Reindel
Eighty Pine Street
New York, New York 10005

Re: Formal interpretation of § 802.70 of the Hart-Scott-Rodino Antitrust Improvements Act of 1976

Dear Mr. Sorkin:

First National City Bank ("Citicorp") has requested an interpretation of § 802.70 of the premerger notification rules as it relates to Citicorp's proposed acquisition of Carte Blanche Corporation ("Carte Blanche"). In accordance with the provisions of § 803.30 of the rules, Commission staff has elected to render, with the concurrence of the Assistant Attorney General in charge of the Antitrust Division of the Department of Justice, a formal response to this request.

Section 802.70(b) of the rules exempts from the reporting and waiting period requirements of the Act and rules acquisitions "subject to an order of the Federal Trade Commission or of any Federal court requiring prior approval of such acquisition by the Federal Trade Commission, such court, or the Department of Justice, and such approval has been obtained." A 1968 consent decree specifically prohibited the reacquisition of Carte Blanche by Citicorp. The court retained jurisdiction, however, to enable the parties to apply for further orders or modifications of the decree. Citicorp obtained the approval of the Department of Justice to petition for vacation of the consent decree and the court vacated the decree on September 7, 1978. Under these facts the proposed acquisition is within the bounds of § 802.70 and thus is exempt from the requirements of the Act and rules.

This formal interpretation is rendered without prejudice to the right of rescission of either the Commission or the Assistant Attorney General. In the event of such rescission, Citicorp will be notified in writing.

Very truly yours,

[Signature]
Malcolm R. Pfunder
Associate Director for Premerger Notification

[CAHILL GORDON & REINDEL LETTERHEAD]
August 25, 1978
Re: United States v. First National City Bank, et. al., 65 Civ. 3963 (S.D.N.Y.)

Dear Mr. Pfunder:

This letter will confirm our contemporaneous oral request for an informal interpretation of Section 802.70 of the Commission's rules implementing Title II of the Hart-Scott-Rodino Act. This request is made pursuant to Section 803.30 of the rules. Section 802.70 exempts an acquisition from the requirements of the act if the acquiring person is subject to a federal court order requiring prior approval of that acquisition by the court or the Department of Justice and such approval has been obtained. Citicorp believes that its proposed acquisition of Carte Blanche Corporation, which will follow vacation of the 1968 consent decree which prohibited it, comes within this exemption.

On August 23, William M. Sayre of this office telephoned you, and due to your unavailability, spoke with Ms. Wilkof of your office. He described to her the proposed acquisition, the steps taken by Citicorp in seeking to vacate the consent decree, and the investigation which was undertaken by the Department of Justice before deciding not to oppose vacation of the decree. He indicated that we were not at that time seeking an informal interpretation, but merely wanted a preliminary reaction to our suggestion that Section 802.70 exempts Citicorp from the requirements of the act. He informed her that before actually seeking an informal interpretation of this Section we would prepare a letter containing the relevant information, which we would then submit to your office; Ms. Wilkof indicated to him that she considered this "an excellent way to proceed". This is the letter which we so promised.

418 *Appendix*

In December, 1965, Citicorp's predecessor (First National City Bank) acquired Carte Blanche Corporation, the operator of the Carte Blanche credit card. The Department of Justice brought suit under Section 7 of the Clayton Act on December 30, 1965, in the United States District Court for the Southern District of New York, 65 Civ. 3963 (Case No. 1882 in the Department of Justice). Subsequently, First National City Bank agreed to sell Carte Blanche to Avco Corporation, and on May 10, 1968 a consent decree was entered by the Court terminating the litigation. The consent decree is reported at 1968 Trade Cases ¶ 72,411 and a copy is attached hereto. This consent decree stated that: "Defendants . . . are hereby enjoined from reacquiring the stock of Carte Blanche, or by any other means acquiring control over the business of Carte Blanche." The decree also provided that:

> "Jurisdiction is retained by this Court for the purpose of enabling any of the parties to this Final Judgment to apply to this Court at any time for such further orders and directions as may be necessary or appropriate for the construction or effectuation of this Final Judgment, for the modification or termination of any of the provisions hereof, for the enforcement of compliance herewith and for the punishment of violations thereof."

On August 18, 1977, Citicorp requested that the Department of Justice consent to modification of the consent decree to permit Citicorp to reacquire Carte Blanche. Citicorp submitted memoranda containing detailed information about the parties' activities, market shares and future plans necessary to permit the Department to analyze all antitrust aspects of the proposed acquisition. In particular, Citicorp pointed out that since the decree was entered Carte Blanche's share of the market for travel and entertainment cards. had declined from about 15 percent to about ½ of 1 percent, and that as a result of the development of the two national bank carafe (Visa and Master Charge) Carte Blanche's share of the "general purpose credit card market" (identified by the Department in its 1965 complaint) had shrunk from 15 percent to about ½ of 1 percent.

The Department investigated the proposed acquisition for more than seven months. During the course of its investigation, the Department requested, and received, additional information and extensive documentary material from Citicorp, Carte Blanche and Avco, and interviewed officers of these companies. In addition, we understand that the Department interviewed other persons and obtained information from sources other than the parties to the proposed reacquisition. On

March 31, 1978, John H. Shenefield, Assistant Attorney General for the Antitrust Division, notified Citicorp that the Department would not oppose a petition by Citicorp to vacate the consent decree, and that if Citicorp filed such petition, it would not oppose the proposed reacquisition of Carte Blanche by Citicorp.

On April 28, 1978, Citicorp filed a notice of motion in the District Court for the Southern District of New York seeking to vacate the consent decree, and filed supporting affidavits and a memorandum at that time. On May 3, 1978, the Department of Justice filed a memorandum setting forth the reasons why it had determined not to oppose Citicorp's motion. In its memorandum, the Department stated that "[I]f the decree were to be vacated, the most probable and immediate effects are likely to be procompetitive." It further stated that the proposed acquisition "does not meet the criteria set forth in the Department's Merger Guidelines for challenging a merger," and concluded that "[i]f the decree were not in effect today, it is unlikely that the Department of Justice would challenge the proposed acquisition under the antitrust laws."

Before acting on Citicorp's motion to vacate the decree, the court entered an order requiring Citicorp to publish notice of its motion and to invite the filing of comments with the Court during a 30-day period. As a result of this invitation, comments adverse to Citicorp's motion were filed by American Express Company (the dominant issuer of travel and entertainment ("T&E") cards) and a Mr. Anthony R. Martin-Trigona (who sought unsuccessfully to intervene pro se). The Department of Justice on July 14, 1978, filed a memorandum in response to the comments filed by American Express. The Department stated in its memorandum that:

> "The most important consideration for the Department in deciding not to object to vacation of this decree was the likelihood that the acquisition would provide important and immediate competition by a revitalized Carte Blanche against Amex and possibly the two bank card systems as well. Nothing in the Amex comments has changed our opinion in this regard. Whether one views the acquisition as a foothold entry by Citicorp into a T&E submarket or as a merger between Citicorp and Carte Blanche in the broader national general purpose credit card market makes no difference. No matter which way one looks at it, vacation of the decree is likely to promote competition among credit cards."

Citicorp's motion to vacate the consent decree came before Judge Cannella for a hearing on August 1, 19?8 [sic]. At that hearing, Citicorp urged vacation of the decree on the ground that the acquisition would be procompetitive, and responded to assertions by American Express that the acquisition could lessen competition. The Department reaffirmed to the Court that it did not oppose Citicorp's motion. Citicorp's motion is now sub judice.

No premerger notification report would have to be filed under the old premerger rules if the acquisition were consummated prior to September 5, because the acquisition would be made by a bank not subject to the jurisdiction of the Federal Trade Commission.

It now appears that favorable action by Judge Cannella and the Comptroller of the Currency may not occur in time to permit consummation of the proposed acquisition by September 5. If consummation occurs after that date, premerger-notification under the new rules would be required unless the transaction is exempted. We are now asking your informal interpretation as to whether the transaction is exempted, in order that the reacquisition may proceed at once if Judge Cannella vacates the decree and the Comptroller approves the transaction on or after September 5.

It is Citicorp's view that the consent decree "require[s] prior approval" of any reacquisition of Carte Blanche by Citicorp, since the acquisition could not be made without favorable action by the decree Court. If the consent decree is vacated by the Court, the purpose and intent underlying the Section 802.70 exemption will have been satisfied. In addition, the proposed transaction has been thoroughly studied by the Department, which is a party to the consent decree, and the Department has advised the Court that vacation of the decree and the resulting acquisition would be procompetitive. Citicorp therefore requests that you or an appropriate member of your staff give us an informal interpretation that the exemption applies to Citicorp's acquisition of Carte Blanche.

If you have any questions or require additional information, please feel free to contact William M. Sayre, William T. Lifland or the undersigned. The individual at the Department of Justice who is familiar with this matter is Gregory B. Hovendon, Assistant Chief of the Judgment Enforcement Section.

Thank you for your prompt attention to this matter.

Very truly yours,

[Signature]
Laurence T. Sorkin

Malcolm R. Pfunder, Esq.
Associate Director for Premerger Notification,
Bureau of Competition
Room 303
Federal Trade Commission
Washington, D.C. 20580

cc: Sandra G. Wilkof, Esq.
Gregory B. Hovendon, Esq.
William E. Swope, Esq.

[¶72,411] *United States v. First National City Bank, FNCB Services Corp., Hilton Credit Corp., Hilton Hotels Corp., and Carte Blanche Corp.*

In the United States District Court for the Southern District of New York. 65 Civ. 3963. Entered May 10, 1968.

Case No. 1882 in the Antitrust Division of the Department of Justice.

Final Judgement

Ryan, D.J.: Plaintiff, United States of America, having filed its complaint herein on December 30, 1965, and each of the defendants having appeared and filed answers denying the substantive allegations thereof; and plaintiff and defendants, by their respective attorneys, having each consented to the making and entry of this Final Judgement, without trial or adjudication of any issue of fact or law herein, and without this Final Judgement constituting any evidence or an admission by any party hereto with respect to any such issue, and the Court having considered the matter and being duly advised,

Now, Therefore, before the taking of any testimony and without trial or adjudication of any issue of fact or law herein and upon the consent of the parties hereto, it is hereby

Ordered, Adjudged And Decreed as follows:

I.
[Jurisdiction]

This Court has jurisdiction of the subject matter of this action and of the parties hereto. The amended complaint herein states a claim upon which relief can be granted against defendants under Section 7 of the Act of Congress of October 15, 1914 (15 U.S.C. § 18), commonly known as the Clayton Act, as amended.

II.
[Definitions]

As used in this Final Judgement:

(A) "FNCB" means defendant First National City Bank, a banking association organized under the laws of the United States;

(B) "FNCB Services" means defendant FNCB Services Corporation, a New York corporation;

(C) "Carte Blanche" means Carte Blanche Corporation, a Delaware corporation;

(D) "Person" means an individual, partnership, firm, corporation, association, trustee or other business or legal entity.

III.
[Applicability]

The provisions of this Final Judgement applicable to any defendant shall also apply to each of its directors, officers, agents and employees acting for such defendant, its affiliates or subsidiaries, successors and assigns, and to all other Persons in active concert or participation with any such defendant who shall have received actual notice of this Final Judgement by personal service or otherwise.

IV.
[Bar to Reacquisition]

Defendants FNCB and FNCB Services are hereby enjoined from reacquiring the stock of Carte Blanche, or by any other means acquiring control over the business of Carte Blanche.

V.
[Inspection and Compliance]

For the purpose of securing compliance with this Final Judgement, and for no other purpose, duly authorized representative of the Department of Justice shall, upon written request of the Attorney General or the Assistant Attorney General in charge of the Antitrust Division, and on reasonable notice to any defendant made to its principal office, be permitted, subject to any legally recognized privilege:

(A) access during the office hours of such defendant to all books, ledgers, accounts, correspondence, memoranda and other records and documents in the possession, custody or control of such defendant related to any matters contained in this Final Judgement; and

(B) subject to the reasonable convenience of such defendant, but without restraint or interference from it, to interview officers, directors, agents or employees of such defendant, who may have counsel present, regarding any such matters.

Upon written request of the Attorney General or the Assistant Attorney General in charge of the Antitrust Division, any defendant shall submit such reports in writing, with respect to the matters contained in this Final Judgement, as may from time to time be requested; provided, however, that no information obtained by the means provided in this Section V shall be divulged by any representative of the Department of Justice to any person other than a duly authorized representative of the Executive Branch of the United States of America, except in the course of legal proceedings to which the United States of America is a party for the purpose of securing compliance with this Final Judgement, or as otherwise required by law.

VI.
[Jurisdiction Retained]

Jurisdiction is retained by this Court for the purpose of enabling any of the parties to this Final Judgement to apply to this Court at any time for such further orders and directions as may be necessary or appropriate for the construction or effectuation of this Final Judgement, for the modification or termination of any of the provisions thereof, for the enforcement of compliance herewith and for the punishment of violations thereof.

Formal Interpretation 3

Cite. 6 Trade Reg. Rep. (CCH) ¶ 42,475, at 42,602 (Dec. 28, 1978) (with inquiry letters and additional information as found at www.ftc.gov/bc/hsr/frmlintrps/fi03.htm).

Text. FORMAL INTERPRETATIONS UNDER 16 C.F.R. § 803.30 CONCERNING AFFIDAVITS FILED BY ACQUIRING PERSONS IN CONNECTION WITH PURCHASES OF VOTING SECURITIES IN CERTAIN OPEN MARKET TRANSACTIONS.

Commission staff have recently received several requests for interpretations of § 803.5(a) of the Commission's premerger notification rules implementing Title II of the Hart-Scott-Rodino Antitrust Improvements Act of 1976 ("the Act"), 15 U.S.C. § 18a, in the context of purchases of voting securities on the open market. These requests relate to the four "notification thresholds" in § 801.1(h) and to the requirement in § 803.5 (a) of an affidavit stating first, that the acquired person has received from the acquiring person written notice inter alia of "(t)he specific classes of voting and nonvoting securities of the issuer, and the number of securities of each such class sought to be acquired" (§ 803.5(a)(1)(iii), and second, that the acquiring person has a "good faith intention . . . to make the acquisition" (§ 803.5(a)(2)). Certain persons have inquired whether § 801.1(h) and § 803.5, read together, require the acquiring person to notify the acquired person of, and to state in the acquiring person's affidavit and response to item 2(e) on the Notification and Report Form ("Form"), the exact number of shares to be acquired and the particular notification threshold with respect to which the filing is made. These persons have suggested that in the context of open market conditions, the acquiring firm cannot know with certainty how many shares (and thus which notification thresholds) will be crossed.

The Commission staff has taken the position that where the exact number of shares to be acquired on the open market is known, the acquiring person must disclose this information in its notice to the acquired person and in its affidavit under § 803.5(a). Where the number of shares to be acquired cannot be determined, the acquiring person's Form must be based on, and the affidavit must attest to, a present good faith intention to acquire a sufficient number of voting securities to meet or exceed at least one of the notification thresholds of § 801.1(h). The precise number of shares to be held as a result of the acquisition need not be stated, but the specific reporting threshold to be crossed must be indicated. Thus, the affidavit may, consistent with § 803.5(a)(2), state that the exact number of shares to be acquired and time of acquisition is subject to market conditions, provided that the affidavit attests to a good faith intention to cross a specific reporting threshold.

A special case exists where the acquiring person crossed a notification threshold prior to the effective date of the rules (§ 801.20(b)), and wishes to acquire additional voting securities of the acquired person. Under such circumstances, the acquiring person's filing for the acquisition of additional shares should indicate the new notification threshold to be crossed. If the acquiring person fails to indicate which new notification threshold the person intends to reach or exceed, the filing will be treated as covering only the highest threshold crossed prior to the effective date of the rules.

Some examples may illustrate:

Example 1

Person "A" currently holds no voting securities (or less than 15% and less than $15 million of voting securities) issued by Person "B" and wishes to acquire such shares on the open market. Person "A" may not file notification unless "A" has the present good faith intention to acquire at least 15% or $15 million worth (whichever is less) of the voting securities of Person "B." It would not be sufficient for Person "A" to send Person "B" a notice that states that Person "A" may, from time to time, purchase shares of Person "B" on the open market, and that the number of shares to be acquired may, at some point, reach 15% or $15 million value. Such a notice would not satisfy the requirement of § 803.5(a)(2) that the acquiring person have a present good faith intention to make a reportable acquisition. A filing containing this notice would be deficient within the meaning of § 803.10(c)(2).

Example 2

Person "C," on the effective date of the premerger notification rules, held 12% of the voting securities of Person "D," with a value of $20 million. Under these circumstances, the acquisition of any additional shares of Person "D" would be reportable, since "C" has already crossed the $15 million threshold (*see* § 801.20(b)). Person "C" wishes to purchase an undetermined number of additional shares on the open market. Person "C" may satisfy the requirements of § 803.5 by providing "D" with written notice that "C" intends to acquire an undetermined number of shares that will, together with present holdings, result in a reportable acquisition. Because the acquiring person has not indicated an intention to cross a specific threshold, the staff, consistent with information contained in the acquiring person's response to item 2(e) (from which pre-acquisition holdings may be determined), will treat such a filing as a filing for the $15 million threshold of § 801.1(h)(1) alone. Further acquisitions meeting or exceeding the 15% threshold of § 801.1(h)(2) or any greater threshold would require another filing and compliance with another waiting period.

Example 3

Person "E," on the effective date of the premerger notification rules, held 20% of the voting securities of Person "F", with a value of $50 million. Person "E" wishes to purchase an undetermined number of additional shares on the open market. Person "E" may satisfy the requirements of § 803.5 by providing "F" with notice that "E" intends to acquire an undetermined number of shares that will, together with present holdings, result in a reportable acquisition. Such a filing will be treated by the staff as a filing for the 15% threshold of § 801.1(h)(2) alone. Further acquisitions meeting or exceeding the 25% threshold of § 801.1(h)(3) would require another filing and compliance with another waiting period.

Of course, Person "E" could cover the 15%, 25% and 50% notification thresholds in a single filing. Thus, if Person "E" wished to acquire control of Person "F," Person "E" would be required to file notification for the 50% threshold of § 801.1(h)(4), specifically informing the agencies and the acquired person of its intention to meet or exceed that level. After expiration of the waiting period, Person "E" would have one year within which to acquire a sufficient number of voting securities of Person "F" to equal or exceed 50%. If that level had not been reached within one year following expiration of the waiting period, Person "E's" notification would expire under § 803.7 of the rules.

Summary

In conclusion, where the acquiring person has no holdings (or holdings valued at less than $15 million) of voting securities of the acquired person, the acquiring person's notice to the acquired person and affidavit required by § 803.5(a) must describe and attest to a good faith intention to cross a specific notification threshold of § 801.1(h). Where, on the effective date of the rules, the acquiring person had holdings of voting securities of the acquired person in excess of one or more of the notification thresholds, the acquiring person's notice and affidavit must describe and attest to a good faith intention to cross one or more additional thresholds. A filing that does not state the additional notification threshold to be reached will be treated as a filing for the highest threshold crossed prior to the effective date of the rules.

The Assistant Attorney General in charge of the Antitrust Division has concurred in this interpretation.

[signature]

Daniel G. Schwartz
Deputy Director
Bureau of Competition

Date: December 28, 1978

Formal Interpretation 4

Cite. 6 Trade Reg. Rep. (CCH) ¶ 42,475, at 42,603 (Jan. 17, 1979) (with inquiry letters and additional information as found at www.ftc.gov/bc/hsr/frmlintrps/fi04.htm).

Text. FEDERAL TRADE COMMISSION
WASHINGTON, D. C. 20580
BUREAU OF COMPETITION
January 17, 1979

Laurence T. Sorkin, Esquire
Cahill, Gordon & Reindel
Eighty Pine Street
New York, New York 10005

Dear Mr. Sorkin:

This formal interpretation is issued by the staff of the Federal Trade Commission under 16 C.F.R. § 803.30 in response to your letter of October 11, 1978. You ask whether an acquiring person that has filed a Notification and Report Form ("Form") under § 7A of the Clayton Act ("the Act"), 15 U.S.C. § 18a, stating an intention to acquire holdings in excess of 10% of the voting securities of an issuer may, during the statutory waiting period, acquire holdings of 10% or less of such voting securities (worth more than $15 million) pursuant to the "solely for the purpose of investment" exemption provided by § 7A(c)(9) of the Act 1/ and § 802.9 of the premerger notification rules ("rules") 2/. You suggest that the acquiring person's stated intention to acquire more than 10% of the voting securities of an issuer might be considered inconsistent with the acquisition of any shares during the statutory waiting period solely for the purpose of investment.

An acquisition of voting securities shall be exempt from the requirements of the act pursuant to section 7A(c)(9) if made solely for the purpose of investment and if, as a result of the acquisition, the acquiring person would hold ten percent or less of the outstanding voting securities of the issuer, regardless of the dollar value of voting securities so acquired or held.

The staff has taken the position that the fact of filing by the acquiring person under these circumstances is not necessarily inconsistent with an investment intention. Thus, the "solely for the purpose of investment" exemption should not be withheld solely because the acquiring person has filed a Form stating an intention to acquire sufficient voting securities to exceed the 10% investment threshold.

The exemption provided by § 7A(c)(9) and § 802.9 comprises two elements. First, the acquisition must be solely for the purpose of investment, as defined by § 801.1(i)(1) 3/, which focuses on the intention of the acquiring person vis-a-vis the basic business decisions of the acquired issuer. Whether or not the requisite intention exists will depend largely on the facts surrounding an acquisition (or series of acquisitions) by the acquiring person and must be determined on a case-by-case basis. 4/

Second, the acquiring person's holdings may not exceed 10% of the outstanding voting securities of the issuer. Once such holdings exceed 10%, the intention of the acquiring person becomes immaterial to the acquiring person's obligations under the Act and rules. 5/ The fact that the reporting person has indicated through a filing that it intends to exceed the 10% investment threshold after expiration of the statutory waiting period does not, of itself, constitute an intention inconsistent with that of investment. Thus, acquisitions that do not result in holdings exceeding 10% may be consummated during the statutory waiting period, provided that the intention of the acquiring person remains consistent with § 801.1(i)(1).

The Statement of Basis and Purpose to § 801.1(i)(1) described various types of conduct that the Commission considered inconsistent with an investment intention. The decision to acquire or seek working control of the issuer (regardless of the percentage of voting securities that may actually confer such control) is clearly inconsistent with investment intent under § 803.1(i)(1). Thus, an intention (indicated through a premerger notification filing or otherwise) to acquire shares resulting in holdings of 50% or more of the shares of the issuer would necessarily eliminate the applicability of the exemption. An intention to acquire less than 50% of the shares of the issuer could also preclude the applicability of the exemption, depending on the extent of the acquiring person's anticipated holdings and all other circumstances relating to the acquiring person's intentions regarding the basic business decisions of the acquired issuer. This interpretation should not be construed to impede the abilities of the Commission and the Department of Justice to investigate the acquisition activity of acquiring persons during the statutory waiting period and to seek civil penalties under the Act where evidence exists that acquiring persons have improperly invoked the exemption provided by § 7A(c)(9) and § 802.9.

The Assistant Attorney General in charge of the Antitrust Division has concurred in this interpretation.

Yours truly,

[Signature]
Malcolm R. Pfunder
Assistant Director for Evaluation

1/ § 7A(c). The following classes of transaction are exempt from the requirements of this section.
> (9) acquisition, solely for the purpose of investment, of voting securities if, as a result of such acquisition, the securities acquired or held do not exceed 10 per centum of the outstanding voting securities of the issuer.

2/ § 802.9 Acquisition solely for the purpose of investment.

3/ (i)(1) Solely for the purpose of investment. Voting securities are held or acquired "solely for the purpose of investment" if the person holding or acquiring such voting securities has no intention of participating in the formulation, determination, or direction of the basic business decisions of the issuer.

4/ *See* Statement of Basis and Purpose, 42 F.R. at 33465 (July 31, 1978).

5/ *See* Statement of Basis and Purpose, 42 F.R. at 33490 (July 31, 1978).

[Cahill Gordon & Reindel Letterhead]
Eighty Pine Street
New York, N.Y. 10005

October 11, 1978

Re: Request for an Interpretation of the Report and Wait Requirements of the Hart-Scott-Rodino Antitrust Improvements Act of 1976

Dear Mr. Pfunder:

I am writing to request an interpretation of the report and wait requirements of the Hart-Scott-Rodino Antitrust Improvements Act of 1976 ("the Act"), with regard to a question which has already risen several times in inquiries made by various clients of my firm.

The typical factual background from which my question arises is as follows:

Company A intends to acquire X% (X% is greater than 10%) of the voting securities of Company B, and states that the acquisition is made "solely for the purpose of investment", pursuant to sub-section (c)(9) of the Act, and § 802.9 of the rules. Company A and Company B each meet at least one of the applicable criteria of the Act with respect to size of parties to the transaction. The purchase of 10% of the voting securities of Company B is, for purposes of the Act, of a value exceeding $15,000,000.

The question which has repeatedly arisen with regard to the factual situation described above is as follows:

After Company A has formed its intention to purchase X% of the voting securities of Company B, and has filed a report and notification form, may Company A purchase shares of voting securities of Company B, so long as its holdings do not exceed 10% of the outstanding voting securities of Company B? Or, must Company A desist from making any further purchases until the end of the waiting period?

It would appear that there is no clear answer to the question in the Act, or in the regulation promulgated thereunder. Arguments of more or less equal weight can be made in support either of allowing continued purchases prior to the end of the waiting period (so long as the acquiring company's holdings do not exceed 10%), or of prohibiting them. They are set forth below.

One factor which may influence your interpretation is the percentage of outstanding voting securities of Company B which is sought by Company A in any particular case. The higher that percentage is, the more suspect the claim of "investment purpose" may be.

Arguments that Further Purchases Should be Stopped Until the Termination of the Waiting Period

(a) The provisions of the Act and the regulations with regard to acquisitions "solely for the purpose of investment" require, by implication, that purchases be stopped until the end of the applicable waiting period, once an intention to purchase X% of the voting securities has been formed. The regulations clearly impose two mutual independent requirements on the availability of the exemption for acquisitions which are "solely for the purpose of investment": (a) that the acquiring person hold 10% or less of the outstanding voting securities of an issuer; and (b) that the acquisition be solely for the purpose of investment. *See* § 802.9, and Statement of Basis and Purpose for § 802.9.

There is no express presumption or determination in the Act or the regulations that the intention to hold more than 10% of the outstanding voting securities of an issuer is or is presumed to be not made solely for the purpose of investment. Unless there is such a determination or presumption, however, the Commission's requirement that the acquisition be "solely for the purpose of investment" will be utterly unenforceable, since the determination of investment purpose must be made on a case-by-case basis, thus necessitating a factual inquiry into the intent of the acquiring person. Such an inquiry is likely to be made only in those cases in which someone strongly objects to the availability of the exemption, or in those cases in which the acquiring person clearly acts in a manner contradictory to its expressed purpose of making an acquisition solely for the purpose of investment.

There are obvious examples of situations in which declaration that an acquisition is solely for the purpose of investment can and should be disregarded. As an extreme example, if a company has expressed an intention to acquire 49% of the outstanding voting securities of an issuer, the claim that the purchase of the first 10% of the issuer's securities is made solely for the purpose of investment would seem incredible and should probably be disregarded.

(b) It would be contrary to the basic policy underlying the Act to allow Company A to increase its holdings of the voting securities of Company B to the 10% level, pending review by FTC and the Department of Justice.

The filing of a notification and report form with regard to the proposed acquisition of X% of the shares of the outstanding voting securities of Company B triggers the operation of the Act, and initiates review by the FTC and Department of Justice. An unfavorable determination will result in the institution of an injunctive proceeding, which may seek the divestiture of all of Company A's holdings. To allow Company A to increase its holdings in Company B may provide a basis for Company A to argue in the injunctive proceeding that it has changed its position and purchased 10% of Company B, and that it would be inequitable to require it to divest itself of holding acquired under these circumstances.

In addition, the interests of shareholders in Company B (other than Company A) should be taken into account. The larger the holding owned by Company A which will be "in limbo" during the waiting period, the larger the block of stock which Company A may be required to divest. Such a large block of available stock may well "hang" over the market, and tend to depress the price which other prospective sellers of the security may obtain, until well after that large block has been sold.

Arguments in Favor of Allowing Continued Purchases

(a) The Act and the regulations clearly operate only at particular threshold levels. There is a sufficient number of opportunities for review at those thresholds to provide a meaningful analysis of the antitrust aspects of any proposed transaction. To prohibit continued purchases up to the 10% level, merely because of an ex- pressed intention to acquire more than 10% of that security, would ignore the plain and clear fact that purchases beyond the 10% level can be made, only if the regulatory authorities decide to forego any challenge to such purchases. Thus, although the ownership of, for example, a 30% block of the voting securities of a widely-held issuer may be inconsistent with an intention to acquire shares solely for the purpose of investment, the holding of a 10% block -- and only a 10% block -- of such stock by Company A which is prohibited from increasing its holding is in no way inconsistent with its expressed intention to hold that 10% block solely for the purpose of investment.

(b) Prior draft regulations would have required acquisitions made for investment purposes to be reported, even if they did not reach the 10% level, provided that they crossed an otherwise applicable notification threshold. The deletion of that requirement is clear evidence that there is little concern that acquisitions of the voting securities of large companies up to the 10% level, under the guise of the investment exemption, pose a significant threat to competition.

The contentions set forth above are representative of arguments which might be made, although they clearly do not exhaust the limits of imagination. No particular resolution of the question appears to be compelled by policy considerations, but it does seem important for there to be a clear answer to this question.

Sincerely,

[Signature]
Laurence T. Sorkin

Malcolm R. Pfunder, Esq.
Associate Director for Premerger Notification
Bureau of Competition
Room 303
Federal Trade Commission
Washington, D. C. 20580

Appendix 435

Formal Interpretation 5
[SUPERSEDED BY FORMAL INTERPRETATION 13]

Cite. 6 Trade Reg. Rep. (CCH) ¶ 42,475, at 42,604 (Aug. 20, 1982) (with inquiry letters and additional information as found at www.ftc.gov/bc/hsr/frmlintrps/fi05.htm).

Text. FORMAL INTERPRETATION UNDER 16 C.F.R. § 803.30 CONCERNING EARLY TERMINATION UNDER § 7A(b)(2) AND § 803.11

Commission staff have received several requests for interpretation of § 803.11 of the premerger notification rules ("the rules"), promulgated pursuant to § 7A of the Clayton Act, 15 U.S.C. § 18a (the "Act"). These requests concern the standards applied by the Commission and the Assistant Attorney General in charge of the Antitrust Division ("Assistant Attorney General") in granting or denying requests for early termination of the waiting period specified in § 7A(b)(l) of the Act.

Section 7A(b)(2) of the Act provides:

> The Federal Trade Commission and the Assistant Attorney General may, in individual cases, terminate the waiting period specified in paragraph (1) and allow any person to proceed with any acquisition subject to this section, and promptly shall cause to be published in the Federal Register a notice that neither intends to take any action within such period with respect to such acquisition.

Section 803.11 of the rules, which implements § 7A(b)(2), specifies the conditions and procedures under which a waiting period may be terminated prior to its normal expiration. However, neither that section nor § 7A(b)(2) sets forth any general criteria to be applied by the Commission and the Assistant Attorney General in deciding whether or not requests for early termination should be granted. This formal interpretation states the position of the staff in this respect.

The staff interprets the early termination provision of § 7A(b)(2) and § 803.11 as a mandate to both agencies to consider each request for early termination on an individual basis and to exercise discretion in making such decisions. No specific criteria can be identified that will be applied invariably in each case; however, the following general principles will be applied by the agency staffs in exercising their discretion.

First, early termination will not be granted unless the staff of the agencies have concluded that neither will take any further action within the waiting period. Second, early termination will usually not be granted unless the requesting party or parties can demonstrate some special business reason that warrants early termination of the waiting period. In other words, the requesting party should explain the need to complete the transaction before the waiting period would normally expire; it may also be helpful to indicate why an earlier expiration date could not have been obtained simply by filing the original notification earlier. Some examples of reasons that may be considered sufficient are the existence of a financing contingency that might fail during the waiting period, the need to infuse cash quickly into a financially weak firm, or the importance of preserving existing contractual relationships that might be placed in jeopardy because of uncertainty generated during a full waiting period. Such reasons are relevant to the early termination decision, of course, only when both agencies have determined that no further action will be taken during the waiting period.

The language of § 7A(b)(2) that permits termination "in individual cases" supports the interpretation that a determination based on the specific facts of the acquisition is contemplated, and that early termination should not be granted as a matter of course. Additionally, the staff notes that the Commission has an advisory opinion procedure (16 C.F.R. § 1.1) and the Antitrust Division has a business review procedure (28 C.F.R. § 50.6) under which prior antitrust agency review of a proposed acquisition may be obtained. The early termination provision is not intended to duplicate or replace such other procedures.

The Assistant Attorney General has concurred in this interpretation.

[signature]
Malcolm R. Pfunder
Assistant Director for Evaluation
Bureau of Competition

Date: April 10, 1979

Formal Interpretation 6

Cite. 6 Trade Reg. Rep. (CCH) ¶ 42,475, at 42,604 (Apr. 10, 1979) (with inquiry letters and additional information as found at www.ftc.gov/bc/hsr/frmlintrps/fi06.htm).

Text. FEDERAL TRADE COMMISSION
WASHINGTON. D. C. 20580
Bureau of Competition

April 10, 1979

Formal Staff Interpretation Under 16 C.F.R. § 803.30 Concerning Incorporation by Reference in the Antitrust Improvements Act Premerger Notification and Report Forms.

With regard to several recent filings of the Antitrust Improvements Act Notification and Report Form, 16 C.F.R. § 803 - Appendix ("the Form"), the following question has arisen: To what extent may a filing person respond to items on, or to requirements that documentary material be supplied with, its Form by referring to information on or to materials accompanying another Form filed either by it or by another person? The issue of incorporation by reference has been raised most frequently in connection with the SEC documents required to be supplied by Item 4(a), although it might arise with other items as well. Persons filing for an acquisition have sought to incorporate by reference documents supplied with the Form relating to a previous acquisition by the same person. The Commission staff has taken the position that Forms which incorporate by reference information not supplied on, or documents not accompanying, the same Form will generally be deemed deficient within the meaning of § 803.10(c)(2) of the premerger notification rules, 16 C.F.R. § 803.10(c)(2).

This decision is based in part on the fact that in the antitrust review of a transaction, the Form and all accompanying documents are frequently sent by the Federal Trade Commission and the Antitrust Division of the Department of Justice to their various litigating groups, including the regional offices of both agencies. These documents may not, therefore, be available to the premerger notification offices of both agencies which must review any subsequent transactions by that person. In view of the time constraints under which the staffs of both agencies must operate, the review of the premerger Forms which is mandated by Title II of the Hart-Scott-Rodino Antitrust Improvements Act of 1976, 15

U.S.C. §18a ("the Act") necessitates that all documentary materials which are required to be supplied with the Form accompany each filing, even though some inconvenience to filing persons may result.

This position will be taken even when the parties to a previously reported acquisition are filing again at a higher notification threshold. Under § 802.21(b) of the premerger notification rules, 16 C.F.R. § 802.21(b), the parties to a reportable acquisition may, after the expiration of the waiting period, make additional acquisitions which do not cross a higher notification threshold. Such acquisitions are exempt from reporting and waiting period requirements for five years. Thus substantial time may elapse between notifications involving the same parties, and the agencies may during that time have destroyed some or all of the information previously provided. Incorporation by reference would, in this situation, tend to interfere with the prompt review of premerger notification Forms required by the Act.

An exception to this restriction seems justified in the following circumstances. For tax or other reasons, parties to a merger or takeover sometimes choose to implement the transaction through an essentially contemporaneous, two step process, such as a cash tender offer for less than 50% of the target's stock, followed by a merger of the acquiring person with the target. The staff is willing to permit incorporation by reference where filings by the same parties are made with respect to a higher notification threshold and are received by the enforcement agencies within ninety days after the earlier filings with respect to the lower threshold.

The above discussion does not restrict incorporation by reference of the answer to one item on the Form, or of accompanying documentary materials, in the response to another item on the same Form. The only limitation to such incorporation is the requirement that the responses to all items must be clear, complete, and unambiguous.

The Assistant Attorney General in charge of the Antitrust Division has concurred in this interpretation.

[Signature]
Malcolm R. Pfunder
Assistant Director for Evaluation

Formal Interpretation 7

Cite. 6 Trade Reg. Rep. (CCH) ¶ 42,475, at 42,605 (May 8, 1979) (with inquiry letters and additional information as found at www.ftc.gov/bc/hsr/frmlintrps/fi07.htm).

Text. UNDER 16 C.F.R. § 803.30 CONCERNING ACQUISITIONS BY CERTAIN BANK HOLDING COMPANIES

Commission staff have recently received several requests for interpretation of the exemption provided by § 7A(c)(8) of the Clayton Act ("Act"), 15 U.S.C. § 18a(c)(8), and § 802.8 of the premerger notification rules ("rules"), 16 CFR § 802.8, which exempt from the general notification and waiting requirements of the Act certain acquisitions approved by the Federal Reserve System. These requests inquire whether the exemption applies to acquisitions by bank holding companies that have filed with the Federal Reserve Board ("Board") irrevocable declarations that the companies, through divestiture of their banks, will cease to be bank holding companies by January 1, 1981. The staff has determined that the regulatory oversight exercised by the Federal Reserve System over acquisitions by such companies does not constitute "approval" within the meaning of § 7A(c)(8) and § 802.8. Therefore, the exemption is not available, and such companies, if planning to engage in acquisitions covered by the Act and rules, must comply fully with the general notification and waiting requirements. A more complete discussion follows.

Section 7A(c)(8) of the Clayton Act exempts from general premerger notification requirements, inter alia, transactions which require agency approval under section 4 of the Bank Holding Company act of 1956 (12 U.S.C. 1843) . . . .

In general, § 4(a) of the Bank Holding Company Act ("Bank Act") restricts the ability of bank holding companies to acquire or maintain interests in firms not engaged in banking. Section 4(c) contains several exemptions to this regulatory scheme. In particular, § 4(c)(12) of the Bank Act provides that the proscriptions of § 4(a) shall not apply to shares retained or acquired, or activities engaged in, by any company which becomes, as a result of the enactment of the Bank Holding Company Act Amendments of 1970, a bank holding company on the date of such enactment, or by any subsidiary thereof, if such company –

(A) within the applicable time limits prescribed in subsection (a)(2) of this section (i) ceases to be a bank holding company . . ., and

(B) complies with such other conditions as the Board may by regulation or order prescribe . . . .

The provisions of § 4(c)(12) are codified in Board rule § 225.4(d), 12 CFR § 225.4(d).1/ This rule provides a separate regulatory scheme for bank holding companies that have filed an irrevocable declaration with the Board that the company, by divestiture of its bank, will cease to be a bank holding company by January 1, 1981.2/ Such bank holding companies, until the time of divestiture, may acquire other going concerns, provided that the company has given the local Federal Reserve Bank ("Reserve Bank") 45 days notice of the company's intention to make the acquisition. Absent opposition by the Reserve Bank, the company may consummate the acquisition after expiration of the 45 day period. Where opposition is expressed, the matter may be forwarded to the Board for further consideration. In exigent circumstances, the Reserve Bank may accelerate the time in which consummation may be made.

The issue presented is whether this procedure provides authority for "approval" within the meaning of § 7A(c)(8) of the Clayton Act. In determining whether authority exists, it is necessary to examine the competitive issues addressed in the course of Reserve Bank review and the Congressional intentions underlying both § 4 of the Bank Act and § 7A of the Clayton Act.

Neither the provisions of § 4(c)(8) and § 225.4(d), nor the regulations of the Board delegating authority to the Reserve Banks to receive notice from bank holding companies (12 C.F.R. § 265.2(f)(19))3/ provide meaningful guidance. Therefore, a review of secondary sources is appropriate, i.e., the legislative history of § 4(c)(12)4/ and a Federal Reserve Board instruction to Reserve Banks dated May 24, 1971. From review of the legislative history, it is clear that Congress intended to permit bank holding companies that filed irrevocable declarations freely to acquire other enterprises, provided that such acquisitions did not afford the company an "undue advantage." Discussing the conference committee version of § 4(c)(12), Senator Sparkman stated that:

> The conference adopted the provision from the Senate bill which will allow any company covered by this legislation to retain or acquire whatever shares, or engage in whatever activities, it wishes so long as, within the applicable divestiture period, it...ceases to be a bank holding company...

> ...It is contemplated that the Board will insure that the authority to make...acquisitions and engage in the activities provided by this particular provision will not be utilized by a bank holding company covered by this legislation to go into activities and make acquisitions which are totally unrelated to its present activities in order to obtain an undue advantage during the applicable divestiture period, or for any other purpose inconsistent with the intent and purpose of the Act. (116 Cong. Rec. 42425 (December 18, 1970)).

It is unclear whether the "undue advantage" alluded to in the Congressional Record was intended to be limited to advantages in the financial markets of the bank holding company, or whether it would include advantages in the financial and (possibly) nonfinancial markets of acquired firms.

This issue is addressed more clearly in the Board letter of May 24, 1971. Regarding the criteria for review of proposed acquisitions, the following guideline is provided:

> In deciding whether a proposed acquisition is appropriate, the Reserve Bank should consider the period of time for which the company will likely continue to own its bank, and base its decision on its judgment as to whether common ownership for that period of time of the bank and the company to be acquired may present undue dangers to the bank or to competitors of the bank or the company to be acquired. Undue danger to the bank would be indicated where, for example, the bank has been criticized in the past for loans to its nonbanking affiliates, the holding company, or related interests. In order to satisfy itself on this question, the Reserve Bank should review the bank's examination report or seek the advice of the bank's supervisor.

Acquisitions by a holding company which has filed the appropriate irrevocable declaration need not be closely related to banking. Therefore, the absence of such a relationship is not, in itself, a cause for concern.

It is anticipated that, with respect to most acquisitions under § 4(c)(12), competitive considerations will not present serious questions. If the company to be acquired is not located within the subsidiary bank's market, no further investigation of competitive effects of the proposal would ordinarily be necessary; such would also appear true, even if the company to be acquired is located within that market, if the bank and affiliated deposit-type institutions have only a small share of the deposits and loans in the area. If, however, the subsidiary bank and other deposit-type institutions within the holding company organization have a large share of the market, the acquisition of a large company within that market would warrant closer inquiry . . . .

Regarding the Board's instructions to Reserve Banks, it is clear that the Reserve Bank's inquiry encompasses both competition in the bank's financial markets and competition in financial and nonfinancial markets in which the acquired firm may be engaged. However, as regards competition in the markets of the acquired firm, this inquiry appears to be limited to the issue of whether the acquired firms access to the capital resources of its affiliated bank will afford the acquired firm an undue advantage, and adversely affect [Formal Interpretation 33] competition, in the firm's product markets. Moreover, Reserve Banks are under no statutory or regulatory obligation to consider the cumulative effect on competition of a series of acquisitions of firms in the same or related product markets. Thus, many issues of primary concern to the antitrust laws are not considered in the course of review by the Reserve Banks. 5/

In light of the limited scope of Reserve Bank review, the Commission staff has concluded that the Congressional intentions underlying § 7A of the Clayton Act are best served by requiring bank holding companies that, pursuant to § 4(c)(12) of the Bank Act, have filed irrevocable declarations to divest themselves of their banks by January 1, 1981, to comply fully with the general premerger notification and waiting requirements of the Act. This conclusion is supported by the comments of the Federal Reserve Board (attached) submitted during the two comment periods preceding promulgation of the premerger notification rules. Nevertheless, nothing contained herein shall affect any acquisition consummated prior to this date.

The Assistant Attorney General in charge of the Antitrust Division has indicated his concurrence with this formal interpretation.

[Signature]
Malcolm R. Pfunder
Assistant Director for Evaluation

MAY 08 1979

Attachment

(a) Comment of the Board of Governors Federal Reserve System (February 18, 1977) in response to Federal Trade Commission Notice of

Proposed Rulemaking Under Title II of the Hart-Scott-Rodino Antitrust Improvements Act of 1976, 41 Fed. Reg. 55488 December 20, 1976.

A. *Section 4(c)(12) Acquisitions*

It is unclear whether section 7A(c)(8) would exempt those acquisitions made pursuant to section 4(c)(12) of the Bank Holding Company Act and section 225.4(d) of the Board's Regulation Y. Under those provisions a company that became a bank holding company as a result of the 1970 Amendments to the Act and has filed with the Board an irrevocable declaration that it will cease to be a bank holding company by January 1, 1981, may make an acquisition of a going nonbanking concern 45 days after the company has informed its Reserve Bank of the proposed acquisition unless the company is notified of the contrary within the time or unless it is permitted to make the acquisition at an earlier date, based on exigent circumstances of a particular case. The status of such acquisitions is uncertain under the FTC's proposed regulations because it is unclear whether an acquisition made pursuant to section 4(c)(12) and section 225.4(d) of Regulation Y is a transaction requiring agency approval under section 4 of the Bank Holding Company Act. From a policy standpoint, there does not appear to be any compelling reason to exempt from the requirements of the Act transactions pursuant to section 4(c)(12). Recommendation: The FTC should consider whether it should assert jurisdiction over acquisitions made pursuant to section 4(c)(12) of the Bank Holding Company Act and section 225.4(d) of Regulation Y and clarify their status under the FTC's proposed regulations.

1/ § 225.4(d). Certain acquisitions by companies that became holding companies on December 31, 1970, as a result of the 1970 amendments: Except as provided in this paragraph, no bank holding company may acquire, directly or indirectly, any shares or commence to engage in any activities on the basis of section 4(c)(12) of the Act. A company may file with the Board an irrevocable declaration, in the form approved by the Board, that it will cease to be a bank holding company by January 1, 1981, unless it is granted an exemption under section 4(d) of the Act. A company that has filed such a declaration may (1) commence new activities de novo, either directly or through a subsidiary, without further action under this paragraph, until such time as the Board notifies the company to the contrary, and (2) make an acquisition of a going concern 45 days after the company has informed its Reserve Bank of the proposed acquisition, unless the company is notified to the contrary within that time or unless it is permitted to make the acquisition at an earlier date based on exigent circumstances of a particular case. . . .

2/ Section 4(c)(12) also governs acquisitions by a bank holding company, that, because it has chosen not to file an irrevocable declaration to divest its bank, must divest its nonbanking interests by 1981. The application of § 7A(c)(8) and § 802.8 to bank holding companies in the latter situation is not addressed in this interpretation.

3/ (19) Under § 225.4(d) of this chapter (Regulation Y), [Reserve Banks have the authority] (i) To notify a bank holding company that has informed it of a proposed acquisition of a going concern that because the circumstances surrounding the application indicate that additional information is required or that the acquisition should be considered by the Board, the acquisition should not be consummated until specifically authorized by the Reserve Bank or by the Board; (ii) To permit a bank holding company that has informed it of a proposed acquisition of a going concern to make the acquisition before the expiration of the 45 day period referred to in that paragraph, because exigent circumstances justify consummation of the acquisition at an earlier time.

4/ S.Rep. No. 91-1084, 91st Cong., 2d Sess. 7 (1970), 116 Cong. Rec. 42425 and 42437 (1970).

5/ *See* Heller, Handbook of Federal Bank Holding Company Law (1976), at 187 n. 87, concerning § 4(c)(12)acquisitions:
> Inaction by the Federal Reserve following notice to it of a proposed acquisition does not mean, for example, that the acquisition will have no significantly adverse effect on competition. Acquisitions by a company that has filed an irrevocable declaration are subject to the antitrust laws and to the jurisdiction of the Justice Department and the Federal Trade Commission in the administration of those laws.

Formal Interpretation 8

Cite. 6 Trade Reg. Rep. (CCH) ¶ 42,475, at 42,605 (Sept. 13, 1979) (with inquiry letters and additional information as found at www.ftc.gov/bc/hsr/frmlintrps/fi08.htm).

Text.
FEDERAL TRADE COMMISSION
WASHINGTON, D. C. 20580
BUREAU OF COMPETITION

September 13, 1979

John W. Barnum, Esquire
White & Case
1747 Pennsylvania Avenue, N.W.
Washington, D.C. 20006

Dear Mr. Barnum:

This is in response to your March 1, 1979, letter to Chairman Pertschuk, discussing the treatment of attorney-client communications in the premerger notification rules under the Hart-Scott-Rodino Antitrust Improvements Act of 1976.

We appreciate your concern that the integrity of the attorney-client relationship not be compromised and we share this concern. The Act, however, mandates that the Federal Trade Commission and the Department of Justice shall require that filing parties submit information and documents relevant to the proposed acquisition that are necessary and appropriate for an assessment of the transaction. Clayton Act § 7A(d)(1). The Act does not exempt any categories of documents from this requirement. We therefore do not believe it is appropriate to amend the rules to provide a broad exemption for "privileged" documents, especially because the rules already provide a mechanism by which the reporting person may assert a privilege.

In appropriate instances a reporting person, both in its initial notification and in a response to a request for additional information or documentary material, may make an incomplete response, provided that each omission is accompanied by a statement of reasons for noncompliance. So long as other required responses have been provided, the inclusion of such a statement begins the applicable waiting period. The content of such a statement is prescribed by § 803.3 of the premerger notification rules. In the situation you describe, the statement should identify each document by author, recipient, date and its subject matter. The statement should also state who has control of the document and where it is located and should invoke the attorney-client privilege as the reason for not supplying it.

As is set forth in the Statement of Basis and Purpose for the premerger notification rules, 43 Fed. Reg 33526 (July 31, 1978), we have responded and will continue to respond to claims of privilege on a case by case basis. Our procedure is to determine (usually through a request for clarification or amplification under § 803.20(d)(2) of the rules) whether the privilege has been properly invoked.

We have no interest in compromising the relationship between a party to an acquisition and its attorney. We are concerned only with fulfilling the main objective of the Act -- evaluation of the antitrust implications of a proposed merger or acquisition prior to its consummation. We believe that a general exemption to 4(c) could frustrate that objective.

I hope that this reply meets your concerns, and I would be happy to continue to discuss these issues with you if you have further questions.

Very truly yours,

[Signature]
Malcolm R. Pfunder
Assistant Director for Evaluation

[WHITE & CASE LETTERHEAD]

March 1, 1979

The Honorable Michael Pertschuk
Chairman
Federal Trade Commission
8th & Pennsylvania Avenue, N.W.
Washington, D.C. 20580

Dear Mike:

Following you appearance at the American Enterprise Institute in January, a BNA reporter who had been present followed up on our discussion of the treatment of attorney-client communications in the premerger notification rules and the result was the attached blurb in the February 15 issue. Although I have not gone back through the comments on the draft regulations to see whether the "chilling effect" point was made or stressed, I would like to repeat the argument that I offered at AEI because I think that the FTC's responses that I see in BNA and have heard elsewhere miss the underlying policy problem.

I believe that the premerger notification regulations should not require production of antitrust counsel's communications to management or a board of directors because the effect of that requirement will be (and already has been) to deter companies from obtaining such opinions when considering an acquisition. Companies will want to avoid having to submit such opinions and then having to risk an incomplete filing and a subsequent argument that the statutory time has not expired because such opinions were not supplied. While companies are still asking antitrust counsel to do much of the same analysis, when they are alerted to the problem that formal delivery of the resulting memoranda may entail they are limiting the transmission of the results of that analysis to an oral presentation to a few members of management.

I do not think that is a very satisfactory way for either counsel or management to do business. I believe that on a major acquisition a board of directors should have an opportunity to study a comprehensive antitrust opinion. Moreover the company should have such a document in its files in order to be able to demonstrate, should the need arise, that the board and management proceeded prudently. I am not just thinking of creating a paper record to defend against possible shareholder suits (or of assuring more work for the antitrust bar); I am concerned with the substance of the record upon which the merger decision is taken. If the board or members of management must proceed on the basis of an oral regurgitation of counsel's opinion, the antitrust implications of the transaction are less likely to receive adequate attention and in any event counsel's views become vulnerable to both conscious and unconscious distortion in their oral repetition. (I note in passing that someone may raise the question whether the regulations now require submission of notes of such an oral presentation that members of the board or management may have taken while counsel is talking or their analysis is being regurgitated).

It is this chilling effect on responsible and effective antitrust analysis and the communication of the results that is unfortunate in the present regulations. It has often been said that the best enforcers of the antitrust laws are the private bar. While sometimes I think that characterization has been overdone, it is nevertheless true that the private bar has deterred management from violating the antitrust laws. Although aborting anticompetitive mergers has probably been less important than, for example, preventing price fixing or similar anticompetitive practices, I still think that you should not create a barrier to complete antitrust analysis of a proposed merger.

It is not enough, in my judgement, for the Commission merely to exercise restraint in requiring actual production of otherwise privileged memoranda. The problem is created by the perception that nonproduction would be an exception to the general rule. It should be the other way around. In a situation where the staff has decided to investigate a transaction more completely after the initial filing, and obviously in any subsequent litigation, there is always the opportunity to attempt discovery of such communications in circumstances where such discovery might be warranted. But it is a different matter to require in the premerger notification regulations that any such opinion be submitted in the first instance as an ingredient of substantial compliance. It puts the company on notice that it will have to either submit the opinion or obtain an exception, either affirmatively or by acquiescence or even by a court ruling, before it can consummate the transaction. If the regulations did not include the express requirement, a corporation that is willing to take its chances on having to submit an attorney-client communication in the course of an investigation or subsequent litigation would be willing to obtain the full written analysis for its executives to study. But after the Commission has expressly rejected the criticism of the requirement and included it in the final regulations, the same company would be less inclined to assume the risks or to invite the dilemma that the regulations may create.

Having the requirement in the regulations also raises the possibility that the antitrust opinion will be prepared more with an eye to its submission in connection with premerger notification than to its consideration by the management and the board of directors. The temptation for counsel to make the best case for the merger, rather than to give the company their most dispassionate advice, presumably would not affect the result of the FTC investigation, but it could have a significantly different effect on the company's decision, no matter what oral caveats accompany its transmission. Obviously I would prefer that antitrust counsel resist that temptation in rendering an opinion, but we should not overlook the fact that your regulation also makes that opinion ipso facto a brief.

If you thing there is any validity to these observations, I would appreciate your forwarding them to the appropriate docket or office of the Commission, and of course I would be pleased to pursue the question with anyone on your staff who would be interested.

Thank you again for your excellent presentation at AEI, and also for your cogent speech on licensing at the Mayflower last week.

Sincerely,

[signature]
John W. Barnum

Enclosure

Formal Interpretation 9

Cite. 6 Trade Reg. Rep. (CCH) ¶ 42,475, at 42,606 (Mar. 20, 1980) (mislabeled as Formal Interpretation 10) (with inquiry letters and additional information as found at www.ftc.gov/bc/hsr/frmlintrps/fi09.htm).

Text.

FORMAL INTERPRETATION PURSUANT TO § 803.30 OF THE PREMERGER NOTIFICATION RULES, 16 C.F.R. § 803.30:

The Treatment of Accounts Receivable under § 801.21 of the Premerger Notification Rules, 16 C.F.R. § 801.21

The Hart-Scott-Rodino Antitrust Improvements Act of 1976 ("the Act") established a requirement that persons of a certain size intending to carry out an acquisition exceeding a certain size must file notification with the Federal Trade Commission and with the Department of Justice and wait a specified period of time before consummating the transaction. Whether an acquisition is subject to the premerger notification requirements of the Act is determined by applying two tests. The size-of-person test ascertains whether the parties to the acquisition are of sufficient size to come under the jurisdiction of the Act and the size-of-transaction test determines whether the transaction itself is large enough to be reportable.

Section 7A(d)(2)(B) of the Act directs the Federal Trade Commission, with the concurrence of the Department of Justice, by rule to exempt from the notification requirements of the Act transactions which are unlikely to violate the antitrust laws. The premerger notification rules, 16 C.F.R. Parts 801-803 ("the rules"), promulgated pursuant to the Act eliminate in two ways the reporting requirements for acquisitions of little antitrust interest. First, certain categories of acquisitions such as those made for investment purposes or those which occur as a result of a stock split or stock dividend are entirely exempted from the Act's notification requirements. Second, § 801.21 of the rules, 16 C.F.R. § 801.21, provides that certain kinds of assets are not counted in determining the size of a proposed acquisition and thus whether it is reportable. Assets which are exempt for purposes of determining whether an acquisition meets the size-of-transaction test include cash, investment securities, and mortgages.

In the past, the Commission staff has taken the position in informal interpretations that accounts receivable are assets which are exempt for purposes of the size-of-transaction test pursuant to the provisions of § 801.21. This position was based on the belief that little antitrust significance would generally attach to acquisitions of accounts receivable. A recent court decision implies, however, that such acquisitions may be of antitrust concern under certain circumstances, and a reevaluation of the position that accounts receivable are covered by § 801.21 is thus called for.

The court held in United States v. Household Finance Corp. */ that cash loans by finance companies constitute a line of commerce within the meaning of § 7 of the Clayton Act. Since the assets of finance companies are primarily accounts receivable, an acquisition of accounts receivable could affect competition in a line of commerce and hence be of significance for purposes of antitrust enforcement.

In view of this decision, the staff has decided that its previous position on the treatment of accounts receivable under § 801.21 should no longer be maintained. To assure that premerger notifications are received for all acquisitions which may violate the antitrust laws, accounts receivable will no longer be treated as exempt assets when acquired and will no longer be covered by § 801.21 of the premerger notification rules. The Assistant Attorney General in charge of the Antitrust Division of the Department of Justice has concurred in this formal interpretation.

[signature]

Malcolm R. Pfunder
Assistant Director for Evaluation
Bureau of Competition
Federal Trade Commission

March 20, 1980
*/ 602 F.2d 1255 (7th Cir. 1979).

Formal Interpretation 10

Cite. 6 Trade Reg. Rep. (CCH) ¶ 42,475, at 42,605 (Mar. 28, 1980) (mislabeled as Formal Interpretation 9) (with inquiry letters and additional information as found at www.ftc.gov/bc/hsr/frmlintrps/fi10.htm).

Text. Formal Interpretation

In accordance with the provisions of § 803.30 of the Commission's premerger notification rules, 16 C.F.R. § 803.30, the Commission, with the concurrence of the Assistant Attorney General in charge of the Antitrust Division of the Department of Justice, issues this formal interpretation.

Section 7A(h) of the Clayton Act, 15 U.S.C. § 18a(h), exempts documents or information submitted pursuant to the premerger notification program from FOIA disclosure and forbids public disclosure "except as may be relevant to any administrative or judicial action or proceeding." Neither the statute nor the premerger notification rules, 16 C.F.R. § 801.1 et seq., require advance notice to the submitting person before premerger submissions are made public in a proceeding, but the Statement of Basis and Purpose to the Premerger Notification Rules states that submitting persons will be given "reasonable notice, when possible," before premerger submissions are placed on the public record in any proceeding to which the submitting person is not a party. 43 Fed. Reg. 33450, 33519 (July 31, 1978).

The Commission and the Assistant Attorney General have determined that a flexible 10 day notice requirement would not hinder the administration of the premerger notification program.

Accordingly, it is hereafter the policy of each agency to instruct its staff to give a submitting person 10 days' notice, whenever possible, before placing on the public record in any administrative or judicial action or proceeding any documents or information submitted pursuant to the Premerger Notification Program, regardless of whether the submitting person is a party to the action or proceeding. In cases where 10 days' notice is not feasible -- for example, where a temporary restraining order is being sought -- staff is instructed to give the submitting person as much advance notice as reasonably can be given, advise the court or administrative agency that the material was obtained under the premerger notification program, and request that the tribunal receive the material in camera for sufficient time to afford the submitting person an opportunity to seek a protective order, if appropriate.

By direction of the Commission.

[Signature]
Carol M. Thomas
Secretary

March 28, 1980

Formal Interpretation 11

Cite. 6 Trade Reg. Rep. (CCH) ¶ 42,475, at 42,606 (Apr. 7, 1981) (with inquiry letters and additional information as found at www.ftc.gov/bc/hsr/frmlintrps/fi11.htm).

Text.
FEDERAL TRADE COMMISSION
WASHINGTON, D. C. 20580
BUREAU OF COMPETITION

April 7, 1981

Formal Interpretation Pursuant to § 803.30 of the Premerger Notification Rules, 16 C.F.R. § 803.30, Concerning Incorporation by Reference in the Antitrust Improvements Act Notification and Report Form

On April 10, 1979, the Federal Trade Commission staff, with the concurrence of the Assistant Attorney General in charge of the Antitrust Division of the Department of Justice, issued a formal interpretation pursuant to § 803.30 of the premerger notification rules ("the rules"), 16 C.F.R. § 803.30, concerning incorporation by reference in the Antitrust Improvements Act Notification and Report Form ("the Form"), 16 C.F.R. Part 803--Appendix. This interpretation specified a narrow set of circumstances in which a person filing notification would be permitted to incorporate by reference in its initial filing documents submitted with an earlier filing and precluded such incorporation in all other cases. This position was based on practical considerations concerning the review of premerger notification filings. Filings are often sent for analysis to divisions in Washington, D.C., or to regional offices in other parts of the country. Filings by the same person with respect to different transactions are not necessarily reviewed by the same office. The analysis of subsequent filings by the same person, within the time limits imposed by the Act, would be made more difficult in such cases if all documentary materials required to be supplied with the Form do not accompany each filing.

Certain documents filed with the Securities and Exchange Commission ("SEC") are among the documentary attachments which are required to be supplied with the Form, provided they are readily available to the filing person. The United States General Accounting Office ("GAO") has recently taken the position that the restrictions imposed by this formal interpretation on the incorporation by reference in later filings of current SEC documents supplied with earlier filings, constitutes unnecessary duplication within the meaning of the Federal Reports Act, 44 U.S.C. § 3512. The Commission staff disagreed with GAO's assertion that these restrictions result in unnecessary duplication. In the interest of cooperation between government agencies, however, the Commission staff will hereafter permit wider use of incorporation by reference of such documents.

In the future, persons filing notification may incorporate by reference all SEC documents supplied with earlier filings which remain current and are called for in the subsequent filing. Item 4(a) of the Form requests specified documents filed with the SEC (or to be filed contemporaneously with the premerger notification filing) if any such documents have been filed within the three years prior to the date of the premerger notification filing and if copies of them are readily available to the filing person. The SEC documents requested are: the most recent Form 10-K, all registration statements and all Forms 10-Q and 8-K filed since the end of the period reflected in the most recent Form 10-K, the most recent proxy statement, and, if the acquisition is a tender offer, Schedule 14D-1. Thus, for example, if a person has made a premerger notification filing in the third quarter following the filing of Form 10-K and has submitted that Form 10-K, Forms 10-Q for the first two quarters, a registration statement, and a Form 8-K, it may now incorporate these documents by reference in a filing made in the fourth quarter. In the latter filing, it must supply only copies of the Form 10-Q for the third quarter and subsequent registration statements and Forms 8-K (assuming that any such documents have been filed with the SEC). After the end of the fourth quarter, however, if a new Form 10-K has been filed, these documents would no longer be called for by item 4(a), and the new Form 10-K would be filed with the premerger notification Form together with any subsequent registration statements and Forms 10-Q and 8-K.

Persons wishing to incorporate documents accompanying an earlier filing should identify that filing by the name of the person and the date on which the Form was submitted. Such persons must also specifically identify each document incorporated by reference from an earlier filing. The formal interpretation of April 10, 1979, remains in effect except to the extent it has been modified here.

The Assistant Attorney General in charge of the Antitrust Division of the Department of Justice has concurred in this formal interpretation.

Formal Interpretation 12

Cite. 6 Trade Reg. Rep. (CCH) ¶ 42,475, at 42,607 (June 2, 1981) (with inquiry letters and additional information as found at www.ftc.gov/bc/hsr/frmlintrps/fi12.htm).

Text. FEDERAL TRADE COMMISSION
WASHINGTON, D. C. 20580
BUREAU OF COMPETITION

June 2, 1981

Lewis A. Kaplan, Esquire
Paul, Weiss, Rifkind, Wharton & Garrison
345 Park Avenue
New York, New York 10154

Re: Sun Company, Inc. 10-3/4% Subordinated Exchangeable Debentures Due 2006

Dear Mr. Kaplan:

This letter responds to your letter of April 8, 1981, and constitutes a formal interpretation under § 803.30 of the Commission's premerger notification rules, 16 C.F.R. § 803.30, in which the Assistant Attorney General in charge of the Antitrust Division of the Department of Justice has concurred.

Your letter requests a formal interpretation stating that the above referenced subordinated exchangeable debentures are voting securities of Becton, Dickinson and Company within the meaning of Section 7A(b)(3)(A) of the Clayton Act, 15 U.S.C. § 18a (b)(3)(A), and § 801.1(f)(1) of the premerger notification rules, 16 C.F.R. § 801.1(f)(1).

Section 7A(b)(3)(A) of the Clayton Act states:

> The term "voting securities" means any securities which at present or upon conversion entitle the owner or holder thereof to vote for the election of directors of the issuer
> . . . .

Section 801.1(f)(1) of the premerger notification rules states:

Voting securities. The term "voting securities" means any securities which at present or upon conversion entitle the owner or holder thereof to vote for the election of directors of the issuer, or of an entity included within the same person as the issuer

. . . .

As we understand it, the above referenced debentures are a debt obligation of Sun Company, Inc., which are convertible into common stock of Becton, Dickinson and Company and allow the owner or holder to direct the manner in which a proportionate number of the underlying Becton, Dickinson shares shall be voted for the election of directors of Becton, Dickinson. The question of interpretation which arises under the premerger notification rules stems from the fact that Sun Company is technically the issuer of the debentures, and the present voting rights which attach to those debentures relate to the election of directors of Becton, Dickinson, which is not technically "the issuer, or . . . an entity included within the same person as the issuer."

We have no doubt that Congress, in enacting Title II of the Hart-Scott-Rodino Antitrust Improvements Act of 1976, intended that the antitrust enforcement agencies have an opportunity to review any antitrust issues arising out of the acquisition of securities with present voting rights such as those which attach to the Sun Company subordinated exchangeable debentures, provided that the statutory size-of-person and size-of-transaction tests are met. In drafting and promulgating § 801.1(f)(1) of the premerger notification rules, the Commission and the Assistant Attorney General did not consider the possibility that, in an unusual case, one company might issue securities which conferred on the owner or holder the right to vote for election of directors of a company that was not controlled by the issuer.

The Commission, in issuing the final premerger notification rules, did state, however:

"Voting securities" are securities that at present or upon conversion entitle the owner or holder to vote for directors of any issuer . . . . [Statement of Basis and Purpose to § 801.1(f)(1), 43 Federal Register at 33462 (July 31, 1978) (emphasis supplied)]

It was not intended that the definition of "voting securities" be limited to securities which give the owner or holder a right to vote for "directors" of a specific "issuer"; rather, that definition contains reference to an "issuer" so that the "acquired person" can be identified.

The fact that a purchaser of these subordinated exchangeable debentures acquires a present right to designate how the votes of the underlying Becton, Dickinson common shares will be cast for directors of Becton, Dickinson means that such a purchaser would, in this respect, be in the same position as a purchaser of an equivalent number of Becton, Dickinson shares. While we do not believe that circumstances such as these arise sufficiently often to justify a change in the Commission's premerger notification rules, we believe it appropriate under those rules to regard these subordinated exchangeable debentures as "voting securities" within the meaning of § 7A(b)(3)(A) of the Clayton Act and § 801.1(f)(1) of the rules. We also believe it appropriate and in keeping with the intent of the Act and the rules to regard Becton, Dickinson and Company as the "issuer" of those debentures under the Act and the premerger notification rules.

Therefore, any purchase of these subordinated exchangeable debentures is a transaction which is subject to the reporting and waiting period requirements of § 7A of the Clayton Act, provided the statutory size-of-person and size-of-transaction tests (in § 7A(a)(2) and (a)(3)) are met. If such a purchase is reportable under § 7A, the acquired person would be Becton, Dickinson and Company, and all other provisions of the Act and the rules would be applied in the normal fashion.

It is theoretically possible that the subsequent conversion or exchange of these debentures for common stock of Becton, Dickinson would give rise to another filing and waiting period obligation under § 7A, since under § 801.32 of the rules a conversion is an acquisition within the meaning of § 7A. It appears unlikely, however, that such a conversion would increase the acquiring person's percentage of Becton, Dickinson's outstanding voting securities above the percentage represented by the subordinated exchangeable debentures held prior to conversion. The conversion is therefore likely to be exempt from reporting and waiting period requirements under § 7A(c)(10).

Note that, while these subordinated exchangeable debentures are "voting securities" under § 7A of the Clayton Act and the Commission's premerger notification rules, they are not "convertible voting securities" under § 801.1(f)(2) of the rules, because they carry a present right to vote. Acquisition of these debentures is therefore not exempt from reporting and waiting period obligations under § 802.31, which exempts acquisitions of convertible voting securities.

Sincerely yours,

SIGNED
Malcolm R. Pfunder
Assistant Director for
Evaluation

[Paul, Weiss, Rifkind, Wharton & Garrison letterhead]

345 Park Avenue
New York, NY 10154
(212) 644-8646

April 8, 1981

Malcolm P. Pfunder, Esq.
Assistant Director, Evaluation
and Premerger Notification
Bureau of Competition

Attention: John Weber, Esq.
Federal Trade Commission
Sixth Street and Pennsylvania Avenue, N.W.
Washington, D. C. 20580

Gentlemen:

    We represent Becton, Dickinson and Company ("BD").
    The purpose of this letter is to request public issuance of a formal interpretation of the Hart-Scott-Rodino Antitrust Improvements Act of 1976 (the "Act") stating that certain subordinated exchangeable debentures of Sun Company, Inc. ("Sun Debentures") are "voting securities" of BD within the meaning of Section 7A(b)(2)(A) of the Act and 17 C.F.R. § 803.1(f)(1) (1980). Put more generally, we ask that the term "voting securities" be construed to include any security which at present entitles the owner or holder thereof to vote for the election of directors of any corporation.
    Briefly stated, the significance of this request is that the Sun Debentures, upon issuance, will carry the aggregate right to cast 32% of the votes for election of directors of BD and are exchangeable into shares of BD common stock ("BD Shares") totaling the same proportion of the

total number of shares issued and outstanding. Thus, acquisition of Sun Debentures, in our view, is equivalent to acquisition of BD Shares for Hart-Scott-Rodino purposes.

The Act's legislative history shows clearly that the purpose of the Act was to provide advance notification of large acquisitions to the antitrust authorities in order to permit effective action to be taken against those acquisitions that may violate the Clayton Act. E.g., H.R. Rep. No. 94-1373, 94th Cong., 2d Sess. (1976).

Acquisition of Sun Debentures entails precisely the risk that Congress sought to protect against in adopting the Act. Because the Sun Debentures carry the right to vote for directors of BD immediately upon issuance, the potential exists for another company to obtain effective control of BD by acquiring Sun Debentures. Accordingly, the policy of the Act, we submit, surely requires its application to an acquisition of Sun Debentures.

Despite this clear legislative purpose, the wording of the Act and the Regulations (which track the language of the statute on this point) create some uncertainty with respect to whether the Act would apply to an acquisition of Sun Debentures.

The background of the relationship between BD and Sun, which explains the reason for the issuance of the Sun Debentures, is set forth at pages 21-22 of the preliminary prospectus for the Sun Debentures, dated March 24, 1981, which is contained in Sun's registration statement on Form S-16, a copy of which is enclosed.*

Hart-Scott-Rodino Treatment of The Acquisition Of Sun Debentures

Sun now owns 6,485,493 BD Shares, which is approximately 32% of all BD Shares issued and outstanding. (PP 12, 21) Sun will issue Sun Debentures that are exchangeable for the BD Shares it now owns. (PP 12) After issuance and sale of the Sun Debentures and prior to their exchange for BD Shares, Sun's BD Shares are to be voted in accordance with and in proportion to (by principal amount) the instructions given by those holders of Sun Debentures who give instructions. (PP 20) Thus, a Sun Debenture in substance will entitle the owner or holder thereof to vote for the election of directors of BD immediately upon issuance.

Assuming Sun Debentures are acquired in a transaction in which the "commerce," "size of person," and "size of transaction" tests are satisfied, the acquisition is subject to the report and wait provisions of the Act if Sun Debentures are "voting securities" within the meaning of the Act.

Section 7A(b)(2)(A) of the Act, 15 U.S.C. § 18A(b)(2)(A), insofar as is relevant here, states:

"The term 'voting securities' means any securities which at present or upon conversion entitle the owner or holder thereof to vote for the election of directors of the issuer . . . "

If Sun is deemed to be "the issuer" of the Sun Debentures, Section 7A(b)(2)(A), if read literally, might indicate that the Sun Debentures are not "voting securities" for Hart-Scott-Rodino purposes because they do not entitle the owner or holder thereof to vote for the election of directors of Sun, which could be considered to be "the issuer." In that event, an acquirer of Sun Debentures could acquire the equivalent of 32% of BD without compliance with the report and wait provisions of the Act.

If, on the other hand, Section 7A(b)(2)(A) is read to define "voting securities" as any security entitling the owner or holder to vote for the election of directors of any corporation, then Sun Debentures are "voting securities." In that event, an acquisition of Sun Debentures subject to the Act would have to comply with the report and wait provisions. This result, we submit, is mandated by the legislative history and the policy of the Act.

Legislative History

The legislative history of the Act shows that Congress intended that a security entitling its owner or holder to vote for the election of directors of any corporation is a "voting security."

S. 1284, 94th Cong., 2d Sess., was the first of the premerger notification bills to be reported out of committee in Congress. S. 1284 applied to acquisitions of "stock or assets", and the term "voting security" was not directly relevant to coverage. The bill, however, would have exempted certain transactions, some of which were defined with reference to "voting security." § 7A(b)(4)(B). "Voting security" was defined for purposes of the exemptions as "any security presently entitling the owner or holder thereof to vote for the election of directors of a company . . . " § 7A(b)(4)(C). Thus, S. 1284 plainly would have treated the Sun Debentures as "voting securities" because they entitle the owner "to vote for the election of directors of a company . . . . " The same language appeared in H.R. 8532, which passed the Senate on June 10, 1976.

The House version of the premerger notification bill, which initially passed the House on August 2, 1976, took a similar approach to this issue. It covered the acquisition of any "voting securities or assets . . . " Section 2 of H.R. 14580, 94th Cong., 2d Sess. (1976) [in a clause denominated 7A(b)(3)(B)] defined the term "voting securities" as "any stock or other share capital presently entitling the owner or holder thereof to vote for the election of directors of a corporation." 122 Cong. Rec. H 8137 (Aug. 2, 1976). Thus, under the House version of the bill, the Sun Debentures clearly would have been "voting securities" because they "presently [entitle] the owner or holder thereof to vote for the election of directors of a corporation."

Following the passage of H.R. 14580 by the House on August 2, 1976 and of H.R. 8532 by the Senate on June 10, 1976, the House asked for a conference. The conference proved impossible to hold, however, in light of the press of adjournment and the threat of filibusters in the Senate. Accordingly, informal negotiations were held between Senators Kennedy, Abourezk and Scott and Chairman Rodino and other members of the House. 122 Cong. Rec. S. 14888 (Aug. 27, 1976). This culminated in an agreement on an amended version of H.R. 8532 which the Senate passed by motion on September 8, 1976. 122 Cong. Rec. S 15420. The compromise bill, of course, contained the definition of "voting securities" that now appears in Section 7A(b)(2)(A) of the Act. (The text of the compromise bill appears at 122 Cong. Rec. S 14867-72 [Aug. 27, 1976]).

On September 16, 1976, the date on which the compromise bill was passed by the House, Chairman Rodino explained the differences between the prior versions of the bill and the final bill. With respect to the definition of "voting securities", Chairman Rodino stated:

> "The House bill covered acquisitions of assets and 'voting securities' -- any debt or equity instrument entitling the holder to elect directors of a corporation. Nonvoting securities were completely exempt from the House-passed bill. However, nonvoting securities that can be converted into voting securities were covered 'upon conversion,' and compliance with the bill's notification and waiting requirements would thus have been required prior to conversion. In contrast, the Senate bill covered acquisitions of assets; voting securities; nonvoting but convertible securities; and, apparently, nonvoting, nonconvertible equity securities. Nonvoting, nonconvertible debt securities were completely exempt from the Senate bill under subsection (b)(4)(B)(ii). The compromise bill completely exempts acquisitions of nonvoting, nonconvertible debt or equity securities. Further, the compromise bill covers nonvoting but convertible securities upon acquisition, not conversion. Finally, the compromise bill covers acquisitions of voting securities in all instances, except

in the case of de minimus [sic] 'solely for purpose of investment' acquisitions expressly exempted by the bill." 122 Cong. Rec. H 10294 (Sept. 16, 1976) (emphasis added).

Thus, according to Chairman Rodino's explanation, the original House-passed bill would have covered the Sun Debentures because they entitled the holder to vote to elect directors of a corporation. The Senate bill also would have covered them because they were "voting securities" as Chairman Rodino used that term. Moreover, there is no suggestion in his comprehensive explanation of the compromise bill that the change in language between (a) the Act as finally passed and (b) the House and Senate bills was intended to alter the substance of the definition of voting securities insofar as is relevant here. Indeed, the Senate floor debate suggests that the change was purely stylistic and not substantive. 122 Cong. Rec. S 14873-88 (Aug. 27, 1976) (Senator Allen). Accordingly, we submit that the Sun Debentures are "voting securities" within the meaning of the Act because they entitle the owner or holder thereof to vote for the election of directors of BD.

The Sun Debentures are "Voting Securities" Even If The Act Is Read Literally

The same result may be reached by another route.
The Act defines "voting securities" as securities that

> entitle the owner or holder thereof to vote for the election of directors of "the issuer." If both BD and Sun are deemed to be "issuers" of the Sun Debentures, then the Sun Debentures are "voting securities" under the literal terms of the Act.

The term "issuer" is not defined in the Act or the Regulations. It therefore might well be construed in light of the lengthy history of its use in the Securities Act of 1933 ("1933 Act") and Securities Exchange Act of 1934. That history, we suggest, shows that both BD and Sun are "issuers" here.

Section 2(4) of the 1933 Act, 15 U.S.C. § 77b(4), provides:

> "The term 'issuer' means every person who issues or proposes to issue any security except that with respect to certificates of deposit, voting-trust certificates, or collateral-trust certificates, or with respect to certificates of interest or

shares in an unincorporated investment trust not having a board of directors (or persons performing similar functions) or of the fixed, restricted management, or unit type, the term 'issuer' means the person or persons performing the acts and assuming the duties of depositor or manager pursuant to the provisions of the trust or other agreement or instrument under which such securities are issued; except that in the case of an unincorporated association which provides by its articles for limited liability of any or all of its members, or in the case of a trust, committee, or other legal entity, the trustees or members thereof shall not be individually liable as issuers of any security issued by the association, trust, committee, or other legal entity; except that with respect to equipment-trust certificates or like securities, the term 'issuer' means the person by whom the equipment or property is or is to be used; and except that with respect to fractional undivided interests in oil, ' , A gas, or other mineral rights, the term 'issuer' means the owner of any such right or of any interest in such right (whether whole or fractional who creates fractional interests therein for the purpose of public offering." (Emphasis added)

Thus, the term "issuer" under the 1933 Act includes "the person or persons performing the acts and assuming the duties of . . . managers" pursuant to a voting trust or other such agreement under which the certificates are issued.

The Sun Debentures are to be issued pursuant to the settlement agreement in the Sun-BD litigation. (PP 22) The BD Shares for which the Sun Debentures are exchangeable are to be deposited in escrow pending their exchange for Sun Debentures. (PP 12, 22) The voting of the BD Shares is to be governed by a voting agreement. The purchase of a Sun Debenture carries with it not only the debt obligation of Sun, but, in substance, the right to vote the BD Shares for which the Debenture is exchangeable. Accordingly, for present purposes, a Sun Debenture may be viewed both as a debt obligation of Sun and as a voting trust certificate governing the voting of BD Shares. Moreover, because the Sun Debentures are to be issued and the BD Shares are to be voted pursuant to agreements to which both Sun and BD are parties, both Sun and BD should be viewed as managers of what amounts to a voting trust containing BD Shares. In consequence, both should be viewed as "issuers" for purposes of Section 7A(b)(2)(A) of the Act.

The Need For Issuance of A Formal Interpretation

We believe that the Sun Debentures are "voting securities" within the meaning of the Act, particularly when Section 7A(b)(2)(A) is considered in light of the Act's purpose and its legislative history. We acknowledge, however, that this conclusion is not necessarily self-evident solely from a literal reading of the language of the statute. Accordingly, one acquiring Sun Debentures might fail to report and wait, as required by the Act, in good faith.

In these circumstances, there is no unquestionably effective remedy for dealing after the fact with a failure to report and wait. There is no private clause of action under the Act. There is little likelihood that the civil penalty provisions of section 7A(g)(1) of the Act would be invoked against a firm claiming that it had acted in good faith. And while the Commission could proceed under section 7A(g)(2) against an acquirer of Sun Debentures, it is unclear whether a district court would prevent the voting of the BD Shares pending compliance with the Act if the failure to comply was inadvertent. Hence, an acquisition of Sun Debentures in violation of the Act could well leave the offender free to vote a 32% interest in BD.

The Commission may readily avoid these potential problems by publicly issuing a formal interpretation of the Act pursuant to Section 803.30 of the Regulations, 17 C.F.R. § 803.30 (1980). Such action would place all potential acquirers of Sun Debentures on notice that the acquisition of those debentures is subject to the Act. This almost surely would avoid the need for any enforcement action by assuring voluntary compliance with the statute. This, we submit, is in the public interest and is exactly what Congress intended in adopting the Act. Indeed, Congress explicitly contemplated such action by empowering the Commission to define terms used in the Act. 15 U.S.C. § 18A(d)(2)(A)

We are ready to provide you with any additional information that may be necessary in connection with this request. In addition, I would appreciate an opportunity to meet with you or your staff to discuss this matter.

Very truly yours

[signature]
Lewis A. Kaplan

* References to the preliminary prospectus are indicated by "PP" followed by the page number.

Formal Interpretation 13
[Supersedes Formal Interpretation 5]

Cite.   Not available in Trade Reg. Rep. (with inquiry letters and additional information as found at www.ftc.gov/bc/hsr/frmlintrps/fi13.htm).

Text.

Formal Interpretation Pursuant to § 803.30 of the
Premerger Notification Rules, 16 CFR § 803.30, Concerning
Early Termination of the Waiting Period under the
Hart-Scott-Rodino Antitrust Improvements Act of 1976.

This formal interpretation of the Premerger Notification Rules concerning "early termination" of the waiting period provided by the Hart-Scott-Rodino Act is issued by the Federal Trade Commission pursuant to 16 CFR § 803.30. It supersedes a formal interpretation issued by the staff of the Federal Trade Commission on April 10, 1979. That interpretation announced criteria that would be used by the Federal Trade Commission and the Department of Justice in determining whether a request under 16 CFR § 803.11 for early termination would be granted. One of those criteria was a requirement that the parties demonstrate some special business reason that warranted early termination of the waiting period.

After experience with the standard for early termination announced on April 10, 1979, the agencies have determined that early termination requests may be appropriately granted in a wider range of circumstances without diminishing the effectiveness of the enforcement process. In the future, the agencies will normally grant a request for termination of the waiting period under the following circumstances:

1. At least one party to the proposed transaction has requested early termination in writing;

2. All parties to the proposed transaction have submitted notification and report forms and any other information required; and,

3. The Federal Trade Commission and the Antitrust Division of the Department of Justice have determined not to take any enforcement action during the waiting period.

Thus, it will no longer be necessary to include in a request for early termination a statement of reasons why the requesting party wishes to consummate the transaction before the end of the waiting period. The amount of time needed to act upon such requests cannot be predicted with precision. It will necessarily vary according to several factors, including the workload of the agencies, the complexity of the proposed transaction, and the seriousness of the antitrust concerns (if any) raised by the proposed transaction.

Notification of each grant of early termination will be published in the Federal Register as required by § 7A(b)(2) of the Clayton Act. 15 U.S.C. § 18a(b)(2). In addition, if any party's request for early termination has been granted, it is the practice of the Federal Trade Commission to so notify by telephone all parties who have filed in connection with that acquisition.

The Assistant Attorney General in charge of the Antitrust Division of the Department of Justice concurs in this interpretation.

August 20, 1982

Appendix 469

Formal Interpretation 14

Cite. 6 Trade Reg. Rep. (CCH) ¶ 42,475, at 42,608 (Nov. 14, 1988) (mislabeled as Formal Interpretation 13) (with inquiry letters and additional information as found at www.ftc.gov/bc/hsr/frmlintrps/fi14.htm).

Text. FEDERAL TRADE COMMISSION

16 CFR Part 802 Premerger Notification:
Reporting and Waiting Period Requirements

AGENCY: Federal Trade Commission

ACTION: Notice of Formal Interpretation

SUMMARY: On November 14, 1988, the Federal Trade Commission, with the concurrence of the Assistant Attorney General in charge of the Antitrust Division of the Department of Justice, issued Formal Interpretation Number 14 pursuant to § 803.30 of the Commission's Premerger Notification Rules, 16 C.F.R. § 803.30. The formal interpretation discusses the effect of the CAB Sunset Act, 49 U.S.C. § 1551(a)(7), on § 802.6(b) of the Commission's premerger notification rules, 16 C.F.R. § 802.6(b). Its primary purpose is to state that any airline merger or acquisition that is to be consummated on or after January 1, 1989, must be reviewed under the Hart-Scott-Rodino premerger notification program, regardless of whether the parties to it have sought or even obtained approval from the Department of Transportation before that time.

EFFECTIVE DATE: November 14, 1988

FOR FURTHER INFORMATION CONTACT: John M. Sipple, Jr., Chief, Premerger Notification Office, Bureau of Competition, Room 301, Federal Trade Commission, Washington, DC 20580. Telephone: (202) 326-3100.

SUPPLEMENTARY INFORMATION: The text of Formal Interpretation Number 14 is set out below:

Interpretation Number 14

Formal Interpretation Pursuant to § 803.30 of the Premerger Notification Rules, 16 CFR § 803.30, Concerning § 802.6(b) of the Rules, 16 CFR § 802.6(b), As It May Relate To Transactions Between Air Carriers And Others Consummated On Or After January 1, 1989.

Mergers and similar transactions between airlines have for decades required federal regulatory approval prior to consummation. Until 1985, that authority was granted to the Civil Aeronautics Board, and since then, to the Department of Transportation (DOT). The Hart-Scott-Rodino premerger notification rules, 16 C.F.R. § 801.1 et seq., have taken account of the prior approval requirement and have attempted to eliminate duplicative notification and review by providing in § 802.6(b)(1) that:

> [A]ny transaction which requires approval by [DOT] prior to consummation, pursuant to section 408 of the Federal Aviation Act, 49 U.S.C. 1378, shall be exempt from the requirements of the act if copies of all information and documentary material filed with [DOT] are contemporaneously filed with the Federal Trade Commission and the Assistant Attorney General.

As of January 1, 1989, under the provisions of the CAB Sunset Act, 49 U.S.C. § 1551(a)(7), DOT will no longer have authority over airline mergers. The Federal Trade Commission is issuing this formal interpretation in anticipation of the following question that may arise concerning the transition: Is a transaction for which DOT approval has been sought or obtained (and for which papers filed with DOT have been contemporaneously filed with the antitrust agencies) but which has not been consummated prior to January 1, 1989, exempt from premerger notification requirements pursuant to § 802.6(b)(1), or is a Hart-Scott-Rodino premerger notification required?

The Commission construes § 802.6(b)(1) as not exempting such a transaction; therefore, Hart-Scott-Rodino premerger notification would be required, assuming that the size thresholds are met and no other exemption applies. A transaction that takes place after January 1, 1989, is not "[a] transaction which requires approval by [DOT] prior to consummation" and thus does not come within the § 802.6(b)(1) exemption. This interpretation is consistent with the most basic policy behind the Hart-Scott-Rodino Antitrust Improvements Act and DOT statutory authority over airline mergers. That policy is to assure that a merger or similar transaction will be subjected to a premerger competitive review. This interpretation eliminates the possibility that a transaction would avoid all premerger review if the parties sought, but did not receive, final approval by DOT of a merger or acquisition.

This interpretation limits the exemption provided by § 802.6 to transactions that are both approved by DOT and consummated by the parties prior to January 1, 1989. Without these limitations, approval of a transaction by DOT might enable the parties to complete a transaction without further premerger competitive review at a much later date when the likely competitive effects of the transaction could be significantly different. This interpretation thus meets the premerger notification rules' concern about the amount of change that can take place in the marketplace between the review and the completion of the transaction. (That concern is addressed by § 803.7 of the premerger notification rules, which requires that the parties complete the acquisition for which notification was filed within a limited time following the Hart-Scott-Rodino review or seek another such review before they complete it).

The Hart-Scott-Rodino premerger notification obligation that may arise for transactions for which DOT approval has been sought need not significantly delay such transactions. Parties may file Hart-Scott-Rodino premerger notification and seek early termination of their waiting period. If the antitrust agencies have, in the course of a DOT section 408 proceeding, actually completed their antitrust analysis of the proposed transaction, early termination could be granted promptly.

In addition, parties need not wait until January, 1989, to submit Hart-Scott-Rodino premerger notifications for proposed transactions. In the unique circumstances of this sunset law, the Commission and the Antitrust Division of the Department of Justice will review a premerger notification notwithstanding that the transaction would be exempt if consummated with DOT approval prior to January 1989. In other words, the parties may both claim the exemption provided for in § 802.6 and separately file for antitrust premerger review of the same transaction. If both procedures are invoked, the parties would be free to consummate a transaction before January 1989 with DOT approval even if the Hart-Scott-Rodino premerger notification waiting period had not terminated.

Section 802.6(b)(2) provides that acquisition of:

> (2) The following...assets will not be exempt under § 802.6(b)(1):
> (i) if the transaction is an acquisition of assets, the assets which are engaged in a business or businesses other than aeronautics or air transportation...;

(ii) if the transaction is an acquisition of voting securities..., the business or businesses of the acquired issuer (and all entities which it controls) which are not engaged in aeronautics or air transportation...

Because there will no longer be any transactions that satisfy the criteria of § 802.6(b)(1), § 802.6(b)(2) will no longer be invoked with respect to transactions that were previously covered by § 408 of the FAA. However, through informal interpretations pursuant to § 803.30, the Commission's Premerger Notification Office has used the method reflected in § 802.6(b)(2) to define the extent to which "assets held as a result of a transaction requiring approval" by other federal regulatory agencies are exempt from premerger notification requirements. The Premerger Notification Office will continue to apply this method to such other transactions consummated after December 31, 1988.

The Assistant Attorney General in charge of the Antitrust Division of the Department of Justice concurs in this formal interpretation.

By direction of the Commission.

Date: November 14, 1988

[signature]
Donald S. Clark
Secretary

Formal Interpretation 15

Cite. 6 Trade Reg. Rep. (CCH) ¶ 42,475, at 42,609 (Mar. 23, 2001) (with inquiry letters and additional information as found at www.ftc.gov/bc/hsr/frmlintrps/fi15amend.htm).

Text. FEDERAL TRADE COMMISSION

Premerger Notification: Reporting and Waiting Period Requirements

AGENCY: Federal Trade Commission

ACTION: Notice of Amendment of Formal Interpretation 15

SUMMARY: The Premerger Notification Office ("PNO") of the Federal Trade Commission ("FTC"), with the concurrence of the Assistant Attorney General in charge of the Antitrust Division of the Department of Justice ("DOJ"), is amending a Formal Interpretation of the Hart-Scott-Rodino Act, which requires persons planning certain mergers, consolidations, or other acquisitions to report information about the proposed transactions to the FTC and DOJ. The Interpretation concerns the reportability of certain transactions involving the formation of a Limited Liability Company ("LLC"), a relatively new form of entity authorized by state statutes, resulting in the combination of businesses into the new LLC.

This Formal Interpretation was first published on October 13, 1998, 63 Fed. Reg. 54713. It was subsequently modified and republished on February 5, 1999, 64 Fed. Reg. 5808; and on June 29, 1999, 64 Fed. Reg. 34804.

On December 21, 2000, the President signed into law certain amendments to Section 7A(a) of the Clayton Act, 15 U.S.C. 18a(a). *See* Pub. L. 106-553, 114 Stat. 2762, effective on February 1, 2001. The current amendments to Formal Interpretation 15 merely reflect the changes in the statutory size-of-transaction test and size-of-person test, and the resultant repeal of 16 CFR. § 802.20.

The reference to § 802.20 at Fed. Reg. 34806 is removed. Example 2 to Formal Interpretation 15 is amended to reflect the new $50 million threshold. Minor typographical errors were corrected in two footnotes, and footnote 7 was revised to reflect the elimination of the size-of-person test for transactions which are valued in excess of $200 million.

DATES: The Amended Formal Interpretation 15 will become effective upon publication.
FOR FURTHER INFORMATION CONTACT: B. Michael Verne, Compliance Specialist, Premerger Notification Office, Bureau of Competition, Room 301, Federal Trade Commission, Washington, DC 20580. Telephone: (202) 326-3167.

SUPPLEMENTARY INFORMATION: The text of Formal Interpretation Number 15, as amended, is set out below. The revision is bolded and italicized. The removed language is bracketed and underlined.

Formal Interpretation Number 15

Formal Interpretation Pursuant to § 803.30 of the Premerger Notification Rules, 16 CFR § 803.30, Concerning the Reporting Requirements for the Formation of Certain Limited Liability Companies ("LLCs").

This is a Formal Interpretation pursuant to § 803.30 of the Premerger Notification Rules ("the rules"). The rules implement Section 7A of the Clayton Act, 15 U.S.C. § 18a, which was added by sections 201 and 202 of the Hart-Scott-Rodino Antitrust Improvements Act of 1976 ("the act").

This Formal Interpretation was first published on October 13, 1998, together with a request for comments, to become effective on December 14, 1998. 63 Fed Reg 54713 (October 13, 1998). The PNO received six comments which were placed on the public record. On December 2, 1998, the effective date of this Interpretation was postponed until February 1, 1999, to give the PNO staff more time to analyze and respond to the comments. 63 Fed Reg 66546 (December 2, 1998).

Formal Interpretation 15 was modified in response to the comments and republished on February 5, 1999. 64 Fed Reg 5808 (February 5, 1999). Under the revised Interpretation, the formation of an LLC which combines under common control in the LLC two or more pre-existing businesses will be treated as subject to the requirements of the HSR act under § 801.2(d) of the HSR rules, 16 CFR § 801.2(d), which governs mergers and consolidations. Because Formal Interpretation 15 had been modified substantially, the effective date of the Interpretation was postponed until March 1, 1999. *Id.*

Shortly after the Interpretation became effective, it became apparent that the Interpretation as it applies to transactions involving existing

LLCs did not give clear guidance. The section of the Interpretation dealing with acquisitions of and by existing LLCs was therefore amended in a number of respects to explain how such transactions are to be analyzed. First, the first full paragraph in the third column at 64 Fed. Reg. 5809 (February 5, 1999) was deleted. Second, the four paragraphs in the notice which begin with the phrase "The acquisition of a membership interest in an existing LLC will be a potentially reportable event . . ." and end with the phrase ". . . whether there is a change in any member's membership interest." was inserted between the carryover paragraph and the first full paragraph in the second column at 64 Fed. Reg. 5810. Third, Example 2, at 64 Fed. Reg. 5811, was revised in a number of respects. Fourth, a new Example 3 was added, and current Examples 3 and 4 at 64 Fed. Reg. 5811 were renumbered as Examples 4 and 5. Fifth, a new Example 6 was added, and current Examples 6-8 at 64 Fed. Reg. 5811 were renumbered as Examples 8-10. Finally, current Example 8 (now Example 10) was revised in a number of respects.

The most recent amendments to Formal Interpretation 15 merely reflect the changes in the statutory size-of-transaction test and size-of-person test, and the resultant repeal of 16 CFR. § 802.20.

The act requires the parties to certain acquisitions of voting securities or assets to notify the FTC and the DOJ and to wait a specified period of time before consummating the transaction. The purpose of the act and the rules is to ensure that such transactions receive meaningful scrutiny under the antitrust laws, with the possibility of an effective remedy for violations, prior to consummation. Under the rules, certain types of transactions, such as mergers, consolidations, and the formation of corporate joint ventures, are treated as acquisitions of voting securities potentially subject to the act, while other transactions, such as the formation of partnerships, are deemed nonreportable. *See* §§ 801.2(d) and 801.40 of the rules, 16 CFR §§ 801.2(d) and 801.40.

The LLC(1) is a relatively new form of business organization that is neither a partnership nor a corporation but a hybrid legal entity that combines certain desirable features of both partnerships and corporations. Specifically, an LLC is taxed as a partnership but shields its members from liability as a corporation shields its shareholders. The first LLC statute was passed in 1977 by Wyoming(2) and a trickle of other states followed. The use of LLCs expanded significantly after 1988 when the Internal Revenue Service ("IRS") concluded that an LLC organized under the Wyoming statute was taxable as a partnership.(3) By 1993 all 51 jurisdictions had LLC laws of one form or another.

When it first encountered these types of organizational structures, the PNO concluded that as "companies" LLCs are "entities" within the meaning of § 801.1(a)(2), 16 CFR § 801.1(a)(2), and that, until it had more experience with them, the PNO would treat LLCs like corporations. Initially, therefore, § 801.40 of the rules, 16 CFR § 801.40, "Formation of joint venture or other corporations," governed the formation of LLCs and an interest in an LLC was treated as a voting security for HSR purposes.

On further analysis, the PNO concluded that this initial approach was too inclusive. LLCs at the time were primarily used as vehicles for the creation of start-up businesses. The PNO's treatment of LLCs resulted in requiring HSR filings in a large number of transactions that did not raise antitrust concerns. Furthermore, the PNO believed that in most LLCs the interest held by the members of the LLC was more like a partnership interest than a voting security interest. Consequently, in 1994, the PNO began to informally advise parties that the treatment of LLCs for reporting purposes would depend on a determination of whether the interest acquired in the LLC was more like a voting security interest or more like a partnership interest.(4)

This treatment of LLCs has not been completely satisfactory. The use of LLCs has evolved, and while LLCs continue to be used as vehicles for start-up enterprises, they are now often used to combine competing businesses under common control. Indeed, the Commission's litigation staff has investigated several transactions raising potential antitrust concerns involving the formation of LLCs. In these transactions, previously separate businesses were combined under common control when they were both contributed to a single, newly-formed LLC. Nevertheless, the creation of the LLC to combine competing businesses under common control was typically not treated as reportable under the PNO's then-current treatment. However, the union of competing businesses under common control is of obvious potential antitrust concern. Since the past treatments of LLCs have not been satisfactory at singling out those transactions that were the most likely to have anticompetitive effects, the PNO staff has decided to revise its approach to LLCs in order to better carry out the purposes of the act.

The formation of an LLC into which two or more businesses are contributed, like other unions of businesses under common control, is a kind of merger or consolidation.(5) Section 801.2(d)(1)(i) of the rules, 16 CFR § 801.2(d)(1)(i), states that "[m]ergers and consolidations are transactions subject to the act ...."(6) A filing requirement for those LLC formations that involve the combination of businesses is appropriate and advances the purposes of the act and the rules, namely, to ensure that the antitrust enforcement agencies have advance notice of, and a timely opportunity to challenge, transactions which may violate the antitrust laws.

This Formal Interpretation, therefore, changes the PNO's treatment of LLC's as follows: The PNO will henceforth treat as reportable the formation of an LLC if (1) two or more pre-existing, separately controlled businesses will be contributed, and (2) at least one of the members will control the LLC (i.e., have an interest entitling it to 50 percent of the profits of the LLC or 50 percent of the assets of the LLC upon dissolution).(7) The formation of all other LLCs will be treated similar to the formation of a partnership which, under the PNO's longstanding position on partnership formations, will not be reportable.

In determining what is a "business" for purposes of this Interpretation, the PNO will look to the definition of "operating unit" for purposes of § 802.1(a) of the rules, 16 CFR § 802.1(a), namely, "...assets that are operated ... as a business undertaking in a particular location or for particular products or services, even though those assets may not be organized as a separate legal entity." In addition, for purposes of this Formal Interpretation, the contribution to an LLC of an interest in intellectual property, such as a patent, a patent license, know-how, and so forth, which is exclusive against all parties including the grantor, is the contribution of a business, whether or not the intellectual property has generated any revenues.

Under this Interpretation, the approach of § 801.2(d) will be used to determine the acquiring person(s) and acquired person(s) for potentially reportable LLC formations.(8) Section 801.2(d)(2)(i) states that "[a]ny person party to a merger or consolidation is an acquiring person if as a result of the transaction such person will hold any assets or voting securities which it did not hold prior to the transaction" (emphasis added). In the context of the formation of a new LLC, this means that any person that will control an LLC in which two or more previously separate businesses will be combined will be an acquiring person. Thus, if "A" and "B" form a 60-40 LLC, the 60 percent member, "A," will be an acquiring person with respect to the contributions of "B." Section 801.2(d)(2)(ii) states that "[a]ny person party to a merger or consolidation is an acquired person if as a result of the transaction the assets or voting securities of any entity included within such person will be held by any other person" (emphasis added). In the above example of the formation of a 60-40 LLC, "B" would therefore be an acquired person. If "A" and "B" were to form a 50-50 LLC to which both were to contribute businesses, both would be both acquiring and acquired persons because both would control the LLC and thus hold assets or voting securities it did not hold prior to the transaction. "A" and "B" would file in both capacities, assuming the relevant size criteria were met. Thus, both the acquiring and acquired persons will be required to file notification and, in accordance with § 803.10 of the rules, the 30-day waiting period will begin when both persons have substantially complied with the notification requirements.

Under this Interpretation, the nature of the acquisition(s) taking place when an LLC is formed, that is, whether it is an acquisition of assets or of voting securities, depends on what is being contributed by the other member(s) of the LLC.(9) In the 50-50 LLC described above, suppose that "A" contributes a group of assets constituting a business and "B" contributes 50 or more percent of the voting securities of a corporate subsidiary, S. In this example, "B" will be deemed to have made an acquisition of assets and "A," an acquisition of voting securities.

In addition, any exemption in the act or rules that would make any other acquisition nonreportable may make the acquisition by one or more of the contributors to an LLC nonreportable. If, for example, "A's" asset contribution consists of hotel properties the acquisition of which would be exempt under § 802.2(e), "B's" acquisition in the formation of this LLC would not be reportable. [Similarly, if S has sales and assets of less than $25 million and the value of the S stock that will be held by "A" as a result of the acquisition is $15 million or less, then "A's" acquisition in the formation would be exempted by § 802.20(b).]

To determine whether a filing is required, the parties to potentially reportable formation transactions also must determine the size-of-person and size-of-transaction, which should be done just as in any other asset or voting securities acquisition in accordance with §§ 801.10 and 801.11 of the HSR rules. Since these transactions are similar to asset exchanges, for most such transactions there will not be a determined acquisition price for the acquired assets or voting securities to use in applying the size-of-transaction test. For such transactions, parties should use the market price or fair market value where another contributor contributes 50 or more percent of the voting securities of an issuer (*see* § 801.10(a)), or the fair market value where another contributor puts assets constituting a business into the LLC (*see* § 801.10(b)).

The acquisition of a membership interest in an existing LLC will be a potentially reportable event (1) if it results in the acquiring person holding 100 percent of the membership interests in that LLC, and (2) that person had not previously filed for and consummated the acquisition of control of that LLC. Such an acquisition is reportable as the acquisition of all the assets of the LLC. This is similar to the PNO's treatment of acquisitions of partnership interests.

Acquisitions of additional businesses by existing LLCs fall into one of two categories. First, those that result in a change in the percentage membership interest of any member will be treated by the PNO as the formation of a new LLC under this Interpretation. In such a new formation, the acquisition by any person that will control the new LLC of the assets or voting securities of the business(es) being contributed that it did not previously control is potentially reportable. Both additional businesses and the business(es) already in the existing LLC are regarded as being contributed to the new LLC. These transactions should be analyzed using the criteria for formations. Accordingly, persons will be regarded as acquiring only those businesses that they come to control as a result of the transaction.

Second, those acquisitions of businesses by existing LLCs that do not result in a change in the percentage membership interest of any member are not treated as new formations but, rather, as the acquisition of the assets or voting securities of the business by the LLC or, if it is controlled, by its ultimate parent entity, or entities, and, as such, are potentially reportable.

The acquisition by an existing LLC of assets or voting securities not constituting a business will be treated as the acquisition of assets or voting securities by the LLC or, if it is controlled, by its post-acquisition ultimate parent entity, or entities, and, as such, is potentially reportable. This treatment will pertain without regard to whether there is a change in any member's membership interest.

This Formal Interpretation will not require reporting of some LLC formations and some acquisitions of existing LLC interests that would have required reporting under the Interpretation announced by the PNO in October of 1998. Unlike the October version, this Formal Interpretation requires reporting of the formation of an LLC only if the formation brings together within the LLC two formerly separately controlled businesses. Comments received suggested that the treatment announced in the October version would have covered a substantial number of LLCs that are not likely to raise competitive concerns. For example, the October Formal Interpretation would have viewed LLCs that are created solely as financing vehicles as reportable. In these transactions, a financial institution (or other party providing financing) in the ordinary course of its business contributes only cash or other financial assets and one other party contributes one or more operating units to a new LLC that the financial institution may control for HSR purposes, at least for a period of time. Under this revised Interpretation, so long as such financing transactions do not result in the contribution of a business to the LLC by two or more members, it will not be treated as reportable.(10)

As described above, except for a situation where, as a result of an acquisition, the acquiring person would hold 100 percent of the interests in an existing LLC, no acquisition of an interest in an existing LLC is reportable under this Interpretation. Several comments indicated that LLC agreements are sometimes entered into in which the right to receive more than 50 percent of the LLC's profits shifts from one member to another upon the happening of some event outside the control – or even the knowledge – of the members. Under the definition of control applicable to LLCs (i.e., § 801.1(b)(ii)), under the October Interpretation, such a shift in the right to receive profits might have created a reporting obligation. The commenters argued that it would be unduly burdensome to require the beneficiaries of such shifts to file and that no substantive law enforcement interest would be served. The PNO does not intend that such shifts be reportable under this Formal Interpretation. Since such a shift would be the post-formation acquisition of an interest in an existing LLC without the contribution of another business, it will not be treated as subject to the reporting requirements of the act.

Some of the reasons for concluding that the formation of certain LLCs should be treated as reportable may apply equally well to partnerships. The position of the PNO, however, is that the formation of a partnership is not reportable and acquisitions of partnership interests that do not result in one person's holding 100 percent of the interests in a partnership are nonreportable. Several comments received on the Formal Interpretation published in October suggested that no change to the treatment of partnerships was necessary at this time. The treatment of partnerships was originally adopted, in part, because of the difficulty of monitoring compliance with HSR reporting obligations since many partnerships can be formed informally or by implication in many typical business arrangements. Furthermore, there has been no suggestion in any of the comments that partnerships are being used with any greater frequency now to combine competing businesses. Consequently, the PNO has decided not to change its treatment of partnerships at this time, but it may re-visit this issue in the future as developments require.

The following examples are an integral part of this Formal Interpretation:

Appendix 481

1. "A" and "B" both plan to contribute businesses to a new LLC in which each will acquire a 50 percent interest. This LLC formation would involve both "A" and "B" making reportable acquisitions if the size-of-person and size-of-transaction tests are met. Each acquisition would be reportable unless exempted by Section 7A(c) of the act or Part 802 of the HSR rules. "A" would file as an acquiring person and "B" as an acquired person for "A's" acquisition of the assets being contributed by "B," and "B" would file as an acquiring person and "A" as an acquired person for "B's" acquisition of the assets contributed by "A." If "A" or "B" (or both) contributed 50 percent or more of the voting securities of a corporation, the acquisition(s) would be treated as an acquisition of voting securities of the issuer whose shares are contributed.

2. "A," "B," and "C" form an LLC in year 1 in which each receives a one-third interest and to which each contributes a business valued at approximately $60 million. "A," "B," and "C" are $100 million persons. This formation would not be reportable because no member controls the LLC. In year 2, "X," also a $100 million person, acquires the membership interests of "A" and "B" for cash. This would not be reportable because acquisitions of membership interests in existing LLCs are potentially reportable only if they result in one person holding 100 percent of the interests in the LLC. Note that if "X" also contributes a business to the LLC in exchange for the LLC membership interest it receives, the transaction will be treated as the formation of a new LLC. The acquisition of the new business will not be reportable because "X" already controls it. "X" may, however, have a filing obligation as an acquiring person with respect to the businesses already in the LLC if the size tests are met and no exemption applies. The existing LLC would be the acquired person because no member controls it. Note also that in the example where "X" contributed only cash and did not file under HSR, if "X" were subsequently also to acquire "C's" membership interest it would then hold 100 percent of the interests in this LLC and would therefore have to file for the acquisition of all of the assets of the LLC.

3. In year 1, "A" and "B" form an LLC to which "A" contributes a business and takes back a 60 percent interest and

"B" contributes cash and takes back a 40 percent interest. This transaction is not reportable. Suppose, however, that in year 4:

a. "B" contributes a new business, "A" contributes cash, and there is no change in percentage membership interests. This would not be analyzed as a new formation but would be treated as an acquisition by the LLC. "A," as the ultimate parent entity of the LLC, would file as acquiring and "B" as acquired for the acquisition of the business.

b. "A" contributes a business, "B" contributes cash, and their interests change so that "A" has 61 percent and "B" has 39 percent. This is a new formation because of the changes in the membership interests but it is not reportable because two or more separately controlled businesses are not being contributed, as "A" controlled both businesses before the transaction.

c. "B" contributes a business, "A" contributes cash, and their interests change so that "A" has 59 percent and "B" has 41 percent. This is also a new formation. "A" will file to acquire the business being contributed by "B."

d. "B" contributes a business and the membership interests change so that "B" has 60 percent and "A" has 40 percent. This is a new formation, and "B" would file to acquire the business contributed by the LLC. "A," as the ultimate parent entity of the existing LLC, would file as the acquired person.

e. "C" contributes assets not constituting a business and the percentage interests are adjusted so that "A" has 50 percent, "B" has 30 percent, and "C" has 20 percent. This is not a new formation because the assets being contributed are not a business. "A," as ultimate parent entity of the LLC, will file to acquire these assets from "C."

Appendix 483

4. "A" and "B" form a new LLC, to which "A" will contribute its widget business and "B" will contribute cash for operating capital. This formation would not be reportable because two previously separate businesses are not being contributed to the LLC.

5. "A," "B," and "C" form a 60-20-20 LLC to which "A" contributes cash and receives a 60 percent membership interest and "B" and "C" each contribute an operating unit for a 20 percent interest. This is a kind of a consolidation of "B's" and "C's" operating units into the new LLC and "A" will control the LLC. There are two reportable transactions (assuming the size criteria are met and no exemption applies): "A" acquiring the operating unit contributed by "B," and "A" acquiring the operating unit contributed by "C".

6. In year 1, "A," "B," and "C" form a new LLC to which each contributes a business and takes back a one-third membership interest. In year 4, the LLC acquires all the voting securities of another business from "D" in exchange for certain assets not constituting a business. This acquisition would not be analyzed as the formation of a new LLC because no member's percentage interest changes as a result of the transaction. Rather, the LLC would be viewed as acquiring the voting securities of the new business from "D." This transaction will be reportable if the size criteria are met and no exemption applies. "D" will, of course, have to analyze its acquisition of assets from the LLC to determine if it is also reportable.

7. "A" proposes to consolidate its widget business, which it has conducted in two subsidiaries and a division, into a newly-formed LLC in which it will hold a 60 percent membership interest. This would not be reportable because, although separate businesses are being combined, they were not under separate control prior to the transaction.

8. "A," "B," and "C" form a new LLC in which "A" will have a 60 percent interest and "B" and "C" each will have 20 percent interests. "A," a large, international pharmaceutical company, contributes $100 million in cash and the assets of a pharmaceutical product which is currently on the market. This

pharmaceutical product line constitutes a business. "B" contributes licenses to several patents which it will also continue to use to manufacture various drugs. "C" will contribute licenses which are exclusive even against itself for several drugs which are still at the testing stage and which have never been marketed. With a 60 percent interest, "A" will control the LLC. Since the licenses "B" will contribute are not exclusive as against it, they do not constitute a business. However, the licenses being contributed by "C" do constitute a business, even though they have not generated any revenue. "A" has a potential reporting obligation for the formation of this LLC for acquiring assets from "C." This formation combines two pre-existing, separately controlled businesses in an LLC which "A" will control.

9. "A" and "B" are both regional grocery store chains which do their data processing in-house. "A's" data processing unit does work only for "A" and "B's" only for "B." "A" and "B" decide to contribute the assets used in their data processing operations to a new jointly-controlled LLC which will provide data processing services to "A" and "B." Assume the size tests are met. This would not be reportable because the assets used to provide such management and administrative support services do not constitute businesses. Cf § 802.1(d)(4) of the rules and Examples 10 and 11, 16 CFR § 802.1(d)(4). This would be the case even if the new LLC intends to begin offering data processing services to third parties, since this would be beginning a new business rather than uniting existing businesses. Note, however, that the result would be different if "A" and "B" had used their equipment to provide any data processing services to others prior to contributing it to the new LLC, for then each would be contributing an existing business.

10. In year 1, "A," "B," and "C" form a new LLC to which each contributes a business in exchange for a one-third interest. This formation is not reportable because no member controls the LLC. Suppose that in year 2 "A" sells additional assets to the LLC for cash. This transaction is not analyzed as a new formation under this Formal Interpretation. However, the LLC has a potential filing obligation as the acquiring person of those assets and "A" as the acquired person. Note that it is irrelevant whether the assets sold by "A" in year 2 constitute a business.

Note also that if assets not constituting a business are acquired by an LLC, even if the percentage membership interests change in the transaction, this is not analyzed as the formation of a new LLC, either, but as an acquisition by the LLC (or its post-acquisition ultimate parent entity).

Donald S. Clark
Secretary

Endnotes:

1. This Formal Interpretation applies only to the reportability of the formation of certain LLCs. The position of the FTC staff on the status and treatment under the act of other non-corporate entities such as partnerships remains unchanged.
2. Wyo. Stat. § § 17-15-101 to -135 (Supp. 1989).
3. Rev. Rul. 88-76, 1988-2 C. B. 360, 361.
4. Specifically, the formation of an LLC was treated as potentially reportable only if the LLC had a group that functioned like a board of directors and the LLC ownership interest resulted in the holders appointing person(s) other than their employees, officers, or directors (or those of entities controlled by such holder or its ultimate parent entity) to that group. In such cases, the LLC interest was treated as a voting security interest. In all other instances, LLC interests were treated as partnership interests and the acquisition of these interests was not reportable (unless the acquiring person would hold 100 percent of the interests as a result of the acquisition).
5. While combining businesses in an LLC may not be a "merger" or "consolidation" in the strictest sense because they do not involve corporations, the rationale of this interpretation is similar to that used by the PNO under § 801.2(d) to require filing for acquisitions of non-profit corporations which, like LLCs, typically do not issue voting securities. (*See* ABA, The Premerger Notification Practice Manual, 1991 ed., Interp. #109.)
6. In fact, as it was originally promulgated in 1978, § 801.2(d)(1)(i), 16 CFR § 801.2(d)(1)(i), stated that "[a] merger, consolidation, or other transaction combining all or any part of the business of two or more persons shall be an acquisition subject to the act...." (emphasis added) 43 Fed Reg 33539, July 31, 1978. In 1983, this section was changed to clarify the treatment of mergers and consolidations under the rules, and the italicized wording was eliminated. However, there is no indication that this change was intended to narrow the scope of § 801.2(d). Rather, according to the Statement of Basis and Purpose to the 1983 changes, 48 Fed Reg 34430, July 29, 1983, the Commission simply sought to make clear that mergers and consolidations are treated as acquisitions of voting securities and to aid the parties to a merger in determining which is the acquiring person and which is the acquired person.

7. Of course, as with all transactions, the HSR size requirements (size of transaction and, if size of transaction is $200 million or less, size of person) need to be met as well, and exemptions may apply.

8. The Formal Interpretation as published in October, 1998 described a method to determine reportability that was based on concepts found in § 801.40 of the HSR rules, 16 CFR § 801.40. Certain comments suggested that such an approach was confusing and would increase the likelihood that parties would make erroneous conclusions on their reporting obligations. In light of those comments, and the change in approach this Formal Interpretation adopts, there will no longer be any need to look to § 801.40 to determine reporting obligations.

9. In this respect, the Interpretation necessarily departs from the text of § 801.2(d)(1)(i), which provides that all mergers and consolidations shall be treated as acquisitions of voting securities.

10. There is no evidence to suggest now that LLC formations where only one business is contributed are being used to accomplish a merger or consolidation of two businesses. However, the PNO will look carefully at these transactions in the future and, if they begin to be used to accomplish a merger or consolidation, will re-visit this issue.

Formal Interpretation 16

Cite. 6 Trade Reg. Rep. (CCH) ¶ 42,475, at 42,614 (Sept. 24, 1999) (with inquiry letters and additional information as found at www.ftc.gov/os/1999/09/frnformalinterpretation16.htm).

Text. FEDERAL TRADE COMMISSION

Premerger Notification: Reporting and Waiting Period Requirements

AGENCY: Federal Trade Commission

ACTION: Notice of the Issuance of Formal Interpretation 16 Changing the Policy of the Premerger Notification Office to Require Filing Persons to Submit Only One Original Affidavit and Certification with their Filings

SUMMARY: The Premerger Notification Office ("PNO") of the Federal Trade Commission ("FTC"), with the concurrence of the Assistant Attorney General in charge of the Antitrust Division of the Department of Justice ("DOJ," collectively, "the enforcement agencies"), is issuing Formal Interpretation 16 addressing the number of original affidavits and certification pages which must accompany Premerger Notification filings. Section 803.5 of the Premerger Notification rules ("the rules") requires all acquiring persons in transactions falling under § 801.30 and all parties to non-§ 801.30 transactions to submit certain affidavits with their premerger notification filings. Section 803.6 of the rules requires a notarized certification for such filings. The PNO has required that each copy of the form be submitted with an original affidavit and certification. Pursuant to Formal Interpretation 16, from now on the PNO will require that one original affidavit and one original certification page accompany one of the two copies of the form submitted to the FTC. The other affidavits and certification pages may be duplicates. Only the originals need be separately notarized.

DATES: Formal Interpretation 16 is effective on September 24, 1999.

FOR FURTHER INFORMATION CONTACT: Marian R. Bruno, Assistant Director, Premerger Notification Office, Bureau of Competition, Room 301, Federal Trade Commission, Washington, DC 20580. Telephone: (202) 326-2846. Thomas F. Hancock, Attorney,

Premerger Notification Office, Bureau of Competition, Room 301, Federal Trade Commission, Washington, DC 20580. Telephone: (202) 326-2946.

SUPPLEMENTARY INFORMATION: The text of Formal Interpretation Number 16 is set out below:

Formal Interpretation Number 16

Formal Interpretation Pursuant to § 803.30 of the Premerger Notification Rules, 16 CFR § 803.30, Concerning the Number of Original Affidavits and Certification Pages Which Must Accompany a Premerger Notification Filing

This is a Formal Interpretation pursuant to § 803.30 of the Premerger Notification Rules ("the rules"). The rules implement Section 7A of the Clayton Act, 15 U.S.C. § 18a, which was added by sections 201 and 202 of the Hart-Scott-Rodino Antitrust Improvements Act of 1976 ("the act"). The act requires the parties to certain acquisitions of voting securities or assets to notify the FTC and the DOJ and to wait a specified period of time before consummating the transaction. The purpose of the act and the rules is to ensure that such transactions receive meaningful scrutiny under the antitrust laws, with the possibility of an effective remedy for violations, before consummation.

The act states that " no person shall acquire . . . any voting securities or assets of any other person, unless both persons (or in the case of a tender offer, the acquiring person) file notification pursuant to rules under subsection (d)(1) of this section . . . ." Section 803.1(a) of the rules states that the notification required by the act is the completed Antitrust Improvements Act Notification and Report Form for Certain Mergers and Acquisitions ("the form"), 16 CFR Part 803- Appendix.

Section 803.5(a) of the rules requires that ". . . [f]or acquisitions to which § 801.30 applies, the notification required by the act from each acquiring person shall contain an affidavit, attached to the front of the notification, attesting [that the acquired person has been notified of certain facts about the proposed transaction, that the reporting person has a good faith intention to make the acquisition, and, in the case of a tender offer, that the intention to make a tender offer has been publicly announced]." Section 803.5(b) requires that ". . . [f]or acquisitions to which § 801.30 does not apply, the notification required by the act shall contain an affidavit . . . attesting that a contract, agreement in principle or letter of intent to merge or acquire has been executed, and . . . to the good faith intention of the person filing notification to complete the transaction." Section 803.6(a) of the rules states that "The notification required by the act shall be certified . . . ."

One of the primary purposes of these requirements - particularly that of certification - is to preserve the evidentiary value of the filing. The Statement of Basis and Purpose ("SBP") for § 803.6 states that ". . . the certification is intended to estop the person on whose behalf the report is filed from later denying the completeness or accuracy of the information provided on the form in the event that either enforcement agency seeks to introduce any such information into evidence in any proceeding." 43 Fed Reg 33511 (July 31, 1978). The certification requirement is also intended to place responsibility on an individual to ensure that information reported is true, correct, and complete and that the form is filled out in accordance with the act and the rules. *Id.*

The affidavit requirement is intended to ensure that several important prerequisites are met before the review process begins. Thus the acquiring person must attest that it has made certain disclosures about the proposed transaction to the acquired person so the acquired person has knowledge of its obligation to file. *Id.* at 33510. In consensual transactions, the parties must also attest that a contract, letter of intent, or agreement in principle has been executed. *Id.* Its contents also ensure that the parties intend to consummate the acquisition and are not using the notification process to vet a purely hypothetical transaction with the agencies. *Id.* at 33511.

The Instructions to the form state that each person filing notification must "[c]omplete and return two notarized copies (with one set of documentary attachments) of [the form] to [the PNO] . . . and three notarized copies (with one set of documentary attachments) to [the DOJ] . . . ." The PNO has interpreted the instructions to require that each certification be originally signed and notarized and that each of the required affidavits also be originally signed and notarized. This has resulted in each party's submission to the enforcement agencies in a non-§ 801.30 transaction and acquiring persons' filings in non-§ 801.30 transactions having ten original signatures and ten original notarizations (five on the affidavits and five on the certifications). Acquired persons' filings in § 801.30 transactions must have five originally signed and notarized certifications.

The PNO has determined that multiple original signatures and notarizations, while not a great burden, is not a negligible one. Accordingly, the PNO has decided to modify its position on the necessity for original signatures and notarizations with premerger notification filings. From now on, filing persons need supply only one original signed and notarized affidavit (if required) and one original signed and notarized certification with one of the two copies of the form submitted to the FTC. The affidavits and certifications accompanying the other copies of the form may be copies of these originals. A copy is acceptable if the signature and notarization (including the embossed notary seal, if required in the jurisdiction of notarization) are clearly visible. Likewise, a person required to re-certify an amended filing because the original was deficient may submit one original certification and four copies with the new information.

This Formal Interpretation affects only the number of original signatures and notarizations which must accompany premerger notification filings. It does not change the affidavit or certification requirements themselves, who may sign the affidavit and certification, or the number of copies of the form and documentary attachments which must be provided. It also remains the case that any filing person, United States or foreign, can swear or affirm under penalty of perjury under the laws of the United States pursuant to 28 U.S.C. § 1746 in lieu of notarization.

Donald S. Clark
Secretary

Formal Interpretation 17

Cite. 6 Trade Reg. Rep. (CCH) ¶ 42,475, at 42,615 (Apr. 3, 2000) (with inquiry letters and additional information as found at www.ftc.gov/os/2000/04/hsrformalinterp17_.htm).

Text. FEDERAL TRADE COMMISSION

Premerger Notification: Reporting and Waiting Period Requirements

AGENCY: Federal Trade Commission

ACTION: Notice of Issuance of Formal Interpretation 17

SUMMARY: The Premerger Notification Office ("PNO") of the Federal Trade Commission ("FTC"), with the concurrence of the Assistant Attorney General in charge of the Antitrust Division of the Department of Justice ("DOJ"), is adopting a Formal Interpretation of the Hart-Scott-Rodino Act, ("the HSR Act," "the Act"), which requires persons planning certain mergers, consolidations, or other acquisitions to report information about the proposed transactions to the FTC and DOJ in order to allow for effective premerger antitrust review. The Act exempts from Hart-Scott-Rodino premerger review certain classes of acquisitions that require premerger competitive review by a specialized regulatory agency. This Interpretation describes the PNO's position regarding transactions that may occur under the recently enacted Gramm-Leach-Bliley Act that have some portions subject to advance competitive review by a banking agency and other, non-bank portions that are not subject to such review. Under the Interpretation, the non-bank portion of such a transaction is subject to the reporting requirements of the HSR Act regardless of whether the non-bank business is housed in an affiliate of a financial holding company or a financial subsidiary of a bank. The Interpretation also addresses HSR treatment of certain transactions in which portions of the transaction require approval under different sections (section 3 and section 4) of the Bank Holding Company Act. This Interpretation does not address questions concerning how to apply the HSR rules to the portion of a mixed transaction that is subject to the HSR Act. These issues will be addressed by the PNO on a case-by-case basis.(1)

DATES: Formal Interpretation 17 is effective on April 3, 2000.

FOR FURTHER INFORMATION CONTACT: Marian R. Bruno, Assistant Director, telephone (202) 326-2846, or Thomas F. Hancock, Attorney, telephone (202) 326-2946; Premerger Notification Office, Bureau of Competition, Room 301, Federal Trade Commission, Washington, DC 20580.

SUPPLEMENTARY INFORMATION: The text of Formal Interpretation Number 17 is set out below:

FORMAL INTERPRETATION 17, PURSUANT TO § 803.30 OF THE PREMERGER NOTIFICATION RULES, 16 CFR § 803.30, REGARDING FILING OBLIGATIONS FOR CERTAIN ACQUISITIONS INVOLVING BANKING AND NON-BANKING BUSINESSES UNDER THE (c)(7) AND (c)(8) EXEMPTIONS OF THE HART-SCOTT-RODINO ACT AS AMENDED BY THE GRAMM-LEACH-BLILEY ACT

Pursuant to § 803.30 of the Hart-Scott-Rodino premerger notification rules ("the rules"), the Premerger Notification Office ("PNO") of the Federal Trade Commission ("FTC"), with the concurrence of the Assistant Attorney General in charge of the Antitrust Division of the Department of Justice ("DOJ", collectively, "the enforcement agencies"), issues this formal interpretation of the Hart-Scott-Rodino Act, as amended.

The Gramm-Leach-Bliley Act

The Gramm-Leach-Bliley Act, Public Law 106-102, was signed into law by President Clinton on November 12, 1999. Title I of Gramm-Leach-Bliley, Facilitating Affiliation Among Banks, Securities Firms and Insurance Companies, generally became effective March 11, 2000. Under the new law, bank holding companies and banks are allowed to affiliate with companies that participate in financial services markets that were previously off limits to such entities. In particular, Gramm-Leach-Bliley repeals the restrictions on banks affiliating with securities firms contained in sections 20 and 32 of the Glass-Steagall Act. The statute creates a new "financial holding company" category under section 4(k) of the Bank Holding Company Act ("BHCA"). Such holding companies can engage in a statutorily provided list of financial activities, including insurance and securities underwriting and agency activities, merchant banking and insurance company portfolio investment activities. Other financial activities and activities incidental to financial activities may be approved if the Federal Reserve Board and the Treasury Department agree. Activities that are "complementary" to financial activities are also authorized and such activities may be specified by the Federal Reserve Board at a later date. A bank holding company that does not become a financial holding company can continue to engage in activities closely related to banking, such as trust services, data processing services, investment advising and ATM network ownership, under section 4(c)(8) of the BHCA.

Gramm-Leach-Bliley also allows a national bank that meets certain standards to engage in the same new financial activities in "financial subsidiaries," except for insurance underwriting, merchant banking (which may be approved as a permissible activity beginning five years after enactment), insurance company portfolio investments, and, unless permitted by other law, real estate development and real estate investment. Other financial activities and activities incidental to financial activities may be approved if the Federal Reserve Board and the Treasury Department agree. The aggregate assets of all financial subsidiaries must not exceed 45% of the parent bank's assets or $50 billion, whichever is less. National banks may continue to have traditional operating subsidiaries. Gramm-Leach-Bliley prohibits operating subsidiaries of national banks from doing anything that a bank cannot do directly.(2)

Amendments to the HSR Act Made by Gramm-Leach-Bliley

The HSR Act exempts from HSR premerger antitrust review several classes of acquisitions that are "already subject to advance antitrust review" by other agencies, thus avoiding duplicative reporting. *See* H.R. Rep. No. 1373, 94th Cong., 2d Sess. 6 (1976).

Section 133(c) of Gramm-Leach-Bliley amended the HSR Act's (c)(7) exemption, pertaining to transactions which require agency approval under section 3 of the BHCA, section 18(c) of the Federal Deposit Insurance Act ("FDI Act"), or section 10(e) of the Home Owners' Loan Act, and the HSR Act's (c)(8) exemption, pertaining to transactions which require agency approval under section 4 of the BHCA or section 5 of the Home Owners' Loan Act. Specifically, the HSR Act's (c)(7) exemption, 15 USC § 18a(c)(7), as amended by section 133(c)(1) of Gramm-Leach-Bliley, provides an exemption from HSR requirements for "transactions which require agency approval under . . . section 1828(c) of title 12 [section 18(c) of the FDI Act], or section 1842 of title

12 [Section 3 of BHCA], except that a portion of a transaction is not exempt under this paragraph if such portion of the transaction (A) is subject to section 4(k) of the Bank Holding Company Act of 1956; and (B) does not require agency approval under section 3 of the Bank Holding Company Act of 1956." (Language added by section 133(c)(1) is italicized.)

The HSR Act's (c)(8) exemption, 15 USC § 18a(c)(8), pertaining to transactions which require agency approval under section 4 of the BHCA, is amended in a parallel fashion by section 133(c)(2) of Gramm-Leach-Bliley. Section (c)(8) of the HSR Act exempts such transactions provided that the materials filed with the agency are contemporaneously submitted to the enforcement agencies at least thirty days prior to consummation.

Treatment of Mixed Bank and Non-Bank Transactions

It has always been the case that some transactions are "mixed," that is, have some aspects or portions subject to regulatory agency premerger competitive review and approval and other aspects or portions not. Such mixed transactions can and have occurred involving all regulated industries, including banking, as discussed below. The PNO's longstanding position has been to treat the portion of a mixed transaction not subject to advance competitive review and approval by a regulatory agency as being subject to the HSR Act.(3) Moreover, when the Commission (with the concurrence of the Department of Justice) promulgated § 802.6(b) of the rules in 1983 to exempt from the HSR Act "any transaction which requires approval by the [CAB] prior to consummation," the agencies made clear in the rule that the non-aeronautic part of a transaction -- which did not require such approval -- was essentially to be treated as a separate transaction potentially reportable under the HSR Act.

The PNO views the amendments of the HSR Act made by section 133(c) of the Gramm-Leach-Bliley Act as confirming that the PNO's longstanding treatment of mixed transactions is to be applied to transactions involving the banking industry. As described below, the non-bank portion of a transaction is subject to the reporting requirements of the HSR Act, regardless of whether the non-bank business is housed in an affiliate of a financial holding company or a financial subsidiary of a bank.(4)

The Joint Explanatory Statement of the Committee of Conference contained in the Conference Report demonstrates that Congress considered section 133(c) of Gramm-Leach-Bliley to be a clarification and affirmation of the existing treatment of mixed transactions under HSR:

> This clarification for the new [financial holding company] structure is consistent with, and does not disturb, existing law and precedents under which mergers involving complex corporate entities, some parts of which are in industries subject to merger review by specialized regulatory agencies and other parts of which are not, are considered according to agency jurisdiction over their respective parts, so that normal H-S-R Act requirements apply to those parts that do not fall within the specialized agency's specific authority. *See* 16 C.F.R. § 802.6.

Cong. Rec. H11296 (Nov. 2, 1999).

The PNO's interpretation of the HSR exemptions amended by Gramm-Leach-Bliley is further guided by the explanatory Floor Remarks of House Judiciary Committee Chairman Hyde:

> Under current law, bank mergers are reviewed under special bank merger statutes, and they do not go through the Hart-Scott-Rodino merger review process that covers most other mergers. Now banks will be able to get into other businesses which they have not been able to do before.
>
> The principle that we have followed is that when mergers occur, the bank part of that merger will be judged under the current bank merger statutes, and we do not intend any change in that process or in any of the agencies' respective jurisdictions. The non-bank part of that merger will be subject to the normal Hart-Scott-Rodino merger review by either the Justice Department or the Federal Trade Commission.
>
> This is, in all likelihood, the result that would have been obtained anyway. Hybrid transactions involving complex corporate entities -- some parts of which are in industries subject to merger review by specialized regulatory agencies and other parts of which are not -- have occurred in the past. In those cases, the various parts of the consolidation were considered according to agency jurisdiction over the respective parts, so that normal Hart-Scott-Rodino Act requirements applied to those parts that did not fall within the specialized agency's specific authority. *See*, e.g., 16 C.F.R.

§802.6. I think the precedents would have already dictated the desired result here.

. . . .

In short, under this bill and the precedents, no bank is treated differently than it otherwise would be because it has some other business within its corporate family. Likewise, no other business is treated differently than it otherwise would be because it has a bank within its corporate family.

Cong. Rec. H11549 (Nov. 4, 1999).

The HSR Act (c)(7) exemption, as amended, expressly addresses acquisitions in which a bank and its financial affiliate are being acquired by a financial holding company (the affiliate structure). The financial affiliate portion of that transaction is not exempt from the HSR Act, because it is subject to section 4(k) and does not require Federal Reserve Board approval under section 3 of the BHCA. Gramm-Leach-Bliley does not expressly address acquisitions of a bank with a financial subsidiary by another bank or holding company (the subsidiary structure). Chairman Hyde explained the absence of an express clarification regarding the subsidiary structure similar to the clarification that expressly addresses the affiliate structure:

> As the shape of the new activities in which banks were going to be permitted to engage through operating subsidiaries became clear in conference, the conferees ideally would have further revised the House language to make a similar clarification, regarding consolidations of non-banking entities that are operating subsidiaries of merging banks. But the operating subsidiary situations so closely parallels the precedents I have mentioned that a clarification for that situation was probably unnecessary.
>
> Of course, whatever aspect of a banking merger is not subject to normal Hart-Scott-Rodino premerger review will be subject to the alternative procedures set forth in the Bank Merger Act and the Bank Holding Company Act, including the automatic stay. So one way or another, there will be some avenue for effective premerger review by the antitrust agencies. These alternative procedures would be in some ways more potentially disruptive to the merging banking entities, particularly when the antitrust concern involves non-banking entities. But it is our intent that the precedents will be followed.

Cong. Rec. H11549, Floor Statement of Chairman Hyde (Nov. 4, 1999).

Accordingly, consistent with the intent of Congress, the PNO interprets the HSR Act, as amended by section 133(c) of Gramm-Leach-Bliley, as reaching the non-bank portion of a transaction when housed in a financial subsidiary of a bank as well as when housed in an affiliate of a financial holding company. Thus, in acquisitions of a bank with a financial subsidiary (or of a holding company in which a bank has a financial subsidiary) by another bank or holding company, the acquisition of the financial subsidiary will be reportable under the HSR Act if the applicable size-of-person and size-of-transaction tests are met and no other exemption applies.

A Related Point

As noted above, the HSR Act (c)(7) exemption covers transactions which require agency approval under section 3 of the BHCA. The HSR Act (c)(8) exemption applies to transactions which require agency approval under section 4 of the BHCA if copies of materials filed with such agency are contemporaneously filed with the enforcement agencies at least 30 days prior to consummation. If a bank holding company acquired another bank holding company that has one or more so-called "4(c)(8) affiliates,"(5) approvals would be required under both section 3 and section 4 of the BHCA.(6) The question has arisen -- and may continue to arise with Gramm-Leach-Bliley in effect -- whether parties to such a transaction need comply with the copies/waiting conditions of the (c)(8) exemption for the section 4 part of the transaction or may instead regard (c)(7) as covering the entire transaction. Based on discussions with Federal Reserve Board staff, we believe that in this type of transaction, the Federal Reserve Board review and approval under section 3 of the BHCA does not entail competitive review and approval of the section 4 portion of the transaction. Accordingly, parties to a transaction that involves approvals under section 3 and section 4 of the BHCA should comply with the copies/waiting conditions of the HSR Act (c)(8) exemption for the section 4 part of the transaction.(7)

The following Examples illustrate the application of this Formal Interpretation. In these Examples, "subject to HSR" means that the parties will have to comply with HSR notification and waiting requirements if applicable size criteria and thresholds are met and no other exemption applies.

1. Financial Holding Company A acquires Bank B. B does not own any financial subsidiaries. This is a transaction which requires Federal Reserve Board approval under section 3 of the BHCA and there is no non-bank part of this merger. The transaction is exempt from the HSR Act under (c)(7).

2. Financial Holding Company A acquires Securities Company B. This transaction does not require banking agency approval under any of the relevant banking statutes, and is thus not covered by the HSR Act (c)(7) or (c)(8) exemptions. The acquisition is subject to the HSR Act.

3. Financial Holding Company A acquires Financial Holding Company B. B owns banks and financial affiliates, including insurance companies and securities companies. While A's acquisition of B's banks is exempt under HSR section (c)(7), the acquisition of the financial affiliates is subject to HSR. This situation is expressly addressed by the language of section (c)(7) as amended by Gramm-Leach-Bliley. The acquisition of the financial affiliates is a portion of a transaction that is subject to section 4(k) of the BHCA and does not require agency approval under section 3 of the BHCA. If in this Example B owned 4(c)(8) affiliates such as thrifts in addition to banks and financial affiliates, A's acquisition of B's 4(c)(8) affiliates would require Federal Reserve Board approval under section 4 of the BHCA. HSR Act section (c)(8) as amended by Gramm-Leach-Bliley would exempt A's acquisition of B's 4(c)(8) affiliates (provided that A complied with the requirements of that section -- *see* Example 7), but the acquisition of the financial affiliates would still be subject to HSR. Under HSR Act sections (c)(7) and (c)(8) as amended, the acquisition of the financial affiliates would be a portion of a transaction that is subject to section 4(k) of the BHCA and does not require agency approval under section 3 or section 4 of the BHCA.

4. Securities company A will acquire Bank B. B does not own any financial subsidiaries. In order to make the acquisition, A must apply to become a financial holding company. Because the acquisition of B requires Federal Reserve Board approval under section 3 of the BHCA and there is no non-bank business

being acquired, this transaction is exempt under HSR Act section (c)(7). *See* Example 1.

5. Bank A acquires Securities Company B as a financial subsidiary under Gramm-Leach-Bliley. This transaction does not require banking agency approval under any of the banking statutes referenced in the HSR Act, and is thus not exempted by HSR Act sections (c)(7) or (c)(8). The acquisition is subject to HSR. *See* Example 2. Note that if Bank A, instead of acquiring a financial subsidiary, had acquired Mortgage Company B as a traditional operating subsidiary, either before or after the Gramm-Leach-Bliley Act takes effect, that transaction also would not require banking agency approval under any of the relevant banking statutes specified in the HSR Act (c)(7) and (c)(8) exemptions, and thus would be subject to HSR.

6. Bank A from Example 5, which now holds Financial Subsidiary B, is acquired by Bank C. While C's acquisition of A requires agency approval (by the Office of the Comptroller of the Currency, Federal Reserve Board or Federal Deposit Insurance Corporation, depending on whether C is a national bank, state member bank, or state non-member bank) under section 18(c) of the FDI Act and is exempt under HSR section (c)(7), the acquisition of financial subsidiary B is subject to HSR. If in this example C is not a Bank but rather a financial holding company, bank holding company or a securities firm, the result is the same. The non-bank portion of a merger is subject to HSR regardless of whether the non-bank business is housed in an affiliate of a financial holding company or a financial subsidiary of a bank.

7. A and B are bank holding companies that have not become financial holding companies under Gramm-Leach-Bliley. They may engage in activities closely related to banking under section 4(c)(8) of the BHCA, but not in the broader array of activities allowed under section 4(k). A acquires B, including the banks owned by B and non-bank section 4(c)(8) affiliates. The acquisition of the banks requires Federal Reserve Board approval under section 3 of the BHCA and is exempt under HSR Act section (c)(7). The acquisition of the non-bank affiliates requires Federal Reserve Board approval under section 4 of the BHCA and is exempt under HSR Act section (c)(8) if copies of

all information and documents filed with the Federal Reserve Board are filed contemporaneously with the FTC and DOJ at least 30 days prior to consummation. Although the parties need not make HSR filings, (c)(7) does not exempt the entire transaction, and the copies/30-day requirements of the (c)(8) exemption must be observed for the non-banking affiliates.

8. A is a national bank that has one or more operating subsidiaries but does not have any financial subsidiaries. Under Gramm-Leach-Bliley, A's operating subsidiaries cannot engage in any activities that A cannot engage in directly. If A is to be acquired by another entity, the PNO will view this for purposes of HSR as a purely banking transaction that requires agency approval under section 3 of the Bank Holding Company Act or section 18(c) of the FDI Act and not as a mixed transaction. The entire transaction will be exempt under HSR Act section (c)(7).

9. Ten entities plan to form and each have a 10% interest in a new corporation, A, which will own and operate an ATM network. Formation of joint venture corporations is generally analyzed under § 801.40 of the rules, which may require one or more of the contributors to the joint venture to file under the HSR Act for the acquisition of voting securities of the joint venture. For HSR purposes, the formation of A involves ten potentially reportable acquisitions. Each contributor that is a bank holding company will require Federal Reserve Board approval for its acquisition under section 4 of the BHCA, and accordingly, each such acquisition is exempt under HSR Act section (c)(8). In addition, a special rule, § 802.42, applies, if at least one of the ten entities forming A is a bank holding company whose acquisition of A is exempt pursuant to the (c)(8) exemption. In that case, under § 802.42, the contributors that are not bank holding companies and whose acquisitions of A are not exempted by HSR Act section (c)(8) receive a partial exemption. These entities can file the affidavits described in Rule 802.42(a) in lieu of filing HSR Forms, but otherwise remain subject to the Act and Rules (*e.g.,* waiting period; second requests).

10. Corporation A from Example 9, an ATM network owned by ten entities, now plans to acquire another ATM network, B. For HSR purposes, there will be one acquisition with A as the

acquiring person. If any of the ten entities that own A is a bank holding company, it will need Federal Reserve Board approval under section 4 of the BHCA. The PNO will apply the rationale of the HSR Act section (c)(8) and § 802.42 in such an instance. Accordingly, the PNO will treat A's acquisition of B as exempt under HSR Act section (c)(8) if: (i) at least one of the entities owning A must get Federal Reserve Board approval under section 4 of the BHCA; and (ii) each such entity that must get such Federal Reserve Board approval complies with the requirements of HSR section (c)(8) by filing copies of all information and documentary material filed with the Federal Reserve Board with the FTC and DOJ contemporaneously and at least 30 days prior to consummation of the proposed transaction. If A's acquisition of B does not require any approval under section 4 of the BHCA (because none of the owners of A is a bank holding company), then A's acquisition of B will be subject to HSR. The PNO believes that this treatment of mergers of ATM networks assures effective premerger competitive review while avoiding duplicative review and minimizing burdens and costs for the parties.

Donald S. Clark
Secretary

1. Parties wishing to determine the application of the HSR Act and the Rules to a particular set of facts will find source materials on the FTC Web site at www.ftc.gov. Parties may also call the PNO for advice at (202) 326-3100.
2. Gramm-Leach-Bliley also recognizes that state banks may have subsidiaries that engage in the same activities as financial subsidiaries, subject to certain restrictions. It does not eliminate existing authority for subsidiaries of state banks to engage in state-authorized activities not permissible for national banks or their subsidiaries, subject to approval by the Federal Deposit Insurance Corporation.
3. This PNO position has been noted by HSR practitioners and commentators. See, e.g., American Bar Association Section of Antitrust Law, Premerger Notification Practice Manual (1991 ed.) Interpretations 33, 36; S. Axinn, Acquisitions Under the Hart-Scott-Rodino Antitrust Improvements Act (1996) §6.06[3][b].
4. Of course, a comparable approach to mixed transactions also applies to transactions involving thrifts or thrift holding companies.
5. A bank holding company can acquire a company engaged in activities closely related to banking if it gets approval under section 4 of the BHCA.

6. By way of contrast, when a financial holding company acquires another financial holding company that has section 4(k) financial affiliates, the acquisition of the financial affiliates does not require Federal Reserve Board approval.

7. In the past, the PNO informally advised that the (c)(7) exemption could be relied on exclusively in such a transaction. This advice was based on the belief that all portions of the transaction were reviewed by the Federal Reserve Board under section 3. This view is no longer held by the PNO.

SUBJECT INDEX

Numbers Refer to Interpretations
Letters Refer to Enforcement Actions
FI Refers to Formal Interpretations

A

Abandonment of Transaction, 266, 267.
    see Withdrawal
Accounting Principles, 140, 144
Accounts Payable, 118
Accounts Receivable, 7, 8, 9, 109, 111, 118, 162, 212, FI-9
Acquired Person
    Civil Penalty, DD
    LLC, 85
    Third Party Voting Securities, 163
Acquiring Person
    Formation, Parties Who Provide Financing, 178
    Former Shareholders of Target, 273
    LLC, 85
Acquisition
    Accounts Receivable, 7, 8, 9, 109, 111, 162, 212, FI-9
    Agent, 49, 78
    Airline, FI-14
    Asset Value, 106, 107
    Automatic Maturation of Inchoate Voting Rights, 69, 164, 231
    Bank Branch, 121
    Banking Industry, 15, FI-7
    Bankruptcy, 255
    Beneficial Ownership, 58
    Broker, 59
    Business as Part of Shopping Center Transaction, 3
    Business Trusts, 71
    Cash Equivalents, 161
    Casino, 207, 208
    Collection Agent, 109
    Collective Investment Trusts, 64
    Consignment, 30
    Consulting Agreements and Retirement Plans Provided to Seller of Business, 33

Consumer Loans, 8
Contingent Liabilities, 113
Contingent Purchases, 56
Convertible Securities, 10, 67, 68, 70
Convertible Securities with Proxy, 70
Covenant not to Compete, 32
Debt Pay-Off, 93
Demand Deposits, 121
Determined Contingent Payments, 101
Dissenting Shareholder, 87
Employment Contract, 113
Exclusive License, 92
Executory Contract, 4, 121
Filing Fee Determination, 112
Fundamental Requirement to Trigger Filing, 159, 172, 190, 230, 231
Government Agency, 12, 34, 35, 36
Hotel, 207, 208
Installment Sale, 28
Instrumental in Causing Transaction, 159, 190, 230
Intellectual Property, 29
Inventory, 3, 5
Investment Bank, 49, 59
Investment Intent. *see* Investment-Only Exemption
Irrevocable Proxy with Convertible Nonvoting, 70
Issuer with Assets Exempt under 802.51, 213
Issuer with Some Exempt Assets, 207
Lease, 3, 4, 28, 103, 104
Liabilities, 122
Life Insurance Policy, 121
LLC Interest, 60, 82, 86
Long-Term Lease, 4
Management Agreement, 53
MLP Interests, 71
Mortgage Loans, 9
Multiple Transactions, 150
Native American Tribe, 35

Numbers Refer to Interpretations
Letters Refer to Enforcement Actions
FI Refers to Formal Interpretations

No Acquisition, but Holder Active in Transaction, 159, 190, 230
No Increase in Percentage Interest, 18, 223, 234
Nonprofit Corporations. *see* Nonprofit Corporations
Nonrecourse Loan, 117
Nonstock Corporation, 74
Nonvoting Securities with Voting Rights. *see* Voting Rights
Notes, 10
Oil and Gas Assets, 6
Open Market Purchase, Point at which Acquisition Occurs, 25
Option with Right to Vote, 31
Option to Purchase Voting Securities or Assets, 31
Partnership Interests, 60, 71, 73, 86, 110
Pension Fund, 121
Price. *see* Valuation
Price Change, 265. *see* Refiling Requirement
Promissory Note, 120
Pro Rata Spin-Off, 19
Purchase Orders, 105
Put-Call Option, 49
Reduction in Percentage of Voting Securities Held, 18, 223, 234
REIT, 197
Related Partnerships, 150
Right to Designate Directors, 70
Step Transaction, 57, 90
Stock Distribution, 87
Subject to Order, FI-2
Supermarket, 5
Transfer of Assets between Controlling Member and Nonprofit Corporation, 42
Transfer of Assets between Parent and Controlled Partnership or LLC, 42
Trusts, 47
Trust Company, 64

Undivided Interest, 60
U.S. Parent with Foreign Subsidiary, 213
Voting Rights. *see* Voting Rights
White Squire Shares, 69
Acquisition Completed after Financials Prepared. *see* Regularly Prepared Financial Statements
Acquisition Vehicle. *see* Formation; Size-of-Person
Formation, 251, 274
Merger or Consolidation, 175
Multiple Acquisitions, 146
Pro Forma Balance Sheet, 145
Size-of-Person for Acquisition when Noncash Assets Contributed, 124, 145, 184
Size-of-Person for Acquisition when Cash Contributed, 145, 146, 184
Advice from Agency on HSR, 270
Aero Limited Partnership, 16, V
Affidavit
 Bankruptcy, 255
 Conditional Transaction, 262
 Dissenting Shareholder in Merger, 87
 Facsimile Copy, 260
 Good Faith Intention, 87, 166, 167, 262
 Notarized, 259
 One Original, FI-16
 Open Market Purchases, FI-3
 Refiling Situation 224, 225
 Tender Offer, 252
 Two-Step Transaction, 252
 Threshold, 264
Agency of Foreign Government, 34
Agency Approval, FI-17
Agent, 49, 78
Aggregation, 156
 Acquired Person, 158
 Asset Acquisitions, 150, 154, 155, 156
 Asset and Voting Securities Multiple Acquisitions, 156, 157

Subject Index 505

Numbers Refer to Interpretations
Letters Refer to Enforcement Actions
FI Refers to Formal Interpretations

Avoidance, 192
   Cash in an Asset Transaction, 5, 160
   Exempt Acquisition, 151, 206
   Inventory with Production Assets, 5
   Multiple Agreements, 154, 192
   Multiple Asset Acquisitions, 150, 154, 155
   Multiple Closings, 154
   Real Property Exemption, 206
   "Related" Entities not under Common Control, 150, 196
   Separate Transactions, 196
   Step Transaction, 154
   Subsidiaries, 157, 158
   Trusts, 64
   UPE, 155
   Unproductive Real Property, 202
   Voting Securities, 150, 156, 158
Agreement
   Amendment, 249. *see* Refiling Requirement
   Beneficial Ownership, 44. *see* Jumping-the-Gun
Airline Industry, FI-14
Amended Filing. *see* Refiling Requirement
Annual Net Sales and Total Assets. *see* Size-of-Person
Anova Holding AG, P
Asset
   Accounts Receivable, 8
   Book Value, 106
   Cash, 5, 160, 212
   Cash Equivalents, 5, 7
   Contingent Liabilities, 113
   Covenant not to Compete, 32
   Distribution, 233
   Employment Contract, 113
   Exempt
      Cash and Accounts Receivable Derived from Exempt Assets, 212
      Goodwill Associated with Rental Property, 204
   Fiduciary, 139
   Inventory, 5
   Lease, 4
   Nonexempt
      Relationship between 802.4 and 802.51, 209, 213
      U.S. Issuer with Voting Securities of Foreign Issuer, 213
   Option to Purchase, 31
   Recruitment Agreement, 115
   Undivided Interest, 60
   Unincorporated Joint Venture, 145
   U.S. and Foreign Assets, 238
   Value of Nonexempt Assets, 215
Asset Purchases
   During Waiting Period. *see* Waiting Period
Assets Located in the United States. *see* Foreign Asset and Issuer Exemptions
Assets Located Outside the United States. *see* Foreign Asset and Issuer Exemptions
Assignment, 104. *see* Lease
Assisted Living Facilities, 205
Associated Exploration or Production Assets, Cash, 212
Assumption of Liabilities, 93, 97, 98, 105, 110, 117, 118, 122
Atlantic Richfield Co., 44, S, W
Attorney-Client Communications, FI-8
Automatic Data Processing, Inc., L
Avoidance
   Aggregation, Q, R
   Beneficial Ownership, Q, X, Y, BB
   Change in UPE, 189
   Choice of Legal Entity, 191, 193
   Consignment, 30
   Debt Pay-Off as Disguised Consideration, 98
   Decision to Form Partnership, 191
   Delayed Closing, 194
   Equalization Payments, 27
   Extraordinary Dividend, 195
   Factors Considered, 196
   Fair Market Value, M
   Instrumental to Redemption, 190

Numbers Refer to Interpretations
Letters Refer to Enforcement Actions
FI Refers to Formal Interpretations

Intermediary Acquisition, FF, GG, HH
Joint Venture Formation, 172, 193
Multiple Acquisitions, 154, 172, 192
Partnership Formation, 27, 191, R, X, BB
Pro Form Balance Sheet, 187
Pre-Transaction Transfer, 186
Regularly Prepared Balance Sheet, Failure to Produce, 187
Related Purchasers, 196
Sham Partnership, 191
Step Transaction, 185, 188, 189
Stock Acquisitions, 188
Stock Redemption, 190
Tender Offer, 219
Transaction Value, CC
Two-Step Analysis, 191
Valuation, M

B

Baker Hughes Inc., AA
Balance Sheet. *see* Regularly Prepared Financial Statements; Size-of-Person
    Accounting Principles, 132, 140, 144
    Asset Values, 144
    Consideration, 142
    Delayed Closing, 194
    Divested Assets, 138
    Error, 132
    Excluding Assets, 142
    Fiduciary Assets, 139
    GAAP or Fair Market Value, 144
    Liabilities, 139
    Natural Person, 275
    Pass-Through, 147
    Preparation, 134
    Pro Forma, 141, 147
    Regularly Prepared, 135
    Restatement, 132
    Size-of-Person, 137
    Special Purpose, 137
Bank
    Hold Customer's Assets, 59

Banking Industry, 15, 59, 121, FI-7, FI-17
Bankruptcy
    Affidavit, 255
    Debt Work-Out, 247
    Foreign, 255
    Second Request, 255
    Trustee, 255
Base Year, Form, 276
Beazer plc, R
Bell Resources Ltd., 16, II
Beneficial Ownership
    Acquisition Agreement, 44
    Agent, 78
    Beneficiary, 56
    Consignment of Goods, 30
    Contingent Purchase Right, 56
    Derivative Agreements, 55
    Escrow Transaction, 88
    Goods Sold, 236, 237
    Indicia of Beneficial Ownership, 44, 54, 55
    Intermediary, 48, 49
    Investment Funds, 54
    Irrevocable Contractual Right, 58
    Jumping-the-Gun, 44, 254, S
    Lease, 28, 248
    Local Marketing Agreement, 53
    Management Agreement, 53
    Nonrefundable Payment, 44
    Open Market Stock Purchase, 25
    Partial Acquisition of Stock Prior to Termination of Waiting Period, 254
    Power of Attorney, 58
    Put-Call Option, 49
    Revocable Proxy, 54
    Shareholders' Agreement, 51
    Step Transaction, 48
    Trust, 56, 139
    Voting Rights, 54
    Voting Securities, 55, 59
    Voting Trust, 39, 43, 63
Blackstone Capital Partners, F
Book Value versus Fair Market Value, 106

Subject Index

Numbers Refer to Interpretations
Letters Refer to Enforcement Actions
FI Refers to Formal Interpretations

Borrowed Funds. *see* Formation; Size-of-Person
Broker
    Holding Customer Assets, 59
Business Trust, 71, 170

C

Civil Aeronautics Board Sunset Act, FI-14
Carbon-Based Mineral Reserves, 211
Cash. *see* Asset; Size-of-Transaction
Cash Tender Offer. *see* Tender Offer
Casino, 207
    Leased, 208
Certification
    Bankruptcy, 255
    Facsimile Copy, 260
    Joint Venture Formations, 268
    Notorization, 259
    One Original, FI-16
    Pending Transactions, 80
    When Refiling, 224, 225, 265
    Withdrawal, 253
Change in UPE. *see* Refiling Requirement
Chi-Chi's, J
Children. *see* Minor Children, 37
Choice of Legal Entity. *see* Avoidance
Civil Penalty. *see* Failure to File
    Acquired Person, DD
    Beneficial Ownership, 44
    Individual Liability, F
    Inadvertent Failure to File, 22, P
    Investment-Only Exemption, 16
    Prosecutorial Discretion, 21
Closed Manufacturing Plant, 201
Coastal Corp., JJ
Collection Agent, 109, 111
Collective Investment Funds, 62, 64
Commission Agent, 236
Common Trust Fund, 62
Compliance Actions. *see* Civil Penalty
Computer Associates, C
Computerized Form, 271
Conceding Size-of-Person
    Natural Person, 134

Conditional Tender Offer. *see* Tender Offer
Conditional Transaction. *see* Affidavit
Confidentiality. *see* Disclosure of HSR Information
Consideration in Cash and Voting Securities, 94
Consignment, 30. *see* Acquisition
Consolidation. *see* Merger
Consulting Agreements, 33
Consumer Loans, 8
Contingent Intention. *see* Affidavit: Conditional Transaction
Contingent Payment, 91, 101, 109, 111
Contingent Purchases. *see* Acquisition: Contingent Purchases
Contract. *see* Valuation
Contribution. *see* Formation
Control
    Aggregation, 150, 196
    Contractual Rights, 40, 43, 46, 51, 58
    Corporation, 40, 41, 43, 46, 51, 63
    Director Appointment, 40, 46
    Familial Relationships, 37
    Group, 46
    Jumping-the-Gun, B, C, E, K
    LLC Formation, 82
    Minor Children, 37
    Multiple Trusts with Common Trustee, 45
    Nonprofit Corporation, 42
    Partnership, 128
    Pension Trust, 50
    Power of Attorney, 58
    Proxy Rights, 43
    "Related" Entities not under Common Control, 150, 196
    Right to Withdraw Filing by New UPE, 168
    Shifting in LLC, FI-15
    Spouse, 37
    Trust, 39, 45, 47, 61, 63
    Voting Agreement, 41

Numbers Refer to Interpretations
Letters Refer to Enforcement Actions
FI Refers to Formal Interpretations

Conversion, 10, 68, 69, 72
   Automatic Maturation of Inchoate
      Voting Rights, 69, 164, 231
   Valuation Issues when Voting
      Stock Held, 152
Convertible Debt
   Voting Securities, FI-12
Convertible Securities, 10, 152, FI-12
   Conversion. *see* Conversion
   Veto Rights, 67
Corporate Dissolution, 232
Corporate Formation. *see* Formation
Covenant not to Compete, 32
Cox Enterprises, Inc., 16, U
Credit Card Receivables, 3, 8
"Crown Jewel" Option, 262
Cruise Ships, 239
Cumulative Voting, 40, 70

D

Debtor-in-Possession, 255
Debt Pay-Off, 93
Debt Work-Out, Debtor Acquisition, 247
Declaration (28 U.S.C. § 1746), 259
Delayed Closing, 194
Demand Deposits, Value, 121
Department of Transportation
   Approval, FI-14
Derivative Agreements, 55
Devices for Avoidance. *see* Avoidance
Disclosure of HSR Information
   Early Termination, 23, 269
   Fact of Filing, 23
   Litigation, 24
   Notice to Parties, FI-10
   State Attorneys General, 23
Discontinued Lines of Business, Form, 283
Discontinued Operations, Size-of-Person, 138
Discounting Future Payments. *see* Valuation
Dissenting Shareholder, 87
Dissolution
   Leasing Arrangement, 248
   Partnerships, 233
Divested Assets
   Information for Form, 283
   Size-of-Person, 138
Drilling Rigs, 6

E

Early Termination
   Criteria, FI-13
   Procedure, 269
   Publication, 23
Effective Period for HSR Approval. *see* Five Year Effective Period; One Year Effective Period
Employment Contract, 113
Enforcement Actions. *see* Civil Penalties
Engaged in Commerce, 36
Engaged in Manufacturing, 1, 2
Entity
   Engaged in Commerce, 35, 36
   Federal, State and Foreign
      Governmental Units, 11, 12
   FDIC, 11
   Foreign Government Agency, 34
   Foreign Governmental Corporation, 36
   Group, 46
   LLC, FI-15
   Native American Tribe, 35
   Partnership, 26
   Pension Fund, 11
Equalization Payment, 27, 191
Equipment Leasing Arrangement
   Dissolution, 248
Equity Group Holdings, X
Error on Balance Sheet, 132
Escrow
   Automatic Conversion to Voting
      Securities when
      Transferred, 72
   Jumping-the-Gun, S
   Secondary Acquisition, 88
Excluding Assets on Balance Sheet. *see* Balance Sheet
Exclusive License. *see* License

Subject Index 509

Numbers Refer to Interpretations
Letters Refer to Enforcement Actions
FI Refers to Formal Interpretations

Executory Contracts. *see* Acquisition; Valuation
Exempt Asset. *see* Asset
Exemptions
   Minority Stock Positions, 214
   Relationship between 802.4 and 802.50, 243
   Relationship between 802.4 and 802.51, 209, 213
Expiration of Notification. *see* One Year Effective Period
Extension of Waiting Period. *see* Waiting Period; Withdrawal; Refiling Requirement

F

Failure to File, G, EE
   Acquired Person Penalty, DD
   Acquisition through an Agent, FF, GG, HH
   Aggregation, I
   Avoidance, M, Q, R, X, Y, BB, CC
   Beneficial Ownership, W
   Fair Market Value, M
   Inadvertent, 22, P
   Individual Liability, F
   Intentional, H, J, M
   Investment Exemption, A, N, O, T, U, V, Z, II, JJ
   Procedures for Making Corrective Filing, 22
   Prosecutorial Discretion, 21
Fair Market Value. *see* Valuation
Familial Relationships, 37
Farley, William, 16, N
Faxed Copy of Form, 260
FDIC, 11
Federal Agency. *see* Entity
Federal Reserve Board Approval, 15, FI-7
Fee. *see* Filing Fee
Fiduciary Assets, 139
Field of Use Exclusivity. *see* License
Figgie International, I
Filing Fee
   Fair Market Value, 112, 272
   Formation, 251, 274

Refile, 173, 224, 253, 267
Refund, 215, 250, 253, 274
Step Transaction, 252
Tender Offer, 263
Withdrawal, 253, 267
Financial Holding Company, 15, FI-7, FI-17
Financial Statements. *see* Pro Forma Financials; Regularly Prepared Financial Statements
First City Financial Corp., 49, FF, GG, HH
Fiscal Year
   Item 5, 285
Five Percent Shareholders, Disclosure on Form, 258
Five Year Effective Period, 220, 221, 222, 223
   Renewal, 220
FOIA. *see* Disclosure of HSR Information
Foodmaker, Inc., J
Foreign Bankruptcy, 255
Foreign Entity
   Formation, 170, 177
Foreign Asset and Issuer Exemptions (802.50 and 802.51)
   Acquisition of Multiple Issuers, 240
   Acquisition of Both U.S. and Foreign Issuers, 240
   Aggregation of U.S. and Foreign Assets, 238
   Aggregation of U.S. Sales, 240
   Asset Acquisitions, 238
   Control Conferred by Contract, 246
   Control of an Issuer, 245
   Divested Assets, 242
   Exempt U.S. Assets, 243
   Formation, 174
   Foreign Issuer, Definitions, 66
   Headquarters, 66
   Intangible Assets, 239
   Joint Venture Formation, 174, 241, 289
   Minority Stock Acquisitions by Foreign Person, 246
   Minority Stockholding, 244

Numbers Refer to Interpretations
Letters Refer to Enforcement Actions
FI Refers to Formal Interpretations

    Movable Assets, 239
    Principal Offices, 66
    Real Property, 209, 243
    Sales in the United States, 174
    Secondary Acquisitions, 245
    Valuation of U.S. Assets, 241
    Securities of Another Person, 244
    U.S. Assets, 239, 244
    U.S. Sales, 235, 236, 237
    U.S. Sales from Divested Assets, 242
Foreign Governmental Corporation. *see* Entity
Foreign LLC, 71, 177
Form
    (The following lists materials relating to specific items of the Form. Additional subject matter entries relating to the Form follow this item list.)

          * * * * * *

Item 2(a)
    List of Shareholders Acquiring Shares as Acquiring Persons, 273
Item 2(d)(i)
    Tender Offer, Undetermined Acquisition Prices, 263
Item 2(d)(iii)
    Requirement to Estimate Fair Market Value to Determine Filing Fee, 272
Item 2(e)
    Requirement to Estimate Fair Market Value to Determine Filing Fee, 272
Item 3
    No Information for One of Joint Venture Partners, 274
Item 3(a)
    Identification of All Persons Forming Joint Venture Corporation, 268
Item 3(c)
    Tender Offer, Undetermined Acquisition Prices, 263

Item 4(a)
    Incorporation by Reference, FI-6, FI-11
    Refiling, 253, 267
Item 4(b)
    Natural Person with no Consolidated Balance Sheet, 275
    Partnerships, 276
    Recent Asset Acquisitions, 276
    Refiling, 253, 267
    Unconsolidated Issuers, 276
Item 4(c)
    Failure to File, D, F, L, AA
    Market Studies, 278
    Offering Memoranda, 278
    Officers and Directors, 280
    Penalties for Failure to File, 277
    Privileged Documents, 279, FI-8
    Scope of 4(c) Documents, 277, 278, 280
Item 5
    Acquired Person, 282, 284
    Assets Being Sold, 284
    Discontinued Lines of Business, 283
    Divested Assets, 283
    Engaged in Manufacturing, 1
    Fiscal Year, 285
    Interplant Transfers of Manufactured Products, 256
    Intercompany Service Revenue, 256
    Intracompany Revenue between Manufacturing and Wholesale Operations, 286
    Limited Response by Acquired Person, 284
    Management Services, 256
    Manufactured in the United States, 281
    Manufacturer Who Also Wholesales, 286
    Manufacturing Revenues, 1
    Natural Person, 282
    Prior Fiscal Year Data, 287

Subject Index 511

Numbers Refer to Interpretations
Letters Refer to Enforcement Actions
FI Refers to Formal Interpretations

Recent Asset Acquisitions, 276
Regularly Prepared Financial
    Statements, 287
When Estimates are Required,
    287
Wholesaling, 281, 286
Item 5(a)
Fiscal versus Calendar Year, 285
Manufacturer that also
    Wholesales, 286
Item 5(b)(ii)
New Company, 288
Prior Fiscal Year versus Calendar
    Data, 287
Products Added or Deleted, 288
Item 5(b)(iii)
Prior Fiscal Year Data, 287
Item 5(c)
Prior Fiscal Year Data, 287
Item 5(d)
Foreign Joint Venturer, 289
No Information for One of Joint
    Venture Partners, 274
Update for Adding Acquiring
    Person, 268
Item 6
Amended Filing, 224, 225
Corporations, 177
Five Percent Shareholders that
    Cannot Be Identified, 258
Foreign Entity Interests, 177
LLC, 290
Partnership, 177, 290
Item 7
Acquired Person, 284
Formation of Joint Venture, 291
Limited Response by Acquired
    Person, 284
Update for Adding Acquiring
    Person in Joint Venture
    Formation, 268
Two Transactions on Same Form,
    251
Item 7(c)
Establishments List, 292
Manufacturer that also
    Wholesales, 286

Item 8
Formation of Joint Venture or
    Other Corporation, 291
Limited Response by Acquired
    Person, 284

* * * * * *

Form, cont'd.
Base Year, 276
Computerized Forms, 271
Corrective Filing, 22
Deficient, FI-6
Disclosure of Information on Form,
    257
Discontinued Lines of Business,
    283
Divested Assets, 283
Faxed Copy, 260
Financial Statements for
    Partnership and LLCs, 276
Fiscal Year versus Calendar Year,
    285
Five Percent Shareholders, 258
Five Year Effective Period, 220,
    221, 222, 223
Foreign Joint Venture, 289
Formation Information, 268, 274
Incorporation by Reference, FI-6,
    FI-11
Information for Natural Person, 275
New Company, 288
Noncompliance, 258
Notarization Alternative, 259
One Original Affidavit, FI-16
One Year Effective Period, 56, 220,
    221, 265, 266
Partnership Financial Statements,
    276
Recent Acquisitions, 276
Two Transactions on Same Form,
    251, 274
Formation
Acquiring Person, 178, 179
Acquisition of Nonvoting
    Convertible Securities, 179

Numbers Refer to Interpretations
Letters Refer to Enforcement Actions
FI Refers to Formal Interpretations

Acquisition Vehicle for Merger or Consolidation, 175
Affirmative Obligation to Determine Jurisdictional Thresholds, 274
Asset Value, 183
Business Trusts, 170
Cash Contributions, 184
Choice of Legal Entity, 193
Conditional Contribution, 172
Contractual Commitments to Acquire Assets or Voting Securities, 181
Contribution, 124, 178, 181
Contributor, 178, 179
Corporation, 95, 99, 119, 124
Foreign Entities, 170, 177
Foreign Exemptions, 174, 241
Foreign Joint Venture, 176
Foreign LLC, 177
Joint Venture, 172
Jointly Controlled Assets, 82
LLC, 82, 85, 177, FI-15
License, 85
Loans/Guarantees, 119, 178, 179, 184
New Partner, 173
Obligation to Refile, 173
Partnership, 191, FI-15
Partnership Conversion to Corporation, 169
Pro Forma Balance Sheet, 123, 135, 137, 141, 145, 146, 148, 149, 182, 187
Post-Formation Acquisition, 171
Required Filings, 268
Second Request, 268
Service Contract Valuation, 183
Size-of-Person, 123, 124, 179, 180
Stock Contributions, 180
Subsidiary Corporation, 227
Third Party Financing, 178
Unincorporated Joint Venture, 145, 170
Value of Shares of New Corporation, 95, 99, 119, 172
Voting Securities to be Acquired, 181
Waiting Period, 268
When Formation Occurs, 171
Future Payments, 107, 120

G

GAAP, 92, 130, 132, 136, 144
Gemstar, B
General Cinema Corp., T
Glass-Steagall Act, FI-17
Good Faith Estimates. *see* Valuation
Good Faith Intention to Complete Transaction. *see* Affidavit
Government Agency. *see* Entity
Government Controlled Corporation. *see* Entity
Government Sale of Voting Securities. *see* Entity
Gramm-Leach-Bliley Act, 15, FI-17
Group Control, 46
Gun-Jumping. *see* Jumping-the-Gun

H

Headquarters, Foreign Issuer, 66
Hearst Trust, D
Hold. *see* Control
  Agent, 78
  Bank, Holding Customer Assets, 59
  Broker, Holding Customer Assets, 59
  Exempt Stock and Assets, 151
  Family Relationships, 37
  Individuals, 37
  Insurance Company Accounts, 54, 65
  Investment Banker, 59
  Investment Funds, 54
  Pension Trust, 50
  Proxies, 43
  Shareholders' Agreement, 51
  Trust, 39, 45, 47, 52, 61, 63
  Trustee, 63
  Voting Rights, 58
  Voting Securities, 51, 55, 59
Honickman, Harold, Q

Subject Index   513

Numbers Refer to Interpretations
Letters Refer to Enforcement Actions
FI Refers to Formal Interpretations

Hostile Tender Offer, Control. *see* Tender Offer
Hotel
   Casino, 208
   Exemption, 207
   Nonexempt Assets, 210
Hypothetical Transactions, 262. *see* Affidavit

I

Illinois Cereal Mills, Inc., CC
Income Statements. *see* Regularly Prepared Financial Statements
Indemnity Reinsurance Contracts, 121
Individual. *see* Natural Person
Individual Liability, F
Informal Interpretation, 270
IPO
   Conversion, 164
   Decreased Percentage Held after IPO, 18
Input/Output, E
Installment Contract, 120
Installment Sale, 4, 28, 248
Instrumental in Causing Transaction, 159, 190, 230
Insurance Company, 54, 65, 136
Intangible Assets, 132
Intellectual Property. *see* License
Intent to Acquire. *see* Affidavit
Intercompany Sales; Size-of-Person, 133
Intercompany Transfers
   Management Services; Form, 256
Interest Payments, 120
Intermediary
   Avoidance Device, FF, GG, HH
   No Additional Filing Required, 48, 57
Intermediate Partnerships and LLCs, 42, 234
Intracompany Debt; Valuation, 98
Intraperson Exemption
   Asset Transfer, 42, 226, 230, 232
   Contractual Power to Appoint Directors, 51
   Control, 228, 231

   Corporate Dissolution, 232
   Corporate Formation, 227
   LLC, 42, 85, 234
   Merger, 231
   Narrower than 7A(c)(3), 229, 232
   Nonprofit: Transaction between It and Its Controlling Member, 42
   Partnership, 42, 233, 234
   Partnership Dissolution, 232, 233
   Reincorporation, 19
   Secondary Acquisition, 223
   Stock Distribution, 229
   Stock Redemption, 230
   Subsidiary Formation, 230
   Transfer of Stock of Unaffiliated Company between Wholly Owned Subsidiaries, 20
   Trust, 228
   Two Ultimate Parents, 226, 227, 229, 232
   Voting Securities Held, 226, 228, 231
   Wholly Owned Partnership or LLC, 42, 234
Inventory. *see* Acquisition Consignment, 30
Investment Advisor: Whether Holding Voting Securities, 54
Investment Bank, Holding Customer Assets, 59
Investment Funds, 54. *see* Collective Investment Funds
Investment-Only Exemption
   Civil Penalty, A
   Competitors, O
   Failure to File, T, U, Z, JJ
   Investment Intent, 16, 17, N, O, T, II, JJ, FI-4
   Intent to Acquire More than Ten Percent, FI-4
   Prosecutorial Discretion, 21
   Waiting Period Acquisitions, 17, FI-4

514   Premerger Notification Practice Manual

Numbers Refer to Interpretations
Letters Refer to Enforcement Actions
FI Refers to Formal Interpretations

Investment Rental Property Exemption
   Mini-Warehouse Business, 218
   Operating Unit, 218
   Portion not Rented, 217
Irrevocable Power of Attorney, 58
Irrevocable Proxy. *see* Proxy

J

Joint Venture. *see* Formation
Jumping-the-Gun, 44, 53, 188, 254, B, C, E, K, S, W. *see* Beneficial Ownership
   Management Agreement Combined with Buying Business, 53
Jurisdictional Thresholds
   Filing before Surpassed, 250
   Obligation to Determine, 274
   Time of Filing, 250

L

Land. *see* Real Property Exemption
Lease
   Acquisition, 103
   Assignment, 28, 104
   Beneficial Ownership of Asset Being Leased, 28, 248
   Duration, 4
   Exempt Property, 3, 4, 28, 103
   Installment Sale, 4, 28
   Lease Payments, 89
   Long-Term Lease, 4, 89
   New, 4, 28
   Sublease, 104
   Transfer, 3, 4
   Valuation, 103, 104
Lease Financing, Dissolution, 248
Leveraged Buyout, 171
Liabilities. *see* Balance Sheet
License
   Exclusive, 29, 81, 91, 92, 132
   Exclusive Field of Use, 29
   Formation, Contribution of Exclusive License, 85
   March In Rights, 29
   Marketing and Distribution Rights, 29
   Termination Rights, 29
   Valuation, 91, 92
Life Insurance Policy, 121
LLC, FI-15
   Acquiring LLC Interests, 60, 71, 82, 85, 86
   Acquired Person, 85
   Acquiring Person, 85
   Acquisition, 86
   Avoidance Device, 193
   Control, 82
   Exclusive License, 81
   Foreign, 71, 177
   Form, 276, 290
   Formation, 81, 82, 83, 84, 85, 170, 177, 193
   Intraperson Exemption, 42, 85, 234
   Merger, 81
   Size-of-Transaction, 84
   Step Transaction, 90
   U.S. LLC, 71
   Wholly Owned, 42, 234
Limited Partnership. *see* Partnership
Limited Voting Rights. *see* Voting Rights
Loan Guarantee. *see* Valuation; Formation
Local Marketing Agreement, 53
Lock-up Agreement, 262
Loewen Group, F, G
Lonrho, PLC, 22, DD
"Look Through" Wholly Owned Partnerships and LLCs, 234

M

Mahle GmbH, H
Management Agreement, 53
Management Buyout. *see* Leveraged Buyout
Manufacturing Plant Closed, Unproductive Real Property, 201
MLP, 71
Merger
   Acquisition Vehicle for Merger or Consolidation, 175
   Airline, FI-14
   Creation of New Shell Parent, 19

Subject Index 515

Numbers Refer to Interpretations
Letters Refer to Enforcement Actions
FI Refers to Formal Interpretations

Dissenting Shareholder, 87
Former Shareholder of Target Form, 273
Intention to Acquire Shares, 166
LLC, 81, FI-15
Multiple Corporation Consolidation, 80
Nonprofit Corporation, 79, 102
Reincorporation, 19
With Same Controlling Member, 42
Nonstock Membership Corporation, 74
Notification as Section 801.30 Filing, 166
Sequential Analysis, 80
Simultaneous Transactions, 80
Three or More Corporations, 80
Methane Gas Reserves, 211
Mini-Warehouse Business, 218
Minor Children, 37
Minority Partnership Interests, 73
Minority Stock Positions, 73, 214
Mixed Transaction, 13, 14, 15, FI-17
Modification of Transaction. *see* Refiling Requirement
Mortgage Loans, 9
Movable Assets, 6
Drilling Rigs and Platforms, 239
Multiple Transactions. *see* Aggregation; Form, Two Transactions on Same Form
Municipal Hospital. *see* Entity
Mutual Fund Held by Insurance Company, 65

N

NAAG Compact, 23
National Bank and Collective Investment Funds, 62
Native American Tribe. *see* Entity
Natural Gas Sales, where Located, 235
Natural Person
  Aggregation, 38
  Annual Net Sales, 127
  Balance Sheet, 134, 275
  Control, 38
  Financial Statements, 130
  Form, Limited Item 5 Response, 282
  Investment Assets, 128
  Investment Income, 282
  Own UPE, 38
  Pro Forma Financial Statements, 140
  Size-of-Person with no Financial Statements, 134
Netting Accounts Receivable and Accounts Payable, 118
New Shell Parent, 19
Newly Formed Entity. *see* Size-of-Person
Noncompliance with Form Requirement, 258
  Attorney-Client Communications, 279, FI-8
Noncontrolling Interests. *see* Secondary Acquisition
Nonconvertible Stock. *see* Voting Securities
Nonexempt Assets. *see* Asset
Nonprofit Corporation
  Acquisition, 74, 102
  Controlling Member, 42, 79, 102
  Consolidation, 79
  Disclosure of Information, 257
  Intraperson Exemption, 42
  Membership Interest, 102
  Merger or Consolidation, 74, 79, 102
  Religious Organizations, Disclosure of Information, 257
  Valuation, 74, 79, 102
Nonrecourse Loan. *see* Valuation
Nonrefundable Payment of Purchase Price before Closing. *see* Jumping-the-Gun
Nonstock Corporation. *see* Acquisition
Notarization, 259
Notes Receivable. *see* Accounts Receivable
Notice Letter
  Tender Offer, 263
  Threshold to be Crossed, 264

Numbers Refer to Interpretations
Letters Refer to Enforcement Actions
FI Refers to Formal Interpretations

Notice to Parties before Disclosure of HSR Information. *see* Disclosure of HSR Information
Notification Thresholds, 51, 153, 159, 219, 220, 221, 222, 223, 254, 264, 265, 267, FI-3
Nursing Home, 205

O

Offsetting Assets and Liabilities, 139
Oil and Gas Exemption
    Long-Term Sales Contracts, 211
    Methane Gas Reserves, 211
    Sales Inside and Outside United States, 235
One Year Effective Period, 56
Open Market Purchases, 25, 100, 114, 147, 153
    Affidavit and Notice, FI-3
    Notification Thresholds, FI-3
Operating Unit, 5, 8, 81, 198
Option
    Exercise, 31
    Nonconsensual Transaction, 165
    Purchase Assets, 31
    Purchase Voting Securities, 31
    Section 801.30, 165
    With Irrevocable Proxy, 31
Ordinary Course Exemption
    Accounts Receivable, 7, 8, 9, 162
    Acquisition of Issuer, 199
    Credit Card Receivables, 3, 8
    Inventory, 3
    Lease, 3, 4
    Loan Portfolio, 8
    Oil and Gas, 6
    Operating Unit, 198
    Realty, 3, 4
    Scope, 3
    Timberland, 200
    Used Durable Goods, 198, 199
Original Affidavit and Certification, FI-16

P

Partial Year Statement of Income, 135
Partnership
    Acquisition, 73, 86
    Avoidance Device, 191, 193, BB
    Conversion to Corporation, 169
    Dissolution, 233
    Equalization Payment, 27, 191
    Existence, 26
    Formation, 26, 27, 73, 146, 149, 191
    Interests, 60, 71, 73
    MLP Interest, 71
    Option to Buy-Out Minority Partner, 191
    Payments to Partners, 27
    Related, 150
    Valuation, 110
    Wholly Owned, 42, 234
Passive Investment. *see* Investment-Only Exemption
Pass-Through Rule. *see* Size-of-Person
Pass-Through Revenues. *see* Regularly Prepared Financial Statements
Patent License. *see* License
Pennzoil Co., 16, O
Pension Fund, 121
Pension Trust, 50
Persons Contributing to the Formation. *see* Formation
Portfolio of Contracts, 121. *see* Valuation
Power of Attorney, 58
Present Value, 107
Principal-Agent Relationship, 78
Principal Offices, Foreign Issuer, 66
Privileged 4(c) Documents, 279
Products Added or Deleted
    New Company, Form, 288
Pro Forma Financials. *see* Regularly Prepared Financial Statements
Promissory Note, 120
Pro Rata Stock Distribution, 229
Prosecutorial Discretion, 21
Proxies. *see* Voting Agreement
    Beneficial Ownership, 58
    Control, 43, 63

Subject Index 517

Numbers Refer to Interpretations
Letters Refer to Enforcement Actions
FI Refers to Formal Interpretations

Investment Advisor, 54
Irrevocable, 31, 39, 43, 46, 63, 70
Irrevocable with Option, 31
Irrevocable with Convertible Nonvoting, 70
Revocable versus Irrevocable, 43, 46
Rights, 43, 70
Publication of Early Termination, 23, 269
Purchase Orders, 105
Put-Call Option, 49

Q
Quiet Period, 164

R
Rales Brothers, X
Real Property Exemption. *see* Residential Property Exemption; Unproductive Real Property
    Aggregation, 202, 206
    Foreign Acquirer, 243
    Foreign Issuer with Exempt Real Property, 209
    Golf Course/Restaurant/Campground, 210
    Hotels, 210
    Hotels/Casinos, 208
    Interaction with Foreign Issuer Exemption, Manufacturing Plant, 201
    Nonexempt Assets, 207, 208, 209, 210
    Productive/Unproductive, 200, 201, 203
    Shopping Center, 3
    Timberland, 200, 202
Realty. *see* Real Property Exemption
Realty Management Company
    REIT, 216
Receivables. *see* Accounts Receivable
Redemption, 230, 232

Refiling Requirement, 48, 173, 220, 249, 265, 267. *see* Withdrawal; Five Year Effective Period; One Year Effective Period
Tender Offer, 224, 225, 265
Regularly Prepared Financial Statements. *see* Balance Sheet; Size-of-Person
    Accounting Principles, 130
    Assets Used for Consideration, Balance Sheet 142
    Avoidance, 187
    Cash, On Balance Sheet, 142
    Discontinued Operations, 138
    Errors, 132
    Fiduciary Assets, 139
    Form Item 5, 287
    Formation, 123, 135, 137, 141, 145, 146, 148, 149, 182, 187
    Intercompany Sales, 133
    Natural Person, 127, 130, 140
    Netting Assets and Liabilities, 139
    Partial Year, 135
    Pass-Through Revenues, 133
    Post-Preparation Events, 129
    Prior Year, 125
    Pro Forma Statements, 123, 125, 127, 130, 135, 137, 140, 141, 145, 147, 148, 149, 182, 187
    Regularly Prepared Requirement, 137
    Regularly Prepared Balance Sheet Requirement, 141, 143
    Restatement, 129
    Restatement Obligation, 130
    Requirement to Produce, Balance Sheet, 187
    Size-of-Person, 126
    Unavailable, 125, 126
    Unconsolidated Financial Statements, 130
    Unconsolidated Subsidiary, 131
Regulatory Approval, 13, 14, 15, FI-7, FI-14, FI-17

Numbers Refer to Interpretations
Letters Refer to Enforcement Actions
FI Refers to Formal Interpretations

Reincorporation, 19
REIT Exemption, 197
    Valuation Realty Management Companies, 216
"Related" Entities not under Common Control, 150, 196
Reliance Group Holdings, 16, Z
Religious Organizations. *see* Nonprofit Corporations
Required Withdrawal. *see* Withdrawal
Residential Property Exemption. *see* Real Property Exemption
    Assisted Living Facility, 205
    Nursing Home, 205
    Timeshare Facilities, 204
    Trailer Parks, 204
Restructured Transaction, 48, 249, 265.
    see Refiling Requirement Withdrawal
    During Investigation, 249
    Refiling Requirement, 267
    Withdrawal, 267
Retail Property Rental, 3
Retirement Plans, 33
Revenue. *see* Form, Item 5
Reversionary Interest. *see* Trust
Revocable Proxy. *see* Proxies
Revocable Trust. *see* Trust
Roscoe Moss Co., EE
Running of Time. *see* Waiting Period; Five Year Effective Period

S

Sales in or into the United States. *see* Foreign Asset and Issuer Exemption
    Commission Agent, 236
    Designed for U.S. Market, 237
    Divested Assets, 242
    Foreign Assets or Issuers, 174
    Future Sales, 174
    Intermediary Sales, 237
    Natural Gas, 235
    No Control where Sold, 235, 236
    Telecommunication Sales, 237
    Title, 237
    Transfer of Beneficial Ownership, 236
Sara Lee Corp., M
Schedule 13D and Investment Intent, 16
SEC Documents
    Incorporation by Reference, FI-11
Secondary Acquisition
    Escrow, 88
    Exempt Asset for 802.4, 214
    Foreign Issue Holding Stock of U.S. Issuers, 244
    Foreign Issuer Stock, 245
    Subsequent Acquisitions, 223
    Waiting Period, 88
Second Request
    Bankruptcy, 255
    Joint Venture Formation, 268
Sequence in Multiple Transactions. *see* Simultaneous Transactions
Service Corp. International, Y
Settlement Date, for Open Market Purchases, 25
Shareholders' Agreement, 51. *see* Voting Agreement; Trust
Shopping Center, 3
Simultaneous Transactions, 48, 80, 230. *see* Step Transaction
Size-of-Person. *see* Regularly Prepared Financial Statements; Balance Sheet; Valuation
    Acquisition Vehicle, 124, 145, 146
    Aggregation, 150
    Annual Net Sales and Total Assets, 129, 130
    Balance Sheet, 132, 134, 135, 141, 142, 144, 147
    Capital Contributions, 182
    Cash, 142
    Conceding for Natural Person, 134
    Consideration, 142
    Controlled Entities, 128
    Delayed Closing, 194
    Discontinued Operations, 138
    Divested Assets, 138

Subject Index 519

Numbers Refer to Interpretations
Letters Refer to Enforcement Actions
FI Refers to Formal Interpretations

Due Diligence Audit, 126
Engaged in Manufacturing, 1, 2
Extraordinary Dividend, 195
Formation of Corporation, 99, 119
Guarantees, 148
Insurance Company, 136
Intercompany Sales, 133
Joint Venture, 123, 146
Loans, 148
Multiple Acquisitions, 146
Natural Person, 128, 134, 140, 275
Natural Person's Annual Net Sales, 127, 134
Newly Formed Entity, 99, 119, 135, 137, 140, 145, 146, 148, 149, 182, 184
No Income Statement, 135
Partial Year Income Statement, 135
Pass-Through, 124, 145, 146, 147
Possible Change in Size, 250
Post Balance Sheet Acquisition, 129
Post-Formation Joint Venture, 124
Regularly Prepared Financial Statements, 125, 126
Restated Financials, 129, 130
Subsidiary to be Divested, 131
Unconsolidated Subsidiary, 131
Unincorporated Joint Venture, 145
Size-of-Transaction. *see* Valuation
  Accounts Receivable, 162
  Acquisition of Control of Subsidiaries, 158
  Acquisition of Partnership Interest, 73
  Aggregation, 196
  Cash, 5, 160
  Cash Equivalents, 161
  Collective Investment Trust, 64
  Contingent Purchase Price, 101
  Consulting Agreements, 33
  Debt Pay-Off, 93
  Exclude Exempt Assets, 240
  Fair Market Value, 112
  Formation of Corporation, 99
  Interest Payments, 120
  Joint Venture, 119, 172

Lease, 89
Loan Guarantee, 102, 108
LLC, 84
Nonprofit Acquisition, 102
Possible Change in Size, 250
Retirement Plans, 33
Trust Department, 64
Undivided Interest, 60
Voting Securities, 94
Smithfield Foods, 16, A
Solely for the Purpose of Investment. *see* Investment-Only Exemption
Special Purpose Balance Sheet, 137
Spin-Off, 19
Spouse, 37
State Agency. *see* Entity
Statement of Reasons for Noncompliance, 257, 258, 279
State Pension Fund, 11
Step Transaction, 27, 80, 90, 185, 191, 230
  Avoidance, 185, 186
  Cash Tender Offer and Subsequent Merger, 252
  Intermediary, 48, 57, FF, GG, HH
  Multiple Filings, 274
Stock Dividends, 19, 223
Stock-for-Stock Transaction, 96, 99
Stock Redemption, 230
Stock Split, 19, 223
Sublease, 104
Subpoena for HSR Material, 24

T

Telecommunications Transactions, Sales in U.S., 237
Tender Offer
  Acceptance for Payment, 25, 168
  Acquisition Price, 263
  Amended Offer, 224, 225
  Beneficial Ownership, 168
  Canadian Law, 168
  Cash Tender, 73, 75, 76, 88, 219, 224, 252
  Conditional, 261, 262
  Conditional Acquisition, 262

Numbers Refer to Interpretations
Letters Refer to Enforcement Actions
FI Refers to Formal Interpretations

    Contingent Tender Offer, 167
    Control, 168
    Existence of Purchase Agreement, 76
    Filing Obligation, 168
    Foreign Issuer, 75
    Friendly Merger, 225
    Hostile, Control, 168
    Issuer's Shares, 159
    Loan Note Option, 75
    Notice Letter, 77, 263
    Open Market Purchases, 219
    Partnership Interests, 73
    Point at which Acquisition Occurs, 25
    Post-Waiting Period Acquisitions, 219
    Privately Held Company, 77
    Public Announcement, 77
    Refiling Requirement, 265
    Section 801.30, 167
    Shareholder Acceptance, 159
    Subsequent Merger, 252
    Target Notification, 167
    Threshold, 264
    Valuation, 263
    Waiting Period, 75, 88, 219, 252
    Waiting Periods for Second Request, 224
    Withdrawal, 168
Tengelmann, BB
Termination of Waiting Period. *see* Waiting Period
Thresholds. *see* Notification Thresholds
Timberland, 200, 202
Time. *see* Waiting Period; Five Year Effective Period; One Year Effective Period
Timeshare Facilities, 204
Titan Wheel International, K
Title Transfer and Risk of Loss to Determine Location of Sale. *see* Sales in or into United States
Tolling Arrangement, Not Engaged in Manufacturing, 2, T

Total Assets. *see* Regularly Prepared Financial Statements; Size-of-Person
Trade Date, for Open Market Purchases, 25
Trademark License. *see* License
Trailer Parks, 204
Transactions or Devices for Avoidance. *see* Avoidance
Transition Rules
    Change in Notification Thresholds, 221, 222
    HSR Act Implementation FI-1
Transmission Towers, 217
Treasury Department Approval, 15
Trump, Donald, 49, FF, GG, HH
Trust
    Acquisition, 47
    Aggregation, 39, 50
    Beneficiary, 46, 52
    Business Trust, 71, 170
    Control, 45, 47, 61, 63
    Employee Stock Ownership Plan, 52
    Formation, 47
    Hold, 39, 61, 63
    Investment Funds, 54
    Minor Children, 61
    Reversionary Interest, 61
    Revocable Trust, 47
    Right to Vote Securities, 45, 52
    Settlor, 39
    Stock Voting Rights, 63
    Trustee, 39, 45, 63
    Trustee, Remove and Replace, 47
    Trustee, Resignation, 47
    Trustee, Right to Vote Shares of Trust, 45
    Voting Trust, 39, 63. *see* Voting Agreement; Shareholder's Agreement, Proxies
TV Guide, B
Two Column Balance Sheet, 144
Two-Step Analysis of 801.90, 191

Subject Index 521

Numbers Refer to Interpretations
Letters Refer to Enforcement Actions
FI Refers to Formal Interpretations

U

UPE. *see* Entity; Hold; Control
    Familial Relationships, 37
    Foreign State or Government, 35
    Intraperson Exemption, 226
    Native American Tribe, 35
    Natural Person, 38
    Trust, 47
Unaudited Financials. *see* Regularly
    Prepared Financial Statements
Undivided Interest in an Asset, 60
Unincorporated Joint Venture, 145
    Formation, 170
University, 11
Unproductive Real Property. *see* Real
    Property Exemption
    Closed Facilities, 203
    Closed Manufacturing Plant, 201
    Mixed Transaction, 200
    Separate Purchase, 202
    Timberland, 200
    Timberland, Separate Parcels, 202
Used Durable Goods
    Internal Administrative Support, 199

V

Valuation
    Accounts Receivable, 111, 118
    Asset Value, 106, 107, 112
    Bank Branch, 121
    Banking Industry, 15
    Best Estimate of Fair Market Value, 116
    Board Determination, 91, 92, 106, 111, 112, 116, 215, 272
    Board of Acquiring Person, 91, 92
    Book Value versus Fair Market Value, 106
    Collection Agent, 109
    Consulting Agreements, 33
    Contingent Liabilities, 113
    Contingent Payment, 91, 101, 109, 111
    Contracts, 4, 107, 121, 183
    Conversion, 152

Corporate Formation, 99
Covenant not to Compete, 32
Debt Assumption, 97, 98
Debt Pay-Off, 93
Debt Restructuring, 97, 98
Delegation by Board, 92, 215
Demand Deposits, 121
Discounting Future Payments, 91, 92, 107
Employment Contract, 113
Exclusive License, 91, 92
Executory Contracts, 4, 107, 121, 183
Exempt/Nonexempt Assets, 215
Fair Market Value, 92, 106, 111, 112, 116, 122, 215 272, M
Future Income Stream, 183
Future Payments, 91, 92, 107
Good Faith Estimate Determination, 111
Installment Contract, 120
Intellectual Property, 91, 92
Interest Payments, 120
Intracompany Debt, 98
Inventory, 5
Joint Venture Contributions, 119
Lease, 4, 89, 103, 104
Lease of Nonexempt Property, 103
Liabilities, 107, 122
Liabilities and Obligations, 107
Life Insurance Policy, 121
Loan Guarantees, 97, 98, 102, 108
Loans, 117, 119
Netting Current Accounts, 118
Nonprofit Acquisition, 102
Nonrecourse Loan, 117
Open Market Purchases, 100, 114, 153
Partnership, 110
Pension Fund, 121
Portfolio of Contracts, 121
Previously Acquired Voting Securities, 114
Privately Held Voting Securities, 94
Promissory Note, 120
Publicly Traded Voting Securities, 94

Numbers Refer to Interpretations
Letters Refer to Enforcement Actions
FI Refers to Formal Interpretations

Purchase Orders, 105
Recruitment Agreement, 115
Regularly Prepared Financials
    Different Than Fair
    Market Value, 106
Retirement Plans, 33
Shares of New Joint Venture, 95,
    119, 172
Stock-for-Stock Transaction, 96, 99
Sublease, 104
Third Party Valuation, 116
Unable to Determine, 215
Voting Securities, 94, 96, 97, 98, 99
Voting Securities Held, 114
Voting Securities of Joint Venture
    During Formation, 95, 99,
    119, 172
Valuation of U.S. Assets, Formation of
    Foreign Corporation, 241
Vehicle. *see* Acquisition Vehicle
Veto Rights, 67
Violation. *see* Failure to File
Voting Agreement, 41, 46. *see*
    Shareholders' Agreement;
    Trust; Proxies
Voting Rights
    Automatic Maturation of Inchoate
        Right, 69, 164, 231
    Combined with Nonvoting
        Securities, 31, 70
    Corporate Votes Other than for
        Directors, 31, 69
    Veto Rights, 67
Voting Securities
    Acquisition, 69
    Beneficial Ownership, 25
    Business Trusts, 71
    Contractual Rights, 58, 67, 70
    Conversion, 10, 68, 69, 72
    Convertible
    Convertible Securities, 10, 67, 70,
        FI-12
    Convertible Voting Securities, 68,
        70, 72
    Convertible Nonvoting with
        Irrevocable Proxy, 70
    Debt Pay-Off, 93

    Definition, 71, 170, 177, FI-12
    Dividend, 19
    Escrow, 72
    Foreign, Entities Including Foreign
        LLCs, 71, 177
    Formation Analysis, 172, 177
    Gain or Loss, 55
    Irrevocable Proxy, 31, 70
    MLP, 71
    Nonconvertible Stock, 68
    Open Market Purchases, 25, 100
    Option and Right to Vote, 31
    Options, 31, 68
    Partnership Interests, 71, 73
    Preferred Stock, 69
    Proxy Rights, While Holding Vote
        Securities, 43
    Purchase Order, 25
    Spin-Off, 19
    Stock Split, 19
    Subordinated Exchangeable
        Debentures, FI-12
    Transfer between Subsidiaries, 20
    Unincorporated Joint Venture, 170
    Valuation of Stock Held, 152
    Veto Rights, 67
    Voting Rights Alone, 54
    Warrants, 68
    White Squire Preferred Shares, 69
Voting Security Purchases
    During Waiting Period. *see* Waiting
        Period
Voting Trust. *see* Trust; Shareholder
    Agreement; Voting
    Agreement
Vulture Fund, 247

W

Waiting Period
    Asset Purchases During, 254
    Cash Tender Offer, 75
    Early Termination Criteria, FI-13
    Formation, 268
    Step Transaction, 252
    Tender Offer, 224

Subject Index 523

Numbers Refer to Interpretations
Letters Refer to Enforcement Actions
FI Refers to Formal Interpretations

Voting Security Purchases During, 254
Withdrawal, 253
Warrants, 68
White Squire Shares, 69
Wholesaling. *see* 286, Item 5, Item 7
Wickes Cos., 49, FF, GG, HH
Withdrawal. *see* Refiling Requirement
   After Expiration of Waiting Period, 266

   After New UPE in Hostile Takeover Context, 168
Effect of Withdrawal, 168, 253
Filing Fee, 267
Refile to Give Agencies More Time, 253, 267
Requirement, 267
Withheld 4(c) Documents, 279

INDEX BY SECTION
OF THE ACT AND RULES

Numbers Refer to Interpretations
Letters Refer to Enforcement Actions
FI Refers to Formal Interpretations

Section 7 of the Clayton Act
  Generally, 25, 30
  §7A(a), 47, 159, A, B, E, G, I, J, K,
    M, N, O, P, Q, R, S, T, U,
    V, W, X, Y, Z, BB, CC,
    DD, EE, FF, GG, HH, II,
    JJ
  §7A(a)(2), 1, 2, 46, 150, 158, 160,
    161, 163, 195
  §7A(a)(3)(B), 97
  §7A(b)(1)(B), 252
  §7A(b)(3)(A), 31, FI-12
  §7A(c), 159, C
  §7A(c)(1), 3, 4, 5, 6, 7, 8, 162, 200,
    243
  §7A(c)(2), 9, 10, 162, 212, 247
  §7A(c)(3), 73, 79, 188, 223, 229,
    232
  §7A(c)(4), 11, 12
  §7A(c)(6), 13, 14
  §7A(c)(7), 14, FI-17
  §7A(c)(8), 13, 14, 15, FI-7, FI-17
  §7A(c)(9), 16, 17, A, N, O, T, U, V,
    II, FI-4
  §7A(c)(10), 18, 19, 20, 172, 223,
    234, FI-12
  §7A(d), D, F, L, AA
  §7A(e)(2), 224
  §7A(g), A, B, C, D, E, F, G, H, I, J,
    K, M, N, O, P, Q, R, S, T,
    U, V, W, X, Y, Z, AA,
    BB, CC, DD, EE, FF, GG,
    HH, II, JJ
  §7A(g)(1), 16, 21, 22
  §7A(g)(2), 255
  §7A(h), 23, 24, FI-10

Part 801– Coverage Rules
  Generally, 25, 26, 27, 28, 29, 30,
    31, 32, 33
  §801.1(a)(2), 11, 12, 34, 35, 36,
    FI-15
  §801.1(a)(3), 37, 38, 50

§801.1(b), 37, 38, 39, 40, 41, 42,
  43, 44, 48, 50, 196, 223
§801.1(b)(1), 27
§801.1(b)(2), 45, 46, 47, 51, 58, 61,
  63
§801.1(b)(ii), FI-15
§801.1(c), 39, 44, 45, 48, 49, 50,
  51, 52, 53, 78, 223, B, C
§801.1(c)(1), 54, 55, 56, 57, 58, 59,
  60, 248, K, S, W
§801.1(c)(2), 37, 38
§801.1(c)(3), 47, 61, 62, 63, 228,
  230
§801.1(c)(4), 47, 61
§801.1(c)(5), 47
§801.1(c)(6), 62, 64
§801.1(c)(7), 65
§801.1(c)(8), 42
§801.1(e), 66
§801.1(f), 10, 67, 68, 69, 70, 170,
  177, 179, 231
§801.1(f)(1), 31, 42, 71, 72, 73, 74,
  FI-12
§801.1(f)(3), 31, 164
§801.1(g), 75
§801.1(g)(1), 76, 77
§801.1(h), 159, 219, 263, 264, 265,
  I, FI-3
§801.1(h)(1), 161, 163
§801.1(i)(1), 16, 17, FI-4
§801.1(i)(2), 128
§801.1(j), 1, 2
§801.2, 53
§801.2(a), 78, 179, B, C
§801.2(b), 158
§801.2(d), 74, 79, 80, 81, 102, 175,
  FI-15
§801.2(e), 87, 273
§801.4, 88, 214, 223, 244, 245
§801.9, CC
§801.10, 85, 89, 90, 91, 92, 93, 94,
  95, 152, 153, M

Numbers Refer to Interpretations
Letters Refer to Enforcement Actions
FI Refers to Formal Interpretations

§801.10(a), 96, 97, 99, 100, 101, 172
§801.10(a)(2), 119
§801.10(a)(2)(i), 98
§801.10(b), 32, 33, 101, 102, 103, 104, 105, 106, 107, 108, 109, 110, 111, 112, 113, 118
§801.10(c), 96, 99, 100, 101, 102, 106, 109, 111, 114, 115, 116, 117
§801.10(c)(2), 97, 107, 108, 118, 119, 120, 121, 122
§801.10(c)(3), 107, 112, 113, 122, 215, 272
§801.11, 123, 124
§801.11(a), 125, 126, 127
§801.11(b), 128, 187, 195
§801.11(b)(1), 129, 130, 131
§801.11(b)(2), 125, 126, 132
§801.11(c), 133, 134, 135, 136, 137, 187
§801.11(c)(1), 138
§801.11(c)(2), 126, 139, 140, 141, 142, 143, 144, 147, 194
§801.11(d), 128, 130, 140
§801.11(e), 125, 130, 135, 137, 141, 142, 145, 146, 147, 148, 149, 181, 182, 187
§801.11(e)(1)(ii), 184
§801.11(e)(i), 47
§801.11(i)(2), 127
§801.12(b), 40
§801.12(b)(3), 258
§801.13, 30, 150, 151
§801.13(a), 100, 114, 152, 153, 156, 158
§801.13(a)(3), 157
§801.13(b), 160, 161, 163, 192
§801.13(b)(2)(ii), 154, 155, 156, CC
§801.14, 151, 156, 157, 158
§801.15, 5, 151, 206, 238
§801.15(a), 152
§801.15(b), 186
§801.20(c), 159
§801.21, 9, 160, 161, 162, 163, FI-9

§801.21(a), 5
§801.30, 76, 87, 164, 165, 166, 224, 264, 266, 269
§801.30(b)(2), 167
§801.32, 10, 152
§801.33, 25, 168
§801.40, 95, 99, 148, 169, 170, 171, 172, 173, 174, 175, 176, 177, 227, 251, 268, 274, 291, FI-15
§801.40(a), 178
§801.40(b), 80, 119
§801.40(c), 179, 180
§801.40(d), 123, 124, 140, 147, 179, 180, 181, 182, 183, 184, 241
§801.40(d)(2), 119
§801.90, 27, 30, 43, 73, 83, 89, 90, 98, 150, 154, 172, 185, 186, 187, 188, 189, 190, 191, 192, 193, 194, 195, 196, 219, M, Q, R, X, Y, BB, FF, GG, HH

Part 802– Exemption Rules

§802.1, 3, 6, 162, 197
§802.1(a), 5, 7, 8, 198, 199
§802.1(d), 198
§802.1(d)(4), 199
§802.2, 6, 9, 103, 206
§802.2(c), 200, 201, 202
§802.2(c)(1), 203
§802.2(c)(2)(ii), 203
§802.2(d), 204, 205, 243
§802.2(e), 204, 207, 208, 209, 210
§802.2(f), 210
§802.2(h), 3, 218
§802.3, 3, 6, 211, 235
§802.3(a), 212
§802.4, 3, 6, 9, 197, 199, 206, 207, 209, 212, 213, 214, 243
§802.4(c), 215
§802.5, 3, 6, 197, 204, 208, 216, 217, 218
§802.6, 13
§802.6(b), 14, 15, FI-14, FI-17
§802.8, 13, FI-7

Numbers Refer to Interpretations
Letters Refer to Enforcement Actions
FI Refers to Formal Interpretations

§802.9, 16, 17, 21, 49, A, N, O, T, U, V, Z, II, JJ, FI-4
§802.10, 19, 151, 223
§802.2 1, 7, 157, 159, 219, 220, 223, 266
§802.21(b), 221, 222
§802.23, 224, 225, 265
§802.30, 19, 20, 42, 51, 73, 79, 85, 190, 223, 226, 227, 228, 229, 230, 231, 232, 233, 234
§802.31, 10, 31, 67, 68, 70, 72, 152, FI-12
§802.50, 209, 215, 235, 238
§802.50(a), 236, 237, 239
§802.51, 167, 168, 174, 186, 209, 213, 215, 235, 240, 246, P
§802.51(a), 176, 241, 242
§802.51(b), 241
§802.51(b)(1), 243, 244, 245
§802.52, 174
§802.63, 247, 248
§802.64, 21, 49
§802.64(b)(3), 16
§802.70, FI-2
§802.71, 47

Part 803– Transmittal Rules

Generally, 249, 250, 251, 252, 253, 254, 255, 265
§803.1(a), 271
§803.2, 282
§803.2(a), 168
§803.2(b), 284
§803.2(c)(1), 289
§803.2(d), 256
§803.3, 257, 258, 274, FI-8
§803.3(d), 279
§803.5, 166, 224, 259, 260, 262, FI-16
§803.5(a), 167, 261, 263, 264, FI-3
§803.5(a)(2), 77
§803.5(b), 87, 252
§803.6, 259, 260, FI-16
§803.6(a), F
§803.7, 220, 264, 265, 266
§803.10, 173, 253, 267
§803.10(a)(2), 171, 268
§803.10(b), 75
§803.10(c)(2), FI-6
§803.11, 269, FI-13
§803.30, 270

Note: For a detailed list of information relating to specific items of the Notification and Report Form, see listings in the Subject Index under "Form."

INDEX OF CASES AND FORMAL INTERPRETATIONS

Numbers Refer to Interpretations
Letters Refer to Enforcement Actions
FI Refers to Formal Interpretations

Cases

    Aero Limited Partnership, 16, V
    Anova Holding AG, et al, P
    Atlantic Richfield Co., 44, S, W
    Automatic Data Processing, Inc., L
    Baker Hughes Inc., AA
    Beazer plc., R
    Bell Resources Ltd., 16, II
    Blackstone Capital Partners II Merchant Banking Fund L.P., 277, F, G
    The Coastal Corp., 16, JJ
    Computer Associates International, Inc., C
    Cox Enterprises, Inc., 16, U
    Equity Group Holdings, X
    William F. Farley, 16, N
    Figgie International Inc., I
    First City Financial Corp., 49, FF, GG, HH
    Foodmaker, Inc., J
    Gemstar-TV Guide International, Inc., B
    General Cinema Corp., T
    The Hearst Trust, 277, D
    Harold A. Honickman, Q
    Illinois Cereal Mills, Inc., CC
    Input/Output, Inc., E
    Loewen Group, Inc., F, G
    Lonrho PLC, 22, DD
    Mahle GmbH, H
    Pennzoil Co., 16, O
    Reliance Group Holdings, Inc., 16, Z
    Roscoe Moss Co., EE
    Sara Lee Corp., M
    Service Corp. International, Y
    Smithfield Foods, Inc., 16, A
    Tengelmann Warenhandelsgesellschaft, BB
    Titan Wheel International, Inc., K
    Donald J. Trump, 49, FF, GG, HH

Wickes Cos., 49, FF, GG, HH

Formal Interpretations

FI-4, 17
FI-5, FI-13
FI-9, 7, 8, 9, 162
FI-12, 31
FI-13, FI-5
FI-15, 71, 81, 82, 83, 84, 85, 86, 116, 149, 170, 177, 193, 234, 290, FI-15
FI-17, 15

ABA SECTION OF ANTITRUST LAW
COMMITMENT TO QUALITY

The Section of Antitrust Law is committed to the highest standards of scholarship and continuing legal education. To that end, each of our books and treatises is subjected to rigorous quality control mechanisms throughout the design, drafting, editing, and peer review processes. Each Section publication is drafted and edited by leading experts on the topics covered and then rigorously peer reviewed by the Section's Books and Treatises Committee, at least two Council members, and then other officers and experts. Because the Section's quality commitment does not stop at publication, we encourage you to provide any comments or suggestions you may have for future editions of this book or other publications.

SECTION OF
ANTITRUST LAW

ABA
Defending Liberty
Pursuing Justice